BERLITZ

W9-CKE-407

DISCOVER
SPAIN

Edited and designed by
D & N Publishing,
Lambourn, Berkshire.

Cartography by Carte Blanche, Basingstoke, Hampshire.

Our thanks to Norman Renouf for his help in updating this guide.

Although we have made every effort to ensure the accuracy of all the information in this book, changes do occur. We cannot therefore take responsibility for facts, addresses and circumstances in general that are constantly subject to alteration.

If you have any new information, suggestions or corrections to contribute to this guide, we would like to hear from you. Please write to Berlitz Publishing at the above address.

Phototypeset, originated and printed by C.S. Graphics, Singapore.

Photographic Acknowledgements
Copyright © A G E PHOTOSTOCK 145 (both), 218, 219 (upper), 281; Berlitz Publishing Co. Ltd. 6, 18/19, 24/5, 36, 43, 46, 50, 52/3, 101, 108/9, 110, 118, 122/3, 127, 132, 142, 151, 154, 156/7, 160, 164/5, 168, 175, 176/7, 182/3, 198, 204, 207, 209, 212, 216/7, 220, 226/7, 234, 238/9, 244/5, 248/9, 254/5, 256, 258/9, 262/3, 264/5, 268, 272/3, 276, 277, 280, 286/7, 291, 306, 314, 316/17, 320; Colorific! 1, 42, 117, 135, 136, 171 (lower), 178, 185, 193, 196/7, 225, 242, 284, 288/9, 292 (upper and lower); Dany Gignoux 144; Giraudon/Bridgeman Art Library 64; David Price-Goodfellow 10, 11, 14, 28, 56 (lower), 188, 192, 205, 208, 323; André Held 100, 103, 219 (lower); Hulton Deutsch Collection 54, 56 (upper), 60, 61, 199; John Measures 27, 29, 90/1, 140/1, 146, 149, 152, 162, 167, 171 (upper), 173, 231, 236, 250, 251; Paul Murphy 33, 35, 62, 203, 213, 282, 298; Natural Image 39, 240 (Bob Gibbons), 285 (Jean Hall), 107, 113, 166, 271 (Peter Wilson); Nature Photographers 66 (SC Bisserot), 184 (Robin Bush), 303 (NA Callow), 295 (Jean Hall), 300/1 (David Hutton), 186, 247 (Paul Sterry), 38 (Roger Tidman); Telegraph Colour Library 41, 48, 92, 97, 103, 124, 224, 229, 274, 284; Ken Welsh 308/9, 310/11; Neil Wilson 51.

Front cover: City Square, Seville (© Image Bank)

Back cover: Seville (Berlitz Publishing)

Previous page: The Ria-Riav celebrations in Pamplona.

The Berlitz tick is used to indicate places or events of particular interest.

BERLITZ®

DISCOVER
SPAIN

Ken Bernstein
and Paul Murphy

SPAIN

FRANCE

La Coruña Santander Bilbao

GREEN SPAIN

ANDORRA

NORTHERN BORDER

Valladolid Zaragoza CATALONIA

CENTRE Barcelona

Salamanca

BALEARIC ISLANDS Menorca

MADRID Mallorca

MADRID

Toledo Valencia Ibiza Formentera

WEST Albacete EAST

Mérida Alicante

Córdoba

Sevilla SOUTH Granada

Málaga

MEDITERRANEAN SEA

ATLANTIC OCEAN

ALGERIA

CANARY ISLANDS

MOROCCO

La Palma Lanzarote

Tenerife Fuerteventura

La Gomera

El Hierro Gran Canaria

PORTUGAL

N

| 0 | 100 | 200km |
| 0 | | 100 miles |

Contents

MAPS: Spain 4, 8–9; Madrid and Vicinity 94; The Centre 120; Green Spain 148; Northern Border 170; Catalonia 190; The East 222; The South 236; The West 270; The Balearic Islands 284; Canary Islands 293.

Town Plans: Barcelona 202; Granada 261; Madrid 95; Málaga 241; Salamanca 121; San Sebastián 174; Seville 252; Toledo 106; Valencia 224.

Planning Your Trip

Spain is not just one country, with one climate, one landscape, or even one people. It varies from glacier to desert, beach to snow-capped mountain, metropolis to rural idyll. Moreover the distances in between regions are great by European standards. First you will have to decide where you want to go, then you can start thinking about how to get there, when to go, what to take and any other practicalities.

When To Go

As a general rule, late spring to early summer and late summer to early autumn are the best times for visiting most parts of Spain. This avoids the crowds (which congregate even in rural areas), the most oppressive heat and the highest accommodation rates. The sea will be warm enough for swimming in, and you should still get a tan. The north west is the

At the sign of the scallop shell, a symbol of the apostle St James the Great, an eager pilgrim finally reaches his goal in Santiago de Compostela.

only possible exception to this rule. 'Green Spain' is, after all, rainy Spain. You should try to avoid Madrid, Valencia and the big Andalusian cities in July and August. The heat is stifling and even Madrileños depart from the city *en masse* in August, leaving many museums and restaurants closed for the month.

If you want to see Spain in winter, only the Canary Islands guarantee you an all-year tan, with temperatures rarely falling below a monthly average of 17°C (62°F). Back on the mainland itself, the south, and the central and southern parts of the east coast are pleasantly mild almost all year round. Avoid the central plains, where temperatures can plummet sharply. Of course, winter is also the best time for skiing in the Pyrenees, Cantabrian Mountains or Sierra Nevada.

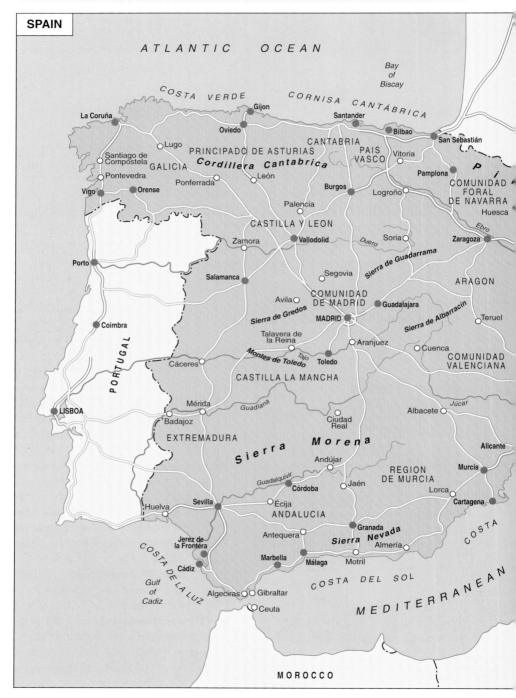

SPAIN

ATLANTIC OCEAN

Bay of Biscay

COSTA VERDE

CORNISA CANTÁBRICA

La Coruña

Gijon

Santander

Bilbao

San Sebastián

Oviedo

Lugo

CANTABRIA

PAIS VASCO

Vitoria

P

Santiago de Compostela

PRINCIPADO DE ASTURIAS

Cordillera Cantabrica

Pamplona

COMUNIDAD FORAL DE NAVARRA

GALICIA

León

Logroño

Pontevedra

Ponferrada

Burgos

Vigo

Orense

Palencia

Huesca

CASTILLA Y LEON

Porto

Zamora

Vallodolid

Soria

Zaragoza

Duero

Ebro

Salamanca

Segovia

Sierra de Guadarrama

ARAGON

Coimbra

Avila

COMUNIDAD DE MADRID

Guadalajara

Sierra de Albarracin

Teruel

MADRID

PORTUGAL

Sierra de Gredos

Talavera de la Reina

Aranjuez

Cuenca

Montes de Toledo

Tajo

Toledo

COMUNIDAD VALENCIANA

Cáceres

CASTILLA LA MANCHA

LISBOA

Mérida

Guadiana

Júcar

Badajoz

Ciudad Real

Albacete

EXTREMADURA

Sierra Morena

Alicante

Andújar

REGION DE MURCIA

Murcia

Guadalquivir

Córdoba

Jaén

Lorca

Huelva

Sevilla

Écija

Cartagena

ANDALUCIA

Granada

COSTA

Jerez de la Frontera

Antequera

Sierra Nevada

Almería

Marbella

Málaga

Motril

Cádiz

COSTA DE LA LUZ

COSTA DEL SOL

Gulf of Cadiz

Algeciras

Gibraltar

Ceuta

MEDITERRANEAN

MOROCCO

You may wish to plan your trip around major fiestas. These can be wonderful experiences but you must book well in advance. Expect to pay inflated accommodation prices and at certain festivals (such as San Fermín at Pamplona), large noisy crowds will mean getting a good night's sleep is almost impossible.

How to Get There

By Air

Transatlantic travellers can fly with Iberia direct to Madrid from New York, Miami and Montreal, though it may be cheaper to re-route via one of the major European airports such as London, Amsterdam or Frankfurt. There are onward connections from Madrid to all other important cities.

Charter flights leave Britain regularly to the main airports of Reus (serving Barcelona and the Costa Dorada), Gerona (Costa Brava), Alicante (Costa Blanca), Málaga (Costa del Sol) and Almería (Costa del Almería). There is always some spare capacity, so as long as you have a little bit of flexibility on dates, hopping on to one of these flights is usually the cheapest way of getting to Spain. It may even be worth taking a cheap package deal; you do not have to stay in the hotel allocated to you and at least you have the first and last night's accommodation sorted out. However, it is also worth looking out for special deals on scheduled flights. Iberia is the national Spanish airline; tel. 0171 830 0011 (UK), 1 800 772 4642 (USA) 514 849 5242 (Canada) and frequently offers special deals. GB airways (UK, tel. 01293 664 239) fly to Murcia and Gibraltar.

If you are not heading to the *costas*, there are also major international airports

*B*arcelona airport, Spain's trendiest "designer" gateway, is an apt entrance to what is the country's most fashionable city.

at Madrid, Barcelona, Oviedo, Bilbao, Santiago de Compostela, Seville, Valencia and Zaragoza. With Spain's domestic airline, Aviaco, you can fly on to another 21 airports. If intend using internal flights, ask about discount air-passes such as the freedom of the Spanish airways pass.

For a visit to the islands there are international airports on Majorca, Menorca, Ibiza, Tenerife, Gran Canaria, Lanzarote and Fuerteventura, and connecting flights to El Hierro, La Palma and La Gomera.

Approximate flying times are: London-Madrid or Barcelona 2 hours; London-Canary Islands 4 hours; New York-Madrid 6½ hours; Montreal-Madrid 7½ hours; New York-Barcelona 8 hours.

By Boat

There is a choice of two ferry crossings to northern Spain from the south of England. Brittany Ferries operate between Portsmouth and Santander in winter (30-33 hours) or Plymouth and Santander the rest of the year (24 hours), while P&O run from Portsmouth to Bilbao (28-29 hours). From Santander or Bilbao it is an 8- to 9-hour drive to Barcelona, a 5- or 6-hour drive to Madrid.

Passenger ships travel regularly to the islands: from Barcelona and Cádiz to the Canaries; from Barcelona and Valencia to Majorca and Ibiza (and less frequently to Menorca); from Denia (on the Costa Blanca) to Ibiza. Boats and hydrofoils link the major and minor islands in the Canaries and in the Balearics.

If you want to arrive on the islands in style you can cruise out of Southampton to the Canaries or the Balearics with either P&O (tel. 0171 930 4343) or the Fred Olsen Line (tel. 01473 292 200), though you will only briefly stop at certain points.

TRAVELLING IN STYLE

The smartest way to see old Andalusia, follow the Wine Trail or do the Pilgrim Tour of St James is aboard the *Al Andalus Express*. This is a luxury vintage train pulling authentic 1920s railway cars, which are claimed to be the most spacious in Europe. Their mahogany panelling and deep velvet brocade has been lovingly restored and you can even dance to live music on board. The train stops at night to ensure everyone gets a good sleep. For more details call MundiColour; tel. 0171 828 6021. From the US or Canada, call Marketing Ahead; tel. (800) 223 1356.

Another charming train runs during summer weekends from Madrid to Aranjuez. The *Tren de la Fresa* (Strawberry Train) follows in the tracks of Spain's second oldest line, opened in 1851 to supply strawberries from the fertile plains of Aranjuez to the capital. The old carriages, built in 1914, are hauled by a steam locomotive. Guides in traditional dress explain the history of the journey and about Aranjuez. Once there, you can spoil yourself even more by taking a *jardinera* (hooded horse-drawn carriage) around the beautiful royal gardens.

A third scenic train covers the mountains of the north, *El Transcántabrico*.

*T*he mountains of Montserrat make wonderful walking country, but let the funicular take the strain of the ascent.

By Road

Express coaches take 26 hours to travel from London to Barcelona, departing most days in the summer. Three times a week they continue south as far as Alicante, stopping at some of the larger towns *en route*. You can also catch the coach to Algeciras, Madrid, Zaragoza, Santiago de Compostela and Santander (contact Eurolines for more information on these services; tel. 0171 730 8235).

If you are driving down through France in your own car, there are numerous routes, depending on your final destination, and what you want to see *en route*.

By Rail

From London take the train to Paris (3 hours by the tunnel, 6 to 7 by ferry); from there you can take either the west coast route to Irun, and on to Madrid, or the east coast route to Port Bou, and on to Barcelona (journey time Paris–Barcelona about 12 hours). All trains must change at the border, so you may prefer to take a local train from here. Contact the British Rail European Travel Centre at Victoria Station in London for further details; tel. 0171 834 2345. See also pages 15-16 for details of rail passes valid in Spain.

Customs and Entry Formalities

Most visitors, including citizens of all EU countries, the USA, Canada, Eire, Australia and New Zealand require only a valid passport to enter Spain. Visitors from South Africa must have a visa.

If you expect to remain for longer than 90 days, a Spanish consulate or tourist office can advise you.

There is no restriction on what you may bring in with you. However, it would be absurd to buy duty-free cigarettes or spirits at your airport of departure, as the same items are much cheaper in Spain.

Tourists may bring an unlimited amount of Spanish or foreign currency into the country and take out (undeclared) up to the equivalent of 1 million pesetas.

Accommodation

All hotels in Spain are government-inspected and graded 1-5 stars depending upon facilities. The majority of tourist accommodation in Spain is provided by 3- or 4-star hotels which conform to a reasonable international standard. As a general rule, book ahead wherever possible.

Hostales are modest hotels with few facilities and are denoted by the sign 'Hs'. The letter *R*, suffixed to a hotel or hostal sign, indicates *residencia*. In theory this means that there is no restaurant facility and the establishment offers bed and breakfast only, but this is frequently not the case. *Pensiones* (boarding houses, denoted by the letter *P*) are the most basic form of accommodation. Both pensiones and hostales are graded 1-3 stars.

PARADORES

Spain's most notable accommodation is usually found in *paradores* (*parador* means 'inn' or 'stopping place'). These are state-run establishments, sometimes housed in stunning historic buildings, sometimes in bland, functional modern blocks with the compensation of being located in outstanding surroundings.

The very first *parador* was set up in 1926. Today there are 86 of them all over Spain. The original aim was to provide good, reasonably priced accommodation in areas away from the main towns and resorts (where there was a lack of places to stay) so that travellers could explore another side of Spain. Today, *paradores* still succeed in showing a more traditional Spain than that of the Costas and all reflect local style in décor and cuisine. However, they are no longer cheap and even in many isolated areas they are no longer the only choice. Moreover, with the growth in provision of accommodation in historic properties, they are no longer unique. Also, being government-run, they sometimes lack that friendly personal touch.

However, nearly all the *paradores* in historic sites are worth a visit as tourist attractions in their own right, and the modern *paradores* for the views they command. Excellent regional food (though it is often quite expensive) is also a *parador* speciality. Some of the best are selected in our list of Hotels (*see* page 326).

There is a central reservation point for *paradores* in Madrid. Contact Paradores de España, Central de Reservas, Velázquez, 18, 28001 Madrid (tel. (01) 435 97 00), fax (01) 435 99 44). *Paradores* also have representatives in other countries. In the UK contact Keytel International (tel. 0171 402 8182). From the USA or Canada contact Marketing Ahead, New York (tel. 212 686 9213). Enquire at the Spanish National Tourist Office in other countries.

You may also come across *fondas* (*F*) and *casas de huéspedes* (*CH*) which are of a similar very basic standard. Youth Hostels (*Albergues Juveniles*) are usually for enthusiasts only. They are rarely located in a convenient place, are usually block-booked by schools and some keep a curfew.

When booking in to any accommodation you will be asked to surrender your passport for a short period. In general, prices are quoted per room (as opposed to per person). A value added tax (*IVA*) of 6 per cent is added to the bill (13 per cent at 5-star hotels).

Under Canvas

Camping grounds are divided into four categories (luxury, 1st, 2nd and 3rd class), and rates and facilities vary accordingly. All sites, however, have drinking water, toilets and showers, electricity, medical facilities, safes for valuables and are under surveillance night and day. Ask the National Tourist Office to send you their free map detailing campsites.

Getting Around

Don't think you can zoom across Spain in a few hours. This is a very large country and even short distances on the map can take hours, locked into traffic-jammed *costas* or serpentine hill roads. If you can cover even most of a single region in a two-week stay, you will be lucky.

By Car

If you want to bring your own car to Spain you will need the car registration papers, a nationality plate or sticker, a red warning triangle, a Green Card extension to your regular insurance policy and a bail

---

A CELL FOR THE NIGHT

If modern hotels turn you off completely, and you think a night in a *parador* castle is a little *passé*, then how about a monk's cell? This traditional hospitality provided for wayfarers has in recent years come to entertain tourists as well. A cell can consist of anything from a room almost as spartan as it sounds, to a pleasant converted apartment with its own little garden (like the one that George Sand and Chopin stayed in when they visited Majorca).

Cells for hire can be found in several places, including the famous monasteries of Santo Domingo de Silos, Las Huelgas and San Pedro de Cardeña (all near Burgos) and also in León, Madrid, Palencia, Segovia, La Coruña and La Oliva at Carcastillo (Navarre). Check with the local tourist office as to availability and restrictions (some cells are single-sex, while others stipulate married couples only).

---

bond that can also be arranged through your insurance company. You will also require an International Driving Permit.

Driving conditions are the same as all over the continent. Drive on the right, overtake on the left and yield right of way to all vehicles coming from your right.

Main roads are very good, and even country roads are usually well surfaced. The *autopista* (motorway or freeway) is usually the fastest way of getting about but it allows you to see nothing of the countryside, and the tolls (*peaje*) charged can be high.

Beware of driving anywhere on a Sunday evening. Massive traffic jams are likely to build up, both on and off the motorway, as city weekenders head back from the beach or country.

Driving and parking is a nightmare in any large city, and the one-way systems in

Armed civil guards (*Guardia Civil*) patrol the roads on their black motorcycles. In towns, the municipal police handle traffic control. If you are fined for a traffic offence, you will have to pay on the spot.

Always carry your driving licence and/or International Driving Permit with you. As the police can demand to see your passport at any time, it is a good idea also to carry a photocopy of the important pages of this with you. Spanish law requires that your car should carry a set of spare headlamp and rear-lamp bulbs. (Check this if you are hiring a car.)

Seat belts are compulsory when driving outside built-up city areas, and children under the age of ten must travel in the rear. Finally, if you are hiring a motorcycle, both you and your pillion rider must wear crash helmets, and motorcycle lights must always be switched on.

An old-fashioned way to see some of the sights of Barcelona – you can find this four-legged option by the waterfront.

towns of even modest size will also have you tearing your hair out; you will probably be able to see where you wish to go, but can never quite get there! If you are on a city-based holiday, it is not a good idea to hire a car, even worse to bring your own car. There is a good chance that your vehicle will be broken into.

Rules and Regulations

Metered parking is quite common in small and large towns, and in the latter your car may well be towed away if you park illegally. It is an offence to park a car facing against the traffic.

Car Hire

You will find local and international car-hire firms all over Spain offering a wide range of cars at varying prices. Always shop around for the best deal. If you want to book in advance in Britain, try Holiday Autos, Europe's largest car rental brokers. They guarantee the lowest hire prices and always use reputable local companies; tel. 0171 491 1111. Their affiliates in the USA are Dollar Rent-A-Car or Alamo, tel 1 800 422 7737. From Canada call any Discount-Rent-A Car office.

Third-party insurance is always included in the basic hire charge, and usually so is CDW (Collision Damage Waiver). Personal accident insurance is normally covered by your standard travel insurance policy.

You must be over 21 if you are paying by credit card and over 23 if you are paying by cash. In the latter case an additional deposit may be required. You should have an International Driving Permit or a recent, pink EU driving licence which supplies translations

Public Transport

Buses are cheap, reasonably comfortable and reliable in most areas, but beware of drastically reduced timetables on Sundays. Buses usually only run into and out of provincial centres so links to smaller places, even if they are quite close to each other, may not be possible.

Train services run all the way along the north coast as far as San Sebastián, and all the way along the eastern Mediterranean coast from Port Bou at the border with France to beyond Murcia in the south. The southern *costas*, however, are not well linked by rail services. Madrid is the hub of the country's network.

There is a bewildering number of types of train. The high-speed *AVE* is similar to the French TGV, and runs during the day between Madrid and Seville (journey time 2 hours); the *Talgo* is a daytime long-distance express; the *Intercity* is a daytime medium-distance express; *Diurno* and *Estrella* are slow day or night long-distance stopping trains; *Regionals* and *Cercanias* are slow daytime medium-distance and local trains.

An *Inter-Rail* pass or *Inter-Rail Plus* (for travellers 26 and over), both available from British Rail (tel. 0171 834 2345), allows unlimited travel on all European railways, with half-price travel in Britain. The *Inter-rail* pass is also available for one, two or three zones of Europe at a lower price (Spain, Portugal and Morrocco constitute one zone). The *Freedom Pass* is more flexible, and allows travel on any 3, 5 or 10 days within one month, in any country or countries of your choice from 26 participating European countries.

COUNTRY STATISTICS

Geography Spain extends over most of the Iberian peninsula on the south-western tip of Europe, with a land mass of 504,788km^2 (194,898 square miles). It is bounded by the Bay of Biscay, the Atlantic Ocean and the Mediterranean, and shares borders with France and Portugal. The two main groups of Spanish islands are the Balearics in the Mediterranean and the Canaries in the Atlantic. Spain also has possessions on the coast of North Africa, namely Ceuta and Melilla.

Highest point: Pico del Teide (Tenerife), 3,718m (12,198ft).

Population 38.4 million inhabitants.

Languages Castilian (Spanish) is spoken everywhere, as a first or second tongue. Official regional languages are Catalan, Basque and Galician.

Capital Madrid (3.2 million inhabitants)

Major cities: Barcelona (1,751,000), Valencia (745,000), Seville (668,000), Zaragoza (595,000), Málaga (538,000), Bilbao (397,000), Las Palmas de Gran Canaria (366,000).

Government A constitutional monarchy with King Juan Carlos I as head of state. A prime minister presides over the *cortes*, composed of the Congress of Deputies and the Senate or upper chamber.

Spain has 17 autonomous communities with legislative assemblies. The 8,022 municipalities are run by elected councils.

Religion Predominantly Catholic, 250,000 Protestants, small Jewish and Muslim communities.

Non-European residents should enquire about the range of *Eurailpasses*; tel. 1 800 TGV RAIL (USA), 1 800 361 Rail (Canada). With all discount passes you may have to pay a supplement for using express trains.

The Spanish National Railways, *RENFE (Red Nacional de los Ferrocar-*

riles Españoles) offer unlimited rail travel passes and these are good for all types of train. If you require further information about travelling within Spain (routes, timetables) write to:

BR International
International Rail Centre
Victoria Station
London SW1V 1YJ.

Taxis

The letters *SP* on the front and rear bumpers of a car (*servicio público*) indicate that it is a taxi. It will probably also have a green light in the front windscreen or a green sign indicating '*libre*' when it is available for hire. Taxis are unmetered in tourist areas. There are fixed prices, displayed on a board at the main taxi rank, giving the fare to the most popular destinations. These are reasonable by north European standards. If in doubt, ask the driver before you set off.

Information

Spanish National Tourist Offices are located in many countries and it is a good idea to write to them before you travel, requesting information on areas of particular interest. The United Kingdom office is at:

57-58, St James' Street
London
SW1A 1LD
Tel. 0171 499 0901

and the main US office is in New York at:

665 Fifth Avenue
NY 10022
Tel. 212 759 88 22.

There are also US offices in Miami, Los Angeles and Chicago.

The main Canadian office is at:

102 Bloor Street West
14th Floor
Toronto
Ontario
M5S 1M8
Tel. 416 961 31 31/40 79.

Gibraltar has its own office:

Gibraltar Information Bureau
Arundel Great Court
179 Strand
London WC2R 1EH
Tel. 0171 836 0777.

Every town or resort of any reasonable size has its own office. The quality of assistance and resources is variable, but in the better places staff are very helpful and are well equipped with maps, leaflets and brochures. Larger towns and provincial centres may also have regional offices.

If you want to know what's on locally (in terms of musical and theatrical events and so on) free listings are often available at the tourist office, large hotels or popular bars. Lookout Publications produce English-language guides to events on the Costa del Sol and the Costa Brava. When in Madrid or Barcelona you can buy *Guía del Ocio* from any newsagents.

Problems

By law, all hotels, restaurants and other establishments dealing with tourists must carry official complaint forms (*Hojas de Reclamación*) and produce them on demand. Once completed, the original of this

FINDING YOUR WAY

alcazaba	*fortress*
alcázar	*castle*
	(fortified palace)
autopista	*(toll) motorway,*
(de peaje)	*highway*
avenida	*avenue*
ayuntamiento	*town hall*
barrio	*quarter, suburb*
calle	*street*
capilla	*chapel*
carretera	*road*
casco antiguo	*old part of town*
casco urbano	*town centre*
castillo	*castle*
convento	*monastery*
correos	*post office*
estación de	*railway station*
ferrocarril	
fortaleza	*fortress*
iglesia	*church*
jardín	*garden*
mercado	*market*
mezquita	*mosque*
murallas	*town walls,*
	ramparts
museo	*museum*
(oficina de)	*tourist office*
turismo	
parque	*park*
paseo	*boulevard*
plaza	*square*
plaza de toros	*bullring*
puente	*bridge*
puerto	*harbour*
río	*river*
ruinas	*ruins*
sierra	*mountain range*
torre	*tower*

And if asking directions...

derecha	*right*
izquierda	*left*
todo derecho	*straight ahead*

document is sent to the Ministry of Tourism, one copy remains with the establishment involved and one copy is given to the person who is making the complaint.

Do try to resolve any problem you may encounter before going through this procedure, as in practice it is difficult to get any redress once you have left the country. The very action of asking for the *hoja* may resolve the problem in itself, as tourism authorities often take a serious view on malpractice, and can revoke or suspend licences. You should also inform the local tourist office, or in serious cases the local police, of any complaints and seek their assistance.

If you are in Catalonia, the regional tourist board has also set up a phone line which acts as an advisory service on any complaints you may have; tel. 900-30 03 03 (calls are free).

Crime

The most common crime against the tourist in Spain is that of theft from hire cars. If you park in the street in one of the big towns or resorts, there is every chance that your car will be broken into. Always look for secure parking areas. Seville is notorious for this, but it happens in all big (and not so big) cities, as well as tourist locations. Never leave anything of value in your car, even in the trunk. Apart from the inconvenience, many insurance policies will not pay out on such losses.

Hotels recommend that you use the safe deposit box in your room for all valuables including your passport. There is usually a charge for this. Burglaries of holiday apartments do occur, so keep doors and windows locked when you are absent and while you are asleep.

*P*uerto Banús, on the Costa del Sol, is southern Spain's classiest marina. Here in this haven of the super-rich, some yachts are so pompous they even fly flags of convenience.

Beware of pickpockets, particularly in crowded places such as markets or bus stations, the metro or busy shopping streets such as Barcelona's Las Ramblas (beware street vendors everywhere). You must report all thefts (or lost property) to the police within 24 hours, who will issue you with a form that you will need for your own insurance purposes.

On a more cheerful note, crimes involving violence against tourists are rare.

Embassies and Consulates

Almost all Western European countries have consulates in Barcelona, and many are represented in other big cities. Citizens of commonwealth countries may also call on the UK consulate. All embassies are located in Madrid. If you run into trouble with the authorities or the police, you can also contact your consulate for advice.
UK: Fernando el Santo, 16; tel. 310 02 08.
USA: Serrano, 75; tel. 577 40 00.
Canada: Núñez de Balboa 35; tel. 431 43 00.

Police

There are three police forces in Spain. The best known are the *Guardia Civil* (Civil Guard). Each town also has its own *Policía Municipal* (municipal police) who wear a different uniform depending on the town and season, but these are usually blue and grey. The third force, the *Cuerpo Nacional de Policía*, a national anti-crime unit, can be recognized by their light-brown uniforms. All policemen are armed. If you need police assistance you can call on any of these forces.

In case of emergency the following numbers are good nationwide: Municipal police, tel. 091 (092 in Barcelona); Civil Guard, tel. 062.

Medical Care

EU residents should obtain form E111 which entitles them to free medical treatment within the EU. It is unwise to travel without health insurance as treatment can be expensive.

Many tourists from northern climes often suffer painful sunburn through overdoing the first day or two. Falling asleep on the beach is a common cause. Take the sun in short doses for at least the first few days. Go steady on the alcohol as well. Spirits are poured in liver-crippling measures, and the beer also packs a punch. Drink plenty of bottled water (*agua mineral*) to avoid dehydration (tap water is safe to drink, but does not often taste particularly pleasant).

A list of doctors who speak your language is available at local tourist offices. There are hospitals in all the principal towns and a first-aid station (*casa de socorro*) in smaller places.

Chemists (*farmacia*) are recognizable by a green cross sign, and are open during normal shopping hours. After hours, at least one per town remains open all night, the *farmacia de guardia*. Its location is posted in the window of all the other *farmacias*.

Post and Telephone Services

Post Offices are for mail and telegrams, not telephone calls. Stamps (*sellos* or *timbres*) are sold at any tobacconists (*tabacos*) and at most shops that sell postcards. Spanish post boxes are painted yellow. The slot marked *extranjeros* is for overseas mail.

If you do not know in advance where you will be staying, you can have mail

---

STEPPING OUT

As evening approaches, most of Europe takes a seat. Britons and Germans gather around their dinner tables, while the café-prone French linger over apéritifs. But not in Spain, where every town and village is abuzz, as if something big is afoot. What is really afoot is the population. The *paseo*, or evening promenade, is an exercise in sociability, rather than physical fitness.

From the Atlantic to the Mediterranean, millions of Spaniards swarm into the streets at sunset for a ritual that even cars and television have not changed. Well-dressed citizens stroll through parks, *plazas*, and streets, exchanging handshakes, nods or conversation with friends and neighbours. Perambulated babies, smartly dressed for the occasion, are ostentatiously admired. Window-shoppers eye the luxurious displays. Feigning indifference, teenagers slyly manoeuvre towards the evening's rendezvous.

---

forwarded to you addressed 'poste restante' (*lista de correos*) at whichever town is most convenient. When collecting, take your passport to the post office as identification.

The cheapest and easiest way to make any sort of telephone call, from local to international, is in a *Teléfonico* kiosk. You go to a numbered booth, dial the number yourself and when you have finished, you pay the person at the desk who has metered your call. Alternatively, you can now dial internationally from any street-corner telephone. Pick up the receiver and when you get the dial tone, dial 07; wait for a second dial tone, then dial the country code, local code (minus the first zero) then the number you are calling. The only snag is that you will need a plentiful supply of 100 peseta coins to feed in to the slot. Easy-to-understand instructions in all languages help you. If you must call home from your hotel (by far the most expensive option), ask in advance how much a three-minute call will cost.

For directory enquiries, tel. 003; international operator (Europe), tel. 008; international operator (rest of world), tel. 005. Big city codes when dialling from within Spain, are: Madrid, 1; Barcelona 3; Seville 5; Valencia 6. These should be prefixed by a 9 if you are dialling from outside Spain.

Etiquette

The Spanish are still by and large an easy-going, friendly people, though you may not think so if caught in a Madrid traffic jam or rush-hour on the Barcelona metro. Away from the big cities, however, many Spaniards still share a belief in the virtues of *mañana*; don't try to rush them. Far from making things better, it might lengthen the delay. In most of Spain work still rotates around the siesta, with whole towns and villages literally going to sleep during the mid-afternoon. Bear this in mind if you are sightseeing so you do not arrive at museums or other attractions during the early afternoon. Small villages also become ghost towns during the siesta. It is far better to arrive in the early evening when the place comes to life as the population gets up to take its *paseo*.

The main exception to this rule is the Catalonians. They are altogether more dynamic and more European, but no less friendly. Politeness and simple courtesies do still matter. Always begin a conversation with *buenos días* (good morning) or *buenas tardes* (good afternoon) and sign off with *adiós* (goodbye), or *buenas noches* (goodnight) when leaving. A handshake never goes amiss.

Eating Out
In a restaurant you must always ask for the bill. It is very rarely offered because no waiter wants to be seen to be actually encouraging you to leave. Since a service charge is normally included in hotel and restaurant bills, tipping is not obligatory, but if the service was good, you might leave around 10 per cent of the bill.

Toilets

The most commonly used expression for toilets is *servicios* or *aseos* though you may also hear or see *WC*, *water* and *retretes*. Public conveniences are rare but all hotels, bars and restaurants have toilets, usually of a reasonable standard. It is considered polite to buy a coffee if you drop into a bar just to use the toilet.

Money Matters

The monetary unit of Spain is the *peseta* (abbreviated *pta*). Coins come in 1, 5, 10, 25, 50, 100, 200 and 500 *pesetas*; banknotes are 1,000, 2,000, 5,000 and 10,000 *pesetas*.

Banking hours are usually from 9am to 2pm Monday to Friday. Banks in the popular resorts also open longer hours and on Saturdays at the height of the season. Beware of hefty transaction charges (often a minimum of 500 pesetas). Outside normal banking hours, many travel agencies and other businesses displaying a '*cambio*' sign will change foreign currency into *pesetas*. Most hotels will also change guests' money, albeit at a slightly less favourable rate than at the bank. Traveller's cheques always get a better rate than cash. You must take your passport with you when changing money or traveller's cheques.

Credit cards, traveller's cheques and Eurocheques are accepted in most hotels, restaurants and big shops.

If you want to report a lost credit card and you do not have the number of your home or local office, the following are Barcelona office numbers (they will circulate details): American Express (217-0070), Eurocard (302-1428), Mastercard or Visa (315-2512).

Disabled Travellers

In general, the provisions for wheelchair travellers in Spain are not particularly good. There are wheelchair ramps at airports and many larger apartments and hotels do make provision for disabled guests. Some of the more modern resorts also provide ramps to cross pavements.

Details of accessible accommodation is given in *Holidays and Travel Abroad* published by:

RADAR
12 City Forum,
250 City Road,
London EC1V 8AF
Tel. 0171 250 3222.

Other sources of information are the Spanish National Tourist Office and the Federation ECOM, who are a group of private organizations for the disabled;

Gran Via de las Cortes Catalanes 562-2a
08011 Barcelona

The latter also publish Access guides to Barcelona and Madrid.

In Britain, contact the Holiday Care Service before you leave. They are experts in the field of holidays for disabled people and will try to answer specific queries; tel. 01293 774 535.

Festivals

The Spaniards gave the world the word *fiesta*, but others can only try to imitate their passion for a celebration. It's a special combination of faith and pageantry, with good-natured boisterous fun always ready to break out, no matter how solemn the occasion seems. No Spanish village is too small to produce a stately saint's day celebration and no city is too big to forget its religious or historical roots.

So many festivals go on all over Spain that you are almost bound to stumble upon one in your travels. The major events, however, are well worth planning for (do book accommodation well ahead). Here's a selection of the very best and also the ones that you are most likely to come across.

February or **March** Santa Cruz de Tenerife, Cádiz, Sitges: Carnival processions.
March Valencia: 'Fallas' – fireworks and bonfires of satirical effigies.
March or **April** Holy Week (*Semana Santa*) processions in all major cities.
April Seville: April Fair, parades, bullfights, dancing. Alcoy (Alicante): 'Moors and Christians' mock battles.
May Jerez de la Frontera: Horse Fair. Almonte (Huelva): Pilgrimage of Rocío. Cordoba: Festival of the Patios and international Flamenco Festival. Granada: Cruces de Mayo – popular festival.
May/June Madrid: Fiesta de San Isidro – bullfighting, concerts, funfairs.
June Granada, Toledo, Sitges, Canary Islands: Corpus Christi festivities. Marbella: San Bernabe Fair. Alicante: St John's Day – fireworks and bonfires. Badajoz: flamenco festival.
July Pamplona: St Fermín Festival – bull runs and bullfights. Granada: Music Festival. Seville: Guitar Festival. Alcalá de Guadaira, Seville: (2nd fortnight) flamenco festival. Barcelona: 'Greek Festival' – daily performances of theatre, dance, song and cinema. Barcelona: Flamenco Festival held concurrently. Tarragona: Dance Festival. Mérida: Theatre Festival. Villajoyosa: Moors and Christians. Santiago de Compostela: Festival of St James. San Sebastián: Jazz Festival.
August Ribadesella (Asturias): international kayak races, processions. La Alberca (Salamanca): traditional Assumption commemoration. Málaga: Summer Fair.
September Jerez de la Frontera: Logroño wine-harvest festivals. Torremolinos: Feria de San Miguel. Barcelona: Merced Festival – music and folklore.

October Zaragoza: Pilar Festival – processions and folklore.

National holidays: 1 January, 6 January, Good Friday, 1 May, 15 August, 12 October, 1 November, 6 December, 8 December, 25 December. Holy Week (4-11) April is celebrated throughout Spain. In addition to these, each region has its own regional holiday and every town and village celebrates its own saint's day.

Carnival and Corpus Christi

The two major fiestas of Carnival (*Carnaval*) and Corpus Christi cover almost the entire range of the Spanish at their celebratory best. The first is pure and simple hedonism and revelry; the second a deeply religious act of devotion.

The places to be at *Carnaval* time are either at Santa Cruz de Tenerife (on the island of Tenerife), Las Palmas (on Gran Canaria), Cádiz, or Sitges. The Tenerifes celebrate loudest of all with pulsating high-energy Latin rhythms, scantily clad Amazonian beauties with skyscraper head-dresses, half the male population in

BURIAL OF THE SARDINE

Of all the carnival festivities, the Burial of the Sardine is surely the most bizarre. A huge board and timber sardine of *Jaws* proportions is hauled solemnly on a large float from an appointed place to the sea. Accompanying it are hundreds of 'mourners' making the most incredible din with their mock anguish, weeping and wailing in the wake of the unfortunate 'deceased' fish. Beauty Queens, transvestites-for-the-night and whole families dressed in stylized black mourning gear make up a funeral party even Dalí could not have envisaged.

At the sea the sardine is ritually burned and a great firework display is given.

*T*he Jerez Horse Fair
(Feria del Caballo), *held each
spring, is an excuse for both horse
and rider to don Sunday best and
parade before locals and tourists.*

self-mocking drag and the other half in all
forms of crazy fancy-dress. Many tourists

don masks and even costumes to join in
the fun.

Corpus Christi

Since mediaeval times, Corpus Christi has
been celebrated all over Spain with religious processions and mystery plays. The
most colourful feature of many Corpus
Christi festivities, however, derives from
the old tradition of covering the route
which the *Corpus* must take with aromatic

herbs. Flower petals are now mostly used, although coloured volcanic sand or coloured salt is sometimes substituted in the Canary Islands, and in Elche de la Sierra (La Mancha), woodshavings and sawdust are used. Whatever raw material is chosen, it is painstakingly arranged on central paved areas to make up enormous artworks. These either take the form of elaborate, carpet-like, abstract patterns or religious pictures, possibly even copied from an Old Master. The most extravagant designs are to be seen in the Canary Islands, Catalonia and Galicia. The pictures are ruined in a matter of moments by the feet of the ensuing procession or by the first rainfall. Only photographs preserve the memory of months of hard work.

Colourful fiestas of song and dance, food and wine, known as *romerías*, follow hard on the heels of Corpus Christi to re-dress the sobriety.

Eating Out

The Spanish take their food very seriously and, as long as you avoid the bland international-style resort hotel and restaurant menus, you will rarely be disappointed by the choice, the flavour or the hearty portions served up throughout Spain. Regional pride is as evident in the cooking as it is in every other facet of Spanish life. No matter where you go, you will be told that the regional version of the dish in front of you is the best in all Spain.

Each region has its gastronomic strengths, from the seafood creations of the north to the rice platters of the east, the roasts of the central area and the succulent hams and fried fish of the south. For every dish there is usually an honest local wine to match.

CHOOSING CAREFULLY

The Spanish are much less squeamish than the British or Americans when it comes to some of the items that appear on the menu. Tapas bars often serve tripe (*callos*) and sometimes offer brains (*cerebros*); restaurants may serve suckling pig complete with head and teeth while *Rabo de Torro* (bull's tail, stewed with onions, tomatoes and a drop of sherry) is considered a classic dish. Around Cuenca you may be offered *oreja de cerdo a la plancha* (grilled pig's ears) while Estremadura confirms its no-nonsense image by putting *lagarto* (lizard) on the menu. In Granada they serve *Tortilla Sacromonte* which includes fried and breaded brain and lamb or veal testicles. *Criadillas* has assumed the inoffensive 'nom de carte' of 'mountain oysters' (presumably so as not to put off more delicate diners). These are in fact bull's testicles! But don't worry if, while in Cádiz, you see *caldillo de perro* (literally, dog soup) – it is really fish soup.

Spanish cooking is currently in a very buoyant mood and has recently spawned its own form of nouvelle cuisine; *nueva cocina Español*, which reigns in the world-class restaurants of Madrid, San Sebastián and Barcelona. However, this does not mean that you should expect tiny portions resembling artworks in the provinces. On the contrary, much of the food is still derived from peasant fare – hearty, filling and generous.

A note for vegetarians and vegetable lovers. The Spanish are, by and large, not great vegetable eaters. Aside from a few inventive salad starters, you will generally have to ask for a salad accompaniment if you want something green to go with the basic dish (potatoes or rice are usually included).

A Little History

The olive, whether black or green, is a versatile fruit. You can eat it marinated or cooked, or press it for the oil, which is widely used for salad dressing and cooking. The ancient Romans, who introduced the olive to Spain, used the oil generously for both internal and external use. Even today, Spanish cooking relies strongly on olive oil and garlic, the latter also introduced by the Romans. The next colonial cooks were the Moors, who brought rice (and the colourful saffron to embellish it) as well as delicious citrus fruits and dates. The Moors also gave the Spanish their sweet tooth.

Thanks to Columbus and company, western hemisphere food exotica, like the potato, tomato and peppers came to be part of the Spanish staple diet. Of course, the really essential ingredients – fresh fish and seafood, plus livestock grazed in the verdant pastures in the north of Spain – have been here all along.

In rural Spain, groves of olives such as these stretching across the rolling Andalusian hillsides, are a common sight.

Where to Eat

Throughout Spain, restaurants are graded by a 'fork' system. One fork is the lowest grade, five forks is the élite. These ratings, however, are awarded according to the facilities and degree of luxury that the restaurant offer, not the quality of the food. If you are in search of the type of restaurant that specializes in local food rather than fancy napkins, the sign *típica*, or *típico*, may be of use in some regions. A brief list of recommended restaurants is enclosed in this guide. All Spanish restaurants should offer a *menú del día* (day's special). This is normally three courses, including wine at a very reasonable set price.

The prices on the menu include taxes and a service charge, but it is customary to leave a tip if you were served efficiently and cheerily. Five to ten per cent is the norm. Bars and cafés, like restaurants, usually include a service charge, but additional small tips are the custom if you have spent any time in the establishment. Prices are 10-15 per cent lower if you stand or sit at the bar rather than occupy a table.

Two notes of caution. The prices of tapas, those tasty snacks on the bar, are not always indicated and can be surprisingly expensive, so do ask before ordering. Also ask how much your bill will be when ordering fish or seafood, which is priced by 100g weight. The price depends on the uncooked weight and can be very expensive. Spain is no longer a cheap place when it comes to seafood.

Meal times are generally later in Spain than the rest of Europe. The peak hours are from 1 to 3.30pm for lunch and from 8.30 to 11pm for dinner. In some parts of the country (like Madrid) meals are taken very late, only starting at around 10pm. However, in the tourist areas or the big cities, you can get a meal at most places just about any time of day.

For a comprehensive menu reader, ask your bookshop for the Berlitz SPANISH-ENGLISH/ENGLISH-SPANISH POCKET DICTIONARY or the Berlitz EUROPEAN MENU READER.

Breakfast

For Spaniards, this is the least significant meal of the day and will probably just consist of *tostado* (toast, which the Andalusians spread with all kinds of dripping) or a roll and coffee. If you have a sweet tooth, look out for places selling *churros*. These are batter fritters, extruded into long strips, deep-fried, and sugared. If you want to go native, dunk them into your coffee or hot chocolate (the latter is more of a thick sauce than drinking chocolate).

Most hotels offer breakfast buffets with an international mélange of cereals, fresh and dried fruits, cold meats, cheeses plus bacon and eggs. Some cafés cater for tourists by offering a full breakfast (*desayuno completo*) of orange juice, bacon, eggs and other trimmings.

Lunch and Dinner

The classic Spanish dish is *paella* (pronounced pie-ALE-ya), named after the black iron pan in which the saffron rice base is cooked in stock. The cook then adds various combinations of squid, *chorizo* (a spicy salami-style sausage), prawns, shrimps, rabbit, chicken, mussels, onion, peppers, peas and so on, according to what is to hand or to the type of paella advertised on the menu. It is always

Snacking in Spain is easy. Tapas, bite-sized morsels of genuine Spanish food, can be found in bars, cafés and restaurants everywhere.

cooked to order (usually for a minimum of two people) and is a feast for the eyes as well as the tastebuds. *Riz* (or paella) *parellada* is a refinement of paella. Bones and shells have already been sorted, so if you want the taste without the fuss (and don't mind paying a little more) it is heaven. You'll find paellas all over Spain, but the home of the dish is Valencia.

There are two other national favourites, which are well known to tourists. The first is *gazpacho* (pronounced gath-PAT-cho), a delicious chilled tomato soup, to which chopped tomatoes, peppers, cucumbers, onions and fried bread croutons are added. Even if the idea of chilled soup does not appeal, try it once: it is a great refresher on a hot summer day. Perhaps not surprisingly, this is an Andalusian dish. The second dish is *tortilla* or potato omelette. There are many variations on this, served hot or cold, and nearly always available on the tapas counter. There is also a cold-weather dish that is all but universal: an extremely rich hotpot called (de-pending on what part of the country you're in) *cocido*, *olla*, *pote*, *escudella* or *cazuela*. The meal starts with a nutritious broth, perhaps with noodles. The next course presents a portion of the ingredients that were cooked to make the broth in the first place: cabbage, carrots, chick peas, onions, potatoes, turnips and whatever else was used. All of which is to whet your appetite for the climax: chunks of beef, ham, sausage, chicken, pork or whatever, which had been cooked in the same pot. Take the rest of the day off.

Regional Tastes

Every province and almost every town in Spain seems to have a different sort of

A splash of seasonal colour – peppers drying in the hot southern sunshine on the outside of a house in the village of Guadix in Andalusia.

sausage, a homemade cheese, a variation on a paella, their own secret ingredients for *cocido* and so on. Here's a suggestion of what's cooking around the country, roughly from north to south.

Galicia *Caldo gallego*, a hearty vegetable soup, which may also contain bits of ham or sausage, is the most common regional dish. The area is particularly recognized as having the best seafood in Spain, and is famous for its love affair with the octopus (*pulpo*). Restaurants devoted almost solely to this odd creature are called *pulperias*. In Santiago de Compostela, the traditional pilgrim dish is *vieira* (scallops) which have always been associated with St James; here they are cooked in butter, then baked on the half-shell with tomato sauce, onions and breadcrumbs. If the weather turns cold, look out for *lacón con grelos* (salted ham with turnip tops). A Galician standby is the *empanada*, a flaky pastry rather like a Cornish pasty, containing anything from meat to seafood, served hot or cold.

Asturias Big white beans and sausage give backbone to the delicious hotpot called *fabada asturiana*. This dish is nationally famous and transcends regional barriers. *Merluza a la sidra* (hake in cider sauce) makes the most of the local apples and fish in an unusual, winning combination. Hake is Spain's most common fish dish. Asturias produces a pungent creamy blue Roquefort-like cheese, *queso de Cabrales*, which is more piquant and more expensive than imported blue cheese.

Basque Country They say that behind every great Spanish restaurant is a Basque chef. Here, in the gastronomic capital of all the Spains, they do wonders with fish and seafood. Try *bacalao al pil pil*, fried cod in a carefully prepared hot garlic sauce; *bacalao a la vizcaina*, cod, peppers and onions; *angulas a la bilbaína*, eels in a hot olive-oil and garlic sauce (always eaten with a wooden fork); *chipirones* (tiny squid cooked in their own ink); and *marmitako* (a spicy tuna, tomato and potato stew). The sublime sauces of the Basque cuisine enrich many a casserole; on menus anywhere in Spain look for the suffixes *a la vizcaina, a la donostiarra* and *a la guipuzcoana*.

Navarre *Trucha a la navarra* (grilled trout with a surprise slice of ham hidden inside), is offered in many parts of the country but, of course, it is best at the source. So is the feathered game and local asparagus.

The Pyrenees Typical here are warming meaty dishes in *chilindrón* sauce (an alliance of tomatoes and peppers, onion, garlic, chopped ham, and wine). Game and trout also figure in the mountain cuisine.

Catalonia The Basques take top honours for the quality of their cooking, but Catalan cuisine is held to be the most sophisticated and comprehensive in Spain. For starters, try *Escalivada* (an olive-oil dressed cold salad of grilled or baked vegetables, including aubergines, peppers and onions); *Esqueixada* – pronounced es-kay-SHA-da – (a stimulating salad of salt-cod, red pepper and tomatoes); or *Xato* – pronounced sha-TO (a salad speciality of Sitges), which comprises anchovies, tuna or cod, in a spicy sauce of oil, vinegar, red pepper, anchovies, garlic and ground almonds, served with olives and endive.

Grilled fish is often accompanied by *Romesco* – a sauce that is the pride of Tarragona. It is made up of oil, ground almonds, hazelnuts, mild chilli, tomatoes, garlic and breadcrumbs, and is delicious with fried fish and shellfish.

Fideuà is a plainer cousin of seafood paella, substituting noodles for rice. Don't miss either of the rich fish and seafood stews that the region is known for – *Suquet de Peix*, or *Zarzuela*. The latter is the showpiece, in a tomato and wine sauce. The Catalans also have a tradition of mixing meat with sweet-sounding sauces (which usually harmonize well and are never as sickly as they sound); so don't be surprised to see partridge with chocolate (it doesn't taste sweet), chicken with peaches, rabbit with almonds and so on.

Castile For starters, try *sopa castellana*, a sort of baked garlic soup with chunks of ham and an egg poaching in it. The star attraction of the region is *Cochinillo asado*, a tender very young Castilian sucking pig, roasted to a golden crispness. *Cordero asado* (roast lamb) is tender and fragrant, and often comes in a gargantuan helping.

The East Coast This is the land of rice and paella is the dish you must try at least once, but there are plenty of other wonderful rice dishes to sample. *Arroz con costra* (rice with a crust) is the pride of Alicante. It's a paella-like dish with added pork meatballs, and the whole thing is topped with beaten eggs and baked in the oven. *Arroz a banda* is a two-part dish where the rice is served first, flavoured with the saffron and fish stock that has been simmering away in it. The fish then follows, possibly served with *alioli* (a garlic sauce).

La Mancha Quixote country is famed for its game. There is a favourite rabbit stew called *tojunto*, an abbreviation for 'all together'. Nationally renowned is *pisto manchego*, an extravagant ratatouille-like vegetable stew emphasizing aubergines, tomatoes and courgettes. Spain's most honoured cheese, *queso manchego*, comes from La Mancha. This is a smooth-textured cheese rather like cheddar, though mild, and is sometimes served with a delicious quince jelly (*membrillo*).

Estremadura Far from the sea in isolated Estremadura, country-style pork is the main attraction; the sausages come in countless styles. The *caldereta* (lamb stew) is a delicious variation on the old shepherds' recipe.

Andalusia The traditional food of Andalusia, sadly, does not often appear on restaurant menus, even off the beaten track. Simplicity and fresh ingredients is the key to *fritura mixta*, the lightest, crispest, most delicious mixed fried battered fish you will taste anywhere. *Pescaito frito* is similar, but usually comprises smaller fish. Both dishes are the pride of Málaga and Cádiz, but are found everywhere in the coastal south. The best ham in the country, the Jabugo variety, comes from Huelva and Trévelez (Granada), but do check the price before ordering. Andalusia is world-famous for its gazpacho, but it also produces an equally refreshing cold soup, *ajo blanco* (also known as *gazpacho blanco*) made from garlic and almonds, and often garnished with moscatel grapes (*con uvas*). *Huevos a la flamenca* is yet another of those classic Spanish dishes where base ingredients, in this case a tomato and vegetable sauce plus eggs, are baked in a casserole with whatever happens to be to hand: *chorizo*, prawns, ham and so on. It is absolutely delicious and takes its name from its colourful appearance.

The Islands Neither the Balearics nor the Canary Islands boast the variety or individuality of the mainland regions. Furthermore, because of the heavy tourist presence, it is more difficult to find the real thing; but don't despair, there are good mainland dishes plus all the local specials to be found.

Canarian specialities include *Papas arrugadas* – new potatoes baked in their skins in seawater, then rolled in rock salt and accompanied by *mojo picón* (a red piquant sauce). *Mojo verde*, is a cool green herb sauce which is a perfect accompaniment to grilled fish. On Majorca you will find *tumbet*, a ratatouille-type of stew plus potatoes, to which meat and fish may be added to form a complete meal.

Sweet-Tooth Specials

When it comes to sweetmeats, the Spaniards outdo almost everybody but the Arabs, who introduced them to their teeth-melting treats. Pastries overflowing with whipped cream are easy to find and hard to resist. Many towns have their own recipes for *yemas*, a monumentally sweet egg-yolk and sugar confection. Marzipan, made of almonds, egg whites and sugar, comes in various guises with regional variations. *Turrón* (nougat), too, varies in colour, consistency and sweetness depending on the source. And there is a big repertoire of cakes, tarts and pastries, flaky or weighty, always sweet, sometimes overpowering. You won't find any of these on the restaurant menu, however, only in the cake shops (*pastelerías*).

When it comes to dessert, the Spanish often seem to lose their inventiveness. The ubiquitous Spanish dessert is *flan* (crème caramel). The Catalans do a de-luxe version of this, known as *Crema catalana*, made of eggs, sugar, milk and flavoured with cinnamon and lemon. It has a glassy-hard caramelized crust which you have to break before entering. Aside from these and the occasional regional specials, however, the choice is usually limited to *helado* (ice cream) or a selection of fresh fruit, which may sound good but is often pretty unexciting.

Wines

Spain has more square kilometres of vineyards than any other European country, producing not only oceans of wine but reefs of controversy. Vintage pundits compare the best Spanish wines with the most respected foreign classics and in 1979 a bottle of Torres Gran Coronas Mas La Plana (often referred to as Black Label) was voted the world's best claret, beating the very best that the French could offer. On the opposite side, critics dismiss much of the crop as plonk – and indeed, much of it is, meant only for home consumption, and never intended to grace the glasses of wine snobs.

In between these extremes, you'll find the average restaurant *vino de la casa*. When a Spaniard sits down to a meal, he simply orders *vino*, and it is understood that he means red wine. In the old days, he would take an empty jug or bottle to the wine shop for a refill of *vino corriente* from a cask inscribed with the degree of alcohol content and the colour: *tinto* for full-bodied red, *clarete* for light red, and *blanco* for white. (Rosé wine – *rosado* – is less common.) Thanks to the tourist invasion and higher living standards, things have become much more sophisticated, although the cask-to-jug supply system still exists. Whether Spaniards buy their wines in the traditional musty-smelling *bodega* or in the supermarket, they are now choosier. To meet this demand and compete with its European neighbours for the export trade, Spain is bottling ever better wines.

Spain's wine-producing regions run from earthy east-coast reds to light, fresh Galician whites. The industry is regulated (and promoted) by a national institute controlling the *Denominación de Origen*. To

If you want to try some local wine, visit a bodega *like this one at Jerez de la Frontera.*

spot a bottle awarded this quality seal, look for a small map on the back label, showing precisely where the wine comes from. It indicates that the vintners follow the strictest rules of their art.

Of all the *Denominaciones* in the field of table wine, the oldest and most vigorously protected is *Rioja*, along the valley of the Ebro in northern Spain. Some truly distinguished wines (mostly reds) proudly bear the Rioja tag. Their distinctive oaky vanilla flavour comes from the casks in which they mature.

East of La Rioja, Aragon contributes some powerful Cariñena reds. The best-known wines from central Spain come from La Mancha, the splendid smooth reds of Valdepeñas. The Penedés region in Catalonia is acclaimed not only for its excellent still wines, but around Sant Sadurni d'Anoía, they produce more sparkling wine by the *methode champenoise* than anywhere else in the world, including the Champagne region itself.

Torres is the most famous label of the Penedés area. This is largely a white wine region but two of the best known Torres labels are on red wines – Sangre de Toro (literally, bull's blood) and their internationally famous, award-winning 'Black Label' (see above).

The best-known *cava* houses are Freixenet and Cordoníu (who will be pleased to show you around). Look for *brut* or *brut natur* on the label if you like it dry. If you want a reasonable quality *cava*, don't buy the cheapest. To the north of Tarragona, the Priorato region is also renowned for its wines – big, full-bodied reds to be precise. Look for the Scala Dei label.

Elsewhere, connoisseurs rave over Vega Sicilia from the Ribera del Duero,

Old Castile (but you will see it in many an expensive restaurant), and as a change to all those hefty reds try the fresh young Albariños of Galicia.

As for southern Spain, where Phoenicians first planted vines 3,000 years ago, the monumental achievement here is sherry from Jerez de la Frontera. It is made by the *solera* method, involving three or four rows of oak casks. The bottom row contains the oldest sherry, which is bottled when needed, whereupon the cask is filled from the one above it, and so on. This makes for uniform quality instead of single-year vintages. As an aperitif, try a bone-dry fino or a medium dry amontillado. A dark, sweet oloroso goes down well after dinner. In Jerez de la Frontera, you can inspect the *bodegas* for yourself.

Lunching on a hot day, it is no social misdemeanour to dilute your table wine if you wish. Adding *gaseosa*, a cheap fizzy lemonade, turns heavy red wine into an imitation of sangría. Real sangría, a popular summer cooler, is a mixture of red wine, lemon and orange juice, brandy, mineral water, ice and slices of fruit – rather like punch, and probably stronger than you expect.

If you are not in the mood for wine at all, have no qualms about ordering a *cerveza* (Spanish beer is often of high quality) or a soft drink or mineral water; nobody will turn up a snobbish nose. In Asturias the standard accompaniment for food is the local cider (*sidre*), refreshingly tart, and traditionally poured from a great height so it bounces off the glass and becomes aerated.

Don't miss out on sweet dessert wines. Some of these are made in the same *solera* system used to produce sherry. Try also a moscatel to accompany your dessert. A good moscatel will have a delicious sultanas-and-honey flavour. Only the poor quality ones are sickly sweet.

Spanish brandy is often sweeter and heavier than French cognac, but not all brands are cloying, so taste around. It is also much better value than buying foreign brandy. Every region has its own liqueur; try, for instance, the herbal concoctions of

TIPS ON *TAPAS*

A *tapa* is a small portion of food which encourages you to keep drinking instead of heading off to a restaurant for a more formal meal. The word *tapa* means 'lid', and comes from the old custom of giving a free bite of food with a drink – the food served on a saucer on top of the glass like a lid. Nowadays it is rare to see *tapas* given away – perhaps the odd olive or dish of peanuts, but bars which specialize in *tapas* are more popular than ever.

Bona-fide *tapas* bars, and indeed many simple bars, have a whole counter display of hot and cold *tapas*, which makes choosing very easy. You can simply point to the one you like the look of. Some of the most common *tapas* are olives, meatballs, Russian salad, local cheese, wedges of Spanish omelette (*tortilla*), *chorizo* (spicy salami-style sausage), octopus salad, prawns in garlic, mushrooms, mountain-cured ham (*jamón serrano*), marinated anchovies (*boquerones en vinagres*).

Tapas are always accompanied by a small basket of fresh bread or Catalan-style *pa amb tomaquet* (bread with tomato). The bread is rubbed with garlic, smeared with tomato, grilled, then drizzled with olive oil. The Majorcans call this *pa amb oli*.

Portion-control: *una tapa* is the smallest amount; *una ración* is half a small plateful, and *una porción* is getting towards a meal in itself. Keep your enthusiasm in check. It is quite easy to spend more on *tapas* than on a good restaurant meal.

Galicia or Ibiza, the monks' secret potion from Montserrat or the potent aniseed drinks from Chinchón, near Madrid.

Wines and spirits are served at all hours everywhere in Spain, so don't raise an eyebrow when you see a local knocking back a large measure of colourless firewater first thing in the morning. You may also be surprised to see that children frequent the bars with impunity. The Spanish consider this quite natural, even quite late at night.

Tea, Coffee and Soft Drinks

The Spanish usually drink coffee (*café*) as opposed to tea (*té*). This can be either *solo*, small and black; *con leche*, a large cup, made with milk, often in a frothy capuccino-style; or *cortado*, a small cup with a little milk. Spanish coffee is nearly always strong and tasty. If it is too strong for you, ask for a Nescafé, and you will be given a sachet of instant granules and a cup of hot water so you can make it up to your desired strength.

Paella is another famous Spanish dish. If on the coast, try the seafood version which will come stacked with prawns, mussels, octopus, and other assorted goodies.

Mineral water (*agua mineral*) is either sparkling, *agua con gas*, or still, *sin gas*. Ice cream parlours sell *granizado*, slushy iced fruit juices in several flavours, and freshly pressed orange juice, *zumo de naranjas*, the latter being surprisingly expensive given that it is one of Spain's main crops.

Around the Valencia and Alicante provinces you will come across *horchaterias* which specialize in the very Spanish, cool refresher, *horchata de chufa*. This is a milky drink made from a fruity, wrinkled little nut with a sweet, almondy taste.

35

THE COUNTRY, ITS HISTORY AND ITS PEOPLE

¡Viva (the New) España!

Put those images of crowded *costas*, third-rate hotels and kiss-me-quick hats to one side. Spain is once again on the fashionable holiday list. Whether it's nightspots of Madrid, Gaudí's Barcelona or the *paradores* of the interior, Spain has shifted its focus from supplying sun, sea and sangria to an altogether more cultured experience.

Imagine a visitor from outer space landing, by chance, in Spain in 1992. What a summer this little green man could have spent: marvelling at the 100-plus exhibiting nations at Seville's Expo '92; moving on to the frenetic night and day delights of Madrid, the reigning European City of Culture; gasping, along with the rest of the world, at the precocious and brilliant staging of the Olympic Games by Barcelona. Surely, he would conclude, this is one of earth's great nations.

The face of new Spain – young, good looking and independent. Trend-setters abound in Barcelona, Madrid, Ibiza and in many university towns.

Yet in historical terms it is less than the blink of an eye (only 20 years) since the end of dictatorship and isolation. If that same alien had arrived between 1936 and 1939 he would have witnessed the ultimate degradation of Spaniard slaying Spaniard. To say Spain has changed radically is an understatement. From the role of Europe's tragic victim it has transformed itself into one of Europe's more dynamic partners. Its cities have been revitalized, its economic and political infrastructure stabilized (Felipe González is now Spain's longest-serving prime minister) and its integration into Europe and NATO realized. Fashion-wise, Spain is also definitely Euro-hip. From the ashes of the Civil War, the New Spain has arisen.

Much has changed, even the workday itself: in parts of the country, economic pressures have forced out the old tradition of the siesta. For better or worse, the chaperones who guarded the morals of young ladies are now but a memory and those young ladies are becoming taller and more independent all the time; some even join the Civil Guard. Hamburgers, pizzas and junk food have won a beach-head in Spain, but the connoisseur of Spanish cuisine will have no problems. In a heartening development in the late 1980s, millions of holiday-makers voted with their feet not to patronize the over-exploited *costas*, and this seems to have stimulated the growth of a more cultured and (to an extent) a more ecologically aware Spain.

Working the land is thirsty work in the heat. Farmers and peasants on mule or horseback are still a common sight in rural Spain.

The good news is that, in spite of its dizzyingly fast Europeanization, Spain remains different.

Spain is the world's most popular tourist destination. Close on 50 million foreign travellers, substantially more numerous than the native population, arrive every year. Although this may sound disconcerting to people who hate crowds, don't worry: the tourist throng is well contained along the beaten path, essentially a very long, narrow strip of highly desirable beachfront. The rest of the country, almost anywhere inland and away from the big international cities, greets the explorer with small-town curiosity and traditional courtesy.

The 'Spains'

The country is so diverse that the ancient Romans gave it a plural name: *Hispaniae*, or 'the Spains'. The internal differences,

*T*he highest peaks in
mainland Spain are the Sierra
Nevada, where you can ski less
than a couple of hours from the
Costa del Sol's broiling beaches.

which began with the landscape and the tribes who settled there, persist. Geographically, 'the Spains' are as varied as snowy mountains and sunbaked sand-dunes, orange groves and rice fields. In the average year the green north west receives six times as much rainfall as the parched plain of La Mancha. From region to region the land, the crops, the houses and the people are vastly different. There is a downside to this. In areas where language and culture diverge from the Spanish mainstream, tensions do sometimes run dangerously high. There are in total four languages: Basque, Catalan, Gallego (the tongue of Galicia) and the unifying Castilian, plus seven dialects. In fact, the very concept of Spanishness has become controversial, although fortunately those most extreme and violent proponents of regional independence, the Basque ETA movement, have now been marginalized. The Catalonians would probably claim to be the least Spanish of all but no doubt the Basques would disagree with that and the Galicians might have something to say on the issue too. The Basques and the Catalans are allowed to run autonomous, (though not independent) states within the country as a whole, and this has greatly reduced tension with Madrid.

Physically Speaking

Bigger than Italy, smaller than France, Spain is about three-quarters the size of Texas but no less proud. (After all, in its Golden Age, Spain ruled Texas – and Florida and Mexico, too.) Most of its national boundaries consist of coastline, about 1,100km (700 miles) along the Mediterranean Sea, and, less touristically, almost over 1,000km (600 miles) along the Atlantic Ocean and Bay of Biscay. In the north east, the Pyrenees wall off Spain from France and the duty-free mini-state of Andorra. The only other contiguous country, Portugal, clings along most of the Iberian peninsula's west coast.

Tourists broiling shoulder to shoulder on Spain's *costas* are often unaware that this is Europe's second most mountainous country after Switzerland. The skiing season here goes on into May. Madrid is Europe's highest capital, even if its altitude at 640m (2,100ft) is unlikely to flutter the heart or strain the lungs. Elsewhere in Spain, the summits soar well over 3,000m (11,000ft). For the record, the country's highest mountain, at 3,718m (12,198ft), is an offshore volcanic peak, a snow-capped mirage on the lush island of Tenerife.

Madrid is a compromise capital built in the middle of Spain's central plateau (*meseta*) almost encircled by mountains. The plateau's climate is officially described as 'continental', which means boiling hot summers and icy winters. Spain offers a choice of two other climates: 'temperate marine' (meaning mild but often wet) in the north and north west, and 'Mediterranean' (the tourist's dream) on the east and south coasts.

In other European countries, the rivers have an economic as well as a scenic importance; it is hard to imagine Germany without the Rhine or London without the Thames. Yet only one of Spain's waterways is notably navigable. The Guadalquivir links Seville to the sea 100km (60 miles) away, hardly an Amazonian challenge. Other rivers dwindle to a trickle for much of the year.

Portrait of a Spaniard

Jutting like a mailed fist south westwards into the Atlantic from the rest of Europe, Spain almost touches North Africa. In turn, North Africa has touched Spain in profound, visible ways. The Moors ruled the country for seven centuries. They left behind their forts and fountains, crafts and music, and their genes, but they were only one of many influences on the face and character of Spain.

The Spanish family tree is a tangle of intertwining cultures. The Arabic influence is clearly visible in the dark-eyed southerners, whereas Celts settled in the north, as you might guess from the sight of red beards and the sounds of the bagpipes. Where the Basques came from is harder to determine, hidden as they are behind an inscrutable language, but they certainly beat the Romans to Spain. Another independently minded group are the Catalans, who once had an empire of their own, and still strongly prefer speaking Catalan to Spanish. With all these variants

RIOTS IN THE STREET

Hand in hand with the Spanish trait of individualism goes a deep distrust of authority. In view of the rulers that have served the people so badly over the last few centuries, this is hardly surprising. A recent incident in Guadalajara, a small town near Madrid, recently demonstrated both this and the gregarious lifestyle of the people. Angry crowds gathered publicly to demonstrate against a proposed new bye-law and even stoned the *Ayuntamiento*. So what caused this outburst: an increase in taxes or cuts in local spending? No, someone had been foolish enough to suggest that drinking-up time should be brought forward to 3am instead of the current 6am!

to choose from, the stereotype of a Spaniard has gone by default to the Andalusian cliché – those dark flashing eyes, clacking castanets and stamping heels. The image is Spanish, but it is only one piece of the whole multi-racial jigsaw.

Whether the eyes are black or blue or green, some traits are representative of the Spaniards. Generosity, for example. Anyone who has been swept up into the embrace of a Spanish family is an expert on the subject. You'll have to get away from the tourist enclaves to appreciate such hospitality. Waiters and barstaff on the costas (though perfectly friendly) are not typical of the nation.

Spanish dignity is apparent in the unwavering gaze of the peasant along the road, to say nothing of the straightbacked posture and meticulous attire of the man or woman in the city. There is a narrow line, of course, between dignity and arrogance, the latter being most manifest in the macho attitude occasionally found in the south.

Quixote was here. There can be no more evocative sight in all Spain than the windmill.

Another Spanish trait is individualism. As the traffic jam in any Spanish city shows, organization and co-operation are *not* national strong points. Spaniards tend not to be team players (even their great football clubs, Real Madrid and FC Barcelona were criticized for taking so long to achieve a major European honour in recent years). Like all the great thinkers and explorers, the Spanish prefer going it alone. Gaudí, Dalí, Picasso and Miró certainly went alone and even Don Quixote, went almost alone (advised only by Sancho Panza). To emphasize the point it has been said that the Spanish are so anarchic that even anarchism strikes them as too organized! That comment, however, was made before the success of the Barcelona

Olympics. This organizational triumph not only surprised most of the rest of Europe, it even shocked the natives of Barcelona. Which only goes to show that when the Spanish put their minds to it, they can be as organized as any nation.

Another generalization is that Spaniards are outgoing and gregarious. Observe them in a restaurant or bar. Loud voices, expansive gestures and hearty expressions. Sometimes these appear to be threatening and angry – but not for long. It is probably just a misunderstanding – everyone is so busy putting their own view across that they sometimes do not hear what the other person has to say. The Spanish tend to behave less like cool, rational north Europeans, and to live life for the moment in the flamboyant Latin style. Here, too, the Catalans diverge – they are the most European of all Spaniards.

THE LUCK OF THE DRAW

On what seems to be almost every street corner in Spain you will see people, often disabled, selling lottery tickets. Behind this huge business (one of the five largest companies in the country) is ONCE, the National Organization for Blind Spaniards. This daily lottery is a subject of great national interest and each evening Tele-5 provides a scantily clad *señorita* to pick out the lucky *cupón* (lottery ticket) in front of the watching nation. The head of ONCE, a blind, dynamic lawyer named Miguel Durán, has for his almost ruthless ambition and dedication to the cause, earned himself the nickname Al Cupone!

The birth rate may be down and divorce (legalized as recently as 1981) may be booming but the sense of the inviolable family seems eternal. Watch the possessive way Spaniards spoil their babies, wrapping them in old-fashioned love and affection. The objects of so much indulgence soon become Europe's noisiest kids, but nobody ever claimed silence was a Spanish virtue.

Religion still plays a vital part in the national psyche. Church-going has declined to a minority activity, yet religious festivals continue as all-consuming as ever and superstition flickers in the subconscious of millions of Spaniards. Once upon a time

The citizens of Cáceres, in Estremadura, share the honour of bearing the image of the Virgin of the Mountain (right).

The annual procession during Holy week in Seville (left).

they would discover lost statuettes of the Virgin and devote shrines to them. The most important (at Montserrat, Zaragoza and Guadeloupe) attract millions of worshippers even today and the cathedral of Santiago de Compostela is still revered throughout Europe.

The Spanish still worship the old traditions, and a few new ones too. They are hooked on games of chance and regularly play the several competing lotteries. After gravely consulting omens, lucky numbers and the success record of the particular ticket vendor, they spend fortunes week in, week out.

Beyond the *Costas*

Mass tourism, much disparaged by sophisticates and environmentalists, seethes along the east and south coasts and the holiday islands. As happy as the sun-blessed millions may be, anchored to packed beaches backed by high-rise hotels and apartment blocks, they are not seeing Spain in the broader sense. It would be the same if tourists visiting the United States never ventured farther north than Florida, or if visitors to Great Britain stayed put in Brighton or Blackpool.

Even the beaches, though, reflect the intriguing diversity of 'the Spains': the hidden coves of the Costa Brava are a world away from the endless sweep of sand on the Costa Almería. Most of the tourist enclaves adjoin towns or villages with more to commend them than just restaurants and souvenir shops. Within walking distance of the most contrived tourist colony, you will probably discover an historic church, buildings of architectural interest, an off-beat museum or a *tapas* bar where you will be welcome to drink and snack

with the locals.

part full of chara

Some of the coa sprawling tourist co ticular attention. The written rule that the to show you far more of th will the coastal resorts tha it for yourself; explore Mála Alicante. Above all, you m capital of the north easter Barcelona; a vital and very Europ which offers everything from me monuments to brilliant 20th-centur chitecture, plus a vibrant street life, and night. Palma, the metropolis of t tourist-inundated island of Majorca, i another treat – crowned by one of Spain's most impressive Gothic cathedrals and an ancient Moorish palace.

On the Ground

A few practical tips to help you get the most out of your stay. If you want to see the most interesting part of town always look for the *casco antiguo* (old town) sign. (Don't be put off by dull or ugly suburbs – just keep going.) The trendiest bars, the oldest buildings, museums and the tourist office are invariably in this part of town.

Your first port of call should always be the local tourist office. Even if they are not all well equipped with local knowledge or leaflets, they will be able to tell you where you can catch a fiesta and a local market within your holiday period (this guidebook covers the major fiestas but lesser ones happen all the time on a local level). It would be a crying shame to leave Spain without witnessing at least one fiesta and markets are also a great slice of real-life entertainment. Moreover, market day may be the one and only day of the week when a town or village comes to life.

If you are staying at a coastal resort where there is fishing activity it is also worth trying to see the *lonja* or fish auction. A siren or bell may announce its commencement (though not all are open to tourists).

The tourist office will help those arriving without accommodation by offering suggestions (although they will not make bookings for you). Beware that Spain is a very noisy place: cars, mopeds, night-life and the stentorian voices of the people themselves. If you want peace and quiet you may be better away from town altogether, though a room set back from the street (and a couple of glasses of the local wine) usually ensures a good night's sleep.

Finally, avoid visiting towns or villages during the *siesta* (from around 1-4pm), when whole settlements literally go to sleep. While there may be some attraction in traffic-free streets, it is deadly quiet when everywhere is closed. Most of the big towns are exceptions to this rule, although even in these places some establishments stick to the old tradition.

History

The history of Spain is as rugged and colourful as the land itself. From Moorish domination to conquerors of the New World; great empires won and lost; brave kings and foolish kings; and through it all, internecine bloodshed, culminating in the ultimate horror of modern civil war and excommunication from the international community. Yet almost unbelievably, less than twenty years post-Franco, Spain's rehabilitation is more than complete.

Early History

The earliest inhabitants of Spain were Neanderthal-like people, sharing the land with lions and even bigger beasts; rhinoceros, hippopotamus and elephant. How did these people and the big game arrive in Spain? Evidently, they walked. In the beginning, it is believed, Europe and Africa were linked by a land bridge between Gibraltar and Morocco. During the Ice Age, lions, rhinos, hippos and elephants wisely headed back to sunny Africa. The first Spaniards put on their bearskin coats, stoked up their fires and stayed. The animals who stayed with them consisted mostly of deer, bison and wild horses – just like those seen decorating the walls and ceilings of caves in Spain; the best known cave paintings being near Altamira, in Cantabria. Prehistoric artists who could convey the concepts of mass and motion left us a vivid notion of the hunter's existence. Their talent dates back at least 15,000 years. By the standards of any age, it is great art.

During the Neolithic period, agriculture and pottery-making developed. In the rock paintings of the new age, simple human figures accompany the images of animals. The women appear to have donned skirts.

Life had changed profoundly by the start of the Bronze Age, not only in the tools at hand but the crops raised and the design of houses and villages. Settlements arose on hilltops, the better to deal with danger. Centuries later, this form of defence planning was to evolve into a network of castles in Spain.

During the Bronze Age, Celtic immigrants populated northern and central Spain, while the south and east were inhabited by various Iberian tribes of North African origin. The Celts were illiterate and rather uncouth, whereas the Iberians had

45

their own written language, sophisticated industry and beautiful art. The supreme work of Iberian art, a stone sculpture of a gorgeous goddess now called *The Lady of Elche*, reigns as the star attraction at Madrid's Archaeological Museum. Some experts find elements of classical Greek style in this statue; the Greeks were among the first foreign influences on the peninsula.

The Celts and Iberians interacted where their territories overlapped, and soon the peninsula had a Celtiberian culture. This does not mean that they intermingled a great deal; it was often a marriage of convenience – the Celts supplied the brawn, the Iberians supplied the brains. The Celtiberians soon gained fame as soldiers and it is said that they invented the two-edged warrior's sword (later to become standard equipment in the Roman army, and to be used against them).

Meanwhile, the Phoenicians, sailing from bases in North Africa, founded several colonies in southern Spain. The first of these, founded in about 1100 BC was called Gadir (now Cádiz). With advanced technology and keen trading instincts, the Phoenicians turned the raw materials of Spanish fish and salt into a big fish-curing export industry.

Carthage, itself a Phoenician colony at the outset, established an empire of its own, which spread to Spain. Carthaginian power extended as far north as Barcelona (named, it is believed, after General

Hamilcar Barca, father of the legendary Hannibal). The dour, ruthless Carthaginians stressed profit instead of political power or cultural interests; they exploited Spain's silver and lead mines and drafted able-bodied young Spaniards into their army.

In the 3rd century BC, the Carthaginians under Hannibal were defeated by the Romans in the Second Punic War, leaving the way open for Rome to take control of the Iberian peninsula. That still left the stubborn Celtiberians.

Spain under the Caesars

After the homeland itself, Spain was to become the most important part of the Roman Empire, and all over the country the stamp of the ancient civilization remains: walls and roadways, villas, monuments and vineyards – and three living languages descended from Latin: Spanish (or Castilian as it is correctly called), Catalan and Galician. Roman law is still the basis of the Spanish legal system. Spain gave birth to Roman emperors as memorable as Trajan and Hadrian and writers such as Seneca and Martial, who are still quoted.

However, the Celtiberians did not yield to the civilizing Roman war machine without a fight. In fact it took nearly 200 years for Rome to complete the conquest of Iberia (by comparison it took the legions just seven years to subdue France). To underline just how seriously this was viewed, the founder of the Roman Empire, Augustus Caesar, personally commanded the Roman legions deployed for the very last battle, in Cantabria in 19 BC.

The Romans divided the peninsula into two: *Hispaniae Ulterior* and *Citerior* ('farther' and 'nearer'). When it was later carved up further, into three provinces, the

*T*he Arco de Santa Maria, part of the 11th-century defences of Burgos. El Cid was a native of the city, and is one of the figures immortalized here in stone.

capital cities were established in what are now Tarragona, Córdoba and Mérida. Soon the symbols of Roman civilization, such as graceful bridges and aqueducts, vast arenas and baths could be found all over Spain. The impact on society was no less obvious. By the turn of the millennium, most of the local languages were muted; to get ahead in the world you had to speak Latin.

Early in the Roman period a new religion called Christianity came to Spain. The word may have been carried by St

Long before the Arabs turned Córdoba into a stronghold, the Romans were here. The bridge they built is still in use today.

Paul himself (he is said to have preached both in Aragon and at Tarragona). However, the pioneering Christian communities suffered great persecution, and martyrdom in the amphitheatres was suffered in Spain as well as in Rome. Ironically, by the time the 4th-century Emperor Constantine had been converted to Christianity, the golden age of the empire was about to yield to the Dark Ages.

The Visigoths

Overstretched and increasingly corrupt, Rome watched its far-flung colonies disintegrate. Germanic tribes, some with a deserved reputation for barbarism, hastened into the vacuum. The Vandals (the name says it all), had little to contribute to Spanish culture, but another of these tribes, the Visigoths, from Gaul (France), did bring a civilizing influence. Formerly allies of the Romans, these were also a military people but aspired to at least some of the Roman ideals. They ruled from Toledo, where they displayed their intricate arts and built opulent churches.

The Visigothic regime was to last for around 300 years, though it never imposed any sort of national unity. The invaders only numbered around 200,000, so subjugation of the far-flung lands and peoples would never have been possible. This new occupation retained many of the old Roman principles. It was finally to self-destruct on the problems of the succession of the crown. The Visigothic monarchy was elective rather than hereditary, and while this may sound commendably democratic, it only prompted a spate of palace intrigues and assassinations to hijack the crown. These and other problems were often blamed on the handiest scapegoat: the industrious Jews. They had fared well in Spain under the Romans and the early Visigoths, but at the start of the 7th century they were either converted to the newly discovered Catholicism or expelled. A century later, a dispute over the succession to the throne was to have far-reaching results. The aggrieved party turned to outside forces to help him claim the crown.

Enter the Moors

In AD 711 an invited expeditionary force of some 12,000 Berber troops from North Africa sailed across the Strait of Gibraltar and poured ashore into Spain. The expertly planned invasion was led by General Tariq ibn Ziyad (the name 'Gibraltar' is a corruption of *Gibel Tariq* – Tariq's Rock). His ambition was to spread the new religion of Islam as far as possible and he cared little for Visigothic intrigues.

The take-over spread nearly as fast as the invaders could march along those long, straight Roman roads, and the Visigoths offered only fitful resistance. Within three years, the Moors or *moros* (as North African Muslims are usually called in Spanish history) advanced all the way to the Pyrenees. By-passing pockets of Christian resistance, the aggressors continued the drive into France. There, much to the relief of the rest of Europe, the relentless Islamic tide was finally turned by the Frankish leader Charles Martel at the Battle of Poitiers, in 732.

The secret of the Moors' initial success was not only their religious zeal. They also cashed in on the military disorganization of the Visigoths, who became casualties of their own internal strife. Nor did the home front help the defenders. For many ordinary citizens the new regime, offering lower taxes and a chance of freedom for serfs, looked like a change for the better. The harried Spanish Jews tended to welcome the Moors as liberators, as, initially at least, the occupation decreed tolerance of other faiths. Conversion to Islam was strongly encouraged though, and throngs of Christians chose to embrace this new religion.

The most tangible relics of this time are now among Spain's greatest tourist attractions: at Granada, Seville and Córdoba. Exquisite Moorish mosques and palaces were designed by engineers and architects whose skills were unknown elsewhere in Europe. The art of the mediaeval Moorish craftsmen is perpetuated

---

A LITTLE MOORISH

Reminders of the Muslim era still live on in the Spanish language. South-coast towns like Algeciras, Almuñécar and Tarifa all bear Arabic names while 'Andalusia' comes from *al-Andalus*, meaning 'the land of the west'. Spaniards often use the wistful exclamation *¡ojalá!*, meaning 'may God grant', derived from *in sha' allah*, or 'if Allah wills it'.

In all, there are some 4,000 Arabic-sourced words still in common use in Spain today. Among the ones you may come across are:

albóndiga	meatball
alcalde	mayor or judge
almohada	pillow
alquilar	to hire or rent
azúcar	sugar
azulejo	a glazed tile

While you are exploring towns such as Seville, Granada or Córdoba remember the following terms:

alcazaba	fortress, citadel
alcázar	fortified place (often a palace)
mezquita	Spanish word for mosque
mihrab	prayer niche (indicating direction of Mecca)

in today's best shopping bets – Spanish ceramics, tooled leather, and silver work.

Thanks to irrigation techniques imported from North Africa, crops like rice, cotton and sugar were planted, and orchards of oranges, peaches and pomegranates blossomed. Other Moorish innovations made possible the manufacture of paper and glass.

Life in the Spanish cities of the Moors, by all accounts, was at least as refined as anywhere in Europe.

The Spanish Strike Back

The Moorish juggernaut that trundled north from Gibraltar in 711 met no serious resistance. It was eleven years before the fragmented defenders of Christian Spain won their first battle. Visigothic nobles

Inscriptions from the Koran and fantastically intricate relief carvings set the Arabian Nights scene in the mezquita at Córdoba.

The rock of Gibraltar was the beach-head for Gibel Tariq's invasion of Spain in AD 711, and is still a promontory of dispute between Spain and Britain.

exiled to the northern territory of Asturias joined with the local mountain folk to fight back. A noble named Pelayo is credited with striking the first blow for the *Reconquista* or Reconquest. Further Christian victories would be a long time in coming, but the Battle of Covadonga (the village is now a shrine) gave heart to a struggle that was to simmer for centuries.

In the middle of the 8th century, the Christians of Asturias, under King Alfonso I, took advantage of a rebellion by Berber troops and occupied the neighbouring region of Galicia. Here at Santiago de Compostela the tomb of the apostle St James (Santiago) was to become the religious focus for all Spanish Christians and a rallying call for the defenders of the

EL CID

Spain's national folk hero was born Rodrigo Díaz de Vivar, near Burgos in around 1040. He is remembered as *El Cid*, from the Arabic for 'the Lord', and is often honoured with the additional title *el Campeador*, 'the Champion'. His exploits in peace and war are recounted in the epic *El cantar de mío Cid* (the Song of the Cid), a poem about knighthood in flower. The legend of El Cid has passed into the Spanish consciousness, but the actual facts are not so easy to come by.

El Cid was an extraordinarily successful soldier of fortune who by some accounts never lost a single battle. He was initially a knight under the command of the kings of Castile, fighting the Moors. When his king, Sancho II, died mysteriously, El Cid forced his successor, Alfonso VI, to swear in public that he had nothing to do with it. This earned him exile from Castile and he joined forces with the Moors, who gave him his title. However this does not seems to have affected his popularity, perhaps because he tended to oppose tyrants of either persuasion, and during these confusing times Moorish-Christian alliances were often formed. His greatest victory was in 1094 when he led a mixed army of Christians and Moors to take Valencia. El Cid died here in 1099 and the Moors, encouraged by the news of his death, grouped to retake the city. Legend has it that his body was propped on his horse and ridden out at the head of his troops to a famous final victory (Valencia fell back to the Moors two years later).

Corneille perpetuated the legend in his tragedy *Le Cid*, in 1636, and in recent years Hollywood and Charlton Heston brought the story to us in the eponymous film epic.

faith. More breathing space from Moorish pressure was won in what became Catalonia. Charlemagne, the powerful king of the Franks, established a buffer zone between Islamic Spain and France, south of the Pyrenees, and pushed further south to capture Barcelona (which gained independence in 878 under a local hero called Wilfred the Hairy). The Christian kingdoms expanded southwards to take advantage of this, and the area between Catalonia and Asturias soon had so many frontier castles that it was called Castile.

For hundreds of years the Reconquest see-sawed according to the state of political alliances, military talent and morale.

The Moors were a fragmented people, often squabbling among themselves and making Christian alliances out of convenience. It is easy to visualize this period of history in black and white, in every sense, but intermingling of the two cultures was commonplace. Christians thrived in Moorish-controlled areas (called *Mozárabes*) while their counterparts were known as *Mudéjars*. To underline the point, the great 11th-century

The town of Alcoy is famous for its 'Moors and Christians' festival. Locals and tourists flock to see battles re-enacted in pastiche costumes.

hero, El Cid, fought for both Christian and Moorish forces at various times.

A romantic portrait of El Cid, from a woodcut of 1541.

Early in the 10th century the Asturian capital was confidently transferred some 120km (75 miles) south from Oviedo to León, a big and symbolic step deep into what had hitherto been 'infidel' territory. But the Muslims were far from on the run. They found a new uniting force under the dictator al-Mansur ('the victorious') and Léon, Barcelona and Burgos fell to his renewed might. Then in a severe blow to Christian hopes, al-Mansur sacked sacred Santiago de Compostela.

The death of the charismatic al-Mansur, in 1002, was a severe blow to the Moors who once again plunged themselves into internecine struggles. The Christian forces moved to regain lost ground. In 1010 they reconquered al-Mansur's headquarters of Córdoba then in 1085 went on to capture the beautiful, cultured city of Toledo from the Moors. King Alfonso VI of Castile and León, who presided over this great victory, had himself crowned 'Emperor of Toledo'.

The fall of Toledo, an intellectual hothouse of Muslim power, sent out shock waves to the Moorish rulers elsewhere in Spain. They called for help from North Africa, from the Almoravids, a confederation of Berber tribes based in Marrakech. These puritanical Muslim zealots, known for their military prowess, succeeded in pushing back the Reconquest, which by now was the longest of the crusades.

ANCIENT CÓRDOBA

The Moors established their capital in Córdoba, and from the 8th to 11th centuries it ranked as one of the greatest cities in the world, famed for its culture and erudition as well as its palaces and gardens. The emirs and caliphs surrounded themselves with poets and philosophers, doctors and geographers, mathematicians and abstract artists. Around the turn of the 10th century, the city boasted Europe's first real university, a library of over 4,000 volumes, 50 hospitals, 27 schools and over 60,000 noble houses alone. Today it is a city of some 280,000 people, less than half the size it was at its peak.

By the time the Almoravids were a spent force, followers of another Berber sect, the even more fundamentalist Almohads, had been called on for further reinforcements in the 12th century. These helped shore up the Moorish gains, but their policy of driving out Jews and *Mozárabes* spurred on the efforts of the outside world to help Spain rid itself of the *infidel*. The turning point of the *Reconquista* is held to be the battle of Las Navas de Tolosa in 1212. After this, the Christian forces regained most of Spain down to Andalusia. Then Ferdinand III of Castile and León retook Córdoba (for the second time) and, after a terrible siege, the most powerful of the *taifas* (small Moorish kingdoms), Seville. Muslim refugees flooded into Granada, the last stronghold, where they lingered for another 250 years amid intellectual and artistic splendour. Ferdinand III, meanwhile was elevated to sainthood, becoming San Fernando.

A Singular Nation

Until the 15th century the Spains had always stayed resolutely plural. There were sporadic moves toward unity, such as a royal marriage between Catalonia and Aragon, and nuptials linking Navarre and Castile. In most cases, however, something divisive happened before the alliance could be solidified.

The royal marriage that was to matter most to Spain brought together the shrewd King Ferdinand of Aragon and the fervently religious and patriotic Queen Isabella of Castile. Under the Catholic Monarchs (as Pope Alexander VI entitled them), a single Spain was created, comprising most of the nation we now know. However, the components of the united kingdom retained their individuality and institutions, and in the long term even this superficial integration failed to endure.

Aiming to unite Spain, Ferdinand and Isabella made history in other ways. To purge the nation of spiritual ills, the Inquisition, an instrument of interrogation and torture, was inaugurated in 1478. Isabella's confessor, the fanatical Tomás de Torquemada, presided over the purge of converts to Christianity: *conversos* (Jews) and *moriscos* (Muslims). Several thousand suspects, judged heretical or at least insincere, died horribly, burned at *auto-da-fés* (Inquisition show trials). With no more non-Christians to murder, the Inquisition then set their sights on Protestants. In 1492 the influential Torquemada convinced Ferdinand and Isabella to expel all the surviving unconverted Jews. Perhaps 200,000 Jews, including some of the country's best-educated and most productive people, were sent to North Africa and various refuges in Europe. The struggle against the Moors was finally won the same year when Ferdinand and Isabella accepted the keys to the Alhambra, Granada's wondrous palace. Religious freedom was guaranteed to the Muslims, then revoked almost immediately and mass conversions were decreed.

*T*he torturers of the Inquisition knew no bounds – rope and pulley, water and fire were used to extract 'confessions' from 'heretics' (above).

*T*his monument to Columbus in Barcelona shows the navigator pointing in the opposite direction to the Americas (right)!

The crowning achievement of 1492 was the voyage of the *Niña*, the *Pinta* and the *Santa María* to what Columbus thought was the Indies. Sponsored by Ferdinand and Isabella (by legend she pawned her own jewels to raise the money), the fortunate Genoese navigator brought back news of a rich New World, which was promptly annexed to the Spanish realm.

The Disastrous Hapsburgs

While Ferdinand and Isabella were Spain personified, their grandson, Charles I, born in Flanders in 1500, could barely compose a sentence in Spanish and was to prove a very poor successor. Soon after his arrival in Spain, the lantern-jawed young man inherited the titles of Holy Roman Emperor and Charles V. A Hapsburg, he assumed the throne in 1516, packed his retinue with Burgundian and Flemish nobles and occupied himself with affairs of state far from Spain.

This did not go down well with the common people (the *comuneros*) and, led from Toledo, they resorted to violent protest while the monarch was off on one of his business trips. The revolt of the *comuneros* was put down by the army and the leaders executed.

Among the emperor's distractions was a seemingly endless series of wars he waged – using mostly Spanish troops – against France, against the Ottoman Empire, and against Germany's new religious sect, the Lutherans. It is said that by the time his reign ended, he had fought just about everyone worth fighting in Europe. All the while Conquistador gold from the New World paid the bills.

In 1556, Charles abdicated in favour of his son, Philip II, which seemed to be good news for Spain. The new king had at least grown up in Spain, and he gave many a top European job to Castilians. Philip proclaimed Madrid his capital, converting an unimpressive town of less than 15,000 into the powerhouse of the greatest empire of the age.

Philip was exhilarated by the rousing Christian victory in the Mediterranean in 1571 when a combined Spanish, Venetian and papal fleet destroyed the Turkish navy in the famous Battle of Lepanto. But not

---

THE 'CATHOLIC DAUGHTERS'

Although Ferdinand and Isabella had a massive effect on Spanish history their offspring were able to consolidate few, if any, of their achievements. Their only son died young and the royal marriages they arranged for their daughters ended in political failure and personal grief. Poor Princess Catherine (of Aragon) was a two-time loser. She was engaged to marry Henry VIII's older brother, Prince Arthur, but he died before the wedding and so she married Henry. Her failure to bear him a male heir led to their divorce. Princess Juana was wed to Philip the Fair, the good-looking son of Austria's Emperor Maximilian. But he, too, died young and the shock caused the already unstable Juana to be considered unfit to rule Spain. History recorded her as Juana la Loca (the Mad) – a label which says much of the intolerant climate her mother and father had created.

---

only did this cause more strain on Spain's reserves, it inspired over-confidence in the emperor, who decided to take on Protestant England. The mission of the vaunted Spanish Armada ended in disaster; England ruled the waves and Spain was left to lick its wounds.

Ten years after the Armada fiasco, Philip died in devout seclusion in El Escorial, the superb palace and monastery he had built in the hills north west of Madrid. In spite of his failures, Spain was still the master of Europe's greatest empire, extending from the Americas (North, Central and South) to the Philippines (named, in all modesty, after himself). However, this Golden Age was to pass swiftly in a rush of reckless spending.

Philip III, who succeeded his father, turned in a lacklustre performance on the throne, delegating his responsibilities to the Duke of Lerma. His most memorable

THE INVINCIBLE ARMADA?

It seems that almost everything went wrong for the Spanish Armada. The commander died just before the fleet sailed and his replacement, the wealthy Duke of Medina Sidonia, barely knew port from starboard. He was certainly no man to face seasoned English aces like Sir Francis Drake and Sir John Hawkins.

Almost as soon as the Armada left Lisbon, it ran into destructive gales and was forced to return for two months of repairs. Even at their best, the 130 clumsy, inadequately armed ships were outnumbered by the more manoeuvrable British fleet.

In the first battle, the Spanish realized that their ships would soon run out of ammunition; but the English, close to home, could easily re-arm.

A planned invasion of England with soldiers based in the Netherlands – the whole point of the exercise – had to be called off. Then the British transformed expendable ships into torches and aimed them at the heart of the Spanish fleet, causing panic and havoc.

Due to a combination of bad luck, ill winds and British naval superiority, the Armada sacrificed thousands of sailors and about half its ships in pursuit of failure. The English not only whipped Philip II, they did it without losing a single ship of their own.

misjudgement was expelling the remaining *moriscos*. Hundreds of thousands were thrown out, depriving Spain of some of its hardest working farmers, and leaving once-fertile lands to become barren.

Religious motives also influenced Spain's participation in the Thirty Years' War, pitting Catholic against Protestant Europe. Philip III and his son and heir, Philip IV were the figureheads during this struggle, which proved as fruitless and costly as it was lengthy.

The last century of the Hapsburg era was a gradual, then rapid, decline in the country's fortunes. The empire lost possessions in the Low Countries, Portugal, and pockets of France and Italy. Emigration, war after war, farm troubles and epidemics contributed to a severe drop in the population.

In counterpoint to all the political and military failures, however, the 17th century was a time of glory in Spanish art: the age of Velázquez, Zurbarán, Murillo and Ribera. Ironically, most of them could not have made a living without the patronage of the otherwise uninspired royal court.

The last of the Spanish Hapsburgs, Charles II, was aged just five when his father died. He grew up to be as useless as his father (some say he was insane), leaving the worries of the empire to others. Having failed to produce an heir, he willed the crown instead to the grandson of France's Louis XIV (the Duke of Anjou) who in 1700 claimed the title of Philip V of Spain. Unfortunately Charles, Archduke of Austria (and a Hapsburg to boot) also claimed the crown and thus began the War of the Spanish Succession. For 13 years (1701-14) this pitted Britain and Austria (joined by Catalonia, Valencia and the Balearics) against the rest of Spain in pursuance of the French claim to a Bourbon Spain.

Bourbons on the Throne

The Treaty of Utrecht which ended yet another unfortunate warring period in the country's history left Philip V on the throne, but at the cost of ceding much of its dwindling empire – Belgium, Luxembourg, Milan, Sicily and Sardinia. Britain won the strategic prize of the Rock of Gibraltar. However, all was not lost: by the end of the war, the unification of Spain was almost achieved. Only Navarre and the Basque country escaped direct rule from Madrid. Catalonia was punished for joining the wrong side and a ban on the official use of the Catalan language was imposed (the Spanish Civil War of 1936-39 provided striking historical parallels).

The most successful Spanish king of the 18th century, Charles III, recruited capable administrators and invigorated the economy. The evil Inquisition was dissolved and out with it went the reactionary Jesuit movement. Charles paved and lit the streets of Madrid and built what became the Prado museum. Under his reign Spain acquired from France the Louisiana Territory, a nice compensation for earlier losses in Europe. However, the expansionist fling lasted only until 1800, when Louisiana was returned to France, which sold it to the United States just three years later.

Spain came increasingly under the power of France during the Bourbon period and things seemed to reach a nadir at the Battle of Trafalgar in 1805 when a combined French-Spanish fleet was soundly beaten by the British under Nelson. Charles IV, barely a competent king at the best of times, was forced to abdicate after a 20-year reign; Napoleon invaded Spain and invested his older brother, Joseph, as King José I. The imposition of an interloper roused Spain to an uprising which developed into the Peninsular War (Spaniards call it the War of Independence). This went on murderously but inconclusively for six years. Finally, with the help of the British, led by the Duke of Wellington, the Spanish expelled the occupying forces.

Another loser of the war was the Spanish empire. Taking advantage of the strife and confusion in Europe, Spain's richest American colonies revolted and won their independence.

Ferdinand VII (son of Charles IV) was reinstated in 1814. His subjects had high hopes of him, so they were bitterly disillusioned when he tore up the constitution and ruled as an absolute monarch. He even reinstated the Inquisition. Political infighting, power struggles and repression followed.

Ferdinand died in 1833 and left the country even more problems. He named his daughter, Isabella II, as his successor, but the conservative factions wanted his brother Don Carlos to rule. Spain was once again at war with itself. The Carlist Wars (as they came to be known) rumbled on, spanning a period of half a century, interrupted by occasional breathing spaces and the proclamation of a shortlived republic. The Carlists were finally defeated by King Alfonso XII, a Sandhurst-educated Bourbon.

This was a very bad period for the church as well. Religious orders were

MODERNISME

Despite the uncertain political times of the late 19th century the arts were flourishing and the movement known as *Modernisme* (the Spanish form of *Art Nouveau*) was to the fore. Basically it was a rebellion against the rigid forms and colourless stone and plaster of the classical architecture that had replaced Gothic. Nowhere did this style thrive quite so well, nor has it been so carefully preserved, as in Catalonia, and particularly Barcelona. Gaudí's Barcelona works are legendary but, elsewhere in the province, you will also see many fine examples of this school, from the grand lines and designs on the most elegant public buildings, to simple adornments gracing humbler homes.

suppressed throughout the country and many beautiful monasteries were destroyed in an orgy of anti-clerical feeling.

Alfonso's reign was destined to be brief. Although he survived a couple of assassination attempts, he died of tuberculosis aged 28. His legacy to Spain was unaccustomed peace and prosperity and a system of limited parliamentary rule.

Some months after he died, Queen María Cristina produced his posthumous son and heir, who became Alfonso XIII (an unlucky number, as it turned out). The queen, who ran the palace until her son came of age, suffered a morale-crushing defeat in 1898. The Spanish-American War cost Spain the last remnants of its empire: Cuba, Puerto Rico and the Philippines. This military debacle jolted the nation; any last pretensions it had to being a world power were now completely gone. Surprisingly, like the military and

political reverses of the 17th century, it inspired the creative renaissance of a generation of Spanish intellectuals.

Spain escaped the horrors of World War I, observing the carnage from a neutral perspective, but a subsequent war in Morocco proved disastrous, with 15,000 Spanish troops killed.

As anarchy and army rebellions caused the government to collapse, Alfonso XIII backed the dictatorship of General Miguel Primo de Rivera. The hard line lost him friends, and in municipal elections in 1931 the anti-royalist forces won a landslide. The king went into exile, from which he never returned.

The Spanish Civil War

Life under the new Republic continued to be turbulent. Bitter ideological conflicts divided parties and factions; the church

was also involved. The 1933 parliamentary elections brought a swing to the right, but in 1936 a Popular Front of left-wing parties won by a squeak and formed a radical government. Conservatives feared that a Marxist revolution was at hand and the fragile alliance of political compromise collapsed. With anarchy in the wind, a large section of the army rose in revolt against the Republican government. The leader of the insurrection was a one-time war hero, General Francisco Franco. As supreme commander of the Nationalist forces he was promoted to *generalísimo*.

Support for the uprising came from monarchists and conservatives, as well as the right-wing Falange organization and the Roman Catholic Church. On the other side a motley band of liberals, socialists, communists and anarchists cast their lot in with the government. The Civil War became one of the great causes of the 20th century; many Europeans saw it as a crucial confrontation between democracy and dictatorship, or, from the other side, as a choice between law and order or chaos and social revolution. Aid for both sides came from abroad, with Germany and Italy in Franco's team and Russia and the volunteers of the International Brigades fighting alongside the Republicans.

Cruel slow-motion battles (and horrific atrocities perpetrated by both sides) kept the blood flowing for three years and cost between 500,000 and 750,000 lives. The sober, wily Franco emerged as *caudillo* (leader) of a shattered post-war Spain.

*G*eneralísimo Francisco Franco (1892–1975) – hero to some, villain to many – in 1938 at the height of the bloody Civil War.

*U*p in arms. The Iberian Anarchist Federation militia at the barracks of Pechralles, near Barcelona.

Many Republicans went into exile; others simply disappeared.

After the war the hardship continued, and the rest of Europe shunned the fascist state. Franco at least managed to slip out of Hitler's embrace, and kept Spain from combat in World War II. The post-war years were hard but American aid (in exchange for permitting US air bases to be located in Spain) started an economic

As Spain speeds into the 21st century, its landscape remains mainly agricultural, as seen here from Arcos de la Frontera.

recovery. Spain was admitted to the United Nations in 1955, opening the gates to an unprecedented tourist invasion, with profound effects on both the economy and the national mentality.

The New Spain

Even while Franco lay protractedly on his deathbed in 1975, Spain was taking the first steps towards liberalization. The pace picked up two days after his death when, in accordance with his wishes, the monarchy was restored in the person of King Juan Carlos. The young grandson of the Bourbon Alfonso XIII surprised his handlers and the world and became Spain's helmsman on the road to democracy. And, in 1981, Juan Carlos's most heroic moment arrived when he thwarted a military coup.

Fundamental changes in the political landscape came thick and fast in the late 1970s and the 80s. The Falange was wound down and the communists regained legal status. In 1982 the socialists swept to power. The church was disestablished and divorce was legalized. Autonomy in varying degrees was granted to those areas Franco had deprived of their cultural identities, most notably Catalonia and the Basque country (although Basque separatist extremists, still dissatisfied, continue their campaign of violence.) Spain joined NATO and, four years later, the European Economic Community – the long separation from Europe's mainstream was finally ended.

The last few years have seen even more remarkable changes in the image that we have of Spain, and in the national psyche. The former poor relation of Europe has become one of its more desirable places; strident culturally and booming economically. The universal

problems of inflation, unemployment, petty crime and pollution may preclude too much over-confidence, but 1992 certainly was an *annus mirabilis* for the country. For the first time in many centuries, Spain can actually look forward confidently to the new challenges of the next hundred years.

*T*he destruction of the Basque village of Guernica by German
planes in April 1937 prompted this outrage against war by Picasso.

HISTORICAL LANDMARKS		
Prehistory	500,000 BC	Hunters may have inhabited Iberia.
	15,000 BC	Altamira cavemen paint realistic scenes.
	3,000 BC	Bronze age traders establish villages.
Colonists	1,000 BC	Celts settle in north, Phoenicians colonize southern Iberia.
	3rd century BC	Carthaginians conquer much of Spain; Punic Wars ensue.
Roman Spain	1st century BC	Romans complete conquest of Spain, imposing Latin language and culture.
	1st century AD	Christianity reaches Spain (legend says St Paul himself brought the word).
	4th century	Empire declining, Dark Ages loom.
Middle Ages	6th century	Conquering Visigoths make Toledo their capital.
	711	Arab-led Berber troops invade Andalusia; soon control most of Spain.
	722	At Covadonga (Asturias), Christian forces win their first victory against Moors.
	758	Córdoba becomes capital of Moorish Spain, ushering in city's golden age.
	1085	Tide is turning: Reconquest of Toledo.

United Spain	1469	Ferdinand, Prince of Aragon weds Isabella of Castile.
	1478	'Catholic Monarchs' unleash Inquisition.
	1479	Ferdinand becomes King of Aragon; Christian Spain united.
	1492	Final triumph of Reconquest: capture of Granada. Ferdinand and Isabella expel the Jews. Columbus reaches America.
The Hapsburgs	1516	Charles I inherits throne and riches from Indies, becomes Holy Roman Emperor.
	1556-98	Philip II rules; Madrid his capital.
	1588	Britain routs Spanish Armada.
	1618-48	Thirty Years' War, Spain the loser; meanwhile, Spanish artistic Golden Age.
Bourbon Spain	1701-14	War of Spanish Succession; Spain loses territories; Philip V wins crown.
	1759-88	Under Charles III economy revives.
	1804	Napoleon invades; 'War of Independence'.
	1805	Battle of Trafalgar: Britannia rules the waves.
	1814	Ferdinand VII regains throne, rules as absolute monarch.
19th Century	1833-76	Carlist Wars: costly, long-running chaos.
	1835	Religious orders suppressed.
	1873	First Spanish Republic proclaimed.
	1875	Monarchy restored under Alfonso XII.
	1898	Spanish-American War: end of empire.
20th Century	1914-18	Spain stays neutral in World War I; domestic unrest.
	1921	Revolt in Morocco; heavy losses for Spanish troops.
	1923	Alfonso XIII backs law-and-order dictatorship of General Primo de Rivera.
	1931	Anti-royalist landslide in local elections; king chooses exile.
War and Beyond	1936	Left-wing Popular Front wins election, forms radical government; chaos in the wind. Army revolts; Franco leads invasion of Andalusia. Civil War, with foreign intervention on both sides.
	1939	Republicans defeated, Franco rules.
	1955	Spain admitted to United Nations.
	1975	Franco dies, Bourbon Juan Carlos crowned. Rebirth of democracy, leading to re-integration into Europe.
	1986	Spain joins the European Community.
	1992	Barcelona hosts Olympic Games.

ON THE SHORTLIST

Just the Essentials

You cannot possibly see all Spain's highlights, but it would be a shame to miss any of the essentials. Our choice of the top sights, although inevitably arbitrary and subjective, may help you decide where to go.

Madrid and Vicinity
Madrid: Plaza Mayor: perfect square.
  The Prado: masses of Old Masters.
  Royal Palace: imperious and
    spectacular.
  Archaeology Museum: La Dama de
    Elche.
Toledo: cathedral, Alcázar, Synagogue of
  Santa María La Blanca.
El Escorial: Palace of the Golden Age.
Valle de los Caídos: Civil War memorial.
Segovia: aqueduct, Alcázar, cathedral.
La Granja: palace and formal gardens.
Ávila: the perfect walled city.

The Centre
Salamanca: Plaza Mayor, cathedrals,
  university.
León: cathedral, Colegiata de San Isidoro
  (Royal Pantheon).
Valladolid: National Museum of
  Sculpture, cathedral.
Burgos: cathedral, Las Huelgas convent,
  Cartuja de Miraflores.
Cuenca: 'Hanging Houses'.

Green Spain
La Coruña: ancient port, glass-front
  houses.
Santiago de Compostela: the Pilgrims'
  goal.
West Coast and north coast: fjord-like
  rías.
Santander: fine port and resort.
Santillana del Mar: perfect mediaeval
  village.
Picos de Europa: picturesque peaks and
  valleys.
Covadonga: cradle of the Reconquest.

The Northern Border
San Sebastián: magnificent beaches and
  cuisine.
Basque Coast: cliffs and creeks.
Estella: churches and charm.
Pamplona: cathedral, baroque city hall.
Leyre Monastery: inspiring setting.
Zaragoza: cathedrals and Moorish palace.
Huesca: stately cathedral.
Ordesa Park: waterfalls and wildlife.

Catalonia
Barcelona: La Rambla: lively street.
  Gothic Quarter: cathedral, Picasso
    Museum, ancient alleys.
  Museu d'Art de Catalunya: magnificent
    mediaeval art.
  Gaudí's Modernisme: Sagrada Familia.
Gerona: oft-besieged city.
Montserrat: mountain pilgrimage.
Poblet: royal monastery.
Lérida: cathedral and Moorish castle.
Figueres: Dalí Museum.
Costa Brava: cliffs, ports, resorts.
Tarragona: Roman and mediaeval remains.
Sitges: good-time, unspoiled resort.

The East
Peñíscola: castle on a rock.
Valencia: cathedral, Silk Exchange,
  ceramics museum.
Alicante: Mediterranean bustle, old town.
Murcia: cathedral and old town.

The South
Marbella: celebrity resort.
Cádiz: ancient atmospheric port.
Doñana National Park: wildlife habitat.
Ronda: cliff-top drama.
Jerez de la Frontera: sherry and horses.
Seville: quintessential Spain.
Córdoba: the greatest mosque of all.
Granada: the Alhambra.
Pueblos Blancos: whitewashed Moorish
  hilltop villages.

The West
Mérida: Roman splendour.
Guadalupe: pilgrim shrine.
Trujillo: home of the *Conquistadores*.
Cáceres: feast of mediaeval architecture.

Islands
Majorca: capital Palma, coastal scenery of
  Tramuntana, fantasy grottoes.
Ibiza: old Ibiza town; trendiest nightlife.
Tenerife: Mount Teide, northern towns
  and mountain scenery.
Gran Canaria: southern beaches,
  mountain scenery.
Lanzarote: Volcanic park.
La Palma: Caldera de Taburiente Park.

Peculiarly Spanish

As places the world over all start to look the same, reflect on what might make your Spanish trip stand out from any other holiday. To supplement or even supplant the standard itineraries, we have devised a number of routes and themes to cater for even the most eclectic tastes. You can, for example, go in search of Roman ruins, visit the country's most impressive cathedrals, take a tour of the best golf courses and walk through spectacular scenery in the national parks.

Castles

In the age of El Cid and al-Mansur, castles were as much a part of the Spanish countryside as today's high-tension pylons. Some mediaeval strongholds have tumbled into disrepair; others have gained a new lease of life, converted into *paradores*. A cross-section of outstanding baileys and keeps in Central Spain:

*F*or the energetic, the mountains of the Canary Islands offer a wealth of opportunity to explore the volcanic upheavals of the Earth. These cliffs tumble down into the beautiful green lagoon at El Golfo in Lanzarote.

1 SEGOVIA (SEGOVIA)
The fairy-tale silhouette dates from an over-enthusiastic 19th-century restoration, but Segovia's *Alcázar* has been making history since the 13th century.

2 COCA (SEGOVIA)
Moorish masons built this massive, oft-photographed Mudéjar masterpiece.

3 CUÉLLAR (SEGOVIA)
Mid 15th-century castle on top of a bare hill with magnificent views. Inside is a sumptuous Gothic-Renaissance palace.

4 PEDRAZA (SEGOVIA)
A thoroughly mediaeval atmosphere is preserved at this castle, famous for having been one of the most impregnable in the country.

From the days of El Cid, the castles of central Spain recall its mediaeval history.

5 PEÑAFIEL (VALLADOLID)
Long, thin and powerful, this ridge-top redoubt was begun in the early 14th century.

6 MEDINA DEL CAMPO (VALLADOLID)
La Mota Castle, powerful and austere, was one of the residences of Ferdinand and Isabella; the latter died here.

7 SIMANCAS (VALLADOLID)
High walls and a deep moat surround this attractive picture-book castle, once a Moorish fortress.

8 TORRELOBATÓN (VALLADOLID)
This simple fortress, built in the 15th century, is today the best preserved castle in all Castile.

9 BELMONTE (CUENCA)
This compelling 15th-century fortress was restored, though not necessarily for the better, in the 19th century.

10 OROPESA (TOLEDO)
An imposing 15th-century stronghold reduced to ruins by dynastic struggles and war with the Moors, now converted to a fine *parador*.

11 GUADAMUR (TOLEDO)
A beautiful castle with an exceptionally graceful keep. Built in the 15th century it was skilfully restored at the end of the last century.

12 *ALCÁZAR* OF TOLEDO (TOLEDO)
Originally the home of El Cid and latterly a Fascist stronghold during the Civil War, this mighty fortress is packed with history.

13 SIGÜENZA (GUADALAJARA)
Originally an Arab *Alcázar*, its warlike appearance was softened by conversion into an Episcopal Palace. The Throne Room, the Romanesque chapels and the sacristy are attractions in themselves. The castle is now a splendid *parador*.

Discovering Columbus

The great navigator made waves in many parts of Spain, inland, on the coast and also in the islands. Columbus-watchers can find milestones and landmarks all over the territory.

Columbus in Andalusia

1 LA RÁBIDA
Columbus endures a long wait in the Franciscan monastery for royal approval. The prior gives vital support to his 'world is

70

round' theory. Columbiana includes models of his ships and the study where he worked.

2 CÓRDOBA

Still awaiting a decision from Ferdinand and Isabella, Columbus fathers his second son, Ferdinand.

Discover some of the more personal journeys of the great Columbus, as well as replicas of his famous ships.

3 SANTA FÉ

April, 1492. Near recently reconquered Granada, Catholic Monarchs finally approve the Columbus expedition.

4 PALOS DE LA FRONTERA

3 August 1492. With many local men in his crew, Columbus sets forth for the 'Indies' from here. (Palos is no longer a port; it has long since silted up.)

5 CÁDIZ

5 September 1493. From this fine harbour, Columbus departed on his second voyage to America with 17 ships and 1,500 men.

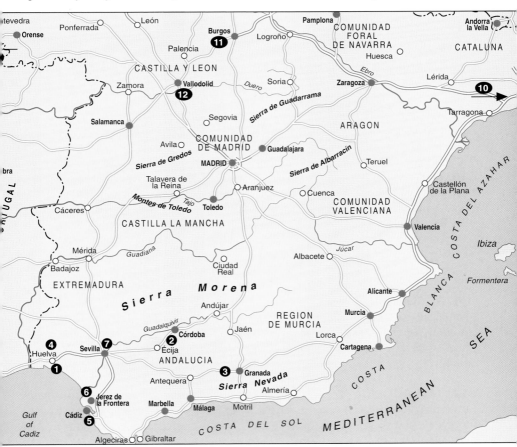

(Cádiz was also the port of departure for his fourth expedition in 1502.)

6 SANLÚCAR DE BARRAMEDA
30 May 1498. A third Columbus venture launched, on a southward course.

7 SEVILLE
Enjoy the pompous 19th-century Columbus mausoleum in Seville Cathedral; Columbus books and marginal notes in Archives of the Indies and the Monastery of La Cartuja where he spent some time in residence.

More Columbus on the Mainland

8 PONTEVEDRA
The local shipyard is said to have built the flagship *Santa María.*

9 BAYONA
1 March 1493. The *Pinta* lands back in Spain.

10 BARCELONA
Ferdinand and Isabella receive Columbus (and some 'sample' Indians) in Plaça del Rei. A full-size replica of the *Santa María* is moored in Barcelona port, overlooked by a fine column and statue to Columbus.

11 BURGOS
Ferdinand and Isabella welcome him back from his second trip in the Burgos town house called La Casa del Cordón (now a bank).

12 VALLADOLID
Columbus lives his last years, alone and forgotten, in what is now the Casa Museo de Colón. He dies 21 May 1506.

Columbus in the Canary Islands

LA GOMERA
Columbus takes leave of the known world from here on 6 September 1492. There are several Columbus-connected sites in the tiny capital of San Sebastián.

GRAN CANARIA
Columbus stops en route to the New World in 1492 at Las Palmas. Visit the church where he prayed and the lovely house in which he resided on three occasions.

LA PALMA
An actual-size concrete and timber replica of the *Santa María*, housing a small naval museum (although Columbus was never here).

Pilgrims' Way

In early mediaeval times, Santiago de Compostela ranked with Rome or Jerusalem as an inspirational destination for pilgrims. Hundreds of thousands of the faithful used to make this pilgrimage annually, traditionally starting in France, crossing the Pyrenees and walking all across Spain to the Galician shrine of St James (Santiago). There were two main routes and several tributaries. Here are some notable stops on one of the most heavily travelled southerly routes; walking is optional!

1 PUENTE LA REINA
An old walled town featuring the Church of Santiago and the Church of the Crucifix with its mediaeval pilgrims' hospice. Also a superb mediaeval bridge.

2 ESTELLA (OFF MAP)

Romanesque churches and monasteries line the pilgrim road (*la Rúa*) of this lovely town.

3 NÁJERA

Ancient capital of Navarre; cliffside Santa María monastery and the magnificent 15th-century church of Santa María la Real.

4 SANTO DOMINGO DE LA CALZADA

St Dominic built a bridge over the river here, with his own hands, to ease the travails of the 11th-century pilgrims. Splendid cathedral and a *parador* for modern pilgrims.

5 BURGOS

A major stopping point and one of Spain's finest cities. Magnificent cathedral, founded in early 13th century; nearby is the royal convent and monastery.

6 FRÓMISTA

The 11th-century church of San Martín is one of the best Romanesque churches on the Way.

7 LEÓN

Another major point of rest. Today an im-

Inspiration for the faithful, but you don't have to walk it today!

portant modern city on an ancient site with a splendid old core; outstanding Gothic cathedral glowing with stained glass.

8 ASTORGA

A fascinating and informative Museum of the Ways to Santiago now occupies the remarkable pseudo-mediaeval palace built by Gaudí for the archbishops of Astorga.

9 PONFERRADA

An iron-mining town with a picture-book Knights Templar castle.

10 CEBREIRO

Thatched village of Celtic origin, featuring an ancient church with holy relics.

11 PORTOMARÍN

The church of the Knights of St John was dismantled and re-erected on its present site to prevent destruction by flooding.

12 SANTIAGO DE COMPOSTELA

End of the line: highlights include the cathedral's baroque façade and Romanesque door and the pilgrim hospital,

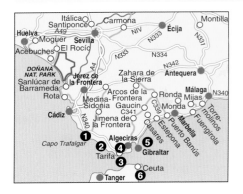

Climb the belvedere above t.
best view across the Strait of G.

4 ALGECIRAS
Busy port with ferries for North Africa,
and an Arab-style market.

5 GIBRALTAR
This tiny British enclave is the European
Pillar of Hercules; the landing point of the
Moorish invasion in AD 711.

*Once they marked the
end of the known world—the
'Pillars of Hercules'.*

6 CEUTA
The North African Pillar of Hercules. A
Spanish enclave and duty-free port.

Artists

After you have seen the Prado, you can
home in on a favourite painter; tracking
down his birthplace, his studio, or a spe-
cialized museum.

founded by Ferdinand and Isabella, now
a magnificent *parador*.

EL GRECO
In Toledo, the Casa de El Greco is
claimed to be the house where he lived. It
is furnished with authentic 16th-century
pieces. Also on show are several of his
paintings. Don't miss *The Burial of the
Count of Orgaz* in Santo Tomás in Toledo.

The Pillars of
Hercules

Marking the end of the known world, the
Rock of Gibraltar and Ceuta, on the North
African coast, were known by the ancients
as 'The Pillars of Hercules'. Here, where
the Mediterranean and Atlantic meet,
are many traces of ancient and modern
history.

GOYA
His birthplace, the village of Fuendetodos
(Zaragoza), is far off the tourist track and
the humble house is sparsely furnished;
upstairs, reproductions of his works are
displayed. The Museo del Grabado de
Goya (Goya Engravings Museum), with
160 prints by the artist, is nearby.

1 CAPE TRAFALGAR
Site of the great naval battle of 1805, won
by Nelson, but at the cost of his own life.

2 PUNTA PALOMA
Northern terminal of proposed fixed link
(bridge or tunnel) between Spain and
Morocco.

SOROLLA
The Valencian impressionist, Joaquin
Sorolla (1863-1923), did much of his

3 TARIFA
Guzman the Good's 13th-century castle.

work in Madrid. His house at Paseo del General Martinez, Campos 37, contains some 300 of his paintings.

PICASSO

During the nine formative years he spent in Barcelona, Picasso lived rather more modestly than the conjunction of 13th-century palaces they have assigned his museum in Carrer de Montcada. It houses an important collection of jottings and finished works from all his phases (though none of his masterworks).

DALÍ

In Figueres, near the Costa Brava, Salvador Dalí converted a stately old theatre into a startling setting for his bizarre but brilliant whims. Visit Cadaqués (his home village), where the Perrott-Moore Museum features more of the madcap maestro's works.

MIRÓ

The Fundació Joan Miró in Barcelona captures all the abstract imagination and wit of Miró and Catalonian modern art. It has won several awards and is a real eye-opener.

Parks and Gardens

The rulers of Spain provided some, but not all, of the country's loveliest garden sanctuaries. Formal, unspoiled, and even unashamedly touristy; here are a few for those with green fingers, or who simply enjoy a peaceful stroll.

1 PARQUE DEL RETIRO (MADRID)

A romantic royal park with a boating lake, gracious buildings and beautiful gardens, providing an essential escape from the city bustle for tourists and *Madrileños* alike.

2 ARANJUEZ (MADRID)

The royal parks and gardens run from flower beds and clipped hedges to luxuriant forests.

3 LA GRANJA DE SAN ILDEFONSO (SEGOVIA)

Thanks to French landscape gardeners, the province of Segovia enjoys a Versailles-style formal garden with lovely woodlands. Don't miss the fountains.

4 SEVILLE (SEVILLA)

Bordering the Guadalquivir, the Parque de María Luisa is another sample of French expertise, this time on the flat.

5 BLANES (GERONA)

Marimurtra, overlooking the Mediterranean, is a collection of 3,000 species of trees, shrubs and flowers.

6 LA CIUTADELLA (BARCELONA)

A botanical garden and Barcelona Zoo are the main features of Barcelona's favourite central park. Don't miss the conservatory in the late afternoon sunlight.

7 CACTUSLANDIA (ALICANTE)

A splendid collection of over 1,500 species of cacti, sub-tropical fruit trees and flowers which cling precariously to a cliff-side high above the sea between Altea and Calpe.

8 ELCHE (MURCIA)

A plantation rather than a garden, featuring Europe's largest collection of date palms. The *Huerta de la Cura* (Priest's Grove) is the centrepiece with cacti, pomegranates, orange trees and over a thousand palm trees.

9 GRANADA

The Moors left a profound mark on Spanish horticulture, and nowhere more so than in the refreshing terraced gardens of the Alhambra's Generalife.

TENERIFE (off map)

Founded in the 18th century, the Botanical Garden (officially called the *Jardin de Aclimatación*) is a cool green luxuriant tropical forest.

Jewish Spain

In the Middle Ages Spain's Jewish community contributed considerably to the national culture. Jewish scientists, philosophers, financiers and administrators made their mark, and in certain epochs relations were good with their Christian and

*P*arks to stroll around *(1–10), and traces of Spain's Jewish golden age (11–22).*

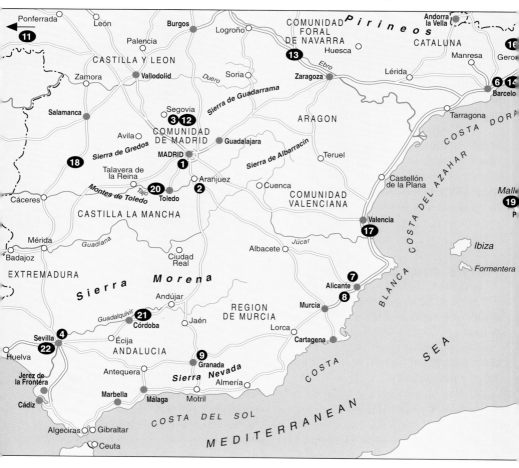

Moslem neighbours. After several expulsions (most notably in 1492), however, the Jewish Golden Age was finished. Yet there are traces all over the country to commemorate this period.

11 GALICIA
The best preserved Jewish quarter is in the quiet town of Ribadavia. In Orense, the former *aljama* (Jewish community) was centred on the present Rua Nova.

12 SEGOVIA (SEGOVIA)
The old Jewish quarter is close to the city ramparts; see also the Calle de la Judería Vieja (Street of the Old Jewish Quarter).

13 TUDELA (NAVARRE)
In what was the province's biggest mediaeval Jewish centre, relics of the synagogue are found in the Romanesque cloister of Tudela's cathedral. The town archive holds important Hebrew parchments.

14 BARCELONA (BARCELONA)
The heart of mediaeval Jewish life was in the narrow streets around Carrer de Sant Domènec del Call and the atmosphere still exists today. Close by, the Crown of Aragon Archive and the City History Museum have documents and displays on the Jewish legacy. So too does the Castle Museum on top of Montjuïc (Mountain of the Jews).

15 GERONA (GERONA)
The Jewish Quarter (Call) is well preserved. The highlight is the Isaac el Çec (the Blind) Centre, a restored Jewish home, showing exhibitions on Sephardic (Spanish Jewish) life. Near the cathedral are Moorish Baths, considered by some to

be Jewish, and in the Archaeological Museum are Hebrew tablets.

16 BESALÚ (GERONA)
This lovely town, still redolent of the Middle Ages, boasts the only *miqwé* (Jewish ritual bath) in Spain. Adjacent is the Plaza del Jueus, where the synagogue once stood.

17 SAGUNTO (VALENCIA)
In the well preserved Jewish Quarter are remains of the old synagogue. Several Hebrew tablets are kept in the town's Archaeological Museum.

18 HERVÁS (CÁCERES)
This mountain village holds one of the prettiest and best-preserved Jewish quarters in Spain.

19 MAJORCA
There are three important Jewish relics in Palma cathedral; a huge lamp and two 14th-century *rimmonium* (scroll supports).

20 TOLEDO (TOLEDO)
Alfonso the Wise had many Jews in his entourage. See two beautifully decorated former synagogues, El Tránsito and Santa María la Blanca.

21 CÓRDOBA (CÓRDOBA)
In the old Jewish quarter, north west of the cathedral, look for the town's last surviving (14th-century) synagogue on Calle Judíos.

22 SEVILLE (SEVILLA)
The old Jewish quarter is now called the Barrio de Santa Cruz; three old churches once were synagogues, the most famous is Santa María la Blanca. See also the Cathedral Treasury Museum.

Conquistadores

Nearly all the famous *conquistadores* who colonized the western hemisphere came from the isolated province of Estremadura. The men of Trujillo alone conceived many American nations. The *conquistadores* exported the Estremaduran tradition of zealous Catholic knighthood, though many joined the adventure to escape grinding poverty. A voyage to their roots:

1 GUADALUPE
Shrine of the conquerors. They dedicated their exploits to the Virgin of Guadalupe and here a school for New World missionaries was founded.

2 MEDELLÍN
Birthplace, in 1485, of Hernán Cortés, conqueror of Mexico. See his statue and read his list of Mexican conquests.

*T*he conquerors of many an American nation came from these parts.

3 TRUJILLO
Home of the Pizarro family (conquerors of Peru and Ecuador) and of Francisco Orellana, explorer of the Amazon.

4 CÁCERES
Returning colonists invested their gold in mansions here. See the Casa Toledo-Moctezuma, the house of Juan Cano de Saavedra, who accompanied Cortés and married the Aztec emperor's daughter.

5 BADAJOZ
Birthplace of Pedro de Alvarado, aide of Cortés and cruel conqueror of Guatemala.

6 JEREZ DE LOS CABALLEROS
Home of Vasco Nuñez de Balboa ('discoverer' of the Pacific) and of Hernando de Soto, explorer of the Mississippi.

7 ZAFRA
The *parador* Hernan Cortés in this Andalusian-style town recalls that the *conquistador* lived here briefly under the patronage of the Duke of Feria.

Golf

For abundance and variety of courses and quality of instruction, golfers would be hard pressed to find a holiday destination to beat Spain. Thanks to its climate, the Costa del Sol is the nation's golfing capital, but the Madrid area and the east coast are also strongholds of the game. Alternatively, in deepest winter, golfers find springtime in the Canary Islands. Of the 90+ courses around the country, here are a few that are special.

PALS (GERONA)
Beautiful course highly regarded by pros.

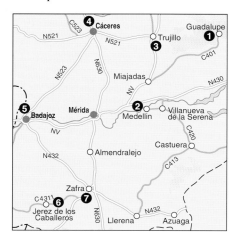

VALDERRAMA (CÁDIZ)

The most famous name in Spanish golf, host to many international tournaments; beautifully manicured, a real test of skill.

LAS BRISAS (MÁLAGA)

This Robert Trent Jones course is a favourite haunt of British show-biz personalities and international jet-setters.

GOLF EL PARAÍSO (MÁLAGA)

Gary Player is the co-designer of this 18-hole course near Estepona.

CLUB DE CAMPO DE MÁLAGA (MÁLAGA)

Fine old 18-hole course with its own small *parador*.

REAL GOLF DE PEDREÑA (SANTANDER)

Fine course where Severiano Ballesteros caddied as a boy.

HERRERÍA CLUB DE GOLF (MADRID)

Beautiful location alongside the majestic 16th-century El Escorial palace.

CAMP DE GOLF EL SALER (VALENCIA)

A *parador* abuts this highly-rated 18-hole course.

EL ESCORPIAN (VALENCIA)

Gary Player designed this course, featuring a number of holes with safe or more adventurous routes.

LA MANGA CLUB (MURCIA)

Three superb courses at the heart of one of Europe's top holiday sports complexes.

CLUB DE GOLF DE LAS PALMAS (GRAN CANARIA)

Established in 1891, this is the oldest and one of the most spectacular courses on Spanish territory; it occupies part of an extinct volcano.

Al-Andalus

For nearly eight centuries the Moors ruled Southern Spain. Their artistic and architectural legacy is remarkably widespread. The best known, most grandiose monuments are in the south: Córdoba, Granada and Seville, and these are dealt with elsewhere in this guide. But beyond these destinations, relics of the Moorish era can also be found in lesser-known places. (An *alcazaba* is a Moorish fortress.)

1 SALOBREÑA

The Arab street-plan and the old castle are reminders of Arab rule in this whitewashed coastal village.

2 VÉLEZ-MÁLAGA

The old provincial capital holds the remains of an important Moorish castle.

3 MÁLAGA

The Alcazaba dates from the 11th century, the adjoining Gibralfaro ramparts came three centuries later.

4 ANTEQUERA

Enjoy the fine view from the ruins of a fortress much fought over during the Reconquest.

5 LOJA

The gateway to the Alcazaba still stands; this fort was the key to the Moors' defence of Granada.

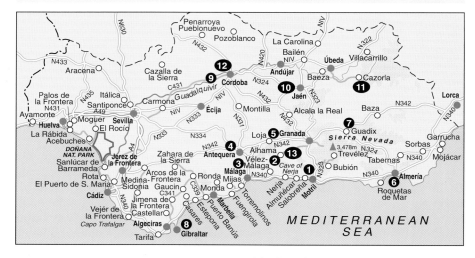

*Legacy of the Moors—
evidence of their long rule.*

6 ALMERIA

A very well-preserved and imposing 11th-century Alcazaba dominates the town. See, too, the remains of the main mosque, found in the church of San Juan.

7 GUADIX

You will find a ruined Alcazaba in this picturesque troglodyte community.

8 GIBRALTAR

Enjoy the view over to the Rock from Tarifa Castle, built in 960, then visit Gibraltar to see the Calahorra Tower.

9 ALMODÓVAR DEL RIO

A magnificent 8th-century castle presides over this small town, near Córdoba.

10 JAÉN

Once capital of a Moorish kingdom; Ali's Bath dates from the 11th century. The old Moorish castle is now a fine *parador*.

11 CAZORLA

The Moors held out in this dramatically sited mountain redoubt for eight centuries. There are two castles to see.

12 MEDINA AZAHARA

Well preserved ruins of a once-fabulous city which may have rivalled the Alhambra, but only survived for 74 years.

13 ALHAMA DE GRANADA

Picturesque small spa town with 12th-century baths at the Hotel Balnearía open to the public. See also the mediaeval quarter and ruined Arab castle.

Traces of the Romans

The legacy of the ancient Romans is clearly visible in many parts of Spain, from the east coast to Estremadura. Some of their monuments are still in use.

1 ALCÁNTARA (CÁCERES)

The drystone 'Legionnaires Bridge' over the Río Tajo outside Alcántara dates from around AD 100. It still carries daily traffic.

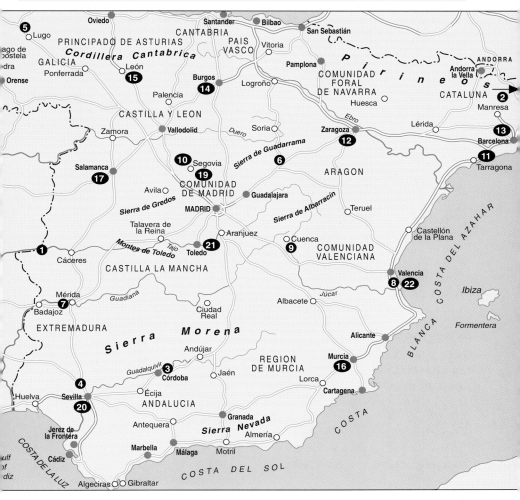

*H*ighlights of ancient Rome (1–12), and the sheer genius of many of Spain's cathedrals (13–22).

2 AMPURIAS (GERONA)

Roman enclave on the Costa Brava, overlooking remains of a Greek town. Wander through the old forum with its ruins of shops and dwellings.

3 CÓRDOBA

The birthplace of the Seneca family. With so many great monuments from the Moorish period in this area, you could easily miss the Roman Bridge across the Guadalquivir.

4 ITÁLICA (SEVILLA)

Just outside Seville, this impressive archaeological site contains the ruins of a huge Roman amphitheatre, a forum and some mosaics.

5 LUGO

The best-preserved Roman town walls in Spain and a column to Augustus Caesar.

6 MEDINACELI (SORIA)

A triple Roman archway (unique in Spain) stands in grand contrast to the small village around it.

7 MÉRIDA (BADAJOZ)

The old capital of Roman Lusitania is strewn with stately monuments, from an arena for 14,000 spectators to a couple of bridges. The outstanding National Museum of Roman Art is here.

8 SAGUNTO (VALENCIA)

Some Roman remains at the Castillo Sagunto and an 8,000-seater amphitheatre is in the process of restoration.

9 SEGÓBRIGA (CUENCA)

Important Roman site only partially excavated. Fine mosaics left *in situ* plus a small museum.

10 SEGOVIA

Engineers, architects and sightseers marvel over Segovia's Roman aqueduct, still supplying some of the city's water.

11 TARRAGONA

Former capital of Rome's biggest Spanish province, Tarragona has an impressive aqueduct plus lots more: a Triumphal Arch, a Roman quarry, a Roman Praetorium building, an amphitheatre, two forums, an archaeological promenade, a necropolis and three important museums.

12 ZARAGOZA

Forum of *Caesaraugusta* (discovered in 1988) is the centrepiece of a large underground *in situ* archaeological museum.

Ten Best Cathedrals

Generations of architects, stonecutters and artists collaborated to create the cathedrals of Spain. In many cases the results are superlative, for the originality of design, the unexpected combinations of style, and the genius evident in the sculpture and painting that decorate the cathedrals. From Romanesque to neo-Gothic, from the manipulation of received ideas to wholly new departures, there is no end to the innovation. Every one of these cathedrals is quite different from every other.

13 BARCELONA

Catalan-Gothic grace with 19th-century amendments.

14 BURGOS

Splendid spires top this truly inspired church; the interior is chock-a-block with art treasures.

15 LÉON

A Gothic classic with a uniquely vast expanse of glowing stained glass.

16 MURCIA

Outstanding baroque façade on a 14th-century Gothic masterpiece.

17 SALAMANCA

Old and new cathedrals combine to celebrate six centuries of great ecclesiastic architecture.

18 SANTIAGO DE COMPOSTELA

Behind the famous baroque façade, a precious Romanesque doorway.

19 SEGOVIA

Last of the great Spanish Gothic cathedrals, begun 1525.

20 SEVILLE
The world's third largest Gothic church, with a minaret for a bell tower.

21 TOLEDO
A Gothic heart with centuries of adornments and innovations.

22 VALENCIA
Mediaeval glory beautifully supplemented by later styles.

Pueblos Blancos
of Andalusia

The 'white villages' (although some are the size of small towns) of mountainous southern Spain are the picturesque legacy of Moorish urban planning. They are a perfect antidote to an overdose of the Costa del Sol.

1 MIJAS
Quintessential whitewashed village, now devoted to coastal day-trippers.

2 MONDA
Reputed site of battle between Julius Caesar and rival, Pompey the Great.

3 RONDA
Distinguished old town in an amazing setting, straddling an awesome ravine.

4 GAUCÍN
Lovely mountain village with ruined castle, much contested during the Reconquest. There are splendid views across to Gibraltar.

5 JIMENA DE LA FRONTERA
Hill town with Moorish castle, Gothic and baroque churches.

W*hite-washed, hilltop villages in southern Spain.*

6 CASTELLAR DE LA FRONTERA
Picturesque hilltop village with a crumbling castle.

7 CASARES
White village spiralling up to a rugged hilltop with sweeping views.

8 ARCOS DE LA FRONTERA
Precariously cliff-perched, one of the region's most stunning white towns.

9 MEDINA SIDONIA
Beautifully situated town with fine Gothic church built atop ruins of castle.

10 VEJÉR DE LA FRONTERA
On a lonely hilltop; 13th-century church built on remains of mosque.

11 ZAHARA DE LA SIERRA (ZAHARA DE LOS MEMBRILLOS)
A picture-book landmark town atop a rocky outcrop, clustered around its church and castle.

12 GRAZALEMA
One of the oldest of the white villages in

a marvellous setting backed by the highest pass in Andalusia and looking down across a broad valley.

Spas

Both the Romans and the Arabs, who gave so much to Spanish culture, were enthusiasts of thermal baths. Mineral waters for every taste and therapeutic prescription bubble forth from hundreds of springs all over the country. Fifty nine of these have been turned into spas. The National Tourist Office will supply you a map, *Guía de Balnearios*, with all the details. In provincial alphabetical order, here's a glance at a few of the places in Spain where you can 'take the cure'.

1 LA CORUÑA
Baños Viejos de Carballo, Carballo. Modern installation on site of baths first exploited by the Romans.

2 GERONA
Vichy Catalan, Caldas de Malavella. The well-known water is bottled here and sold all over; the spa offers everything from mud baths to inhalations.

3 GRANADA
Alicun de las Torres, Villanueva de las Torres. In beautiful hill country north east of Granada, all the medicinal facilities in a relaxed atmosphere.

4 HUESCA
Panticosa. High in the beauty of the snowy Pyrenees near the French border, the spa dates back to the early 19th century.

5 LÉRIDA
Caldas de Bohí. Luxury resort atmosphere

for 'taking the waters', hot and cold, in grand style in the Pyrenees.

6 PONTEVEDRA
La Toja island. Since the turn of the century a luxury resort has exploited the curative waters of this charming little island.

Romanesque Art

In the 11th and 12th centuries a new concept of art and architecture, now called

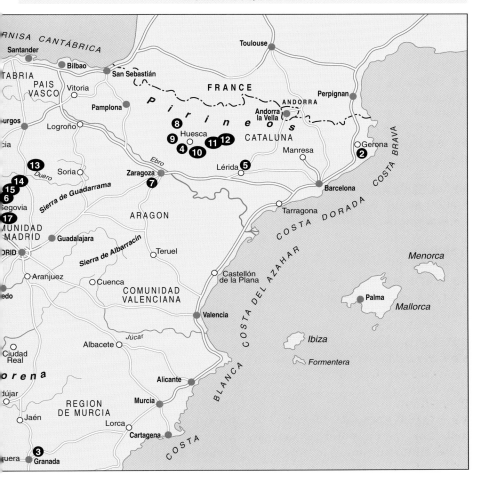

Romanesque, swept Spain. The pinnacle of this achievement is the Cathedral of Santiago de Compostela. At the other side of the country, Catalonia is especially well endowed with Romanesque churches and monasteries, and Barcelona's Museu d'Art de Catalunya is a priceless treasure-house. Among lesser known pockets of Romanesque culture, here are ten suggestions— five each in Aragon and Castile. A few are a little more difficult to get to, by way of mountain roads, a sure way to avoid the crowds.

*C*urative thermal therapy beloved of the Moors and the Romans (1–7), and graceful Romanesque architecture (8–17).

Aragon

8 JACA

The 11th-century cathedral inspired Road to Santiago architects and artists.

9 LOARRE

Lovely Romanesque church alongside a royal castle; a mountain fortress.

10 HUESCA

Gorgeous stonework in cloister of old monastery of San Pedro el Viejo.

11 BIERGE

Remote village with Romanesque church.

12 ALQUÉZAR

A 12th-century castle and remains of Romanesque cloister.

Castile

13 MADERUELO

Two Romanesque churches in a hilltop village.

14 SEPÚLVEDA

San Salvador church, dominating its hill site, is the most original of the town's Romanesque churches.

15 CANTALEJO

Romanesque priory north east of here, but road is difficult.

16 TURÉGANO

Romanesque church overshadowed by one-time castle of bishops of Segovia.

17 SEGOVIA

Romanesque churches of St Stephen, St Martin, St Lawrence and San Juan de los Caballeros.

In Quest of Quixote

Miguel de Cervantes, who wrote Spain's best-selling novel, knew well the vanishing horizons and looming windmills of moody La Mancha. He made the most of it as the background for the exploits of his immortal hero, Don Quixote. Scholars could point you to dozens of places with Quixote connections, but here is a day-trip starting from Madrid to get you going:

In search of Don Quixote's windmills—discover for yourself the landscapes that inspired Cervantes famous novel.

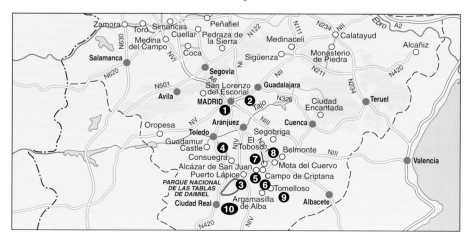

1 MADRID
See the superb bronze statue of Quixote and Sancho Panza in Plaza de España and the exterior of one of his houses on Calle del León.

2 ALCALA DE HENARES
Birthplace (1547) of Cervantes. Two houses claim the honour; one features a museum.

3 PUERTO LÁPICE
Here Quixote was knighted by the local innkeeper.

4 CONSUEGRA
Rebuilt windmills and a ruined castle make this lovely village a photographer's dream.

5 ALCÁZAR DE SAN JUAN
An old castle marks this market town; Quixote and Sancho Panza slept here.

6 CAMPO DE CRIPTANA
Another typical La Mancha village with windmills at which the knight may have tilted.

7 EL TOBOSO
The most authentically mediaeval of the many places on the Quixote trail and the charming home town of Quixote's ideal woman, Dulcinea. 'Dulcinea's House' is now a museum and the town hall holds some rare editions of the novel.

8 MOTA DEL CUERVO
Classic La Mancha village with castle ruins and Quixote windmills.

9 TOMELLOSO
A wine-bottling town. Nearby Peñarroyo castle was used for a Quixote adventure.

10 ARGAMASILLA DE ALBA
Cervantes began writing the book in this Ciudad Real village where he was imprisoned. A local dignitary, Don Rodrígo de Pacheco (see his painting in the parish church), is said to have inspired the character of the knight errant.

Highlights of the Catalonian Pyrenees

After a few days on the beach, or in Barcelona, you may be ready for some exercise, mountain scenery, fresh air and peace and quiet. This is just one of many possible itineraries in the Pyrenees of Catalonia.

1 BELLVER DE CERDANYA
Quaint rocktop village; balconied houses and cobbled streets overlooking Segre Valley.

2 LLES
Dramatic views from approach road.

3 LA SEU D'URGELL
Former princely city with 12th-century cathedral; superb diocesan museum.

4 ANDORRA
Pop across the border into this tiny Catalan-speaking principality of duty-free shopping, isolated hamlets and exclusive ski resorts.

5 COLL DE NARGÓ
Near Grau de la Granta, a lake dramatically confined by cliffs.

6 BÓIXOLS
Impressive scenery around pass leading to tiny village. Caution: steep roads.

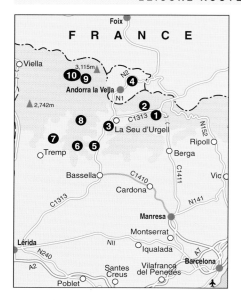

Fresh air and mountain scenery in the Catalonian Pyrenees.

7 NOGUERA PALLARESA VALLEY

Scenic route past towering 'Wild West' gulleys, bluffs and cliffs (especially Collegats Gorge, north of La Pobla) and salt beds towards more verdant mountains.

8 SORT

Turn left for Llessui Valley, lovely site for winter sports centre.

9 RIBERA DE CARDÓS

Beauty-spot resort with trout fishing.

10 ESPOT

Entrance village to Aigües Tortes National Park. From here you need a four-wheel-drive vehicle.

National Parks

After the traffic jams of Madrid and the teeming beaches of the *costas* you may be ready for some wide open spaces. The most refreshing escape roads lead to Spain's nine national parks (ask the Spanish National Tourist Office for a copy of their excellent *Spanish Wildlife* booklet).

COVADONGA MOUNTAIN

Set high in the Cantabrian mountains, this park occupies the western region of the massif Picos de Europa. It includes a series of peaks over 2,400m (8,000ft) high, fast-flowing rivers and two lakes of glacial origin. The park also holds the shrine of Covadonga (*see* page 158-9) and is therefore also of great historical importance.

ORDESA AND MONTE PERDIDO

Rubbing high shoulders with a French national park across the Pyrenean mountain peaks, the scenery here includes breathtaking glacial canyons, and is regarded as one of the great natural wonders of Europe, if not of the world. Ordesa is the last refuge of the Spanish Ibex (a wild goat) and there are numerous Chamois here. There is a visitor centre in Ordesa Valley.

AIGÜES TORTES WITH SAN MAURICIO LAKE

In the Pyrenees of Catalonia the peaks go up to almost 3,000m (10,000ft). The most outstanding features are the beautiful lakes of glacial origin and spectacular *cirques* (curved vertical walls of rock, scoured by glaciation). The melting snow provides a wonderland of waterfalls, mountain lakes and fertile valleys.

LAS TABLAS DE DAIMIEL

Tablas means 'river floodplain' and here comprises fresh water from the Cigüela and brackish water from the Guadiana. A sort of 'Everglades of La Mancha' swamp landscape provides abundant bird and plant life. Visitor Centre at park entrance plus two marked trails.

DOÑANA

This vast wildlife refuge in the province of Huelva is one of the most important ecological sites in Europe. It comprises marshes, spectacular white dunes and pine forests as well as beaches. Among honoured guests are more than 250 species of birds, including huge flocks of geese, ducks and waders in winter, groups of flamingoes, and the rare and majestic imperial eagle, found nowhere else in Europe. Other residents with this status are the Iberian lynx and the Egyptian mongoose. Visits are by guided tour only, starting at El Acebuche.

LAS CAÑADAS DEL TEIDE

Lying at the foot of Mount Teide on Tenerife (the highest mountain in Spain at 3,717m/12,195ft) this whole countryside is parched and volcanic. During the winter months, snow caps Mount Teide and descends down the mountainsides. Despite this, there is a wealth of plant life. However the major appeal is the stunning *malpais* ('badlands') scenery and the chance to ascend Teide by cable car.

GARAJONAY

The only Spanish natural area to be declared a World Heritage site lies in the centre of the Canary Island of La Gomera. Rare *laurisilva* bay tree forests dominate the undulating scenery which is humid and misty most of the year.

LA CALDERA DE TABURIENTE

A wonderful lush park dominated by pine trees set inside the vast crater, (3km across by 900m deep,) (2 miles by 2,950ft) of a huge volcano on the Canary Island of La Palma. Marvellous views over to volcanic plugs and peaks within the park from the viewpoint of La Cumbrecita.

TIMANFAYA (MONTAÑA DE FUEGO)

Lanzarote's 'Mountains of Fire' is an extraordinarily desolate lunar landscape found nowhere else on earth. A 50-minute coach tour (Route of the Volcanoes) is the only way to see the interior of the park. A stunning experience. Excellent visitor facilities include a restaurant which uses the heat of the volcano for cooking.

*T*he serenity of the Embalse de Riaño shows another side of Spain, and offers a measure of tranquillity to soothe the soul of the traveller in search of a little peace and quiet (overleaf).

The Cultured Capital

Madrid is famed all over Europe for its exuberant late-night scene. Where else do you have city-centre traffic jams at four o'clock in the morning – in winter? *Madrileños* work just as hard by day. And, as if the responsibilities of government and industry were not enough, in 1992 Madrid was named the European Capital of Culture. Take it all in, from the Prado to El Escorial to the city street life. You have nothing to lose but your sleep. Madrid is also a city literally at the crossroads. Right in the middle of Spain, it makes a great base for visiting some of the country's most historic towns.

At the geographical heart of Spain, Madrid is also Europe's highest capital – more than 640m (2,100ft) above sea level – and the mountain breezes generate a unique atmosphere. The city is alive with light, the sunshine filtering down through a pale sky barely dense enough to float a cloud on. Velázquez didn't invent these skies, he just painted what he saw.

When the sun goes down, Madrid comes into its own. See the *Madrileños* cramming the promenades and outdoor

Madrid's 18th-century Palacio Real looks out onto lavish gardens. Guided tours inspect the state apartments, except when royal ceremonies take precedence.

cafés at the hour of the *paseo*. So starts Europe's longest evening, for the night people of Madrid (known as *los gatos* 'the cats') dine very late and play even later. It's a wonder how they manage to go to work in the morning, let alone administer the country's affairs.

Madrid's elevation from obscurity to capital in the 16th century was a result of political compromise. However artificial its rise, the city has become a success as a dynamic international metropolis with a character all of its own. There is just never time enough to see and do everything here – perhaps that is why *los gatos* prowl all night.

At the crossroads of Spain, the centre of Madrid is 'Kilometre O' for all the radial highways. On the Castilian plateau beyond the built-up area, some of the most wonderful sights in the whole country are within day-tripping distance. Give top priority to Toledo, a former capital set on a crag, with haunting memories of El Greco and the very essence of historic Spain built into its houses and churches. Don't miss Segovia, a royal stronghold with a fairy-tale castle and classic Roman aqueduct. Tour the ancient walled city of saints, Ávila. Closer to Madrid, see El Escorial, the monastery, college and palace that sums up Spain's Golden Age, and the wonderful gardens of La Granja and Aranjuez.

CAPITAL BY CONVENIENCE

Madrid is a comparatively young European capital, only established as such in 1561 by Philip II. At that time the city was a fairly inconsequential settlement of just 20,000 inhabitants – one quarter of the population of neighbouring Toledo. As Philip trusted neither the clergy of Toledo, nor of Valladolid (the previous capitals), and as he wanted to be close to the construction of his beloved El Escorial project, Madrid was the best choice. Besides, reasoned Philip, Madrid was right in the middle of the country – what better reason to make it the capital!

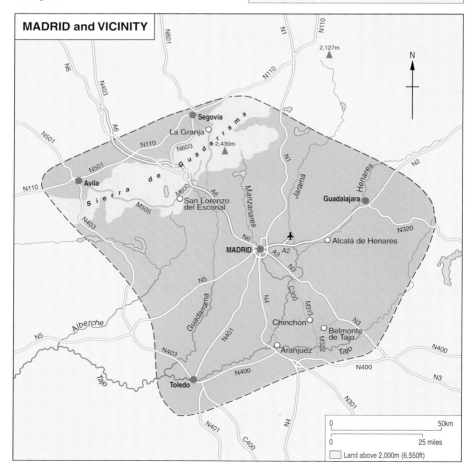

MADRID and VICINITY

Madrid

It is easy to find your way around **Madrid**. Outside every metro station stands a large city map. Signs at bus stops explain the arrivals and departures of buses on that route. The streets are clearly identified, often with wittily illustrated wall tiles.

Don't expect to find peace and quiet in Madrid. All the clatter and shriek makes this one of Europe's noisiest cities. Only very early in the morning does Madrid sound old-fashioned and neighbourly. An itinerant knife-sharpener advertises his trade on a Pan-style flute. A gypsy junk-collector walking beside his donkey-cart chants his call. A grinding, tortured roar from a café means the espresso machine is boiling milk for coffee. Europe's most sleepless people, the Madrileños, are loping off to work again, only six hours (or less) after another late night out.

Madrid and its people run to extremes. Perhaps this is a result of the altitude, or the weather, which is usually either too cold or too hot (roughly one third of the population flees Madrid every August).

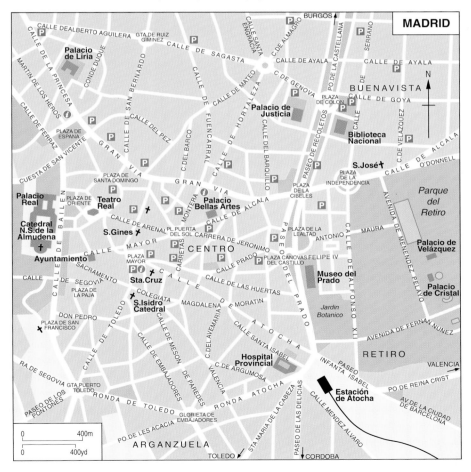

Madrileños seem to be bubbling one moment and sulking the next. They go to church, but they go to porn-shows too. They may bemoan the rush of modern life, but they find time to sit over coffee for an hour in a *tertulia*, an informal conversation club, discussing literature or football – or the rush of modern life.

There is a lot to see in this city of more than 3 million inhabitants (though less than Barcelona) so it's worth considering

a half-day guided tour to get your bearings. Are you going to divide the city geographically or chronologically? Do you feel the pull of the Prado, or the lure of the bars and cafés? Whatever your predilections, you really ought to start by savouring the oldest part of the city, on foot, in the heart of the original Madrid.

Old Madrid

Little is left of mediaeval Madrid except the mood. You feel it in the narrow streets that meander south from the Calle Mayor (Main Street). Dimly lit shops sell religious habits, military medals, books, berets, capes and cheeses. Artisans chip away at their woodwork. A beggar-woman, holding somebody else's baby, asks for a coin. A greengrocer builds a tomato pyramid. A blind lottery-ticket salesman, tapping his white cane to attract attention, recites a poem promising instant riches.

Vendors on foot and in kiosks sell several varieties of lottery tickets around the **Puerta del Sol** (Gate of the Sun), the hub of ten converging streets. For centuries this has been the city's nerve centre. Facing all the plaza's bustle is a statue based on Madrid's coat of arms, showing a bear standing against a *madroño* tree (an *arbutus*, or strawberry tree). This same bear is seen as a symbol all over Madrid – look on the doors of taxis.

The **Plaza Mayor** (Main Square), a few blocks away, is a 17th-century architectural symphony in bold but balanced tones. Broad arcades surround a vast cobbled rectangle. Plaza Mayor may be entered from all four sides through any of nine archways, but mercifully not by motor vehicles. In the past, this was the scene of pageants, bullfights, even executions; residents owning one of the 400-plus balconies overlooking the square used to sell

---

SUNDAY IN MADRID

Some cities sag through sedate Sundays. Not Madrid. Try to take in the sabbatical excitement.

The Rastro On Sunday mornings, the streets of old Madrid, beginning just south of the cathedral, are transformed into one of Europe's biggest flea markets. Tens of thousands of bargain-minded *Madrileños* join the out-of-towners searching out clothing, antiques, pots and pans, and junk of all sorts. Anyone for a used gas mask?

Puerta de Toledo The bait at the former central fish market is a bright collection of shops and galleries featuring antiques, art, fashion, handicrafts, plus a restaurant and cafés. (Open Tuesdays to Sundays.)

The Stamp Market Hundreds of collectors assemble in the Plaza Mayor on Sunday mornings to buy and sell stamps, coins, banknotes, cigar bands, and even used lottery tickets.

The Book Fair Just south of the Botanical Garden, bibliophiles throng to open-air stalls along Calle de Claudio Moyano. New and used books are bought and sold: trashy novels, pornographic comics, foreign fiction and valuable old tomes change hands. After drinks, snacks and, of course, lunch, you will have to decide whether to watch Real Madrid play football, to go to a bullfight, or to follow the horses at the Zarzuela Hippodrome.

tickets for such events. A statue of King Philip III occupies the place of honour but is no obstacle to events ranging from pop concerts to theatre festivals. Take a seat at one of the outdoor cafés in the square and enjoy the perfect proportions of Madrid's most elegant architectural ensemble.

Farther along Calle Mayor, the old Plaza de la Villa juxtaposes stately 16th- and 17th-century buildings of varied style. The **Casa de Cisneros**, built in the mid-16th century by a nephew of the intrepid inquisitor, Cardinal Cisneros, belongs to the fine, intricate style of architecture known as plateresque. The style is so called because it seems as delicate as a silversmith's work (*platero* means 'silversmith'). The **Ayuntamiento** (City Hall) represents the Hapsburg era, with the towers and slate spires characteristic of the 17th-century official buildings all around the capital.

Although there are more than 200 churches in Madrid, very few could be classified as essential tourist attractions. The city is too young to have a great mediaeval cathedral. The present (provisional) cathedral in Calle de Toledo, the **Catedral de San Isidro**, needed a lot of rebuilding; it was badly damaged during the Civil War. Under its massive dome, among many relics, are the revered remains of the city's patron saint, San Isidro Labrador (St Isidore the Farmer).

Just down Calle de Toledo from the cathedral is the site of the **Rastro**, Madrid's famous and phenomenal Sunday flea market.

The Plaza Mayor; unbelievable as it seems today, from these beautifully muralled balconies blood-curdling auto-da fés *and executions were once popular spectator events.*

The city's most formidable church is the mid-18th century **Basílica de San Francisco el Grande**, dedicated to St Francis of Assisi. The curved neoclassical façade somewhat curtails the effect of the church's most superlative feature. Once inside, the dome is out of the ordinary. Indeed, its inner diameter exceeds that of the cupolas of St Paul's, London or Les Invalides in Paris. Imposing statues of the apostles in white Carrara marble surround the rotunda. Seven richly ornamented chapels fan out from the centre. In the chapel of San Bernardino de Siena, notice the large painting above the altar. In this lively scene by Francisco de Goya, the second figure from the right, dressed in yellow, is said to be a self-portrait.

Central Madrid

Plaza de la Cibeles would be perfect were it not for the intensity of the traffic, vehemently directed by pony-tailed police-women. The fountain in the centre shows Cybele, a controversial Greek fertility goddess, serenely settled in a chariot pulled by two lions. The sculptural ensemble is probably the best-known fountain in all Spain. The most obvious building on the plaza is the cathedral-like Palacio de Comunicaciones, a ponderous post office, inaugurated in 1919, and rather sarcastically nicknamed 'Our Lady of Communications'. Across the square, the Army headquarters coyly camouflages itself behind century-old iron railings and a lovely garden dotted with statues of scantily-clad nymphs.

Also facing Plaza de la Cibeles, the headquarters of the Bank of Spain combines neoclassical, baroque and rococo styles. It looks reassuringly solid enough to take care of the nation's money. The financial district, Madrid's 'City' or 'Wall Street', begins here along **Calle de Alcalá**. Mammon does not occupy the whole street, however. Next door to the Ministry of Finance is the **Museo de la Real Academia de Bellas Artes de San Fernando** (Museum of the Royal Academy). The academy owns a celebrated batch of Goya's paintings, including the *Burial of the Sardine* (a bizarre ceremony you may witness at Carnival time), full of action and humour, and a superb self-portrait of the artist. Rubens, Zurbarán, Velázquez and Murillo are also represented among hundreds of works on display.

The **Gran Vía** is the main east-west thoroughfare and lifeline of modern Madrid. It throbs with shops, hotels, theatres, night-clubs and cafés and is the street for strolling and window-gazing. Connoisseurs of traffic jams will marvel at the nightmare of the rush-hour here. Immobile drivers, at their wits' end, lean on their horns, not quite overriding the screech of the police whistles. Thanks to the siesta break, there are four rush-hours a day in Madrid!

At **Plaza del Callao** the pedestrian traffic reaches its peak. This is the centre for department stores (the two biggest glare at each other across a pedestrian mall), cinemas, cafés and bus termini. Yet only a couple of streets south of Callao's turbulence, the **Convento de las Descalzas Reales** clings to a 16th-century tranquillity. The institution was founded by Princess Joanna of Austria and subsidized by generous patrons. Cloistered nuns of the Santa Clara order stay out of sight when the public is admitted (the visiting hours are few and eccentric, so check with the tourist office before you go). The first view of the convent's splendours begins with the theatrical grand stairway. Upstairs are heavy timbered ceilings and walls covered with works of art, mostly of religious or royal significance. In one hall you can see a dozen 17th-century tapestries based on original Rubens' drawings.

From Plaza del Callao, the Gran Vía continues downhill towards the **Plaza de España** through more shopping, strolling and nightlife territory. Skyscrapers of 26 and 34 storeys overlook the plaza, a sanctuary of grass, flowers, trees and fountains. A favourite sight, especially with visiting photographers, is the Cervantes monument. A stone sculpture honouring this author looms behind bronze statues of his immortal creations: Don Quixote, astride his horse, Rosinante; and Sancho Panza, on his donkey.

Calle de la Princesa, which begins at Plaza de España, is actually a north-west extension of the Gran Vía. The **Palacio de Liria**, residence of the Duchess of Alba, at Calle de la Princesa, 22, calls to mind a scaled-down Buckingham Palace. The family picture gallery includes works by

---

FROM SWORD TO PEN

Miguel de Cervantes Saavedra fought at the Battle of Lepanto (1571), was wounded, captured and imprisoned; he escaped, was enslaved by pirates and finally ransomed. Back in Spain, he worked as an army quartermaster, but was beset by problems. He was excommunicated from the church and spent several spells in prison on charges of financial and technical irregularities. Then at the age of 58, with the necessary fund of worldly knowledge at his disposal, he wrote one of the world's best-selling novels, *Don Quixote*. Despite this, his royalties were modest.

Cervantes died on 23 April 1616 in his house in Madrid's Calle del León (by an enormous coincidence, on the same day the world also lost William Shakespeare).

---

such artists as Titian, El Greco, Rubens, Van Dyck, Rembrandt and Goya. The palace is closed to the public except by special arrangement.

The smart thoroughfare of Calle de la Princesa ends where the university district, *ciudad universitaria*, begins. The landmarks here are the Air Force headquarters (a modern copy of El Escorial) and Madrid's youngest triumphal arch (which was built to commemorate Franco's 1939 victory).

The Prado

Madrid's pride and joy, the **Museo del Prado**, houses what is indisputably the world's greatest collection of Spanish paintings. In addition, there are hundreds of foreign masterpieces, especially of the Italian and Flemish schools. This immense treasure trove was assembled from the collections of Spain's Hapsburg and Bourbon kings, patrons of the arts, and various convents and monasteries.

Charles III commissioned architect Juan de Villanueva to design the neoclassical building towards the end of the 18th century. It was supposed to have served as a museum of natural history, but after some eventful delays (Napoleon's invasion badly damaged the building), its mission was diverted to art: the Royal Museum of Painting was inaugurated in 1819, and in 1868 it became *el Museo del Prado*.

A Prado annexe, the gravely colonnaded **Casón del Buen Retiro**, up the hill in Calle de Felipe IV, houses the Prado's collection of 19th-century Spanish art. Works include several paintings of death and daily life by Goya and portraits by Vicente López (Goya's prize pupil). There is a hall of historical paintings, strong on melodrama and Spanish honour, and a collection of early Spanish impressionists.

TACKLING THE PRADO

A serious student of fine art could easily plan an entire Madrid itinerary around repeated visits to the Prado. The average tourist, however, may only want to spend a few hours here. To see more Old Masters per minute, plan ahead. Decide what you want to see and give the remainder a quick glance.

For a hurried dash through the Prado, or an overview at the start of several visits, here are our nominations for the museum's top dozen painters (listed chronologically within their groups). To speed your rounds, we spotlight their most famous works:

Heaven, earth and hell, as represented by the feverish, surrealistic mind of Hieronymous Bosch in The Garden of Delights. *This is just one of several of his Prado works.*

It seems that Goya could turn his hand to any style of painting. The Prado holds some of his greatest works: from the horrors of war to tapestry designs, from unflattering royal portraits to his voluptuous (and anonymous) nude, the Maja Desnuda *(the Naked Beauty).*

Spanish

El Greco (1541-1614). *Knight with Hand on Chest*, an early portrait, realistic and alive, studies a deep-eyed, bearded *caballero* in black. It is signed, in Greek letters, '*Domenikos Theotokopoulos*', the artist's real name. The Prado is also well supplied with El Greco's mystical, passionately coloured brand of religious paintings, such as *Adoration of the Shepherds*.

José Ribera (c. 1591-1652). Most of his life was spent in Italy, where the Valencia-born artist was known as 'Lo Spagnoletto'. His human-interest portraits of saints, hermits and martyrs show impeccable draughtsmanship and keen lighting. A batch of his pictures of the disciples of Jesus are on view in the Prado.

Francisco de Zurbarán (1598-1664). Mysticism and realism are combined in Zurbarán's experiments in space, light and shade. He was versatile enough to excel at still life as well as mythological, religious and historical themes. The Prado owns his strained but fascinating battle picture, *The Defence of Cádiz against the English* and a rarer *Still Life* of a goblet, two vases and a pot.

Diego Velázquez (1599-1660). *Las Meninas* (The Maids of Honour), Spain's all-time favourite painting, featuring the family of Philip IV, proudly has a room to itself. Notice that the artist painted himself with palette in hand at the left side of his own masterpiece. Another vast, unforgettable Velázquez canvas here is *Surrender of Breda*, a pageant with pathos. Elsewhere are his portraits of the high and the mighty, along with studies of ordinary people.

Bartolomé Murillo (1617-82). In *Holy Family with a Little Bird*, Spain's most popular religious artist of his time catches biblical personalities off guard. Tender scenes such as these plus classical religious works with soaring angels brought Murillo international fame.

TACKLING THE PRADO *CONTINUED*

Francisco de Goya (1746-1828). Of all the Prado's paintings, none is more discussed and disputed than *The Naked Maja*, one of Spain's first nudes. The face is awkwardly superimposed on the body, suggesting that the sensuous lady's identity was thus disguised. Rumours of a scandalous affair between Goya and the Duchess of Alba are always mentioned, and usually denied. Goya's most celebrated royal portrait, *The Family of Charles IV*, is daringly frank and unflattering. Demonstrating yet another side of the artist is *The Executions of the 3rd of May*, one of Spanish history's most powerful protest pictures.

Dutch and Flemish
Rogier van der Weyden (c. 1400-64). The powerful composition and brilliant draughtsmanship of the altarpiece, *Descent from the Cross*, confirms this as the artist's greatest painting.
Hieronymus Bosch (c. 1450-1516). The Spanish call him 'El Bosco'. Here you can see three of his all-time surrealist masterpieces, including a large triptych called *The Garden of Delights*. A risqué mix of erotic fantasies and apocalyptic nightmares, it portrays the terrors and superstitions of the mediaeval peasant psyche. The works of Bosch hints at the art that Salvador Dalí was to express some 400 years later.
Peter Paul Rubens (1577-1640). His students ran an artistic assembly line, but the prolific Rubens kept his work as original as his genius. Of the dozens of paintings by Rubens in the Prado, two best demonstrate his versatility: the huge *Adoration of the Magi* is a brilliant religious extravaganza, while *The Three Graces* balances fleshy nudes with an equally voluptuous landscape.

Italian
Raphael (1483-1520). Napoleon showed good taste when he hijacked the Prado's Raphael collection to Paris, but it was soon recovered. However, centuries of investigation have failed to uncover the identity of *The Cardinal*, Raphael's explosive character study of a man with fishy eyes, aquiline nose and cool, thin lips.
Titian (c. 1490-1576). *Portrait of the Emperor Charles V* shows Titian's patron in armour, on horseback at the Battle of Mühlberg; it set the standard for court painters over the next century. Titian also painted religious works, but seemed to have no difficulty changing gears to the downright lascivious. *Baccanal* is about as far as an orgy can go within the hallowed halls of the Prado.
Tintoretto (1518-94). While Titian was painting kings, Tintoretto was aiming slightly lower on the social scale. The Prado owns, among others, his portraits of a prosecutor, a general and a senator. Look for his dramatic bible stories, originally ceiling paintings, and, for something completely different, *Lady Revealing Her Bosom*.

On your way through the Italian rooms, also keep an eye open for these Renaissance prodigies:
Antonello da Messina's intensely tragic *Christ Sustained by an Angel*.
Sandro Botticelli's *The Story of Nastagio degli Onesti*, a storyboard from the *Decameron*.
Fra Angelico's glowing *Annunciation*, with Adam and Eve, clothed, in supporting roles.

Las Meninas (*'Maids of Honour'* or *'Maids-in-Waiting'*) by Velázquez is said to be
Spain's favourite painting, and it is certainly one of the Prado's most visited. It features
the Infanta Margarita attended by two maids and a dwarf (opposite above).
The Prado itself (opposite below).

Opposite the Prado is the elegant three-storey brick Palacio de Villahermosa, which now houses the famous **Museo Thyssen Bornemisza**. This is the kind of collection that curators from all over the world would die for, and it is a measure of Madrid's stature that the city was chosen to house them, neatly coinciding with its nomination as the 1992 European Cultural Capital. More than 800 paintings are exhibited, from the 13th Century to the present day.

Royal Madrid

The **Palacio Real** (Royal Palace) is set among formal gardens on a bluff overlooking the Manzanares valley. An old Moorish fortress on this site burned down in 1734, whereupon King Philip V ordered an immense new palace in French style. His command produced this imperious residence, loaded with art and history.

On certain days, not always predictable, the palace is closed to the public to give priority to regal ceremonies and portentous events. When it is open, visitors are forbidden, for security reasons, to wander on their own, but are escorted in groups. The basic tour takes in 50 rooms (out of a staggering total of 2,000), but their opulence is such that even after this relatively small sampling, you may be relieved that the tour goes no further.

A few highlights: the Gasparini room, rococo at its most overwhelming; the ceremonial dining room, seating 145 guests; the throne room, with ceiling painted by Tiepolo. For an extra charge you can view the crown jewels, the museum of paintings, the royal library, pharmacy and armoury. Called the finest collection of its type in the world, the armoury is packed with battle flags, trophies, shields and weapons.

On the far side of the palace, in Campo del Moro, the **Museo de Carruajes** (Carriage Museum) specializing in royal transport of all kinds, is currently closed while underground railway lines are being built. The collection is interesting and well-organised, so watch out for the re-opening or contact the tourist office to check on the current situation.

More Museums

A wide-ranging, priceless private collection bequeathed to the nation fills the **Museo Lázaro Galdiano**, Calle de Serrano, 122. Ancient jewellery includes a Celtic diadem which dates from the 2nd century BC. There are paintings by Bosch, El Greco, Rembrandt and Goya, but the museum's greatest pride is a portrait of angelic beauty by Leonardo da Vinci, *The Saviour*.

Centro de Arte Reina Sofía, Calle de Santa Isabella, 52. The centre houses one of Madrid's most important collections of modern art. Picasso's monumental Guernica behind its bulletproof glass is undoubtedly the star of the show, a panorama of horror provoked by the Civil War bombing of a defenceless Basque town. The centre also houses the original studies for the work and other paintings of Picasso. The collections of the former Museo de Arte Contemporáneo are now housed here, including important works by Miró, Dalí and Juan Gris.

Museo Sorolla, Paseo del General Martínez Campos, 37. On view are close to 300 paintings by the Valencian impressionist Joaquín Sorolla (1863-1923). This is the city's only museum devoted to a single painter and occupies the house in which he lived and worked.

Panteón de Goya – Ermita de San Antonio de la Florida, Paseo de la Florida. In a rather unglamorous area between the railway yards and the river, Goya's greatest fresco covers the cupola of an 18th-century chapel. An identical chapel built alongside permits the local congregation to pray in peace while tourists crane their necks next door.

Museo Arqueológico, Calle de Serrano, 13. The art of the peninsula's ancient inhabitants is on display, with miraculously preserved mosaics from 2nd-century Roman Spain and earlier Carthaginian statuettes from Ibiza. The highlight of this collection is *La Dama de Elche* (the Lady of Elche), a stone sculpture of an enigmatic Celtiberian deity, perhaps 2,500 years old, found in Alicante province. Here, too, is an accurate reproduction of the cave paintings of Altamira, which date back some 15,000 years to the dawn of art. The underground simulation is well worth seeing, for pictures can't fully reproduce the three-dimensional power of these murals and the actual caves in Cantabria are closed to most visitors in order to protect the paintings – so this may well be as close as you ever get to the real thing.

Museo de América, Avenida de los Reyes Católicos, 6 (Ciudad Universitaria). To Spaniards, 'America' means Central and South America, and there are outstanding pre-Columbian statues and artefacts here. Two rare Mayan *codices* (manuscripts) are displayed in their entirety.

Templo Egipcio de Debod. For a change of ancient pace, have a look at this 25-centuries-old Egyptian temple, dismantled and shipped to Madrid stone by stone. From the temple you can enjoy a panoramic view over Madrid.

Museo Nacional de Artes Decorativas, Calle de Montalbán, 12. The best of old Spanish glassware, woodwork, tapestry, porcelain and jewellery – all the things

genuine antique collectors dream of finding at the flea market.

Museo Romántico, Calle de San Mateo, 13. Spaniards seem incurably nostalgic for the age of love seats, rococo mirrors and petticoated young princesses. (There are several Museo Románticos in Spain.)

Real Fábrica de Tapices (Royal Tapestry Factory), Calle de Fuenterrabía, 2, was founded by Philip V in 1721. Goya himself worked here, creating the designs on which tapestries were based. They are still being copied here, along with contemporary designs.

Landmarks and Parks

Plaza de Colón (Columbus Plaza). Beneath the plaza is the city's cultural centre, where art exhibitions, concerts and plays are staged. Drop in and see what's on. The bus station which serves the airport is also here. Above ground, a colossal abstract sculptural ensemble in the Jardines del Descubrimiento (Discovery Gardens) gives credit to Columbus's unsung crewmen, all of whose names are listed here.

Paseo de la Castellana, Madrid's principal north-south avenue runs for several miles through the heart of the city. Many of the patrician town houses in the central area have given way to banks and other commercial developments, and there are luxurious apartment blocks with landscaped balconies. Surrounded by the traffic, the tree-shaded central strip is wide enough to provide a promenade and a lively zone of outdoor cafés.

Nuevos Ministerios (New Ministries). A bureaucrat's dream along the Castellana, this mammoth 20th-century project is reminiscent of Washington DC at its most monumental. Just north of the ministries is a vast urban development zone called Azca, with housing, offices, stores and gardens; it looks like an Eastern European exercise in gigantism.

Puerta de Alcalá. This giant monumental triumphal arch, surmounted by warrior angels, honours Charles III.

Parque del Retiro. Until little more than a century ago, the Retiro was a royal preserve. Now it is the easiest place for *Madrileños* to take a family outing. Sunday morning is the best time to visit, when they turn out in their best attire. There is a lovely rose garden, a boating lake and carefully laid out gardens to enjoy. Street entertainers, a puppet show and a concert band are usually around too.

Parque Casa de Campo. For a more rural Sunday in the park, this is another former royal preserve, forested by Philip II in 1559, and boasting thousands of acres of woodland, interspersed with attractions and amenities.

Toledo

Everything that is quintessentially Spanish, in terms of tradition, grandeur and art, is crammed into El Greco's adopted home town, set on a Castilian hilltop. The one-time imperial capital remains the religious centre of Spain and an incomparable treasure-house of the fine arts, but **Toledo** is not just a collection of churches and museums. Above all, this is a town to wander in, drinking in the ancient atmosphere, just happening upon vestiges of a glorious past. In season the town fills up with day-trippers, but you can escape them in the back streets; and at either end of the day, before and after the coaches, peace descends.

Toledo's eminence goes back to the first Christian synods and ecclesiastical councils, held here as early as the year 400.

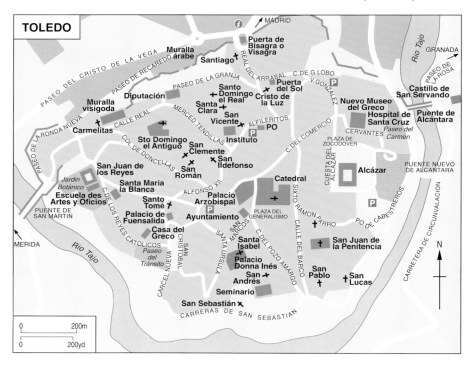

After the Muslim invasion in 711, however, Christianity went underground. Toledo was reconquered in 1085, and mosques were turned into churches. Finally, in 1222, funds were appropriated for a fitting cathedral. The construction lasted two and a half centuries, and the ornamentation took even longer, but it was worth the wait. You can locate the **cathedral** of Toledo from any part of town, thanks to its Gothic tower, topped by a spire strangely ringed by spikes. At ground level, however, the building is hemmed in by a clutter of back streets. No matter; its glory can be seen inside. Its splendid stained glass, wrought iron, sculptures and artworks have been produced by whole armies of inspired artisans.

In the centre of the five-aisled basilica, the **coro** (choir) is a marvel of wood-carving, but the main altar outdoes even this. Just behind the back wall of the main chapel, the **Transparente** is the cathedral's most unforgettable innovation. It is the work of one man, Narciso Tomé, an 18th-century architect, sculptor and painter who opened the ceiling and drew heavenly light into the sanctuary. While the cathedral's 750 stained-glass windows illuminate with sublime restraint, Tomé's bronze, marble and jasper ensemble of colour, shape and symbolism startles as it inspires.

The **Sala Capitular** (Chapter house) is an interestingly oriental room with an intricate ceiling in the style called Mudéjar (the work of Muslims converted to Christianity after the Reconquest). In the **Tesoro** (Treasury), all eyes focus on the towering gilded monstrance (the receptacle for the Host), composed of 5,600 sections, plus many precious stones.

The **sacristy** is a museum of art. The pictures are clearly labelled (a rarity in

*T*his wood turner at Toledo is carrying on the town's centuries-old tradition of craftsmanship.

Spanish churches), so you won't have to wonder whether the picture in front of you could be a genuine El Greco. It certainly could. In all, there are 16 of them in this small collection.

The cathedral's only competitor for domination of the Toledo skyline is the **Alcázar**, a fortress which has been destroyed and rebuilt many times since the Roman era. During the Spanish Civil War it was a stronghold of the pro-Franco forces, who held out during a 72-day siege which all but destroyed the stronghold. Today, the building is something of a shrine to those defenders, with all sorts of

Toledo's unforgettable hilltop skyline, ringed by the Tagus river, is almost unchanged since the days when El Greco painted it.

improbable propaganda stories of heroism and martyrs to Franco's cause, and an intriguing Army (Ejercit) Museum.

The triangular-shaped **Plaza de Zocodover**, also rebuilt after Civil War destruction, is where the Moorish market (*zoco*) was held in the Middle Ages. It was also the scene of fiestas, tournaments and executions. Appropriately, the horseshoe arch leading from the square towards the river is called *El Arco de la Sangre* ('Arch of Blood').

Just down the hill beyond the arch, in Calle de Cervantes, the 16th-century **Hospital de Santa Cruz** (Holy Cross Hospital) is now a museum. The main portal, built of stone, is carved in plateresque style. Inside, great wooden ceilings add to a feeling of opulent spaciousness. Among a wide selection of El Greco's works here is his *Altarpiece of the Assumption*, painted a year before his death.

The parish church of **Santo Tomé** is a landmark because of its stately Mudéjar tower. Here they charge an admission fee to view a single painting. . . but what a painting! El Greco's *Burial of the Count of Orgaz* magically fuses the mundane and the spiritual. It depicts local noblemen at the count's funeral, which was also attended, according to tradition, by two saints. El Greco shows St Augustine and St Stephen lifting the count's body, while up above, angels and saints crowd the clouds. The whole story is told in perfect pictorial balance and with the artist's unpredictable colours.

El Greco spent the most productive years of his prolific career in Toledo. Just down the hill from Santo Tomé, a house in which he is said to have lived has been reconstructed and linked to a museum. The **El Greco House** was originally built by Samuel Levi, a 14th-century Jewish financier and friend of King Peter I of Castile.

As devout as he was rich, Levi built a synagogue next to his home, known as **La**

Sinagoga del Tránsito. Muslim artists adorned the walls with filigrees intricate beyond belief, as well as inscriptions in Hebrew from the Psalms. After the expulsion of the Jews from Spain, the synagogue was converted into a church, hence the Christian tombstones in the floor. Today it is a national monument. Attached to the synagogue, a **Museum of Spanish Judaism** exhibits mediaeval scrolls and vestments.

TOLEDO STEEL

Toledo is famous all over the world for the quality of its steel, and swords have been forged here since the times of the ancient Romans. According to legend, the special property of the steel is inherited from the magical water of the river Tagus which surrounds the town. Look out for *damascene* steel souvenirs. This is a craft unique to the city, which involves inlaying black steel with decorative gold, copper and silver filigree.

Ávila

The fairy-tale stone **walls** protecting **Ávila** are perhaps too perfect: they make the city look like a Castilian Disneyland. These all-embracing fortifications, built in the last decade of the 11th century, boast 88 towers and an estimated 2,500 niches suitable for sentries or marksmen. Yet there is more to this city than its defences. In fact, the whole of Ávila has been nominated as a national monument (which means it cannot be altered). In some ways, this seems to have worked against the city, stifling its development and almost hermetically sealing it from the outside world. But for most tourists it remains very much a 'must see' town.

The **cathedral** of Ávila, built between the 12th and 16th centuries, includes Romanesque, Gothic and Renaissance elements. It has a fortivied apse, **cimorro**, which is actually part of the wall itself. The high retable was begun by Pedro Berruguete, Spain's first great Renaissance artist. Behind the principal chapel is the alabaster tomb of Bishop Alonso de Madrigal, whose dark complexion won him the splendid nickname *El Tostado* ('the Toasted One'). The 16th-century sepulchre portrays the bishop in full regalia, accurate right down to the embroidery on his robes. A museum of relics and art attached to the cathedral houses a silver monstrance as tall as a man.

Like the Tránsito, the **Sinagoga de Santa María la Blanca** (St Mary the White) underwent a change of name and religion. Constructed by Muslim artisans, with 24 columns supporting horseshoe arches, it looks more like a mosque than either a synagogue or a church.

A final Toledo church, with regal connections: Ferdinand and Isabella built **San Juan de los Reyes** (St John of the Kings) in a combination of Gothic, Renaissance and Mudéjar style. Look for a poignant souvenir on the outer wall – the chains that held the Moors' Christian prisoners before their liberation. The superb double-layer cloister has elaborate stone carvings.

Just outside the city walls, the **Basilica de San Vicente** is noted for an extraordinary tomb topped by a bizarre oriental-looking canopy. Knights of old used to place their hands on the 12th-century sepulchre when they took their oaths. Commemorated here are St Vincent of Zaragoza and his two sisters, martyred in the 4th century.

One of the multi-faceted rose windows that illuminate the fabulous ornamentation within the Gothic masterpiece that is Toledo Cathedral. Generations of craftsmen have since added to this landmark. The exterior is best viewed from afar.

Melancholy history also surrounds the royal **Monasterio de Santo Tomás**, sponsored by Ferdinand and Isabella. Their only son, Prince Don Juan, died here at the age of 19. His two tutors are buried in a small chapel near the tomb of the prince. Incidentally, this monastery was the headquarters of the notorious Torquemada, Spain's first Grand Inquisitor.

Many visitors come to Ávila in honour of the frail but tireless reformer, St Teresa of Jesus. Teresa de Cepeda y Ahumada was born in Ávila in 1515 and the convent of Santa Teresa marks the site of her birthplace. She spent some 30 years in the convent of the Incarnación (outside the city walls) as a novice and later as prioress. The convent of San José, founded in 1562, was the first of 17 Carmelite convents that she established. She was canonized in 1622 and proclaimed the first female doctor of the Church in 1970. In Ávila you can see relics and manuscripts, and even the habit worn by St Teresa.

After you have seen Ávila up close, drive or take a bus across the Río Adaja to the monument called **Los Cuatro Postes** ('the Four Posts'). This rocky hill offers a panoramic view of the whole of mediaeval Ávila. At sunset, this invulnerable walled city looks too good to be true.

El Escorial

Sheer statistics cannot do justice to the extravagant scale of this 16th-century royal palace complex. By official count, **El Escorial**, which comprises living quarters, a church, a monastery, a mausoleum and a museum (all under one roof), has 86 stairways, more than 1,200 doors and 2,600 windows. In a distinctly Spanish version of Italian Renaissance style, it

sums up the physical and spiritual superlatives of the empire's Golden Age, at the time when it ruled some 75 per cent of the known world. Hilaire Belloc called it 'the supreme monument of human permanence in stone; the supreme symbol of majesty'. Those even more charitably inclined have labelled it 'the 8th Wonder of the World'. However, it is not to everyone's taste. It is undoubtedly vast, and stark and bleak in places too.

The overwhelming effect is eased by the adjoining town of San Lorenzo de El Escorial. Because of the altitude of 1,055m (3,460ft), it is a popular retreat for *Madrileños* escaping the searing summer heat, hence the generous supply of hotels, restaurants and bars.

Inside the **basilica** of El Escorial, the mood is one of devout magnificence. The immense main retable is composed of red marble, green jasper and gilded bronze. The 124 finely carved seats in the choir include a slightly roomier one for its founder, King Philip II. Of the dozens of works of art collected here, none attracts more admiration than the life-sized marble crucifix by Benvenuto Cellini of Florence.

Philip II, who ordered El Escorial to be built, died here in 1598. He is buried in a family tomb tunnelled beneath the high altar of the basilica. The royal **pantheon** contains the remains of almost all of Spain's kings, queens, princes and princesses over a period of four centuries. In the central hall, marble sarcophagi are stacked four high.

Above ground again, 40,000 rare books as well as manuscripts of immense beauty and value are preserved in the **library**. In the **Palacio Real**, each room is more lavish than the one before. The tapestries are based on original designs by Goya and

The fabulous library at El Escorial, which houses one of the world's greatest collections of rare books.

Rubens, but the most striking wall covering belongs to the **Sala de las Batallas** (Hall of Battles). Here, frescoes depict hundreds of soldiers, with each detail carefully painted.

The **apartments of Philip II** are modest in comforts but rich in works of art. The king died here among cherished paintings, including a fantastic triptych by Hieronymus Bosch and works on religious themes by German, Flemish and Italian artists.

In addition to the fine paintings scattered through El Escorial, the **New Museums** display great works commissioned or collected by Spanish monarchs. In these stately surroundings hang pictures by Bosch, Ribera, Tintoretto, Velázquez and Veronese and El Greco. It is a worthy gallery by any standards.

The last monarch at El Escorial was Ferdinand VII, who died in 1833. By 1861 this great palace was no longer the royal residence.

Valle de los Caídos

A giant stone cross said to weigh 181,740 tons marks the **Valle de los Caídos** (Valley of the Fallen). This grandiose memorial ostensibly honours all the dead of the Civil War, but in reality it is far more of a shrine to Franco's forces. Franco himself chose this beautiful site in a forested valley, and here he is buried.

The church of the Valle de los Caídos is claimed to be the 'largest basilica ever built in the history of mankind', and has an entry in the *Guinness Book of Records* to prove it. It was hewn out of the side of the mountain like a railway tunnel (most of the labour provided by Franco's prisoners). Statues and tapestries fill out the colossal dimensions and add to the subterranean pomp. The nave runs 262m (860ft) into the mountain, making the church floor area over 50 per cent bigger than that of St Paul's Cathedral in London.

Whatever your feelings about the architectural, artistic, religious or political merits of the Valley of the Fallen, it's an unforgettable visit.

Segovia

Just as you are taking in the glory of **Segovia**'s natural setting, the magnificent man-made skyline hits you. It's a mirage of mediaeval Spain with a fairy-tale castle at its heart. Segovia suddenly juts out from the clean-air plateau in the heart of Old Castile. Normally these wide-open spaces are interrupted only by the occasional clump of trees, a lonely farmhouse, a monastery or a solitary castle.

Marching through the centre of town, Segovia's **Roman aqueduct** is both a work of art and a triumph of engineering, the whole structure being held together without the aid of mortar. Composed of thousands of granite blocks arranged in graceful arches, sometimes two-tiered, it is nearly 1km (half a mile) long and up to 30m (99ft) high. Almost as astonishing as the engineering achievement is the fact that the aqueduct has been in constant use for 100 generations. A few details have been changed, but it still brings water to Segovia.

The **Alcázar**, Segovia's royal castle, was built in the most natural strategic spot. It dominates a ridge overlooking the confluence of two rivers, the Río Eresma and the Río Clamores, and has an unimpeded view of the plateau in all directions. The present story-book castle is a far cry from the simple stone fortress that took shape in the 12th century. As it grew bigger and more luxurious, it played a more significant historical role. By the 13th century, parliaments were convened at this castle. Here in 1570, Philip II married his fourth bride, Anne of Austria. In the 16th century, the Tower of Juan II became a dungeon for political prisoners. In truth, the castle's romantic superstructure dates only from the second half of the 19th century. It was destroyed by fire in 1862 and restored, perhaps a little too enthusiastically, twenty years later. From the top of the Alcázar there are marvellous views over Segovia.

The pinnacles and cupolas of Segovia's **cathedral** look as if they belong to a whole complex of churches, but, in fact, it's all one single elegant monument. Begun in 1525, this is the last of the great Spanish Gothic cathedrals. It was even taller until a lightning bolt lopped off the main tower in 1614.

Fine stained-glass windows illuminate the cathedral's majestic columns and arches. Two 18th-century organs present

TRAGEDY IN THE ALCÁZAR

The saddest item in the museum chapter house of the Segovia Alcázar is the 14th-century tomb of the baby Prince Pedro, son of Enrique II. As his nurse was holding him and admiring the view from an open upper window of the Alcázar he squirmed free and slipped from her arms. Scarcely hesitating, she leaped after him to death in the moat. Whether this was an attempt to save the child, an act of hysterical remorse, or suicide to cheat the executioner, we will never know.

a strikingly flamboyant sight. Less obvious are the altarpieces in the chapels. Look for the 16th-century polychrome *pietà* (image of the dead Christ) by Juan de Juni.

On show in the museum and chapter house is the baroque carriage propelled through the town every Corpus Christi, with its huge 17th-century silver monstrance. Facing Segovia's most charming square is the church of **San Martín**, a 12th-century Romanesque beauty. The primitive sculptures in the square, which resemble hippopotami, are a legacy of the Celtiberians.

So much of Segovia is superlative that you could almost miss the 11th-century **city wall** that stretches for 3km (1½ miles). Just outside the wall and almost in the shadow of the Alcázar, the 12-sided church of **Vera Cruz**, which dates from the early 13th century, is perhaps the best of the town's many fine ancient chapels. The Knights of the Holy Sepulchre held court here in the circular nave, and the Maltese Order, church-owners for centuries, last renovated it in the 1950s. It remains very atmospheric. Climb the tower for another good view over the town. Another fine Segovian church is the Romanesque **San Esteban**, behind Plaza Mayor.

Villages and Palaces

La Granja de San Ildefonso

Climbing the stately drive from the village of San Ildefonso to the palace of **La Granja**, you'll be impressed by the giant pines, the diligently tended lawns and flower beds. All this, however, is just a foretaste to the magnificent gardens within the gates of the estate.

San Ildefonso was founded in the mid-15th century as a modest hideaway for King Henry IV. More than 250 years later, the first Bourbon king of Spain, Philip V, had the idea of building a Versailles-style summer palace on the spot. Philip made history at La Granja when he abdicated in 1724 in favour of his son Louis, but Louis died soon afterwards, and Philip resumed his rule for another 20 years.

The hillside escape from Madrid turned out more lavish than anticipated. The sumptuous baroque rooms are all in a row, so you can look down the whole length of the palace. Several of the halls now comprise a **tapestry museum** containing textile masterpieces collected by the Spanish royal family. Visits are conducted in guided groups and numbers are strictly limited. The severely clipped gardens contain artificial cascades, forests of poplar, oak, elm, maple and horse chestnut trees, and all with the cooling sight of the mountains in the background. The highlight is the spectacular fountains, which only play on certain days and times. Try to arrange your visit accordingly – you won't be disappointed if you do manage to see them.

Guadalajara

Spain's **Guadalajara** is a regional market town and industrial centre, founded in the days of the Iberians. It fell to the Moors early in the invasion tide and stayed under Muslim control until late in the 11th century. The name comes from the Arabic for 'River among the Stones' and was transported to the New World to name the Mexican city.

From the 15th to 17th centuries, the town was the seat of a powerful political and sometimes literary family, the Mendozas. They built the **Palacio del Duque del Infantado**, one of the glories of 15th-century Spain. Five centuries later, during a Civil War battle, misdirected bombs almost obliterated the palace, but it has been rebuilt. The façade, profusely ornamented, is a brilliant introduction to the flamboyant Gothic two-storey patio. Here King Philip II married his third bride, Elizabeth of Valois. A provincial **museum of fine arts** has been installed on the ground floor.

Alcalá de Henares

The relatively small town of **Alcalá de Henares** has spawned some famous sons and daughters. It was the home town of Miguel de Cervantes, who grew up here in very modest circumstances, then saw the world and wrote *Don Quixote*. He would no doubt be amused that two houses now claim to be his birthplace (one features a small museum). The town is also the provenance of a king and a queen. The Holy Roman Emperor Ferdinand I, and Catherine of Aragon (who became the wife of England's Henry VIII) were born here within a few years of each other, but you will search in vain for any great monuments to them.

Alcalá de Henares has undergone some violent ups and downs: thriving under the Romans, and again after the Reconquest, it became a battleground in the Civil War

and lost much of its glorious heritage. Near the Plaza de Cervantes, stands the major exception to this destruction, the **Colegio de San Ildefonso**. The old university is a beautiful, harmonious three-storey structure with a fine plateresque façade. It is the work of Rodrigo Gil de Hontañón, a star of the Spanish Renaissance. The university, founded around the turn of the 16th century, published the first polyglot Bible with texts in four ancient languages. In the 19th century it was merged with the University of Madrid.

Chinchón

Chinchón is charming proof that you only have to travel 20km (12 miles) from Madrid to immerse yourself in old Spain. The town square here could easily be a film set. Two- and three-storey white stucco houses with wooden arcades surround an irregular, vaguely oval plaza. Watch burdened donkeys labouring through the cobbled streets and locals washing their laundry in the town fountain. In season, bullfights are held right in the square.

The town is celebrated as the home of various aniseed liqueurs. It also grows a much-vaunted variety of garlic.

Aranjuez

As you cross the Río Tajo (the Tagus) into the centre of **Aranjuez**, the roomy, geometric town plan becomes apparent. The balanced main square is faced by arcaded buildings on two sides and the porticoed church of San Antonio on a third.

These sights, however, take second place to the royal palaces, parks, gardens and forests. Spanish monarchs from Ferdinand and Isabella have retreated to this oasis to escape Madrid's summer heat. Since the mid-19th century, they

The Alcázar, the royal castle of Segovia, dates from the 12th century. The present array of turrets dates from the 19th century.

have enjoyed the luxury of a country palace reminiscent of Versailles.

Guided tours of the **Palacio Real** (Royal Palace) reveal a cross-section of royal taste in furniture, paintings, sculpture, tapestries, clocks, pianos and bric-a-brac. Among the highlights: the Throne Room, ceremonious except for the Louis Seize chairs standing in for thrones; the Porcelain Room, dazzlingly designed with decorations created in Madrid for King Charles III in 1760; the Smoking Room, an Arabian Nights fantasy.

Downstairs, the **Museum of Court Dress** shows reproductions and, where possible, the actual costumes worn by Spain's kings and queens from the 16th to 20th centuries.

Two kilometres (just over 1 mile) from the Royal Palace, the **Casita del Labrador** (Farmer's Cottage) is the amusingly rustic name for a small palace the kings used for weekends. Tours begin in the Billiard Room, filled by a behemoth billiard table beneath a formal chandelier. In the Statue Gallery a far-fetched folly of a clock incorporates simulated water jets and a large music box. The Ballroom is small by royal standards but could still accommodate around 200 noble dancers. The Platinum Room leads to the king's own toilet, wittily arranged as a plush throne.

Within the same park you can also visit the **Casa de Marinos** (Sailor's House) which holds the 'Tagus Squadron' in which kings of Spain were rowed along the river. This extravagant royal fleet is the last word in rococo canoes, fancy feluccas and gilt gondolas.

STRIKING A CHORD

If you are a music lover, particularly of the Spanish classical guitar, then you will probably know that the correct title of Rodrigo's famous guitar concerto is *Concierto de Aranjuez.* Rodrigo published the concerto in 1939 and following its première in 1940 it was an immediate success. It is perhaps no great surprise that such a beautiful place as Aranjuez should inspire a great masterpiece. The enormous pathos behind the piece, however, is that Rodrigo was blind.

THE CENTRE

Land of El Cid
and Don Quixote

Central Spain is home to the most soul-stirring and archetypal Spanish landscape – great plains dotted with ancient windmills and isolated castles. On the windswept *meseta* (plateau) of Castile, the infinity of the sky is the limit. Here, vast spaces open up with a scale and grandeur unusual in Europe.

Together, Castile and León cover some 94,000km² (36,300 square miles); an area bigger than the whole of Portugal. Acre upon acre of grain fields, grazing land and vineyards. You will either love it or hate it. Among the wide open spaces are three of Spain's greatest cities – Salamanca, León and Burgos.

In this chapter we include much of the regions of Castile and León, an enormous area stretching all the way to the Portuguese border and almost within striking

Grotesque contemplation for the Dominican nuns in a Salamanca cloister, provided by 16th-century sculptors.

distance of the Bay of Biscay. This chapter also embraces La Rioja, Spain's prime wine country, and part of the ancient kingdom of Aragon. Finally, we cover the atmospheric plateau of La Mancha, Don Quixote's old stamping ground.

Salamanca

What keeps this ancient city young is its university, four centuries older than Harvard and nearly as venerable as Oxford (although academically not in the same league as either since the Franco days). Students are always in evidence in the town, and consequently there are good cheap bars, lively budget restaurants and a reasonable nightlife. A large summer language school means that these students

CENTRE

N

Gijon
Santander
Bilbao
Villacayo
Pamplona
Cervera de Pisuerga
León
Orense
Astorga
Burgos
Logroño
Santo Domingo de Silos
Calahorra
Palencia
Tudela
Soria
Zaragoza
Torrelobatón
Valladolid
Duero
Zamora
Toro
Simancas
Peñafiel
Cuéllar
Pedraza de la Sierra
Medina del Campo
Coca
Medinaceli
Calatayud
Alcañiz
Salamanca
Sigüenza
Monasterio de Piedra
Segovia
San Lorenzo del Escorial
Guadalajara
Avila
MADRID
Ciudad Encantada
Teruel
Oropesa
Aranjuez
Cuenca
Toledo
Segobriga
Guadamur Castle
El Toboso
Belmonte
Valencia
Consuegra
Alcázar de San Juan
Mota del Cuervo
Puerto Lápice
Campo de Criptana
PARQUE NACIONAL DE LAS TABLAS DE DAIMIEL
Tomelloso
Ciudad Real
Argamasilla de Alba
Albacete
Murcia
Córdoba

0   80km
0   50 miles
National Park
Land above 2,000m (6,550ft)

THE PLATERESQUE TREATMENT

You will see plateresque art in many forms and places all over Spain but the finest examples are to be found in Salamanca, possibly because the soft sandstone here is so easy to work. This style is basically an intricate and usually very elaborate form of shallow relief carving which became popular in the 16th century. At its most decorative, it seethes with curlicues, cherubim, medallions, coats of arms and many other sculptural flourishes. The name derives from its similarity to the delicate work of the *platero*, the silversmith.

are not only Spanish, either. You are just as likely to meet someone from Maryland as from Madrid. You will also hear students busking for the tourists; dressed in mediaeval finery, strumming guitars and singing in the main square, in groups known as *tunas*.

The 18th-century **Plaza Mayor** (Main Square), the magnet for tourist and resident alike, is acknowledged to be the most perfect plaza in Spain. Eighty-six round arches, including three that are two storeys high, form the arcades surrounding the cobbled square. Three floors of balconied

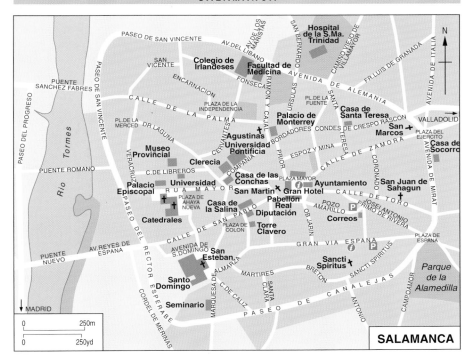

SALAMANCA

```
0        250m
0        250yd
```

windows on all four sides add to the soothing symmetry of the design, broken only by the elegant façades of the Town Hall and the Royal Pavilion. Much of the credit for this magnificent ensemble goes to Alberto Churriguera, a member of an artistic dynasty responsible for some of Spain's most distinctive baroque buildings. (The family is remembered in an adjective, *churrigueresque*, describing an elaborately decorated style found in Spain and Latin America.)

Dating from Iberian times, Salamanca first enters historical records in the 3rd century BC, when it became the western-most conquest of Hannibal. As part of the Roman province of Lusitania, Salamanca rated the title of municipality, with city walls and a bridge (still standing) across the Río Tormes. Vandals and Visigoths followed the decline and fall of the

Romans, and then the tide of Islam swept through. Salamanca was fought over, on and off, for three centuries until the final triumph of the Christian forces. In 1178 Ferdinand II of León assembled his parliament in the city, to which he granted special privileges. By the 16th century, Salamanca was so special and splendid it was nicknamed 'Little Rome'.

Salamanca's two cathedrals, which throw up a thicket of spiky spires and turrets, are contiguous; you enter the old through the new. The **Catedral Nueva** (New Cathedral) is not really so modern; construction began in 1513, when Gothic architecture was going out of fashion. Although baroque and plateresque elements were added, it has been called Gothic's last gasp. Among the architects were two generations of the Gil de Hontañón family, father Juan and son

The setting sun brings a warm glow to the golden sandstone of Salamanca's Plaza Mayor, arguably the most perfect plaza in the world. It was once the tradition that boys and girls walked in opposite directions around the square. Nowadays they dance together in the clubs.

Rodrigo. The main (west) **façade** is a study in arches upon arches, further embellished with coats of arms, statues and reliefs. Inside, the triple-naved cathedral is longer than a football field. Outstanding here are the baroque **choir stalls**, an 18th-century **organ** that sounds as good as it looks, and 18 side chapels, most notably the **Capilla Dorada** (Golden Chapel) with 110 sculptures.

After the grandeur of the New Cathedral, the **Catedral Vieja** (Old Cathedral) seems as intimate as a private chapel. Work started here in the 12th century when Romanesque architecture was giving way to the new Gothic style. The main **altar**, dating from the 15th century, includes 53 paintings by Nicholas of Florence. The highlight is a 12th- or 13th-century statue of the Virgin, and above the retable is Nicholas's dramatic, detailed *Last Judgement.*

The **cloister** is an 18th-century replacement for the Romanesque original, which became a distant victim of the dreadful Lisbon earthquake of 1755. The first chapel on the left, the **Capilla de Talavera**, has an unusual Mudéjar dome; services in the old Mozarabic rite are held here. (*Mozárabes* was the name given to

123

Christians, during the period of Moorish rule from the 8th to the 11th centuries.) Next door, in the Santa Barbara chapel, candidates for university degrees have traditionally spent the night before the big exam praying for success, and maybe doing some last-minute studying.

The 16th-century plateresque Dominican monastery of San Esteban is one of Salamanca's loveliest and most intimate churches.

In the cathedral's old chapter house, a **diocesan museum** has a collection of paintings by Fernando Gallego, an underrated master of the 15th-century Hispano-Flemish style. He did some of his finest, brightest work in Salamanca. Another museum highlight is a sensitive triptych by Juan of Flanders, a contemporary of Gallego.

The **Universidad** (University) of Salamanca, founded in 1218, was one of Europe's greatest centres of learning in the Middle Ages. The 16th-century plateresque **façade** of the main building has such intricate stonework you might think it was modelled in clay. In the lecture halls around a central patio, you can admire centuries of architectural and decorative details; the mood is broken only by the presence of modern audio-visual devices. Take a stroll around the **Patio de las Escuelas Menores** across the square, a spacious grassy courtyard surrounded by columns supporting wide, scalloped arches. Salamanca is noted for its number of stately patios and cloisters, conducive to calm thoughts and meditation.

Closer to the centre of the city, the **Casa de las Conchas** (House of Shells) is an extraordinary representative of 15th-century originality, and is considered by some to be the zenith of plateresque design. Its exterior walls erupt in hundreds of scallop shells. There are few windows, indicating its initial purpose as a fortress. The patio here contains a generous collection of coats of arms tracing the family trees of the building's first owners.

Another severe building, the 16th-century **Palacio de Monterrey** is also strong on coats of arms. Its airy rectangular towers, typical of Spanish Renaissance style, have inspired many copies elsewhere within the country and in Latin America.

Salamanca to León

Zamora

The Italians say 'Rome wasn't built in a day', the Spanish say 'Zamora wasn't conquered in a day'. When you see the city's position above the right bank of the Río Duero, and the remains of its ramparts, you will understand why.

Often besieged, **Zamora** changed hands several times during the centuries of the Reconquest of Spain from the Arabs. Later, it became the stronghold of the Portuguese supporters of Princess Juana, who claimed the throne of Castile from Ferdinand's wife, Isabella. Doña Juana's forces surrendered in 1475, opening the way for a unified Spain.

For the best overall view of this appealing historic city, cross the Duero by the 14th-century, 16-arched bridge. From the south bank you can admire the Byzantine cupola of the **cathedral**, roofed in curved stone tiles laid like fish scales. The Romanesque cathedral is one of half a dozen well-preserved 12th-century churches around town. Inside, there is a notable retable by Fernando Gallego, as well as some risqué wood-carvings in the choir that illustrate monks and nuns in a number of rather unclerical positions. In the cathedral's cloister, a **museum** highlights a prized collection of Flemish tapestries of the 15th and 16th centuries, with dramatic and often violent scenes from legend and history.

Parts of the **city wall**, including impressive gateways, still surround the remains of the castle. On the north side, the **Postigo de la Traición** (Traitor's Gate) marks the supposed spot where the assassin of the Castilian, King Sancho II, entered Zamora to find refuge in 1072.

Toro

On the dividing line between wheat- and wine-country east of Zamora, the tersely named **Toro** (meaning, among other things, 'bull') is a mediaeval hilltop town, so well preserved that it has been proclaimed a national monument. Like Zamora, it has been much fought over.

Its greatest pride is the **Iglesia Colegiata de Santa María la Mayor** (Collegiate Church of St Mary the Great), a 12th-century Romanesque classic with a two-storey turreted cupola. The west portal, which came later, is beautifully carved in Gothic style. Inside the Collegiate is a most unusual 16th-century painting called *The Virgin and the Fly*, much studied because of the common housefly inexplicably resting on the Virgin's left knee. The greater point of interest, however, is that this is widely considered to be the best-known likeness of the Catholic monarch, Isabella.

Toro also boasts some fine Romanesque churches, convents, mansions, and the ruins of a 10th-century castle.

Astorga

Astorga, once an important town on the Pilgrim Way to Santiago de Compostela is famous for its neo-Gothic **Palacio Episcopal**, a mad, wonderful experiment, effectively a two-tier cathedral pastiche combining pomp and fantasy. If you have been to Barcelona or you are a fan of *Modernisme* (Spain's Art Nouveau movement) you will have no difficulty recognizing this as the work of Antoni Gaudí, the creator of Barcelona's trademark, the Sagrada Familia church. He was commissioned to design the palace by a fellow Catalonian, the bishop of Astorga.

Unfortunately, it turned out so overwhelmingly palatial that it became a local

'WHO IS THE FAIREST OF THEM ALL?'

Astorga was once famous as a stopping-point on the *Camino de Santiago* (Way of St James), and there is a story of an over-zealous knight, who guarded the bridge at Hospital de Orbigo, near Astorga, which would have taxed the imagination of even Cervantes.

It is said that this errant fellow, Suero de Quiñones, stopped every knight and would only let them pass if they agreed that his lady was the most beautiful of all! At least 70 knights did not agree, some blood was shed and the chivalrous lunatic passed into local lore. The bridge, since renamed the Paso de Honor, still stands.

embarrassment and no bishop of Astorga would ever agree to live in it. In recent years, however, the building has at last been put to excellent use as the **Museo de los Caminos** (Museum of the Pilgrim Ways). The exhibits illustrate the pilgrim tide, with maps and a hoard of saintly statues, sacred paintings and reliquaries.

A Romanesque church was demolished to make way for the present **cathedral**, begun in the 15th century in Gothic style. The baroque façade tastefully disguises its flying buttresses, as if they were Victorian piano legs. Inside, take a look at the impressive, towering, 16th-century retable. In the diocesan museum you can see 10th-century documents, Romanesque wood-carvings, and enough historic vestments to clothe a conclave of cardinals.

León

León is a prosperous, modern city with an ancient, welcoming heart. As a result of its location far north of Madrid, it does not re-ceive too many tourists, but those who do make the effort are amply rewarded. Although *león* means 'lion' in Spanish, the name is a corruption of the Latin *legio* meaning 'legion', as this was an outpost of the Roman troops.

Latin is also used to dignify the nick-name of the city's most magnificent mon-ument. *La Pulchra Leonina* ('the beauti-ful Leonese') is what they call the **Catedral de Santa María de Regla.** León's cathedral, constructed in the 13th century and clearly inspired by the French Gothic cathedral at Chartres, has the most glorious complement of **stained-glass** in all Spain. Indeed, the top half of the walls are almost entirely glass. This may worry modern engineers, but delights visitors as the interior floods with inspiring, multi-coloured light.

The west face of *La Pulchra* is sur-prisingly asymmetrical, with a couple of mismatched towers. Otherwise, all is har-mony – a rose window high above the main portal, with three tall Gothic arches interspersed with acute mini-arches. Take a long look at the sculptural details of the middle portal, with the dra-matic contrast between the happy pilgrims and the shrieking sinners in the Last Judgement.

Inside, crane your neck and admire the splendour of the stained glass: 125 huge windows and 57 other openings of various shapes and sizes for coloured light. They

Glum faces peer through the stained glass, among the glories of the 125 huge windows of León cathedral. With great delicacy, firemen saved the treasures during a blaze in 1966.

illustrate the history of this art from the 13th to the 20th centuries.

There are tours of the **cloister**, an elegant conjunction of Gothic and Renaissance elements. This leads to a **diocesan museum**, exhibiting ancient relics, sculpture, painting and applied arts.

A few streets west of the cathedral, the **Colegiata de San Isidoro** (Collegiate Church of St Isidore) honours an early archbishop of Seville, noted for his voluminous and influential writings. When Seville fell to the Moors, St Isidore's remains were evacuated to the safety of León and his relics still attract pilgrims. On the south façade, on top of all the other sculptural achievements, the saint himself is carved in stone, riding a horse as if off to battle with the Moors.

Although it houses the tombs of assorted kings and princes, there is nothing funereal about the **Panteón Real** (Royal Pantheon), alongside the church. The naïve frescoes covering its arched ceilings are so wonderful that the place has been dubbed the Sistine Chapel of Romanesque Art. There are uplifting biblical stories and everyday asides picturing ordinary, local people. The **treasury** features some beautifully worked 11th-century caskets and an even older chalice.

The former **Monasterio de San Marcos** has a formidable plateresque façade. This immensity is divided into dozens of intricately ornamented compartments, with never a dull detail. San Marcos began as a hospice for mediaeval pilgrims on the way to the shrine at Santiago de Compostela. King Ferdinand the Catholic poured more money in to make it a showpiece monastery for the Knights of St James. Now it is back in the hospitality business, neatly transformed into one of Spain's most expensive *paradores*

(government-run inns). You're quite welcome to look inside even if you are not staying here.

Not all of the vast ex-monastery is used for hotel purposes. Here, too, is the **Museo Arqueológico Provincial**, occupying the cloister and sacristy. The collection rounds up everything from Roman mosaics and sarcophagi to Romanesque sculptures. Note the exquisite 'Cristo de Carrizo', a small 11th-century ivory crucifix with some touching features.

For an architectural change of pace in the centre of León, see the building called the Casa de los Botines, designed by Gaudí. In spite of some original details, this once controversial construction is *not* one of his triumphs. It looks like a school building with neo-Gothic airs, and is best seen at night, with the white spotlights bleaching it.

ON THE ROAD

The Way of St James – *el Camino de Santiago* – is one of those roads that fire the imagination, like the Silk Road in China, the Old Chisholm Trail in the American West, or the Road to Mandalay. By the 11th century, the pilgrims' way through France and across northern Spain to Santiago de Compostela had become the busiest 'tourist' route in Europe. Everyone from cardinals to criminals made the trip, an exhausting, sometimes dangerous hike, as well as an uplifting religious experience. The pilgrims travelled in groups, the better to protect themselves from the perils along the way and the Order of the Knights of St James was founded to afford additional protection.

The scallop shells – symbols of St James – sculpted on the façade of León's San Marcos monastery, identify it with the pilgrimage. The city's position as a vital way station along the pilgrim route assured its prosperity.

A few kilometres west of León the contemporary sculptor José María Subirachs has created striking, tormented statues of the disciples, flanking a slim Virgin, for the modern façade of the church of the **Virgen del Camino** (Virgin of the Way). Inside the church is a revered baroque retable. The 'Way' in the name refers to the well-beaten path to Santiago de Compostela, for this is on the pilgrims' road.

Valladolid

On the map, great stretches of the road from León to **Valladolid** appear as a straight line. This is neither slipshod cartography nor poetic licence. For many kilometres, the N601 goes straight through flat farmland. There is little to divert the gaze except for a few horses and sheep basking in the sun. Valladolid is the biggest and most industrialized city of this region, and it lacks the historical charm and grand boulevards of León. Yet there is much here for students of architecture and sculpture, and there are also glimpses of Cervantes and Columbus.

Valladolid is one of the hotbeds of the Isabelline style of art, a form of overblown plateresque expressed in extravagant, florid ornamentation. The style is named after Isabella of Castile, whose fateful marriage to Ferdinand of Aragon took place here in 1469. Valladolid was the capital of Castile until the end of the 16th century, and was then, briefly, the capital of all Spain.

Plunge right into the mainstream of Isabelline decoration at the **Colegio de San Gregorio**, founded by Brother Alonso of Burgos, Isabella's confessor. The royal coat of arms in the upper centre of the façade is surrounded by a riot of sculptural effects from statues and escutcheons to flora. It's all so overwhelming that your eye is distracted, as the builders intended, from the essential simplicity of the architecture. The first impression is no flash in the pan. Inside, the double-decker **patio** is decorated almost as riotously as the front entrance. From the upper deck, you can look the gargoyles right in the eyes.

The college houses the **Museo Nacional de Escultura** (National Museum of Sculpture), the Prado of religious statues. Even if this is not your cup of tea, you may be surprised by the variety of style and content. The works range from the 13th to the 18th centuries, but the star here is the woodcarving genius of the Spanish Renaissance, Alonso Berruguete, said to have studied under Michelangelo. His martyrs seem to shed real tears and blood. Other important sculptors on show include Juan de Juni, an Italian-trained Frenchman of the mid-16th century, and the sensitive Gregorio Fernández (1566-1636). When you have finished looking at the exhibits, note the spectacular ceilings of the college.

Valladolid's **cathedral** has a long history. Based on the remains of a 13th-century church, it was designed in 1580 by Juan de Herrera, co-creator of Philip II's grandiose Escorial project. Delays kept cropping up and the cathedral never has been finished, but much of Herrera's strength still shows in the interior design. An altarpiece by Juan de Juni is the highlight of a rich ration of art within these walls.

Some famous names are associated with Valladolid. In this city several kings, including Philip II and Philip IV were born, and Christopher Columbus died (surprisingly, in obscurity). The arcaded two-storey house where the much-honoured explorer embarked on his final voyage has been restored. The **Casa Museo de Colón** (House-Museum of Columbus) is stocked with relics and documents from the age of discovery.

The **Casa de Cervantes** commemorates another local celebrity. Miguel de Cervantes lived in Valladolid for several years late in his literary career. His ivy-covered house, facing a peaceful, shady garden, contains furniture and books from his time. *Don Quixote* fans can visit the room in which he is said to have written a couple of his later, lesser-known books. It was also here that Cervantes had an unpleasant brush with the law, being wrongly accused of a sensational murder on his doorstep.

The splendid and exotic works of art in Valladolid's **Museo Oriental** were contributed by Augustinian monks. For centuries the Augustinians worked as missionaries in Asia, and the 'souvenirs' they collected range from thousand-year-old Buddhist paintings to colourful Chinese opera-style demons. The museum is inside the Augustinian monastery, at the south end of the fan-shaped **Campo Grande**, the main city park.

Around Valladolid

Coca Castle

In Castile it is only natural to expect to see castles. They come in all sizes, shapes and degrees of ferocity, but few, if any, are finer than the masterpiece in the small town of **Coca**.

It was constructed in the late 15th century for the Archbishop of Seville, Alonso de Fonseca, who hired Moorish craftsmen to work on the project. The brilliance of the architects and the artistry of the masons make this fortress a showpiece of Spanish Mudéjar military construction.

Three layers of walls surround an impenetrable keep, and there are towers and clusters of battlements at all levels. It is unclear why the archbishop required such awesome, if beautifully decorated, walls around his Coca retreat.

These days it is home to a forestry school, but it is open to the public.

Palencia

Not to be confused with the bigger and better-known east-coast city of Valencia, **Palencia** was also catalogued by ancient geographers. Unlike Valencia, however, which became an important Roman colony, Palencia declined to submit to the empire. Its valiant Celtiberian defenders were unable to resist later invasions by the Visigoths and Moors, however, and Palencia was wiped out.

Rebuilt in the 11th century, Palencia became the political hub of Castile, where royal courts and church conclaves were held. Spain's first university was founded here at the beginning of the 13th century and in the 14th and 15th centuries, a Gothic **cathedral** was built. It is laid out in the form of a Latin cross, with three naves. The church and adjoining museum contain a superlative array of 15th- and 16th-century works of art – woodcarvings, paintings, statues and tapestries. Among the famous sculptors well represented here are Pedro Berruguete, Gil de Siloé and Simon of Cologne. The cathedral's best-known treasure is a painting of St Sebastián by El Greco.

Peñafiel

The castle of **Peñafiel**, 35km (22 miles) east of Valladolid, is one of a kind. From afar it looks like the age of chivalry's most improbable shipwreck. High on a lonely hilltop, the long, low, thin fort – over 200m (220yd) long, but less than 25m (28yd) across – tapers at the ends into the shape of a ship. The equivalent of the bridge is a stern square keep.

One of the legends linked with this elegant stone castle explains its name. When King Sancho conquered it from the Moors in the 11th century, he is said to have raised his sword and sworn, 'Henceforth this shall be the faithful rock *(peñafiel)* of Castile'.

This castle has everything a well-made stronghold could have needed in the Middle Ages: a double set of ramparts, 30 towers, and turrets enough to make any enemy think again.

In the village below, the big open sandy plaza is used for bullfights in August.

Pedraza de la Sierra

In this lovely, isolated mountain village, the houses crowd together protectively. Yet despite the advantage of standing on a hill and being girdled by town walls, **Pedraza** still looks quite vulnerable. Houses with evocative names line the twisting, narrow streets and a *parador* occupies the former House of the Inquisition.

The castle of Pedraza offers fine views and has a story, too. For four years the eldest sons of King François I of France were held hostage here. Their imprisonment was a postscript to the Treaty of Madrid of 1526, which brought a breathing space in the long-running feud between the French king and the Holy Roman Emperor Charles V. François eventually bought back the princes for a ransom of 2,000,000 gold crowns and bankrupted France.

Burgos

The one-time capital of the kingdom of Castile is an oasis of urban beauty, halfway on the main road between Madrid and the French border.

When the pious pilgrim traffic to Santiago de Compostela was at its peak, mediaeval **Burgos** was one of the most significant stopping places and had more than 30 hospices and hostels. The welcome mat is still out, and it is an excellent place for today's tourists to stop.

What a relief – and joy – it must have been for the weary mediaeval pilgrims to glimpse the delicate but prickly towers of the Burgos cathedral on the horizon. Nowadays, spotlighted at night, it has become even more of a beacon for travellers. The best approach, though, is from the south, crossing the usually lazy Río Arlanzón to the most flamboyant of the city gates. The **Arco de Santa María**, part of the city wall since the 14th century, was reconstructed in symmetrical grandeur two centuries later. As dramatic as a backdrop for grand opera, the massive gate honours, among others, Emperor Charles V and the great warrior El Cid, sculpted in niches on the front.

Along the river here, three parallel promenades follow the path of the original city wall. Trimmed trees and bushes, flower gardens, fountains and statues adorn the walks. Towards sunset most of Burgos converges here to stroll and unwind from the day's stresses. Although a few brave palm trees try to deny it, Burgos is hundreds of miles from the Mediterranean, where the tradition of the *paseo* was born. Yet the daily promenade is quite at home here.

The great **cathedral** of Burgos was begun in 1221 by order of Ferdinand III of

Castile and Bishop Maurice of Burgos (said to be an Englishman). Construction dawdled on until the 19th century, though the Gothic style was sealed early in the project. The bristling, lacy spires of the west front date from the 15th century. Before you enter, walk right around this complex building and take in all its faces and moods. There are ceremonial doors on all four sides, each very different, with architectural effects ranging from grand to cozy. The main **façade,** facing the Plaza de Santa María, is a stirring sight from any angle, with its high-rising balustrades and arches, statues, and a rose window with a Star of David in the middle, known here as Solomon's Seal.

This is the third-biggest cathedral in Spain (after Seville and Toledo), but somehow there is a reassuring intimacy to it. The vast interior is divided into precincts by walls, fences, screens and railings; there is never a view of the whole. If you are in a rush, have a glance up at the delicately decorated octagonal dome and keep going to the far end and the **Constable's chapel**. Here, a splendid golden altar with beautiful statuary, and a most uplifting cupola is the setting for the tomb of Fernández de Velasco, the eponymous Constable of Castile during the reign of the Catholic Monarchs.

Strolling players in doublet and hose known as tunas serenade tourists and locals alike in towns such as Burgos and Salamanca. The airy towers of Burgos were a sight for sore eyes for pilgrims on the way to Santiago.

CURIOSITIES IN THE CATHEDRAL

Why are all those Spaniards milling about expectantly just inside Burgos cathedral's main door, staring up at the top of the arch, waiting for something to happen? The clock here is surmounted by a manikin in red, called the *Papamoscas*, or 'Flycatcher'. When the hour strikes, the comic character astride the clock opens and closes his mouth. Next to him a much smaller figure appears between two bells every quarter hour. The *Papamoscas* has been telling the time in Burgos for more than six centuries.

A far more curious figure lies within the cathedral. Look for the Capilla del Santo Cristo and here you will find the famous *Cristo de Burgos*. This is a rather disturbing life-size effigy of Christ made from buffalo hide and human hair. They say the finger nails, beard and hair need trimming regularly and there are even claims that this is the true body of Christ, mysteriously washed ashore in Galicia.

The **altar** of St Anne, with its sculptured portraits of distinguished local women, is by the German artist Gil de Siloé. His son, Diego, designed the exquisite **golden stairway** inside the Coronería portal. Diego is also the sculptor of *Christ at the Column,* a vivid statue in the **sacristy**. High on the wall here hangs the iron-bound **coffer** of El Cid, the legendary 11th-century hero, who is buried beside his wife under the cathedral's dome. There is a somewhat implausible story that El Cid tricked money-lenders into financing one of his military campaigns by leaving this heavily laden locked coffer with them as collateral. Instead of the jewels which were promised to be inside, there was only sand. Fortunately, the collateral was never called upon.

For a sculptor's impression of the immortal Cid, see the equestrian **statue** of the armoured warrior, in flowing beard and cape, a few streets east of the cathedral at the San Pablo bridge. The square, the Plaza del General Primo de Rivera, is named after the pre-Franco dictator of Spain. After Franco himself died, many towns expunged his name and those of his closest collaborators from the directory of streets and squares, but conservative Burgos was the headquarters of the *generalísimo* during the Civil War. The city still honours him in the name of a riverfront avenue.

Burgos is a fine city for wandering. There are stately apartment blocks with artistic touches, bustling shopping streets, inviting squares and parks, and distinguished mediaeval town houses. Outstanding among them is the Casa del Cordón, the mansion in which Ferdinand and Isabella welcomed Columbus back from his second trip to America. Beautifully restored, it is now the home of the local savings bank.

Another noble Renaissance house, the Casa de Miranda, serves as the **town museum**. Three floors of exhibits, with thousands of items from the Stone Age to the Roman era, plus a fine art collection, surround a neoclassical patio. Just across the street is the colourful and mouth-watering municipal food market selling a plethora of fish, meat, cheese, fruits and vegetables.

On the western outskirts of Burgos, the **Convento de las Huelgas** was the place princesses were sent for a strict education. The institution, founded in the 12th century, soon became a powerful force in Castile, and kings were crowned and buried here. You can inspect some of the treasures – religious relics, tapestries, even battle trophies – amassed by the convent's abbesses. Behind the fortress-like walls, the complex contains a mixture of architecture: Romanesque, Cistercian and Mudéjar.

A few miles east of Burgos, in a forest park, the 15th-century Carthusian monastery called the **Cartuja de Miraflores** also has royal connections (*cartuja* means 'chapter house'). Founded by King Juan II, it features his sepulchre which also holds his second wife, Isabella of Portugal. This alabaster masterpiece, sculpted by Gil de Siloé, is considered to be one of the finest tombs in all Spain.

The Cartuja's many-pinnacled white granite church is bigger and more lavish than you would ever guess from the exterior.

Around Burgos

Santo Domingo de Silos

Three dozen Benedictine monks still live in this ancient monastery in the isolated Burgos village of **Silos**. In the entrance hall they sell medicinal herbs and local honey. The monastery's pride, however, lies within: a two-storey cloister with pillars of capital importance in the history of Romanesque sculpture.

Monks have been drawn to the tranquillity of Silos since the time of the Visigoths. The first primitive monastery was rebuilt in the 10th century, only to be levelled by the Moors. A monk named Domingo thereupon undertook a whirlwind reconstruction programme, winning fame as a miracle worker, which is how the institution comes to bear his name.

The **cloister**, which surrounds lawns and a giant, slim cypress tree, is a festival of stonework. The carvings on top of the columns portray biblical personalities, but also abstractions and fanciful animals. The styles suggest that several very distinct artists were involved, but every one of the 64 columns on the ground floor is worth a close look. Just off the cloister is an **old pharmacy** with a rich library of antique medical and pharmaceutical books in several languages. Benedictine specialists looked after the health of the villagers as well as the monks. There are mortars, pestles and vessels, and a still any moonshiner would covet, although it was dedicated only to the distillation of medicines (or so they say).

A short but twisting drive east of Silos takes you to a limestone gorge called the **Garganta de Yecla**. This chasm is more remarkable for its width than its depth; in places the walls are only just far enough apart to squeeze through. A daring walkway has been built, jutting over the rushing stream far below.

Logroño

The leafy main square of this spacious modern city is big enough for a fiesta, and when it's fiesta time in **Logroño** you can be sure of a certain amount of wine-tasting. For this is the lively capital of Spain's premier wine region, La Rioja.

Among mediaeval travellers (the pilgrim road passes right through town) the province of La Rioja was famous for its cheerful and attentive hospitality. Presumably the local wine, which has been known since the 12th century, had something to do with this.

Rioja wine has been made in the region for centuries. Today, it is known throughout the world.

These grapes, from the Muga vineyard in Rioja, go to produce wines which are currently among the best in the region.

Logroño is built alongside the Río Ebro, spanned here by two bridges, one of iron, the other of stone. It is essentially the same stone bridge that the pilgrims crossed. Their first stop would have been the church of **Santa María de Palacio,** which dates from the 11th century, and is topped by a tall, graceful, pyramid-shaped tower. A few streets to the south, matching Baroque bell towers mark the **cathedral,** which is considerably younger. The generously sculptured main portal, deeply recessed, is flanked by unexpectedly blank stone walls. Behind the cathedral lie the atmospheric, narrow streets of the old town.

ST JAMES THE MOORSLAYER

Some 15km (9 miles) south of Logroño is the village of Clavijo. Little remains to indicate its importance in Spanish legend but apparently, in 844, the Christian forces of King Ramiro I were taking a heavy beating here when divine intervention appeared in the form of St James the Apostle (known to the Spanish as 'Santiago'). He and his band of angels slew some 70,000 Moors and thus the legend of Santiago, *Matamoros* (St James the Moorslayer) was born.

There are numerous equestrian statues of St James in vengeful mood but few are so famous as the 18th-century version on the church of Santiago el Real in Logroño. Infamous may be a better term, as the statue's notoriety rests with the horse, blessed with what Edwin Mullins called 'the most heroic genitalia in Christendom, a sight to make any surviving Moor feel inadequate and run for cover' (from *The Pilgrimage to Santiago*).

THE FRUIT OF LA RIOJA

The good soil, relatively mild climate, adequate rainfall and irrigation along the Ebro make La Rioja one of the most productive agricultural regions in the country. Rioja wine has been produced here since at least the beginning of the 12th century, but the big boom came after a 19th-century phylloxera epidemic wiped out France's vines.

Rioja wines come in all colours, but the most prized are the full-bodied reds, considered to be Spain's best table wines.

Wine intoxicates the scenery. The hills north of Logroño are traced by vines planted to follow the curvature of the land. They look like tightly combed scalps.

Moving Southwards

Soria

Spain's smallest, calmest provincial capital spreads along a poplar-shaded bend of the Río Duero. The scene is Old Castile at its most poetic, and in spite of some unchecked modern development, little has changed here since the Middle Ages.

The axis of **Soria** runs along a pedestrian street linking the main square with a roomy, restful city park, called the Alameda de Cervantes. At the park entrance a small chapel, the **Ermita de la Soledad**, contains a treasured wooden statue from the 16th century. Exuding pathos, the *Cristo del Humilladero* (Christ of the Roadside Chapel) is a classic of Spanish baroque art.

Across the street, the **Museo Numantino** (Museum of Numancia) specializes in relics found in the Roman ruins just north of town. Numancia was a Celtiberian city of some 10,000 inhabitants. Legend has it that when the besieged occupants finally realized their struggle was hopeless, they destroyed their own town and committed mass suicide rather than give in to the Romans. The Romans built a new city, but this too has long gone, although fractured columns and outlines of walls survive at the site, and a reconstruction is under way.

Soria's collection of churches, in mellow toast-coloured stone, is bountiful and beautiful. All date from the 12th century, and among the most important are: **Santo Domingo**, with an expansive Romanesque façade; **San Juan de Rabanera**, with Byzantine touches and an early hint of Gothic; and the **Co-catedral de San Pedro**, with a plateresque portal and a Romanesque cloister.

Across the river, at the end of a romantic, tree-lined road, the **Ermita de San Saturio** is an octagonal church built on a rocky outcrop above caves. You can only reach the church by climbing through a series of connecting caves, but this is not as difficult as it sounds.

All but hidden on the left bank of the river, just north of the bridge, **San Juan de Duero** used to be a monastery of the Knights Templar. The remains of the original Romanesque-Oriental **cloister** reveal finely carved capitals, picturing animal, vegetable, mineral and abstract themes. The church now serves as the mediaeval section of the Museo Numantino, with exhibits on Christian, Jewish and Islamic culture.

Sigüenza

What, you may ask, is a town this small doing with a cathedral fit for a metropolis and a classic fortress big enough to house a regiment under siege?

The **fort**, overlooking the town, started as a Visigothic castle. The Moors took it over, building a formidable *alcázar*.

137

Reconquered by the Christian forces early in the 12th century, it became the headquarters of the bishops of Sigüenza. In the 15th century it could house approximately 1,000 soldiers and more than 300 horses. Between wars, cardinals and kings used to be wined and dined behind these stern walls. Now it has been spruced up as a *parador*.

At first sight the **cathedral** also seems to be a fortress. In the dangerous days of the 12th century, its fiercely crenellated towers were useful for ringing bells, watching for attackers and firing from. The cathedral was begun in Romanesque style, but construction went on into the Gothic and then baroque periods. It is particularly well supplied with sculptural features. The most celebrated is the **sepulchre of 'El Doncel'** ('the page'). Most Spanish tombs tend to show defunct dignitaries in perpetual sleep. However, 'El Doncel', Don Martín Vázquez de Arce, is sculpted in extraordinary detail, reclining on one elbow, engrossed in a book. The monument was ordered by Queen Isabella to honour her young page, who was killed in action, fighting in Granada in 1486.

The **Museo Diocesano de Arte**, opposite, is bigger and better than you might expect from its unprepossessing entrance. In its 14 halls you can see everything from prehistoric axes to an ethereal Virgin painting by Zurbarán.

Locals claim that Sigüenza's **Plaza Mayor** is one of the most beautiful main squares in Spain, and in spite of a lack of harmony, there are indeed some lovely arcaded mediaeval houses here.

Medinaceli

High on a hill above the main Madrid-Zaragoza road, in the southernmost part of Soria province, is the startling silhouette of a Roman triumphal arch. Drive up to see it and you will find **Medinaceli**, a village that time has passed by.

Not that the arch (which dates from the 2nd or 3rd century) is very grand, or in mint condition; its embellishments are all but gone with the wind. It is, however, unique in Spain and the view from the summit, out over the Castilian plain, catches the heart.

While you're here, have a look at the town's mediaeval houses and 10th-century church.

Piedra

In order to encourage meditation, many monasteries are deliberately isolated, and some are all but inaccessible. **Piedra**, however, is reached by good, if twisting, roads, broad enough to accommodate all the excursion coaches. The scenery on the way changes with almost every bend, from hostile cliffs to great plains of grain, from vineyards to orchards.

If you have had your fill of church architecture by now, don't worry. The ancient **Monasterio de Piedra** has been beautifully converted into a hotel and the main attraction is the natural splendour of the surrounding countryside.

Piedra, one of four monasteries the Cistercians founded in the kingdom of Aragon, was established in 1195, but the buildings fell into disrepair after the government sold off church property in 1835. Not much is left of artistic value, but for an indication of the old monastic way of life, have a look at the kitchen, which is big enough to barbecue several whole cows at a time.

The other memorable sight here is the woodland preserve around the monastery, something of a tropical rainforest oasis,

FAREWELL, YOUNG LOVERS

Once upon a time, in the Middle Ages, a young Teruel couple fell impossibly in love. There are various versions of the story of the star-crossed couple; here is one.

Diego de Marcilla asked for the hand of the girl in his life, Isabella de Segura, but to the grievous distress of both, Isabella's father deemed the lad to be too poor to be his son-in-law and sent him packing. Diego joined the Crusades and five years later returned a hero, and rich enough to marry Isabella. Alas, as he wandered into the parish church, he found his beloved at the altar with another man. Isabella, believing him dead, had finally stopped waiting. His heart broken, Diego collapsed and died on the spot. At his funeral, Isabella's own grief overtook her and she, too, died. They were buried in the same grave.

inexplicably found in arid northern Spain. It has waterfalls, cascades, torrents and rapids enjoying romantic names such as Horse's Tail Falls, Diana's Bath and Devil's Rock.

Teruel

The Golden Age of **Teruel** occurred under the Moors. When Alfonso II of Aragon captured the town in 1171, however, most of the Muslims chose to stay. A special law granted them liberal rights, encouraging the development of a mixed tradition in art, which distinguishes the provincial capital today.

Christian generosity to Teruel's Muslims lasted until the beginning of the 16th century. This was time enough for the creation of lasting works of Mudéjar art. The greatest threat to these architectural treasures came during the Civil War, when the town served as a bloody battlefield.

Spanish tourists are likely to make a beeline for the Gothic **Iglesia de San Pedro** (St Peter's Church). It has a fine 13th-century Mudéjar tower but in all probability these tourists are not here for either architectural or religious reasons. Adjoining the church is the **chapel** containing the mausoleum of the 'Lovers of Teruel'. The story of this star-crossed 13th-century couple has inspired many writers, from Boccaccio to Tirso de Molina. The lovers are commemorated in a 20th-century alabaster sculpture. Their bones are on view as a symbol of their eternal togetherness (and also to show that they really existed).

Teruel's **cathedral** has some intriguing Mudéjar elements, especially the finely decorated 13th-century brick tower and the lantern in the dome.

Two other local towers are also considered classics of Mudéjar style. The **Torre San Martin** and **Torre del Salvador** are almost identical in design; square and divided vertically into three parts, from street-level arch to belfry. The brick and ceramic decorations on the outer walls call to mind the design of an oriental carpet.

Cuenca

It's hot in summer, cold in winter and well away from the main roads, but picturesque **Cuenca** is on most tourist itineraries, and with good reason. The old town is perched on a precipice above the rivers Huécar and Júcar, with mediaeval houses hanging over the void. There are twisting narrow lanes to explore, and a 13th-century cathedral and a museum of modern art to visit.

Cuenca's famous **Casas Colgadas** ('Hanging Houses'), date from the 14th century. Until the beginning of this

WORKMANSHIP BY THE VANQUISHED

The Moorish craftsmen who stayed on after the Reconquest and created the Mudéjar style contributed a bright chapter to the history of Spanish architecture and the decorative arts. Mudéjar means 'subjugated', which indeed post-Reconquest Muslims were, to a greater or lesser degree.

Some of the more obvious aspects of Mudéjar style are the geometrical designs, the horseshoe arches, the use of meticulously laid bricks, and the enthusiasm for ornamentation.

right after the Reconquest, on the site of a mosque. The original plan was Gothic, influenced by some Norman features attributed to itinerant mediaeval architects. Among the treasures here is a 14th-century Byzantine diptych embellished with precious stones, said to be the only one of its kind in Spain.

century they were known as 'the Houses of the King', leading to the belief that they provided some sort of retreat for mediaeval monarchs. The views (to and from here) are certainly fit for a king. In the evenings, spotlights heighten the dramatic effect.

The **Museo de Arte Abstracto Español**, a collection of outstanding contemporary Spanish paintings and sculpture, is installed in the hanging houses. The interior décor and the view outside may distract from the works on show, but the exposition is very well arranged.

The **Museo de Cuenca**, a provincial archaeological museum, occupies a 14th-century mansion near the cathedral. The collection starts in prehistory, goes on to Roman mosaics and statues, and also gives space to local artists.

Construction of the **cathedral**, now protected as a national monument, began

The charming Moorish hill village of Albarracin, 39km (24 miles) west of Teruel, has been declared a national monument.

In good weather, take the scenic mountain drive north to **Ciudad Encantada** (the Enchanted City). This series of rock formations is best explained by their own peculiar names: *Hongo* ('toadstool'), *Las Barcas* ('the ships'). *Elefante* and *Cocodrilo* are obvious. This is a good spot for walking.

Albacete

An important road junction, **Albacete** is surrounded by the moody scenery of La Mancha. It was founded by Iberians, developed by the Romans and later developed more by the Moors. The **Museo Arqueológico Provincial** (also known as the Museo de Albacete) is housed in a

splendid modern building opposite the Abelardo Sanchez Park. It has a large and interesting collection of prehistoric, Roman and mediaeval relics. If you are on the Quixote trail, this may be a good place to stay overnight. The *parador* of La Mancha on the outskirts of the town is modern, comfortable and reflects the regional style. There is also a very worthwhile diversion 14km (9 miles) south east of Albacete. Chinchilla de Monte-Aragón is a beautiful, small hill town with a mediaeval castle, a charming plaza and the Gothic-Renaissance church of Santa María del Salvador.

Today's town is a growing modern industrial centre that is noted for its steel. Not girders and pipes, but scissors and knives, known for their high quality and beauty.

Ciudad Real

The name of **Ciudad Real** (Royal City) may arouse expectations of grandeur, but don't get your hopes up too high. This may have been the 'seat of the God of smiles' to Cervantes, but, and more prosaic, to that other man of more recent letters, Gerald Brenan, Ciudad Real appeared a 'dull, one-horse little place'. Notwithstanding some historical royal connections, this provincial capital is extremely provincial.

*P*recipitously ensconced on a clifftop, Cuenca is officially dubbed a 'picturesque site' – which is putting it mildly. Because of its isolation, and parched weather that is usually too hot or too cold, this provincial capital has remained very provincial.

MAN OF LA MANCHA

The vast, parched plain of La Mancha, with its endless horizons and potential for blurry mirages, was the perfect setting for the adventures of Cervantes' myopic knight, the immortal Don Quixote.

The home town of Quixote is never specified in the novel, but it is clearly somewhere in La Mancha. The location has to be inferred from passing references, none of which are conclusive. Could it have been the traditional windmill village of **Mota del Cuervo** in Cuenca province? Or **Argamasilla de Alba** in the province of Ciudad Real, where Cervantes started writing the book? A modern windmill has been erected in his honour. Many a squat, whitewashed and otherwise undistinguished hamlet would love to be honoured as Quixote's birthplace.

Cervantes was a place name-dropper throughout the novel, so we can closely follow the knight's adventures. For instance, there is no doubt about the importance of the village of **El Toboso** (in Toledo province). In this typical village of La Mancha lived Dulcinea, the woman of Quixote's dreams. Today 'Dulcinea's House' is open to visitors.

Alfonso X (the Wise) is credited with founding the original town in 1255 but it did not become a Royal City until 1420. The town's only memorable impact on Spain's history was in a period when the Inquisition was based here before moving its terror machine to permanent quarters in Toledo.

Sightseeing focuses on the remains of the 14th-century town wall, specifically a Mudéjar gate, the Puerta de Toledo. There are also three Gothic churches, including the cathedral, noted for its choir stalls. The church of San Pedro boasts fine Mudéjar and Gothic portals.

143

MIRROR ON SPAIN

Cervantes waits for inspiration at his desk in Madrid Wax Museum.

Spanish literature unerringly mirrors every step in the evolution of the country: its varied heritage, its violence and mysticism, its code of honour and harsh religious values, its alternating eras of glory and despond.

In the beginning, Spaniards bumbled through a babel of languages; Latin was the *lingua franca*. But medieval troubadours, who moved effortlessly between the warring Christian and Muslim courts, tended to choose Castilian Spanish over other dialects. Anonymous epic poems like the famous *Cantar de Mío Cid* sang the praises of Christian nobles and warriors. Late in the Reconquest, King Alfonso the Wise sponsored translations into Castilian of classical, Arab, Hebrew and Christian knowledge.

By the 14th century there was a boom in a more creative field of writing. After a spell in jail for his satirical style, **Juan Ruíz,** archpriest of Hita, wrote *El Libro de Buen Amor*, a typically lusty Spanish mixture of eroticism and devotion. Some 150 years later, *La Celestina*, a kind of Spanish *Romeo and Juliet*, appeared.

The end of the 15th century, with the Moors expelled, Spain reunited, Columbus triumphant, and movable-type printing in use, heralded Spain's *Siglo de Oro* (Golden Age). Spanish poetry soon began to match the refinement of the Italian model. But the content—religious sincerity and a profound feeling for nature—took priority over the form. One of the 16th-century literary names to remember: **St. Teresa of Ávila,** the prolific author of searching spiritual books.

On quite another level, books about *pícaros*, cynical rogues who survived through outsmarting others, were a 16th-century Spanish invention. The first picaresque novel, the anonymous *Lazarillo de Tormes,* dramatized the decaying social climate, showing the anti-hero living by his wits. The trend reached its apogee in the reign of **Miguel de Cervantes,** the greatest Spanish novelist of all time. In *Don Quixote* he presented reality on two levels: the ''poetic'' truth of the knight errant's fuzzy vision and the ''historic'' truth of Sancho Panza, more earthy and rational. Cervantes used their adventures to develop a philosophic commentary on existence.

Drama came into its own with **Lope de Vega,** a theorist who was practical enough to write, or have a hand in, some 1,800 plays—action dramas, full of deceit, honour and romance. On his heels came the monk **Tirso de Molina,** creator of the infamous Don Juan. But the greatest of the Golden Age playwrights, **Pedro Calderón de la Barca,** introduced deep philosophical themes and dramatic unity.

After a couple of centuries of on-and-off decline, with literary movements coming one after another and poetry overrefined and pompous, the novel came to the fore. **Pedro Antonio de Alarcón** wrote a jolly, earthy story, *El Sombrero de Tres Picos* (The Three-Cornered Hat), and it struck a popular chord. **Benito Pérez Galdós** used the recent wars against Napoleon as the backdrop for the 46 novels of his *Episodios Nacionales*.

The Spanish-American War of 1898, which Spain lost, shook the nation into taking stock and gave rise to a literary group called the Generation of '98. The pseudonymous novelist and critic **Azorín** took inspiration from the Spanish countryside and rethought earlier literary values. The influential **Miguel de Unamuno** analysed the national problem in perceptive essays. A contemporary, **Pío**

Baroja, wrote easy-to-read novels advocating social action at the expense of tradition.

In the 1930s the Spanish Civil War drove many promising novelists into political exile. But the Andalusian poet and dramatist **Federico García Lorca** stayed at home, to die a martyr. Fascinated by jazz rhythm, he presented elemental passions so intense that his characters became mere puppets, symbols of man against fate. His dramatic poetry was personal yet universal, truly modern yet solidly built on traditional foundations.

The poet **Antonio Machado,** who died in exile, explored memory and soul through recurrent symbols, seeking islands of stability in the sea of consciousness. For many Spaniards, Machado still lives; as many as 500 letters a year are delivered to a mailbox fixed to his tombstone.

In 1989 the Nobel prize for literature went to a onetime bullfighter, **Camilo José Cela.** Franco censorship rejected his stark, provocative first novel, *La familia de Pascual Duarte*.

With democracy restored, the turmoil in Spanish letters shows signs of producing new big names, even if the centre of creative gravity remains in Latin America. In the meantime, literature in the Catalan and Galician tongues, banned under Franco, steers a lively comeback course.

A poet and an essayist: Federico García Lorca, Miguel de Unamuno.

Beaches, Peaks and Pastures

If your idea of Spain is whitewashed houses under a baking sun, high-rise *costas*, swirling Flamenco dancers and cascading guitar rhythms, then think again. For this is a very different country – a green, rural, Celtic land of fishermen and farmers; in fact this is where the rain in Spain falls mainly. Fjords split the scenery and sometimes bagpipes split the ears, but discos are few and far between, and off the beaten track you could go for days without seeing a fellow tourist.

The bright green of the countryside of northern Spain is the colour of an hallucination. As unreal as the tint is the tilt of the hillsides: the sheep, even cows, seem pinned to vertiginous, almost vertical fields. From this steep, bucolic backwater you can almost smell the sea, just around the corner, crashing against cliffs or caressing a sandy beach.

In the rural areas of Galicia, farmers make their living in much the same way as they have for centuries. Sheep can traverse the steep fields, provide wool for the cold Galician winters and milk for the area's delicious cheeses.

Galicia

The ancient kingdom of Galicia, in the north western corner of the Iberian peninsula, is a rugged isolated land battered by the Atlantic tides. It is around the size of Belgium or Maryland and rises rapidly from romantic sea inlets to 2,438m (8,000ft) high snow-topped mountain ranges. Yet, in spite of its remoteness, you could not say that Galicia is off the tourist track. Rather, the original such track leads here. History's first tourists, millions of sandal-shod pilgrims, hiked from all over Europe to the supreme shrine of Spain, Santiago de Compostela.

Even by Spanish standards, the Galicians are a fiercely independent folk. Their ancestry and isolation have given them this character, and they still preserve their

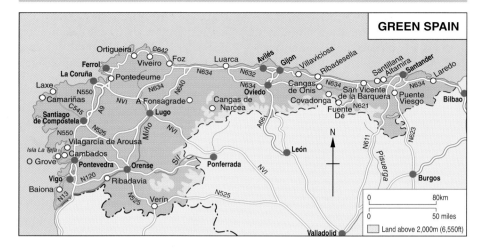

own language, culture and folklore. On bilingual road signs in Galicia you may see that the Castilian spelling has been blacked out by graffiti spray. The language issue is less intense than in Catalonia, but nationalistic forces vehemently promote the use of *gallego* over Castilian.

The energetic Celts arrived in Galicia around the 6th century BC, settling in thoroughly enough to put up fierce resistance to subsequent invasions by Romans (led by Julius Caesar) and Moors. Under Spanish rule, Galicia reached its greatest heights as the tomb of St James was discovered – conveniently at just the ideal moment to rally the Christian Reconquest. The great number of churches in Galicia is a legacy of St James's miraculous intercession.

Cows and ploughs are common sights in the Galician landscape. When the cows are not being milked, they are hitched up to plough the fields or pull wagons. Though much slower and more ungainly than horses, the overworked cows, like the farmers they serve, do their best with what they have.

La Coruña

The English call it Corunna, the Spanish **La Coruña**. In the Galician language, which is very close to Portuguese, it's A Coruña. This historic port and provincial capital is now very built-up, but worth a visit for the port and old town.

You can't get much more historic than Spain's oldest lighthouse. La Coruña's **Torre de Hércules** is said to be the only ancient Roman lighthouse still in operation. Of course, there have been some changes made since its first gleam in the 2nd century. The square five-storey tower is an 18th-century design, incorporating an interior staircase, and sadly there is none of the original stonework on view. If you climb the 242 stairs, you will be rewarded with vistas of the city and the Atlantic. The tower, so much a landmark that it is incorporated into La Coruña's coat of arms, stands on a peninsula near the northern tip of the city. Leading to it, the centre of town occupies a relatively narrow isthmus with a crescent beach on one side and the port on the other.

The large **port** is shared by oil-tankers, freighters, ferries, fishing boats and yachts.

This was the point of departure for the re-grouped Spanish Armada as it headed for England, and disaster, in 1588. Behind the port, the Avenida de la Marina presents shining examples of local 19th-century architecture. The **solanas** (or *miradores*) of La Coruña, glassed-in porches on the upper floors of apartment houses, are designed to warm the houses in winter and insulate them from the heat in summer. La Coruña has so many multi-storey houses with these floor-to-ceiling balconies that it is sometimes called the 'City of Glass'.

The **Castillo de San Antón** at the front of the harbour was built in the 16th century and now holds an archaeological museum which includes some fine jewellery.

*T*he Ortigueira estuary, or riá, *one of Galicia's Rías Altas. A quiet corner of Spain for walking, boating and contemplation.*

The **old town**, east of the port, has more than its fair share of historic churches and monasteries, set amid winding streets and restful gardens. La Coruña's oldest church, the 12th-century **Iglesia de Santiago**, is Romanesque in style with some Gothic additions.

The **Palacio Municipal** (town hall), La Coruña's most pompous public building, really is quite palatial. Built at the beginning of the 20th century, it has a wide, arcaded façade and three cupolas.

The North Coast

Galicia's coastline is characterized by *rías*: fjord-like estuaries where sunken valleys have been invaded by the sea. The scalloped coastline is perfect for boating, fishing, and when the sun shines, swimming. Although the Atlantic coast, south from La Coruña, has the more spectacular *rías*, the northern indentations, called the **Rías Altas**, have their enthusiasts too. Along the inlets are unspoiled resort towns and some quiet beaches where solitude is easy to find.

Try to visit at least one of the attractive little towns of the Rías Altas between La Coruña and the border of Asturias. **Pontedeume** is a mediaeval village and old-fashioned resort with a long sandy beach; **Ortigueira** is noted for its fine sandy beach and verdant hills; **El Barqueiro**, a picture-postcard fishing village, boasts a white sandy beach; **Viveiro**'s historic monuments provide a contrast to the fishing port and resort atmosphere; and **Foz** is popular with fishermen and bathers, and claims a particularly mild microclimate.

El Ferrol

A few *rías* north east of La Coruña, **El Ferrol** is a naval base with a perfect, protected port. It has figured in both mediaeval and modern history. The main part of town has a harmonious layout dating from the 18th century, when the town's shipyards were built.

This was the birthplace of Francisco Franco; during his reign, the town's name was expanded to El Ferrol del Caudillo in his honour. An equestrian statue of the late ruler still stands in the main square. Despite being a native of Galicia, Franco suppressed its regional aspirations in the cause of national unity, and like Ferdinand and Isabella, he even outlawed the Galician language. No wonder the town's name is back to El Ferrol.

Santiago de Compostela

This is the one major town of the region, a name recognizable to millions of people all over the Christian world, even though they may never have heard of Galicia. It is the third holiest shrine in Christendom (after Jerusalem and Rome) and consequently, almost everybody, pilgrim or plain tourist, approaches the town with some degree of awe. But don't worry, **Santiago de Compostela** is not a holier-than-thou place with a single solemn interest. Besides piety, so much else is going on: politics, education, commerce and tourism in some fairly irreligious guises. Chaucer's Canterbury pilgrims would have felt right at home here.

Modern Santiago is a well-rounded, mellow community which is so well preserved that it has been declared a national monument. This does not mean it is a historically cocooned city, however. In the streets and squares among the stately buildings, life goes on at a brisk pace, but you needn't worry about traffic, as much of the central area has been pedestrianized. This only adds to the town's attraction as a tourist destination.

The postcard picture of Santiago, the view every pilgrim has been awaiting, is the main façade of the **cathedral**, looming high above the plaza, with baroque adornments and twin towers – all the surfaces stained with rust-coloured moss. The cathedral is unique in Spain in that it is surrounded by four plazas which blend everything together into a splendid architectural whole.

Historically, this is supposed to be the spot where the 9th-century Asturian kings, Alfonsos II and III, built churches over the

*H*ostal de los Reyes Católicos parador. *Now this is what you call a hotel entrance! This magnificent* parador *in the centre of Santiago de Compostela started life as the Hospital Real in 1511 catering for pilgrims. It still does – they are just a little richer these days.*

A hillside chapel at Tosantes. This is one of many which may be found on the Camino de Santiago.

tomb of St James (Santiago). In 997 the whole town, including the church, was wiped out by the Moorish general al-Mansur, but he is said to have spared the tomb itself. As soon as Santiago was re-taken by the Christian forces, construction of a proper Romanesque cathedral was undertaken. The European pilgrim tide was unleashed even before the cathedral had been completed in 1211. The monumental baroque **façade**, the work of Fernando Casas y Novoa, dates from the mid-18th century.

Climb the stairs from the square to the main entrance. The first surprise is just inside: the 800-year-old **Pórtico de la Gloria** (Door of Glory) is a marvel of

A SAINT'S SAGA

According to legend, St James the Apostle, one of the innermost circle of the disciples of Jesus, brought Christianity to Spain. Around AD 44, back in Jerusalem, the former fisherman became the first of the apostles to be martyred – beheaded by order of Herod. The story goes that his followers sailed back to Spain with his body, which they buried somewhere in Galicia. After the upheavals of the Dark Ages, no one could remember where the grave was situated. Then, early in the 9th century, a star in the sky directed some shepherds to the place. Further miracles ensued when embattled Christian soldiers were helped in beating back the Moors by St James on horseback. All of which gave the Reconquest a hefty boost during its darkest days.

Modern scholars scorn the legends, maintaining that St James never visited Spain in the first place and that the whole story was merely a propaganda exercise to unite the fragmented Spain during the Reconquest. They are probably right, but whisper it very quietly in Santiago de Compostela.

Romanesque sculpture. Look up to see the stories and character studies in stone around its arches. About the only thing we know about the genius who carved it is his name, Master Mateo.

Note the fingerprint-shaped indentations on the column directly below the statue of Christ, which represents the tree of Jesse (Christ's family tree). Here you can rest your hand in the same spot where millions of devout pilgrims have rested theirs.

A 13th-century polychrome statue of St James takes the spotlight on the main altar. Don't be startled if you suddenly see hands come out of the darkness to touch the saint's shoulders or neck. They belong to the pilgrims standing in the passageway behind the altar. A crypt below the altar contains what are said to be the saint's remains.

The gardenless Gothic cloister leads to a **museum of tapestry** with rich old hangings, unfortunately displayed without captions. Facing the Plaza del Obradoiro, opposite the cathedral's main entrance, is the **town hall**, an 18th-century neo-classical palace by a French architect, Charles Lemaur.

On the north side of the square, the **Hostal de los Reyes Católicos** has a stupendous plateresque façade. The institution was founded in 1499, by Ferdinand and Isabella (hence the name) to receive pilgrims. It is now a luxurious *parador.*

Wherever you meander in Santiago de Compostela, you will be within sight of a historic church or monastery. On the secular front, the city has a charming, relaxed provinciality. The local university students balance the sobriety of some of the pilgrims. Bars and restaurants bulge with patrons snacking on seafood, fresh from the *rías,* washed down with the light local wines. Even when it rains, which it often does in these parts, the water gushing off the mediaeval roofs and from the gaping gargoyles is a sight in itself.

The principal sightseeing attraction in Santiago, away from the cult of St James, is the **Museo do Pobo Gallego**, which is a museum of Galician folklore and crafts, housed in the old convent of Santo Domingo.

The West Coast

The road from Santiago de Compostela to the **Rías Bajas** (Lower Estuaries) goes through the legend-shrouded village of **Padrón.** This is supposed to have been the spot where the ship (without sails or crew) carrying the remains of St James arrived. The stone to which the ship is said to have moored may be seen beneath the main altar in the local church of Santiago.

The *rías* themselves form a jagged coastline softened by the blue calm of the water and the warm, green curves of the hills.

Villagarcía de Arousa has a bright, cheerful appearance, but beyond the

---

THE COAST OF DEATH

Long before public relations wizards began inventing glamorous names for beach zones, there was already a named *costa* in north west Galicia. Its title was hardly calculated to lure the tourists, however. With awful frankness, it is called Costa de la Muerte (the Coast of Death).

When the ocean is calm you would never guess that this coast has claimed more than its fair share of seafarers. The local festival in Laxe in August features a simulated shipwreck and rescue. Near Camariñas, an English cemetery contains the remains of victims of the 1890 shipwreck of a British training ship, the *Panther.*

When the tide goes out in Galicia's *rías* in the shellfish season, hundreds of people flock to the beaches to collect a prodigious crop. It is tough work amassing a bucketful of clams, cockles, oysters, scallops and eminently edible barnacles (*percebes*). Between the spoils collected by barefoot scavengers and those of *mariscadores* in boats, the harvest is valued in billions of pesetas.

One of the advantages of a holiday in Galicia is the freshness and variety of the seafood. Above all, do try *pulpo* (octopus). This is so popular that you will find bars and restaurants (called *pulperias*) specializing in just this one creature. At fairs and fiestas hundred of octopuses are cooked in great pots and eaten off wooden dishes.

municipal gardens it is a big, working port. The highway goes right through the main square of **Cambados** – not around the square but through the middle – which seems slightly disrespectful to such a stately town. Note the elegant *pazos* (historic mansions). The local Albariño wine is said to be descended from vines hand-carried here by pilgrims from the abbey at Cluny, in Burgundy, and is highly rated by connoisseurs.

La Toja, a holiday isle of pines and palms, has been linked to civilization by

On the island of Arosa, just off the indented coast of Pontevedra province, live mussels are returned to the sea to grow fatter and more valuable in captivity. Galicia's seafood harvest is also rich in scallops, oysters, crabs and lobsters.

a bridge for most of this century, and in recent years has become quite developed, with some large hotels springing up. On the mainland side is O Grove, a fishing port which has also expanded into a popular resort.

Pontevedra

In the Middle Ages, **Pontevedra** was an important port and shipyard; they even say that Columbus's flagship, the *Santa María*, was built here. The city is one of the most charming in Galicia. It preserves many fine old buildings, and the squares and gardens are spacious and inviting. The city's pride and joy is the plateresque **Iglesia de Santa María la Mayor** in the old fishermen's quarter, which has been declared a national monument. The **façade** is divided into sculptural compartments, each telling a New Testament story; the crucifixion tops the towering slab. The stone carving is attributed to a Dutch artist, very active in these parts, known only as Cornelis.

BLACK MAGIC

Galicians not only believe in the benevolent intervention of the supernatural (as personified by Santiago), they also believe in the dark side. In late June the fiesta of Nuestra Señora de Corpiño (a small town in the Pontevedra province) is the gathering place for people who believe themselves to be possessed by evil spirits. Penances are paid, exorcism rites are performed and it is generally no place for the faint-hearted.

The following month at Nieves, also in Pontevedra province, another bizarre ceremony is held. People who have had a close shave with death during the year are transported in coffins around the church of Santa Marta as thanks to the local saint for their salvation.

The city's patron saint is commemorated in the baroque **Iglesia de la Virgen de la Peregrina** (Church of the Pilgrim Virgin). The curvaceous, Italianate, 18th-century façade adds to its grace. Nearby, the **Iglesia de San Francisco**, with Romanesque touches, was begun in the 14th century.

The **provincial museum** of Pontevedra is housed in interconnecting historic mansions. There are departments of archaeology, art and some enlightening exhibits on the Galician seafaring way of life.

Vigo

In this industrial city of 250,000 people, modern fishing boats share a splendid natural harbour with pleasure craft. **Vigo** was known to Phoenicians and Romans, and attacked by Normans, Saracens and Moors, but did not become Spain's leading **fishing port** until relatively recently.

Vigo was formerly a mainstay of trade between Spain and its American colonies. This brought prosperity but also danger; buccaneers frequently swooped on the harbour to hijack the incoming gold shipments. Vigo also had the misfortune of a visit from Sir Francis Drake, the renowned English naval 'hero' ('pirate' to the Spanish), who pillaged the town in 1589.

Drake's band burned down the church of Santa María, which was subsequently

Near the gorges of Sil in Galicia it may look like paradise, but not all is rosy in the garden. The old farming practice of dividing the land up into small parcels is uneconomic in today's mass markets.

rebuilt in neoclassical style as Vigo's co-cathedral. The Rua Real leads from the cathedral down to the colourful fishermen's district, El Berbés. The early morning fish market attracts tourists and the local cats. Nearby, you can soak up the atmosphere at the anything-goes flea market called A Pedra.

Bayona

Bayona (or *Baiona* in the vernacular) was the first place to hear of the discovery of the New World, for it was here that the *Pinta* landed on 1 March 1493 after Columbus's triumphant expedition. Nowadays, Bayona is one of the most attractive resorts in Galicia, developed enough to have a life and ambiance all of its own, but as yet undiscovered by the masses.

The charming fishing port is full of traditional old houses and tapas bars. It is set in a *ría*, and overlooked by a wooded promontory that once held a castle, lately converted to an excellent *parador*. The views from here, particularly at sunset, are wonderful. Bayona has its own beaches, but these are small and soon get crowded in the season. A few miles out of the village is the excellent large beach of Playa de América.

Orense

Orense is set in inland Galicia. It is surrounded by beautiful scenery, but economically it is poor, with farmers eking their living from plots of land much too small to be efficient.

Straddling the Río Miño (here on its way to becoming the frontier with Portugal), Orense has been around since the time of the ancient Romans. They built a stone bridge now known as the *Puente Romano*. Actually, this is newer than it looks, dating (above the original foundations) from the 13th century. The Romans, connoisseurs of therapeutic baths, were drawn here by the hot springs.

Today, the provincial capital of Orense is an unprepossessing place with modern soulless suburbs. Still, it's worth persisting to get to the town's historic hub. The **cathedral**, Romanesque and Gothic, was consecrated at the end of the 12th century. Of special interest is the triple-arched **Paradise Portal** (Pórtico del Paraíso), patterned after Santiago de Compostela's Door of Glory. The down-to-earth bars crammed into the narrow Calle de Lepanto, almost in the shadow of the cathedral, will give you a good impression of the unaffected nature of the people of inland Galicia.

Lugo

The centre of **Lugo** is enclosed by the best-preserved **Roman walls** in Spain. You can climb to the top and walk all the way around the bulging battlements, a distance of nearly 2km (1½ miles). Within these walls stands a well-preserved mediaeval enclave.

Lugo is proud of its past. In Plaza de Santo Domingo stands a Roman column topped by a huge sculpture of an eagle; the inscription honours Augustus Caesar, who brought peace to the empire. However, the Roman walls failed to fend off the Suevi in the 5th century, the Moors in the 8th,

the Normans in the 10th, and later the Moors again. Napoleon's troops won the town in 1809. You can learn more about the town's history in the **Museo Provincial**, housed in an old palace which also encompasses the cloister of the convent of San Francisco. There is a good fine arts collection here too.

Old Lugo is a pleasant town for strolling, with a big, tree-shaded main square, fine old houses, and historic palaces and churches. Work started on the cathedral in 1129 but continued for so long that it includes Romanesque, Gothic and baroque elements.

Asturias

They say that this is the true Spain, not in any tourist context, but because it was the only region which did not succumb to the Moors. It is a wild, rugged place, known for its fiercely independent people and its potent cider.

Covadonga

After the seemingly invincible Moors had overrun most of Spain in the 8th century, a spearhead of the Christian forces, hidden among these harsh mountains, began the Reconquest. The Battle of Covadonga in AD 722 was the first Christian success in a struggle that was to go on for another seven centuries. The victory was a symbolic one rather than a major turning point, but no less celebrated for all that.

It was led by Pelayo, a local hero with royal connections, who may have been a Visigothic noble or a member of the king's entourage. There is a statue in the main square dedicated to him, but it is modern, and is based on little more than the sculptor's imagination.

Across the esplanade from the basilica is an unexpectedly large neo-Romanesque church, less than a century old. Down the hill is the **Santa Cueva** (Holy Cave) where Pelayo saw a vision of the Virgin Mary which inspired his victory. The remains of Pelayo and his consort are kept here. Every good Asturian is supposed to walk to this shrine at least once in a lifetime, and so this is the most visited place in the province.

Cangas de Onís

The village of **Cangas de Onís**, now on the tourist map as the western gateway to the Picos de Europa, was once the capital of Asturias, and from here Pelayo led the forces of the Reconquest.

Aside from the natural beauty surrounding Cangas, there are two monuments to see. The first is the humpbacked ivy-covered 12th-century Romanesque bridge over the Río Sella; a Christian cross hangs from its high arch. The second is the Capilla de Santa Cruz, a 15th-century rebuild of an early monastery that may have been used by the Visigothic kings and is one of Spain's earliest Christian sites.

Villaviciosa

This small town, north west of Cangas at the head of an estuary, is an atmospheric old place with plenty of mediaeval architecture to admire. The biggest event in its history occurred in 1517. A royal armada turned up unexpectedly, carrying the French-speaking prince who would later become the Holy Roman Emperor, Charles V. Apparently, he had meant to land in Santander, but his navigators brought him instead to this backwater. A monument shows the king coming ashore in a craft which looks uncomfortably like a rubber dinghy.

The *viciosa* suffix to the town refers not to any violence, past or present, but to the luxuriant vegetation of the area. It is the centre of an important apple-growing region, so if the smell of Asturian cider is in the air, you'll know why.

Gijón

The major port and sometime resort of **Gijón** is the biggest city in Asturias, with over 250,000 inhabitants. It was badly damaged during the Civil War and has been almost totally rebuilt. There are ancient remains to be found, however, most notably the small, well-preserved Roman baths. Today's bathers head for roomy San Lorenzo beach, although this is busy and not terribly attractive.

Bagpipes are as much at home in Asturias as in Aberdeen or Ayr and they have a museum all to themselves, the **Museo de la Gaita**, on the right bank of the Río Piles in Gijón.

Oviedo

This is the political and cultural capital of Asturias, founded in the 8th century. At that early stage in the Reconquest it became the seat of King Alfonso II (son of Pelayo, see above). Despite royal status moving south soon after that, **Oviedo** still has a certain grandeur and many a fine monument graces its compact historic centre.

The **cathedral** culminates in a flourish with a tall, richly turreted tower in Flamboyant Gothic style. The **high altar** features an immense 16th-century retable, divided into 24 delicately carved compartments. The 14th-century **cloister**, with lovely Gothic tracery, surrounds an exceptionally green garden.

The most significant part of the cathedral is the **Cámara Santa** (Holy Chamber), a shrine built by Alfonso II to

protect the holiest relics evacuated from Toledo in the face of the Moorish onslaught. It also serves as a pantheon for the Asturian kings. At the entrance notice the outstanding statues of the apostles, carved in the 12th century.

Behind the cathedral is the **Museo Arqueológico**, housed in a splendid old palace-convent with a gorgeous plateresque cloister. Within the museum is a good section on folklore.

There are two other notable churches within a few minutes of the city centre. The ancient church of **Santullano**, built in the early 9th century, is a short walk to the north east. It is claimed to be the oldest pre-Romanesque church in Spain and boasts frescoes reminiscent of a Roman villa. **Santa Maria del Naranco**

The season's harvest of maize is kept safe and dry under the roof of an Asturian farmer's hórreo.

and the old palace chapel of **San Miguel de Lillo** are beautifully located on a wooded hill, some 3km (2 miles) outside the centre.

If you would like to take in some fresh air after all those churches, visit the **Parque de San Francisco**, a 6-ha (15-acre) garden with some splendid shady trees, almost right in the centre of town.

Cantabria

Behind the ports and resorts and miles of sea-front wilderness rises a great wall, the Cantabrian Mountains (*Cordillera Cantábrica*). The peaks are higher than 2,500m (over 1½ miles) culminating in the Picos de Europa, so you can fit in snow and sea all in a day's excursion.

Cantabria is world famous as the home of prehistoric cave artists of true genius.

Laredo

West from Bilbao stretches the beach-lined Cantabrian coast, with fishing villages and summer resorts little known abroad. Yet times are changing, and restaurants in **Laredo**, half-way between Bilbao and Santander, now post menus in English, French and German. In the high season the population multiplies eight-fold to around 100,000, and some uncomplimentary comparisons have been made with Torremolinos, although here the visitors are mostly French and German, rather than British.

Laredo's beach, though far from town, is beautiful in the San Sebastián style and is even bigger than the beach at that resort. Apartment blocks and comfortable holiday houses proliferate. The old town is still attractive, however, with narrow, steep streets, though it has now sprouted souvenir shops and many of the other accoutrements of mass tourism.

Because sailors from Laredo joined the expeditions of Columbus, Pizarro and later adventurers, the town's name is perpetuated in several western hemisphere communities, such as Laredo, Texas.

Santander

Santander successfully combines the roles of major port and tasteful resort, although there is little of cultural or historic interest here. This is due in large part to two major disasters in the last hundred years. In 1894 a freighter laden with explosives blew up in the port, killing hundreds of people and demolishing much of the harbour area. In 1941, a devastating fire ravaged Santander. Casualties were miraculously minimal, but two-thirds of the city was destroyed and 20,000 inhabitants made homeless.

For the rebirth of Santander, a far-sighted plan decreed that new buildings must be held to low-rise proportions and interspersed with parks and gardens. To make life easier, some inconvenient hills were razed and laid out the new streets and boulevards in a grid plan.

After the fire the **cathedral**, overlooking the ancient port, had to be reconstructed almost from bottom to top. It was restored to resemble the mediaeval original, something between a fortress and a watch-tower. The oldest part of the building is the Romanesque crypt. Other elements of the cathedral were tacked on over the centuries in the style in vogue.

Santander's **Museo Provincial de Prehistoria** has some notable finds from excavations around the province. Also displayed are axes, arrows, and skilfully carved staffs or batons made from deer antlers. The town also boasts a fine **Museo de Bellas Artes**, featuring some powerful and disturbing images by Goya.

The antidote to Santander's clanging port, the district called **El Sardinero** gives the city its resort mood. A grand casino (now downgraded to a bingo hall) is complemented by small seafood bars. The beaches, parks and gardens are spacious, though not quite the measure of the crowds that congregate on a sunny day in

Across the bay from Laredo lies Santoña, a fishing town with some good, sandy beaches, a fortress and a mediaeval church.

summer. Overlooking the sea on its own rugged peninsula, the Victorian-style **Magdalena Palace** was built for Alfonso XIII as a summer escape and features a host of architectural eccentricities. It is now home to a summer university.

Santillana del Mar

Jean-Paul Sartre called this 'the prettiest village in Spain', and he may have had a point. In this perfectly preserved ancient community, only the television aerials, tacked to some of the red tile roofs, reveal which century this is. There is nothing contrived about the mediaeval village effect. In a stone barn 30 paces beyond the main square, cows are mooing while being milked.

The name *Santillana* is a contraction of Saint Juliana (martyred by Emperor Diocletian). *Del Mar* means 'of the sea', but it actually lies a few kilometres north across the protecting hills.

You don't need a map to explore the narrow cobbled streets of Santillana. Just wander at will and soak up the atmosphere: old stone houses with flowered balconies, mediaeval towers and inns, grand mansions built by '*Indianos*'; local folk who returned, rich, from adventures in the Americas.

In front of the *Ayuntamiento* (town hall) stands a modern sculptor's vision of a prehistoric bison. On the stone next to it is engraved:

Santillana
Al Hombre de
Altamira

(from Santillana to the Man of Altamira).

This is the village's tribute to the cavemen of nearby Altamira (*see* below) who left a magnificent artistic legacy – featuring the local bison, which is sadly, long-since extinct.

At the north end of the village, the **Collegiata** (Collegiate Church) is dedicated to St Juliana. Her statue is in a niche above the Romanesque portal, and her tomb is inside. Built seven or eight centuries ago the **cloister** is well worth a few minutes of meditation, if only for the beauty of the sculptural work.

In the **convent** at the other end of the village, the **Museo Diocesano** specializes in carvings of saints and angels gathered from outlying churches.

Altamira

The caves (*cuevas*) of **Altamira**, about 2km (1 mile) inland from Santillana del Mar, contain some of the most inspiring

AUTHENTICATING ALTAMIRA

In 1868, a hunter's dog ferreting through heavy undergrowth unearthed the hidden entrance to a cave later named Altamira. The hunter tipped off Marcelino Sanz de Sautuola, an amateur archaeologist in the area, who discovered amazing paintings deep within the caves.

In 1880, Sautuola published *Brief Notes on Some Prehistoric Objects of the Province of Santander*. The leading French experts on prehistory dismissed Altamira as either a misunderstanding or a hoax. One French palaeontologist who condescended to go down and look judged the paintings to be less than ten years old. Humiliated and forgotten, Sautuola died in 1888.

Towards the turn of the century, however, cave paintings remarkably similar to Altamira's were discovered in France, and confirmed as palaeolithic art. Altamira was reappraised and pronounced the genuine article. In 1902 one of the French experts published an apology, offering posthumous rehabilitation to Sautuola and his daring vision. Today, Altamira is designated as a site of World Heritage.

*O*ne *of the favourite Picos de Europa walking trails is here above Fuenta Dé. Take the cable-car up the 800m (2,500 ft) cliffs, then it's a 4km (2½ mile) walk to the Refugio de Aliva, where you can enjoy some refreshment.*

ancient works of art in Europe. They were painted some 15,000 years ago, but that is not the sole reason why they are rated so highly. For these are neither antique doodles nor cave graffiti. The draughtsmanship is astonishingly keen and like all great art, the paintings convey the artists' intense sensitivity and feelings.

The most sublime of these occupy a part of the cave network dubbed the 'Sistine Chapel of Prehistoric Art'. The bison

and other muscular beasts painted on the ceiling didn't get there because a few cavemen were sitting around a fire with nothing better to do. This is a special part of the cave, far removed from the living quarters, presumably some form of religious sanctuary. Like Michelangelo, the artists would have been too close to the low ceiling to have been able to see the 'big picture'. Yet they took advantage of the curvature and protuberances in the rock to give life and motion to their subjects.

The Altamira paintings were discovered more than a century ago and, perhaps not surprisingly, foreign experts suspected a hoax. Once they were finally authenticated, however, they became a major tourist attraction for decades. Alas, the very breathing of the gaping crowds (causing a build- up of moisture) threatened their existence and so the caves were closed to the public in 1977. Nowadays, entry is restricted to a mere handful of visitors per day (usually bona fide researchers), who have to obtain permission well in advance. Write to the Centro de Investigación de Altamira, 39330 Santillana del Mar, Santander, Cantabria. It may also be worth turning up on a standby basis. If you have not obtained permission, enquire at the local tourist office.

As a second best, there is a museum above the caves which contains the 30,000-year-old remains of a caveman, nicknamed 'Pipo' by the locals. To simulate the cave experience though, you have to go to Madrid, where parts of it have been replicated under the gardens of the Archaeological Museum.

There are, however, other caves in the vicinity that are open to visitors. Some 30km (48 miles) out of Santander on the road to Logroño and near Torrelavega are four caves at **Puente Viesgo**. The main one, **Cueva del Castillo**, also features bison and some curious handprints in the style of a photo negative, thought to be the artist's signature.

Picos de Europa

The road west from Santillana to Oviedo runs parallel to the sea but is rarely in sight of it. Occasionally though, you'll see a *mirador* sign pointing to a look-out spot. Take the opportunity to pull over and take

Real bears can be found if you are very lucky in the Picos de Europa, but this strong fellow guards the Puerto Glorioso at the entrance to the Picos National Park.

in that salty Atlantic breeze while enjoying the distant seascape. Landwards, the Cantabrian countryside can be idyllic; steep green fields spattered with wildflowers, red-topped white houses, tinkling cow-bells and the sweet smell of haystacks.

Soon after you pass the beach resort of San Vicente de la Barquera, road signs offer the adventurous the first of several turns inland to the Picos de Europa. This mountain range begins just 25km (15 miles) in from the sea and extends across three provinces.

The peaks of the Picos rise beyond 2,600m (8,500ft), so a single view may encompass snow at the top right the way down to olive blossom. The valleys between the rugged walls of grey limestone are green Shangri-Las. There are three *massifs*, delineated by the Rivers Deva, Duje, Cares and Sella. They make their

T he Picos de Europa rising to over 2,600m (8,530ft), are snow-capped even in summer. On a clear day they are visible from the beaches.

way to the sea in many moods from trickling, refreshing brooks to shimmering pools and torrents roaring through microchasms.

Complete wilderness is never very far away, but the roads are in good repair. Of course, if you want to get off the beaten path on to the mountain roads you will need a four-wheel-drive vehicle. Chamois and wolves are quite at home here, but your closest encounter with the native wildlife will probably be waiting patiently for the cows to move out of the road.

Basque Country to the Pyrenees

Spain's entry into the European Community may have toppled the economic wall that always divided the country from northern Europe but the physical barrier, the Pyrenees, still stands tall – a harshly beautiful monument to the differences between Iberia and the rest of Europe.

Our definition of the Northern Border actually starts at Bilbao, some little way from the border, and progresses east along the Bay of Biscay (the Spanish call it the Mar Cantábrico). It ends in the fastness of the Pyrenees. This chapter of the guide includes the Basque Country, Navarre and northern Aragon, but excludes Catalonia which is covered separately. It all adds up to a remarkably diverse sweep of Spain.

*G*audily garbed Basque dancers prepare for a holiday procession in the remote valley town of Oñate, in Guipúzcoa province. The flat cap, or boina, originated in the Basque country, and migrated to France as a beret.

Basque Country

The Spanish Basque Country (Pais Vascos) is an autonomous region which has its own language, traditions, and what most gourmets consider to be the finest cuisine in Spain.

Bilbao (Bilbo)

Bilbao is the capital and the industrial heartland of the Basque country. This big city houses more than 400,000 people and is Spain's most important port. It is unfortunately, a badly polluted city, although it does have many pleasant aspects, like boulevards and parks, to compensate for the smoke-stacks. The central district, full of banks as well as stores and shops, reflects Bilbao's position as the powerhouse of the Basque economy.

For tourists, and for art lovers in particular, there is one sight that clamours for attention. The **Museo de Bellas Artes** (Fine Arts Museum) is one of the country's very best collections, providing a rich survey of Spanish classics plus Flemish and Italian masterpieces. After you have caught up with Goya and El Greco, Brueghel the Elder and Teniers the Younger, have a look at the upper floor, devoted to Basque and international 20th-

century art. Here are luminous portraits by Ignacio Zuloaga, blue folklore scenes by Valentin de Zubiaurre, a room full of Impressionist landscapes by Dario de Regoyos Valdés, and the fishermen and country folk of Aurelio Arteta. It's a unique chance to see the Basque version of the faces, scenery and way of life in their country over the last couple of centuries.

The old town, currently undergoing heavy restoration, is full of good, cheap eating and drinking places. If you visit in late August, the *Semana Grande* is a notoriously lively fiesta.

HATS OFF TO THE BASQUES

When you think of a beret, you probably picture a Frenchman, perhaps a fisherman or an artist, with a Gauloise dangling from his lips and a glass of red wine in his hand. But, while the black beret is right at home in Paris or Marseilles, it is not a native style – the familiar, round, flat cap is a Basque invention.

You don't have to be a farmer, fisherman or poet to wear one. In several countries, elite military units wear them as a fraternal badge, to symbolize their bravery and exclusivity. The Basque police wear bright red berets, or, more correctly, *boinas*.

Guernica (Gernika)

You have almost certainly heard of the place and by now you may have seen the picture (in the Centro de Arte Reina Sofia in Madrid); here is the town that inspired it. Picasso's *Guernica* is the ultimate artistic outcry against war. This typically stylized Picasso painting was the reaction to the bombing by Nazi planes of this defenceless Basque town in April 1937. In the world's first test of mass aerial terror, the death toll was in the region of 2,000.

A Basque village nestles in the hills, well away from the bustle of the coast.

T he fiesta of Semana Grande, held in Bilbao in mid-August, is one of Northern Spain's biggest celebrations.

EUSKADI

The Spanish Basque Country (Euskadi in the Basque language) has been an autonomous region since 1980.

As soon as you enter the Basque country, you know you are somewhere very different. Suddenly all the signs seem threateningly foreign, in an archaic-looking typeface, with names and words full of the letters x and k.

The origin of the Basque language is disputed. Although theories have linked it with Iberian or the ancient language of the Caucasus region, these are inconclusive. The Basques themselves think it evolved from the language spoken by the region's original cave-dwelling inhabitants, before the first intruders arrived.

Forbidden under the Franco regime, the language (called *Euskara* in Basque) was clandestinely treasured as the symbol of a culture that refused to surrender. In the post-Franco liberalization Basque has achieved regional equality with Castilian Spanish. Nearly all Basques are bilingual.

Now rebuilt, **Guernica** (Gernika) is rather an ordinary modern place. It does have another strong historical association besides the Civil War atrocity, however. Basque parliaments have been held in the town on and off ever since the Middle Ages, and it was this assertion of independence that provoked the attack in 1937. The town still honours the ancient oak tree in whose shade the mediaeval conclaves were held. A miniature Greek temple-like building protects the stump of the historic tree, a symbol of Basque freedom. Nearby, its descendant and successor, in good health, stands behind a dignified official building called the Casa de Juntas.

If Guernica, the town, is an anti-climax after *Guernica*, the picture, you can seek solace in another fine work of art which predates Picasso by some few millennia. Head inland to the cave of **Santimamiñe** to see charcoal renditions of animals which were once common in this part of the world, including bears, horses and stags. Speaking of charcoal, this bucolic spot is an excellent place for a barbecue, or picnic.

Vitoria (Gasteiz)

Sancho the Wise, king of Navarre, 'discovered' this place, on a plain half-way between Bilbao and Logroño, in 1181. At the time it was an undistinguished village called Gasteiz, but Sancho proclaimed it a city, gave it a rousing, victorious name, and built what became a charming walled town. Sancho's son, known as Sancho the Strong, lost **Vitoria** and the surrounding province of Álava to Castile. The Castilian kings greatly expanded and upgraded the town.

The growing city of Vitoria had to wait centuries for a victory that might justify its name. In the 1813 Battle of Vitoria, the Duke of Wellington's Anglo-Spanish army trounced the troops of Napoleon's brother Joseph. An overblown monument in the **Plaza de la Virgen Blanco** (White Virgin Square) commemorates the battle.

On the north side of the plaza, a niche on the outside of the Gothic church of **San Miguel** contains a polychrome statue of the city's patron saint. The square (actually more like a triangle) is a fine example of the local architectural style of multi-paned balconied windows. Elsewhere in the city, modern architects have adapted the typical sun-porched style with great success.

Just east of this plaza, the city's spacious main square, **Plaza de España,** is a classic 18th-century Spanish ensemble,

*O*n this spot near Miranda de Ebro, a shepherd was struck dead by lightning. This statue was erected to all shepherds.

with the *Casa Consistorial* (town hall) on the north side.

Vitoria offers a choice of cathedrals, new and old. The **Catedral Nueva**, in the modern city, is a big 20th-century neo-Gothic affair. The **Catedral de Santa María**, in the middle of the crowded old town, dates from the 14th century.

The city's mediaeval centre is laid out in a concentric pattern, a logical design for a fortified hilltop. The streets bear the names of the trades that congregated in them; Calle de la Zapatería (shoemakers); Herrería (blacksmiths); Cuchillería

(cutlers), and so on. Look out for original mediaeval houses with walls of thin bricks, alternating with equal horizontal layers of mortar. In a restored 16th-century house just north of the old cathedral, the well-ordered **Museo Provincial de Arqueología** features Iron Age and Roman relics unearthed in the area.

San Sebastián (Donostia)

In mediaeval times, this was the first stop in Spain for pilgrims on the arduous journey to Santiago de Compostela. The dreamy curve of **San Sebastián**'s great long beach (reminiscent of Rio de Janeiro's Copacabana) must have been a wonderful sight for sore eyes. And for sore feet too. It would surely have been an irresistible temptation – as it still is – to dip tired feet in the cool Bay of Biscay.

The magnificent **Bahía de la Concha** (Seashell Bay) is a perfect semicircle and more, stretching to a 270-degree arc. At low tide the perimeter of the beach stretches well over a mile. The sand is protected from wave erosion by the embrace of two peninsulas and a small island between them. Guarding the right flank, the steep **Monte Urgull** is now a municipal park scattered with the remains of a mightily fortified castle. Taking the brunt of the waves in the middle is the **Isla de Santa Clara**, a green excursion spot which can be visited by boat. On the left, **Monte Igueldo** has an amusement park, a hotel and some great views at the summit (reached by funicular).

The main beach, **Playa de la Concha**, adjoins the business district and a zone of luxurious high-rise housing. The smaller **Playa de Ondaretta** runs out at the tennis club. Both beaches are of excellent quality, but can become unbearably crowded in high season.

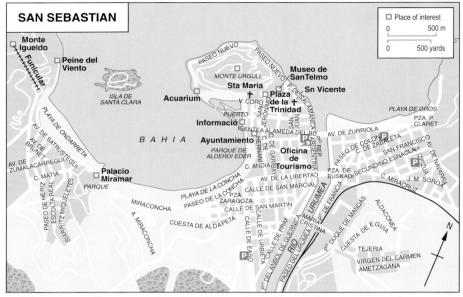

The cosmopolitan atmosphere is only a little more than a century old. What had hitherto been a fishermen's village, a mercantile port and then an industrial centre was finally 'discovered' when the royal family chose San Sebastián as a cool relief from Madrid's infernal summer. The 'Pearl of the Cantabrian Coast' had come of age. Many *belle-époque* villas and buildings still survive and lend San Sebastián its 'high society' cachet, although it is very much an established family resort. San Sebastián is often referred to as one of Spain's most beautiful cities, but it is not a place to visit in search of historic monuments. Much of the antique aspect was wiped out in 1813 when Napoleon and a combined British-Iberian force decided to do battle here. The burned-out town was promptly rebuilt with wide modern streets laid out in a grid pattern and today it has a very French feel to it.

In the **Parte Vieja** (Old Section) of town, in the lee of Monte Urgull, the atmosphere still recalls an old-time fishing village. If you want to learn more about Basque seafaring, look in at the **Palacio del Mar**, which is an aquarium and a museum. The narrow streets here are the focus for the early evening walkabout, with locals and tourists cramming the multitude of bars and restaurants. San Sebastián is internationally famous for its culinary delights, and several of its smarter establishments enjoy a liberal sprinkling of Michelin rosettes, but there is good food available at all prices.

The colourful old streets of the Parte Vieja radiate from the arcaded **Plaza de la Constitución**. Note the numbers painted on the balconies; when bullfights were staged in the square, the residents rented out space to spectators.

A whale of a beach – La Concha Bay in fashionable San Sebastián. Only the dubious weather keeps it uncrowded.

*A*ll the family join in the fun and put on their best clothes at fiesta time, from the youngest to the oldest.

So many special events take place in San Sebastián that you may arrive to find it brimming with visitors at any time: Carnival time, the jazz festival, Semana Grande ('Big Week') in mid-August or the Cannes-style international film festival in September. Even off-season a feeling of fiesta reigns; a *joie de vivre* that makes San Sebastián special.

The streets of the characterful old town are cheered by the colourful touches on the houses – wooden balconies and shutters painted red, green or blue. There is a good sandy beach here, too. Overlooking it all is a pockmarked castle (known as the castle of Emperor Charles V, but said to have been built in the 10th century). It is now home to a *parador* recently re-opened after restoration.

Irún

Even though they sell plenty of kitsch bullfight-and-flamenco souvenirs to tourists nipping over from Biarritz, **Irún** the gateway to Spain's Basque Country, is a bigger, more serious border town than you might expect from first sight. Most of the buildings and the wide streets were built after the destruction of the Civil War. Irún is separated from the French town of Hendaye by the Río Bidasoa. Pleasure boats and visiting birds bob about in these frontier waters.

Navarre

From west to east the mountains gain altitude, and the Basque character of the countryside and the people recedes. In the middle of the Navarre Pyrenees, the most crucial of the ways through the peaks is the legendary **Roncesvalles Pass**. This was the scene of a rather routine 8th-century battle later blown up into a heroic saga of knighthood in full flower. The prosaic facts are that the Navarrese pounced on the rear guard of Charlemagne's army, caught in the pass in 778, and massacred them in revenge for an attack on Pamplona. However the *Song of Roland*, the first great French epic poem, rewrote this incident as a glorious struggle against

Fuenterrabía (Hondarribia)

The road signs now use the Basque name, **Hondarribia**, to identify this charming, picturesque and historic fishing port. All along the sea wall, the local amateurs cast their lines for whatever fish the trawlers may have missed. The best of the catch ends up in the cluster of Hondarribian fish restaurants, which can be found on the lively main street alongside some pleasant bars and cafés.

the Moors. Nonetheless, this all added a splash of glamour to Roncesvalles Pass, through which hordes of French pilgrims were to enter Spain on the hike to Santiago de Compostela. The village of Roncesvalles, just after the pass, is quite small and simple, the kind of place where a traveller was glad to settle for spartan lodging and a hot meal. In that respect not too much has changed over the centuries. For more sophisticated facilities, it is less than 50km (30 miles), all downhill, to the buoyant forward-looking capital of the kingdom of Navarre, Pamplona.

Pamplona (Iruña)

In the 1920s, Ernest Hemingway soaked up the atmosphere at the famous festival of **Pamplona** and immortalized it in *The Sun Also Rises* (published in Britain under the title *Fiesta*). Perhaps not knowing whether it was a good or bad thing to invite the world to the greatest street party in Spain, it took forty years for the locals to express their appreciation by erecting alongside the Pamplona bullring a bust of the bearded author, known locally as Don Ernesto. The street it stands on is named Paseo Hemingway.

The *encierro* or the 'running of the bulls' is Pamplona's trademark through-out the world, and is a perennial curiosity feature on the international television news. Perhaps the rest of the world enjoys seeing the bulls getting their revenge for the misery that is inflicted on them in the *corrida*. This is the best-known aspect of the feast of St Fermin, but there's much more, and if you can get to Pamplona in the second week of July (you must book well ahead and be prepared for double the usual prices) you're guaranteed some vivid experiences in exchange for your usual quota of sleep.

Pamplona is also good on a non-festive day. Its compact old centre is full of lively

*B*ull running at Pamplona: a quick bull can run the half-mile course in three minutes – few runners can match this!

restaurants and bars, many enjoyed by the trendy young university students who are much in evidence here, though you can easily escape them if you wish. The city's attractions are grouped tightly and it's a good place for walking.

Pamplona was founded by the Roman general Pompey the Great; *Pompeiopolis* evolving into Pamplona. Look in the elegant **Museo de Navarra**, which occupies a 16th-century hospital, for remnants of this period. There are some fine Roman mosaics and funerary relics, and interesting Romanesque and Gothic artefacts too.

The **cathedral** is a huge complex backing on to the ancient city wall; the defences have been integrated into a park. The overblown west façade went up in the 18th century, but the gloomy Gothic interior dates from the 14th and 15th centuries. Alongside, the beautiful Gothic **cloister** is a haven of sunshine and calm, with some notable sculpture.

Between the old and new parts of the city, Pamplona's main square, the **Plaza del Castillo**, is an attractive spot. There are shady trees, benches, a bandstand, plenty of space for promenading, and outdoor cafés along the edges.

As impressive as the cathedral is, however, the most extraordinary single building in town is the baroque **Ayuntamiento** (city hall), a glorious fantasy of frills, with statues of awesome giants on the roof and plenty of balconies for festive occasions.

'A DAMNED FINE SHOW'

These were the words of Ernest Hemingway describing the *encierro* (the running of the bulls), in Pamplona. Effectively it's a stampede through the main street down into the bullring. The crowd runs with the bulls trying to keep ahead of them, but often failing, although if anyone arrives in the ring well ahead they are jeered as cowards! It is said that you have to be young, brave, crazy or drunk to take part and many of the macho participants are all of these, even at 8am when the *encierro* is held. Tourists can and do take part but beware. It may 'seem like a good idea at the time', but people are maimed and killed quite regularly in this outbreak of ritualized lunacy.

It may be hard to believe, but there is another festival custom which makes the *encierro* look as safe as a Sunday morning stroll. Pamplona's other suicidal spectacle involves young locals throwing themselves off high buildings in the hope that their friends below will catch them. Sometimes they don't. Surely even Hemingway would have blanched at that.

Estella

Estella was a favourite stop for pilgrims hiking to Santiago de Compostela, and their legacy is an unspoiled mediaeval town of beautiful Romanesque structures.

During the 11th century, thanks to another one of those miraculous discoveries of a holy image, Estella was built at a bend in the Río Ega. The site adds much to the beauty of the town (nicknamed 'Estella la Bella') and you will probably see horses grazing along the river banks. Don't try to drive across the pretty **Puente de la Cárcel** (Floodgate Bridge). It's so steeply humpbacked that it will gouge the bottom right out of your car.

In **Plaza de San Martin** is the regional tourist office, enviably ensconced in a 12th-century palace. There's no entry, but you can get a good look at the splendid exterior from the top of the steps of the church of **San Pedro de la Rúa** (St Peter of the Road – the 'road' being the Way of St James). This has a most unusual portal, with a scalloped arch and elements influenced by both the Moors and the

Cistercians. Have a look at the remains of its Romanesque **cloister**. Half of it went up in smoke in a 16th-century explosion at the castle next door, but the surviving sculpture on the capitals of the columns is worthy of detailed examination.

Another extraordinary church here is the unfinished **Iglesia del Santo Sepulcro** (Church of the Holy Sepulchre), which boasts a superlative Gothic portal.

Across the river, don't miss the church of **San Miguel Arcangel**. Its portal is chock-a-block with biblical scenes and characters, carved to inspire the pilgrims on their way. The hilltop church of **Santa María Jus del Castillo**, is a reminder of less glorious religious times. It was was a synagogue before a mediaeval pogrom scarred Estella.

Estella is not cocooned in its magnificent mediaeval architecture, however. It really comes alive in August, when they hold their own *encierro* here. And, just to show they are more sexually liberated than their Pamplona neighbours, women as well as men run with the bulls.

A couple of kilometres south of Estella, the **monasterio de Irache**, another important stop on the pilgrim way, once contained a university. Its big 12th-century church looks fit enough to stand for another eight centuries. Take a look at its 'new' and 'old' cloisters; the latter boasts some fine plateresque details. If you need physical as well as spiritual refreshment, pop into the monastery's wine museum and try the Navarre *rosado* that was such a favourite with Hemingway.

Olite

This charming small mediaeval town is for the most part unspoiled, and careful restoration is bringing it back to a pristine state. You can't miss the local palace, the **Palacio Real**, a splendid royal castle with turrets, pinnacles and crenellations, right in the middle of town. The kings of Navarre lived here in the Middle Ages, until their realm was swallowed up by Castile. Nowadays, part of the castle houses a *parador*.

Alongside the rambling palace, and actually a part of it, the **Iglesia de Santa María**, begun in the 13th century, served as a royal chapel. Its sculpted portal is a distinguished example of Navarre Gothic. A few kilometres south east of Olite is **La Oliva**.

This was an early Cistercian monastery renowned for its architecture and the size and scope of its library. Of special interest is the **portal**, with some pleasing Romanesque sculptural details. The Gothic cloister is perfectly proportioned.

Tudela

You can see the soaring tower of **Tudela**'s cathedral from miles away, yet once inside the labyrinth of narrow streets you may end up having to ask directions to it. Built soon after the Reconquest on the ruins of a mosque, the **cathedral** is a 12th- and 13th-century classic of the earliest Gothic style. There are three monumental **portals**, the most dramatic facing west and devoted, with terrifying detail, to the Last Judgement. Among the highlights inside is the **Capilla de Santa Ana** (St Anne's Chapel), a baroque spree with flights of angels all the way up the walls to the top of the chapel's dome. The chapel holds the Gothic statue of Tudela's patron saint, which figures in the local festival on 26 July. Don't miss the Romanesque **cloister.**

Sanguesa

The ancient town of **Sanguesa** guards a crucial bridge across the Río Aragón, much disputed during the struggle against the Moors and later a crossing point on the Pilgrims' Way.

There are many handsome mediaeval buildings in the town, but the *pièce de résistance* is the church of **Santa María la Real**, built up against the river, right by the bridge. At the outset, in the 12th century, it was a royal chapel. Its south **portal** is a wonder of stone carving, and its remarkable rendition of the Last Judgement and other holy scenes seems determined to set a record for the number of figures sculpted per square foot.

Leyre

The mountain setting of **Leyre** monastery is inspirational, yet it remains quite accessible to visitors. A well-paved road climbs from the main Pamplona–Huesca road to the monastery, perched between Pyrenean cliffs and the Yesa reservoir far below. During the 11th century, Leyre was the religious powerhouse of all Navarre.

The venerable **church** retains its original Romanesque arches and the west **portal** is lavishly carved, hence its Latin nickname, *Porta Speciosa* ('Splendid Doorway'). The sculptural repertoire here consists of saintly figures interspersed with a nightmarish parade of monsters. If you can, stay for the Evensong Gregorian Chant, which is an atmospheric treat.

Northern Aragon

The sparsely settled mountains and valleys of northern Aragon compensate for their isolation with striking scenery and regal history. Here began the mediaeval kingdom of Aragon, which grew to hold sway as far afield as the Mediterranean. Aragon was a key factor in what became the

---

THE PYRENEES PEAK IN ARAGON

The tallest peaks of all the Pyrenees belong to Aragon, most pointedly the Pico de Aneto, at 3,404m (11,169ft). Not for nothing is this called the *Maladeta* ('Accursed') region. Only an accomplished mountain climber could love these dangerous summits. They may be very poetic when seen from afar, but you can always start a snow-slide here, even in midsummer.

Snow is a great attraction, however, and the Pyrenees of Aragon are equipped with international ski resorts like Astún, Candanchú and Formigal. This high above sea level, nobody could doubt that Spain is Europe's second most mountainous country (topped only by Switzerland).

---

mighty realm of Castile. This really is 'undiscovered Spain', and (with the exception of the Ordesa National Park) foreign tourists are few and far between.

Sos del Rey Católico

Ferdinand of Aragon, destined to become King Ferdinand the Catholic, ruler of all Spain, was born in this hilltop village in 1452. Today **Sos del Rey Católico** is all spruced up in his honour. This is definitely a village for walking; if you drive you will not only lose your way (the quaint, narrow streets tend to be unnamed), but you will probably have to back out after a long, twisting adventure into a dead-end.

The population today is less than a thousand, but the church of **San Esteban** (St Stephen) is big enough for a congregation twice the size. Here is preserved the font in which the future king was baptized. Have a look at the spooky **crypt**, reached down a tight spiral staircase. Back up top, enjoy the **view** over the soft, furrowed green hills surrounding the charming old village.

In the foothills of the Pyrenees in Upper Aragon, a shepherd looks after his far-flung flock. Since time immemorial the livestock has been kept on the move, changing altitude with the season to avoid climatic extremes and to find the richest pastures.

Jaca

Gateway to the Aragon Pyrenees and an old stop on the Pilgrim Way, **Jaca** has been fraught with military significance for at least a dozen centuries, ever since it figured in one of the earliest victories over the Moors. The enormous, low-lying 16th-century **fortress** at the edge of town is a symbol of its former strategic importance.

Jaca's other notable monument is its **cathedral**, which dates from the 11th

surviving in the Pyrenees. The dramatic canyon of the Ordesa valley has been a national park for more than 70 years, and its aficionados claim it to be one of the best-kept secrets in Europe. Its a little bit of the Grand Canyon, a little bit of Victoria Falls and certainly one of Europe's greatest natural wonders. The canyon walls are almost 1,000m (3,250ft) high, dwarfing the forests of ancient beech, silver fir and mountain pine far below. You can enjoy the canyon from the comfort of your car but you will get so much more from the experience if you have your hiking boots with you.

The tourist office and local shops have maps of suggested walking tours requiring varying degrees of energy and proficiency, but anyone can enjoy the general park atmosphere. Note that during the summer the park can become quite busy, but snow cuts off access completely from about October to April.

Huesca

The 'H' in **Huesca** is silent, and so is the legendary bell. An old Spanish saying describes bad news as resounding like 'the bell of Huesca'. The story behind it tells of the 12th-century king, Ramiro II, who invited rebellious nobles to see a great bell cast, seizing the occasion to behead them. News of the 'bell' incident soon reverberated throughout Aragon and beyond.

A century or so after the alleged bell affair, construction began on the stately **cathedral** of Huesca, on the site of a Roman temple and a Muslim mosque. The Gothic **façade** is divided into upper and lower halves by an unusual little projecting roof. There are three ample naves, and the alabaster **altarpiece** is a splendid 16th-century carving by Damián Forment, who was based in Zaragoza.

century and is one of the oldest in Spain. Look out for its fine Romanesque frescoes, as well as afterthoughts like Renaissance sculpture and a plateresque retable.

Ordesa National Park

Graceful Pyrenean chamois perch on the cliffs here. So do wild goat, roe deer, wild boar and the only ibex (a handsome mountain goat with back-curved horns)

The Valle de Arazas, the main valley of the Ordesa National Park.

Across the calm square is the Renaissance **Ayuntamiento** (town hall), with corner towers and a patio, altogether a most impressive place to go to pay your taxes. A 19th-century painting here illustrates the story of the bell of Huesca in vivid detail (you may have to ask to see it). You can even tread in the footsteps of the victims as the old palace room where unlucky nobles lost their heads is now the **Museo Provincial**. This houses a good collection of early local paintings.

Ramiro II is buried in the church of **San Pedro el Viejo**; a coin-operated lighting system reveals the sepulchres of the king and his brother, Alfonso I. The Romanesque **cloister** has been much restored, and so too have most of the fine carvings on the capitals; unfortunately they have been redone like new, and are too perfect to be true.

Some of Spain's most breathtaking scenery lies just a few miles north of Huesca. Huge pink sandstone sugar-loaf cliffs, known as **Los Mallos**, rise vertically above the tiny village of Riglos in the foothills of the Pyrenees, dwarfing man's attempt to colonize this hostile terrain. You can catch the train to Riglos, so even car-less travellers can enjoy the spectacular landscape.

Zaragoza

The unusual name, precipitating a double lisp in Spanish (pronounced thar-a-GO-tha), can be traced back to before 24 BC, when an ancient Iberian settlement named Sálduta stood here. Around this time it fell to the Romans, became a colony under Augustus Caesar, and was called *Caesaraugusta*. The Moors captured the town very early in the 8th century and pronounced it Saraqustah. From there, it is (almost) an effortless evolution to **Zaragoza** (Saragossa in English), which is how the town was re-named after its Reconquest in 1118 by Alfonso I.

Zaragoza is the capital and one big town of the region, and in fact is the fifth-largest town in the country. It's a mixed place of broad stylish avenues and attractive streets displaying *Art Nouveau* touches, alongside unpleasant slums. Much of the old town is undergoing restoration.

The River Ebro, refreshed by mountain streams, is at its best here, more than half-way from its origin in the Cantabrian mountains to its outlet in the Mediterranean. The Romans built the first bridge; the present **Puente de Piedra** (Stone Bridge) was revived after its demolition at the hands of Napoleon's troops and shows elements of Mudéjar, French, Italian and baroque architecture.

Backing on to the Ebro is Zaragoza's favourite church, one of two cathedrals on its skyline. The basilica of **Nuestra Señora del Pilar** (Our Lady of the Pillar) contains a small Gothic statue of Spain's patron saint. The cathedral is vast and bright and always packed with pilgrims. According to tradition the Virgin Mary appeared here in AD 40, standing on a pillar, and the cathedral was built in the 17th century around the jasper column in question.

Pilgrims queue up to kiss the pillar, which is housed in the elaborate **Capilla de Pilar**. The cathedral's main **retable**, as big as the side of a barn, is the greatest work of the sculptor Damián Forment. It looks intricate enough to have taken a lifetime.

The **Plaza del Pilar** has recently had a face-lift and been expanded to become the largest square in all Spain, and one of the largest squares in Europe. Fountains and floodlights have been added, including a row of 15m (50ft) high lights which

The many towers and domes of the basilica of Nuestra Señora del Pilar in Zaragoza – Spain's second most important place of pilgrimage.

illuminate the basilica so brightly that it becomes a beacon from almost 32km (20 miles) away. Try approaching the city from Barcelona by night and you will be amazed by the sight! The plaza is home to religious souvenir shops (selling all sizes of statuettes of the revered image, with or without lights) and outdoor cafés.

Just off the plaza, the Aragon tourist office occupies the Zuda tower, a 14th-century Mudéjar relic between the Roman wall Nuestra Señora de Pilar (the municipal tourist office, across the square from the basilica, uses a mock Roman temple).

Zaragoza's other cathedral, **La Seo**, was built hundreds of years earlier, on the site of a mosque. Construction, in brick, lasted from the 12th to the 16th centuries; the architecture is mainly Gothic but there are Romanesque remnants as well as striking Mudéjar decorations and baroque postscripts. The belfry is a 17th-century addition, chiming in with the look of the towers on the Pilar church, a couple of hundred metres to the west. Inside is one of the finest **tapestry** collections in Spain.

Another fine collection is being developed in front of the cathedral. In 1988, workmen stumbled on the site of the 3rd-century Forum of Caesaraugusta, and this has opened recently as a large *in situ* archaeological museum showing remains of the Forum's temple, homes, shops and offices, plus assorted statuary, ceramics and general artefacts.

*T*he Aragonese
countryside around Zaragoza is in
places harsh, unyielding and
spectacular, as typified by this
eroded sandstone stack.

FROM ZARAGOZA TO THE NEW WORLD

A pilgrimage to Zaragoza is the second most devout journey in Spain after the journey to Santiago de Compostela. By legend the Virgen del Pilar appeared to Santiago (St James) on 2 October AD 40. How the date can be so precisely measured is almost as mysterious as the legend itself, but suffice to say it sets off 10 days of festivities which culminate on 12 October. This is a double landmark date as not only is it the Virgin del Pilar's day, but it is also the day when Columbus set foot in the New World, and is celebrated throughout Spain as the *Día de la Hispanidad*. To complete the local connection, Columbus actually took a piece of the Zaragoza *pilar* on his voyage as a good-luck charm.

Between the two cathedrals stands Zaragoza's most imposing civil structure, a Renaissance palace that served as the 16th-century equivalent of a stock exchange. **La Lonja** (the Exchange) brought commercial traders in from the cold. They made their deals in a most palatial triple-naved trading room, which is only open to the public on special occasions.

The Moors' most lasting bequest to Zaragoza, the **Aljafería**, looks from the outside like a rendering of an ambitious child's sand-castle. When you cross the moat (now a sunken garden) you enter a world of Muslim Spain rarely seen this far north. After the Reconquest, the pleasure palace of the Moorish rulers was much tampered with, but it is now splendidly restored, with delicately filigreed arches and panelled ceilings. There are even lemon trees planted around the reflecting pools in the patio.

Homage to Catalonia

Catalonia is different from the rest of the country. Whereas southern Spain was historically influenced by the Moors, this northern part has always looked towards the rest of Europe. Andalusians may dance the fiery flamenco, but Catalonians hold hands in a circle for the stately measured *sardana*. This is a strongly independent region, and wherever you go you will find evidence of the Catalonian separatist movement. Don't be surprised by the language – most locals prefer to speak Catalan rather than the Castilian Spanish that Franco tried to impose.

Spanish traditions mean less here; the siesta is largely eschewed in favour of work, or an active lunch-break; menfolk are less macho than their southern brothers; women are now entering the professions; bullfighting is not a Catalonian pastime. But be in no doubt as to the passion of the people – attend any fiesta, talk to them about Catalan history, or food, or just watch a Barcelona football match in a crowded bar.

Catalonia is a large, autonomous (although not independent) part of Spain

The entrance to the monumental monastery at Poblet, one of Catalonia's two great working religious fraternities.

which stretches north to the French border and far west across the Pyrenees. This dynamic region of 6 million people has its own history, tradition, folklore and language. (Its name is Catalunya in Catalan, Cataluña in Spanish.)

The major metropolis of Catalonia is, of course, the booming, fashionable city of Barcelona. It's not only good to visit, it also produces almost 20 per cent of Spain's industrial output.

The other major city in Catalonia is Tarragona, relatively unknown to international tourism, but well worth a day or two for its rich Roman legacy. Sitges is the most complete resort on the Costa Dorada coast, while inland the mountains offer wonderful natural scenery in the Pyrenees and the great monasteries of Montserrat, Poblet and Santes Creus.

Northern Catalonia

The Pyrenees of Catalonia

The rugged peaks of the Pyrenees over-shadow more than just the pine forests, waterfalls and glacial lakes of a most picturesque countryside. History marks this scene with charming old hamlets, Romanesque churches and monasteries.

For raw scenery, the natural place to go is the **Parque Nacional d'Aigües Tortes y San Mauricio**, a national park measuring over 100 km² (nearly 40 square miles)

Snow-capped peaks exceeding 3,000m (9,850ft) serrate the skyline. Chamois, ibex and wild boar frequent these wide open spaces, but you will need a four-wheel-drive vehicle to penetrate the park. After that, comfortable hiking shoes are essential.

Seo de Urgel (La Seu d'Urgell)

Just across the frontier from Andorra, the small town of **Seo de Urgel** is a tourist centre with a glorious history going back to the days of the Romans. Since the 13th century the local bishop has been the co-ruler of Andorra.

The 12th-century cathedral of **Santa María**, built under Lombard influence, stands on the site of earlier churches going back to the 4th century. The diocesan Museum keeps on show an illuminated manuscript of great importance and beauty – a 10th- or 11th-century copy of *Commentary on the Apocalypse* by the 8th-century monk, Beatus of Liébana. It's a vivid, dream-like illustration full of action.

Ripoll (El Ripollès)

Wilfred the Hairy, Catalonia's first hero, who died in battle in AD 878, is buried in the royal pantheon of **Ripoll**'s ancient Benedictine **monastery**. Built in the shape of a cross, the monastery has five aisles and a transept with seven apses. The 12th-century **portal** and adjacent wall space are sculpted into a sort of storyboard of the Bible, illustrating *Old* and *New Testament* dramas. The **cloister**, from the same era, also features important stone carving. The district of Ripoll is said to contain more than 60 Catalan Romanesque churches.

Central Catalonia

Lérida (Lleida)

The province of Lérida stretches from the snows of the Pyrenees to rolling grazing land and orchards. The capital city, also called **Lérida**, is safely in the sunny south.

The Iberians settled here, and the Romans fought over the town. The Moors moved in early in the 8th century and held Lérida for more than 400 years. You can see the Moorish influence in the **Seu Vella** (Old Cathedral), built on a promontory at the beginning of the 13th century. The **cloister**, somewhat oddly placed in front of the church, has unusual dimensions and

---

ANDORRA: SHANGRI-LA IN THE PYRENEES

The tiny principality of Andorra hasn't got an army, an airport, a railway station, nor even a currency to call its own: Spanish pesetas and French francs are equally valid here. They do have border posts, though, so take your passport.

After seven centuries of fiercely defended independence, power is shared equally, and with no visible strain, by the president of France and the bishop of Urgel, just across the border in Spain.

Andorra is the world's only country whose official language is Catalan. Spanish and French are almost universally understood, while English and German are spoken in the shops. It's all very cosmopolitan.

Since Andorra is free of the taxes afflicting neighbouring countries, the price of many things, especially imported luxury goods, is lower than in France or Spain, so every year, millions of shoppers cross the Pyrenees to the bulging **shops** of Carrer Meritxell, the main street of the capital, Andorra-la-Vella. Here they splurge on cut-price whisky, cheap perfume and electronic gadgets. Beware, however, as not everything is a bargain compared with prices at home. Furthermore, you may be subject to taxes and duties at the vigilantly patrolled border. Until well into the 20th century, Andorra was a lonely shepherd's domain, all but inaccessible to the outside world. Now it shares Europe's traffic problems.

It may seem a shame that Andorra's spectacular **scenery** takes second place to the scrum of bargain hunting, but if you are in search of solitude, perhaps this is to your advantage. Many villages boast fine old **Romanesque churches** and the countryside is as invigorating as it is rugged. Andorra's other claim to fame lies in its well-equipped **winter sports** resorts.

fascinating sculptural effects. Overlooking the city is the mediaeval Arab fortress of the **Zuda**. The castle suffered many misfortunes, most recently in the Civil War, but the surviving defensive walls and towers give a good idea of its one-time importance.

Montserrat

For 700 years, pilgrims have been climbing the mighty rock formation to the monastery of **Montserrat**. Now that donkeys and foot power have been replaced by cable cars and excursion coaches, around 1 million people every year make the trip to the spiritual heart of Catalonia.

There have been hermitages here since mediaeval times, possibly established to escape the Moorish invasion. One such hermitage was enlarged to become a Benedictine monastery and in the 12th

century it became the repository of a small brown statue of the Virgin Mary, known as **La Moreneta** ('the little dark madonna'). According to legend, this had been made by St Luke and brought to Barcelona by St Peter. La Moreneta was adopted as the patron saint of Catalonia and pilgrims, from commoners to kings, have come to worship her ever since.

The original monastery was destroyed by Napoleon's troops in 1808 and the present one dates from 1874. However, Montserrat is very much a living, working monastery and public entrance is only allowed into the basilica and museum. A highlight of any visit is the famous **Escolania choir**, who sing angelically

The monastery at Montserrat huddles beneath the eroded, serrated mountains which give it protection as well as its name.

La Moreneta (the little black Madonna) is the most revered religious icon in Catalonia; be prepared for lengthy queues to see her.

every day at 1pm. The monastery also boasts a good **museum**, with works of art by such masters as Carravagio, El Greco and Picasso; a fine collection of modern Catalan paintings; and a number of archaeological treasures from the biblical orient, including Egyptian mummies. Look out for the beautiful Gothic cloistered section next door.

Complaints are frequently voiced about the commercialization of the monastery grounds, and souvenir stalls do proliferate alongside a hotel and restaurants. If Montserrat disappoints the religious soul, its magnificent setting in beautiful protected **mountain parkland** provides inspiration to the most wooden of hearts.

There is only one way to arrive here in style, and that's by cable-car. The terminal is on the C1411 Barcelona–Manresa road. Join the queue, then it's up and away, over 1,000m (3,280ft) to the mountain top, probably breaking through the clouds en route. The **view** of the mountains, which certainly live up to their name (*montserrat* means 'serrated' or 'sawtoothed' mountain) is magical.

Poblet

When you've seen one monastery, you have definitely not seen them all. The mediaeval fortress-monastery of **Poblet** contrasts sharply with Montserrat.

For a start, few tourists crowd Poblet, even though it is the largest and best preserved Cistercian monastery in Europe. While Montserrat clings to its granite eyrie, Poblet sprawls upon a green open plateau amid fertile hillsides, and while both have been ruthlessly plundered, Montserrat is only a structural replica of its former glory; Poblet is as close to its original mediaeval state as is possible.

Poblet was founded in 1151 by the Count of Barcelona, Ramón Berenguer IV, as a gesture of thanksgiving for the reconquest of Catalonia from the Moors. Continuous royal patronage brought the monastery fame, fortune and historical importance. The ultimate accolade of royal pantheon was bestowed by Peter the Ceremonious in the 14th century. He and seven other kings of Aragon are interred here in a unique style of **tombs** which are suspended on low arches in the cross vault of the church. Only fragments of the original tomb sculptures were preserved, so the carvings of today are skilled reproductions, but still very impressive.

As you enter into the grounds, the **front** of the monastery is a majestic sight. Its towers, belfrys, lanterns and walls are as imposing as any castle. Poblet is still a working monastery, so you are not allowed to wander at will. A guided tour takes you past the vaulted wine cellars, the library, chapter house, refectory and into the great Gothic-Romanesque church. The latter is big, airy and, in accordance with the Cistercian way of life, shuns ornamentation.

Perhaps the real appreciation of the monastic mood comes in the **cloister**. This, too, is large and atmospheric, with four brooding poplars and a rose garden. Only the trickle of water and birdsong disturbs the serenity. At one time around 200 monks lived and worked here. Today there are around 30 of them.

Santes Creus

About 40km (25 miles) from Poblet, another great monastery sprawls among the vineyards. The Cistercian foundation of **Santes Creus** (holy crosses) was founded just six years after Poblet in 1157. Comparisons with Poblet are obvious. Santes Creus is much smaller and less grand, but even within the shadow of its bigger and more famous brother it is still an architectural masterpiece. The cloisters are once again a highlight (here there are two). The Great Cloister is classic Catalan Gothic, dating from the 14th century, and includes some uncharacteristically light-hearted touches. Look out for heraldic designs, animals and humorous faces carved on the arches and walls. The Infirmary cloister is quite plain and very peaceful.

There is a superb vaulted **chapter house** with tombs of 16th-century abbots set into the floor and, upstairs, a spacious dormitory with a large timber-arched roof.

Santes Creus was the royal resting place before the honour passed to Poblet, and two kings are buried here. Peter the Great (Pere II or Pedro el Grande, died 1285) lies in a splendid **Gothic tabernacle** and close by is the beautifully sculpted tomb of Peter's son, James the Just (died 1327).

Santes Creus also reveals its regal connections with the remains of the living quarters known as the **Royal Palace**, built by order of Peter II. These surround a perfect 14th-century patio of delicate arches and a lovely staircase.

The monastery was disbanded in 1835 and subsequently pillaged, but unlike Poblet, did not arise again. Instead, it became a parish church and was recently taken over by the state.

Vich (Vic)

Vich rhymes with rich; and it's doing very well as a bustling market town surrounded by farm country.

An indication of the grandeur of the original **cathedral**, founded in the 11th century, is its seven-storey Romanesque belfry. The cathedral was rebuilt in neoclassical style at the end of the 18th century. In the 20th century a leading Catalan painter, Jose Maria Sert y Badía, covered its walls with powerful **murals**. (Among Sert's other major commissions were murals for the Waldorf Astoria Hotel in New York.) During the Civil War the church was sacked and burned but Sert was able to return to redo his greatest work, which was all but finished before he died in 1945. He is buried in the cathedral.

The cathedral also boasts an excellent **Museu diocesa**, which claims to hold the best collection of Romanesque Art outside Barcelona. Food fans know Vich for its delicious local sausages, which you will see in butchers' shop windows around the old town.

Gerona (Girona)

The Iberians built a fortified city on **Gerona**'s hilltop, and over the next couple of thousand years it was coveted and assaulted by invaders of many sorts – Romans, Visigoths, Moors, Franks and so forth. Thus its odd nickname, 'City of Sieges'. The area's latest invaders, however, hordes of tourists who alight here for the Costa Brava, generally choose to leave the town alone, and head off instead to their coastal destinations. Although it is some 30km (20 miles) inland from the Mediterranean, the capital of Gerona province is, by extension, the capital of the Costa Brava.

It's a good town for simply wandering around. You can feel its mood best by strolling along the banks of the Río Oñar (Riu Onyar), which bisects the town, then up into the narrow streets of the old town. The most typical street of mediaeval Gerona is the beautifully preserved and quite steep **Carrer de la Força**, once the heart of the old Jewish quarter. It climbs to the base of the hill, climaxed by the Gothic **cathedral**, more than 90 ceremonial steps above. This cathedral represents a remarkable feat of mediaeval architecture: its single nave, said to be the widest in the world at 22m (72ft), creates an immense vault, like a precocious design for an aircraft hangar. The alabaster high altar has served the church since its consecration in 1038.

The cathedral's **treasury** (the Museu Capitular) is chock-a-block with precious articles. Do look in, even if this type of collection does not ordinarily appeal to you. There are gold and silver monstrances, rare illuminated manuscripts, a statue of Charlemagne, and a unique **tapestry** from the 12th century. In a room of its own, the *Tapestry of the Creation* summarized the Bible for illiterate church-goers, explaining everything, in logical order, from Adam and Eve to the winds and the months. The **cloister** features some delightful *Old Testament* sculptures.

Close by, on Carrer Ferràn el Catolic, are the 12th-century **Banys Arabs** (Arab Baths). These are the best preserved in Spain after Granada, and you can visit several of the rooms, which display both Roman and Moorish influences.

Figueras (Figueres)

The second-biggest town in Gerona province, otherwise undistinguished, happens to contain the second most visited museum in all Spain (after the Prado). The **Teatre-Museu Dalí** is just the sort of witty, surreal museum you would expect in the birthplace of Salvador Dalí. In and out of the museum, piles of truck tyres stand as solemn columns; you can't get much more iconoclastic than that.

In a typically outrageous Dalí plan, they gutted the very proper municipal theatre and put surreal sculptures on stage and in the loges. An ancient Cadillac parked in the patio supports a statue of a gilt-breasted Amazon. Giant representations of hens' eggs stand on the battlements, the roof line topped by a geodesic dome.

It's great fun, impossible to describe and the perfect antidote to the surfeit of 'serious' art on display in the vast majority of galleries. See Dalí's version of the Sistine Chapel, walk into a room arranged in the shape of the face of Mae West (her lips are a great red voluptuous sofa) and much more. Shocks and jokes aside, however, the institution contains a very good cross-section of Dalí's work; even the most sceptical come away admitting he was a genius.

A couple of hundred metres down the hill, the **Museu de l'Empordà** includes

*D*alí was so prolific that he might well have had six hands! A typically off-the-wall portrait, taken in 1955.

*Y*ou don't have to go to the Dalí museum to be shocked in Figueres. The surrealist master was born here in 1904 and attracts innumerable tourists yearly.

*C*alella de Palafrugell, a pretty resort on the Costa Brava near Gerona (pages 196-7).

an eye-opening collection of Greek and Roman vases, statues and implements unearthed by archaeologists in the region. Just opposite the museum, a statue honours the man who was the greatest local hero until Dalí came along. He was Narciso Monturiol (1819-85), the designer of a pioneering six-man submarine.

Costa Brava

The *brava* in Costa Brava was coined in 1908 by the Catalan poet, Ferran Agulló, to sum up Spain's north-easternmost coast. It has several meanings – wild, savage, craggy, stormy and steep. It hardly sounds conducive to sun and sand holidays for the masses, yet this is a fitting adjective to this 214km (133-mile) stretch of cliffs, coves and beaches. That intrepid explorer, Rose McCauley, captured it exactly when she described it in the late 1940s as 'Cornwall with sunshine'.

With France just across the border, a wonderful climate and such striking scenery, this was the first part of Spain's Mediterranean shore to achieve international fame. Since its discovery early in the 20th century, wrenching changes have occurred all along the Gerona coast. The Costa Brava became the birthplace of package tourism in the early 1960s, and soon bustling modern resorts were brushing aside indigenous fishing villages. Thankfully, that kind of thoughtless tourism development seems to have had its day. Avoid the overdeveloped concrete resorts of the south and you can still find some charming, authentically Spanish places along this beautiful coast.

Sant Pere de Roda

This is as good a place as any to appreciate the savage beauty of the Costa Brava's rugged coastline. The 10th-century fortified monastery of **Sant Pere de Roda** was once the most influential religious centre in the region. Nowadays only ruins remain, but the climb to the top of Mount Vedera is worth it for the view. You can see for kilometre after kilometre from here. It's an energetic hike from bottom to top, but you can drive most of the way there, then walk for some 15 minutes to the summit.

Cadaqués

Cadaqués is the whitewashed fishermen's village everyone has dreamed of, the sort of place where you could settle in, breathe the sea air, and become a great artist. Which is almost exactly what Salvador Dalí did. In 1929 he moved into a one-roomed fisherman's house on the edge of Cadaqués at Port Lligat. Cadaqués is the place where he held court and it now draws a very chic crowd, hoping perhaps that some of that Dalí magic will rub off. It has become a great place for people-watching, but it is also relatively expensive and crowded in season. Despite this, Cadaqués remains a working fishing village, and still inspires painters.

HAND IN HAND IN CATALONIA

The most famous Catalan folklore expression is the dance known as the *sardana*. To the outsider this seems a sedate, even dull affair, but to the Catalans it evokes an uncommon degree of participation and a literal bonding between people of all ages.

A group join together in a circle, hold their hands high and to a musical accompaniment, alternate between slow, thoughtful steps and medium-tempo bouncy kicking. It's not really a spectator sport, so once you think you know roughly what is going on, break into the circle (don't get in between a man and the woman to his right) and follow the dancers' example. Each *sardana* lasts for around ten minutes. The band is traditionally an 11-piece ensemble, often made up of rather crusty-looking old men who look as though they have been dusted off and brought out specially for the occasion. *Sardanas* are danced at festivals, parties, family gatherings or simply because it's the weekend.

You can see some modern masters in the **Perrot-Moore Museum** (founded by Dalí's ex-secretary) and this is often referred to as an appetizer for the feast in Figueres. The local Museu d'Art also includes works by household names.

The long, eventful history of Cadaqués, marked in particular by pirate attacks, has added to the reputation of the local people as indomitable, self-assured and independent (and also the coast's most skilful smugglers). The old church was burned down by the infamous Barbary pirate Barbarossa in 1543. The replacement, built in the 17th century, has a rich baroque altarpiece by Pau Costa.

About the only thing missing in Cadaqués is a good beach, but perhaps that is also its saving grace.

Rosas (*Roses*)

From **Rosas** south, the character of the coastline softens from cliffs that look as if they were dynamited from the mountainside to gently sloping, sandy beaches. It proved just too irresistible from the point of view of tourism development, and now holds dozens of high-rise blocks.

Thanks to the contortions of the coast's geography, the **port** of Rosas faces due west; sunset-lovers gather here for the best end-of-the-day spectacle on the whole coast. Add to this vista the sight of the local fishing fleet returning from a day on the high seas and you have a perfect picture-postcard scene.

Ampurias (Empúries)

Ampurias was built by the Greeks, improved by the Iberians and then greatly expanded by the Romans. What makes it so interesting (aside from the unusual presence of Greek remains) is that the site was continuously occupied for some 1,500

years and therefore provides a rich legacy to sift through. Archaeology buffs will enjoy an hour wandering through the digs of Ampurias – the **remains** of villas, temples, baths, and the old market-places. Non-enthusiasts will be content to view the sea from the vantage point of the lovely Roman-style landscaping.

The ancient settlement was only remembered in local legend and the buried treasures were not revealed until early in the 20th century. The most sensational find was a larger-than-life **statue** of Asclepius, the Greek god of medicine, sculpted in marble from an Athenian quarry. The original has been moved to the Barcelona Archaeological Museum, but a copy stands in its place in the ruined temple. Another copy is in the **museum** right on the site, which exhibits most of the local discoveries – ceramics, jewels, household items, weapons, mosaics and statues rescued from centuries of oblivion. Outside the museum, still intact on the mosaic floor, is the touching Greek inscription 'Sweet Dreams' which has survived the ravages of time and invasions. Note that 'Ampurias' figures in a number of place names along the Costa Brava – it meant 'trading post'). If you are driving, look for L'Escala, the nearest resort, and then the signs for the '*Ruinas*'.

Palamós

In 1299, the Catalonian fleet set out from here to conquer Sicily. Today the **Palamós** fleet casts off at dawn and returns in time for the 5 o'clock auction in La Llotja, the Exchange. With warships gone, the lovely bay is now shared by local fishermen and holiday-makers. The heart of the high-rise resort remains the inner beach of the port, where fishermen and their wives still mend their nets by hand.

Tossa de Mar

In dramatic cliff country south of Bagur, **Tossa** was an artists' colony before it became a fully developed international tourist resort. Despite its dubious claim to being the first package resort and its proximity to the overblown (and eminently avoidable) Lloret de Mar, Tossa remains a surprisingly attractive spot.

The brooding 12th-century walls and three great towers that defend the **Vila Vella** (the old town) have not only been spared the bulldozers and concrete mixers of the developers, they don't even have to compete for the skyscape. Here old and new co-exist quite happily. Paintings by Marc Chagall (who called Tossa 'Blue Paradise') and other artists who frequented the town, hang in the local museum.

Blanes

At the southern border of the Costa Brava, **Blanes** is a prosperous centre of farming, industry and fishing; tourism does exist but is generally understated. Blanes' greatest assets are the wild beauty of the cliffs, and its **Marimurtra** botanical gardens, with more than 3,000 species of trees, shrubs and flowers.

Barcelona

Barcelona is a sophisticated city where the creative energy of modern Europe and the relaxed pleasures of the Mediterranean meet in happy union. It may only be Spain's second city, but it is very definitely a capital, though now of a culture, rather than a country.

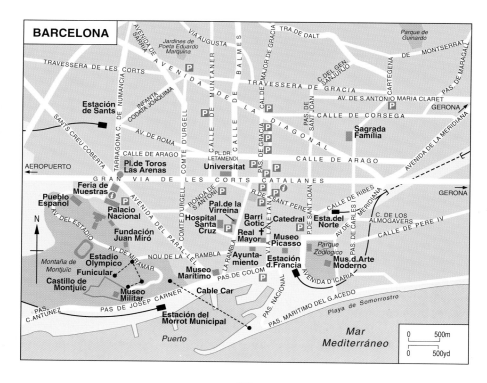

Go straight to the famous Ramblas, half promenade and half bazaar, to get into the feeling of the city. Barcelona avenues are broad and leafy, with plazas, statues and fountains at the main intersections. Few skyscrapers destroy the human scale of the city profile. The buildings which impress are usually banks, almost as numerous as bars, and a reminder that for all its southern European flair, this is a city of big business.

If you only have a couple of days to see the city, or if you want an easy introduction without the restrictions of a tour coach, then jump aboard the **Bus Turistic** (mid-June to September only). This is an excellent hop-on, hop-off service which circles around all the most interesting parts of the city. Buses turn up regularly, so once you have seen a sight and you're ready to move on, another bus will soon be along. As a bonus, the bus fare also gives you free cable-car, funicular and tram rides and discounts on admission to

several attractions. Pick up a leaflet from any tourist office.

La Rambla

The start of La Rambla is marked by the statue of Christopher Columbus, on top of his 50m (164ft) **Monument a Colom**. On this famous street there is a bustle and energy unmatched almost anywhere else in Europe. Resist the temptation for just a while and look out over the waterfront.

A replica of the **Santa María**, Columbus's flagship, is berthed by the fleet of pleasure boats that tour the harbour, and you can clamber aboard them all. There is

*V*iew down La Rambla *from near Plaça de Catalunya. The name derives not from the multitude who 'ramble' here but from the Arabic word for dry river bed.*

a cable-car which flies above the harbour to the characterful dockside area of **La Barceloneta**, famed for its fish restaurants. If you are interested in seafaring history, don't miss the **Museu Marítim** (next to the Monument a Colom), which charts over seven centuries of shipbuilding in Barcelona.

La Rambla stretches nearly 2km (1 mile) up a gentle incline to the city's hub, the **Plaça de Catalunya**. It changes name seamlessly five times, though you will notice the character and denizens do alter throughout. The lower stretches are the seediest and the Barri Xino (Chinatown), to the left, is best avoided, especially at night. A little further along and just off the Rambla is the **Palau Güell**, the splendid fortress-like mansion Gaudí built in 1885 for his patron.

On the opposite side of La Rambla is the handsome but decayed **Plaça Reial**. Until recently, this arcaded square was a notorious haunt of low-lifers, but now it is regaining its past fashionable image. On this stretch of La Rambla you will start to encounter street entertainers: jugglers, fire-eaters, musicians, human statues, or whatever the latest craze is.

The next building of note is the **Gran Teatre del Liceu**, a monument of the Catalan Renaixença period, opened in 1847, and very plush inside. It was gutted by fire in January 1994, but every effort

*G*audí's architectural influence in Barcelona may undoubtedly be the most original expressions of Modernisme, but the most perfect example is usually agreed to be Luís Domènech's Palau de la Música.

*T*he lobster strikes back! In Barcelona, even eating out can be an artistic experience.

is being made to reopen it as soon as possible. Across the way is the venerable **Café del'Opera**, a good spot for refreshment.

The heart of La Rambla is the Pla de la Boqueria. The 19th-century covered market here, known as **La Boqueria**, is a city highlight. Huge, lovingly arranged mounds of fruit, vegetables, seafood, sausages, meat, poultry, herbs, spices and sweetmeats form a cornucopian mosaic under the high-ceilinged ironwork naves. It opens at dawn but closes down in mid-afternoon, so time your visit accordingly.

The next part of La Rambla is famous for its flowers and is one of the most photographed scenes in the city. The blossoms give way to birds and their vendors and La

205

Rambla finishes at Plaça de Catalunya.

Montjuïc

In 1992, the 'Hill of the Jews' was transformed into a new Mount Olympus as millions of TV viewers thrilled to the pictures of high-board divers in the open-air Olympic swimming pool, spectacularly perched above the city. The hill is no stranger to big events, however. In 1929 it was the site of the International Exhibition and the ornate fountains of the **Plaça d'Espanya** were created to grace the entrance. The gateway is also marked by two huge brick columns, modelled on St Mark's Campanile in Venice. A number of large hangar-type halls, still used for commercial exhibitions, lead up to the **Palau Nacional**, domed like the US Capitol and dominating the skyline. This was the Spanish Pavilion in 1929 and now houses the **Museu d'Art de Catalunya**, one of the world's finest collections of mediaeval art.

There are so many attractions on Montjuïc alone that it would be easy to spend several days here. Chief among them is the **Poble Espanyol** (Spanish Village), where you can see the whole of Spain in a couple of hours, though you can easily spend much longer here. The village is a showcase of the country's various regions, represented by replicas of houses, church towers, fountains, plazas and palaces. There are 115 of them in total, interspersed with shops, restaurants, tapas bars and artisans' workshops. It may not be the real thing, but it's a good crash course to the delights of the country and the Barcelona Experience is an easy audio-visual introduction to the city.

If you are in search of more cerebral institutions, there are many other museums and galleries on the hill – don't miss the witty abstract art of the highly rated **Fundació Joan Miró**.

If you really want a bird's-eye view of the city, take the **cable car** (Telefèric de Montjuïc). This takes you on a breathtaking ride up above the Olympic swimming pool and the city skyline to the fairground, **Parc d'Atraccions de Montjuïc**. At the very top of the hill is the 17th-century **Castell de Montjuïc**, which houses a military museum.

Barri Gòtic

If you step off La Rambla about half-way along and walk two to three hundred metres east, you will find yourself in the **Barri Gòtic** – the oldest part of town. It's an atmospheric place of narrow alleyways, and old buildings coming back to life as museums, hotels or restaurants. You'll find the best bits in a remarkably preserved concentration of mediaeval architecture clustering round the **Cathedral**. It's not hard to find this huge, imposing, time-blackened building. It was begun in the 13th century, although its florid Gothic façade wasn't finished until 1892. Don't miss the beautiful cloister.

Next door is the **Palau Reial** (Royal Palace), which is famous as the place where Columbus met Ferdinand and Isabella in 1493, to report what he had found in the New World.

There are also two excellent museums here. The **Museu d'Història de la Ciutat**

*D*on't forget to pack your sense of humour when you visit the quirky Fundació Joan Miró in Barcelona – it's one of the city's liveliest galleries.

(Museum of the History of the City), housed in a rebuilt 15th-century mansion, is a must if you want an historical perspective of Barcelona, while the **Museu Frederic Marés** is a wonderful eclectic collection of religious objects, art and miscellany from all over the world.

Just outside the Gothic Quarter is Barcelona's most popular museum, devoted to the works of Picasso. The **Museu de Picasso** occupies a gorgeous mediaeval palace in the Carrer de Montcada, which is one of the most untouched streets in the mediaeval city. You won't see Picasso's greatest paintings in here, and there are few Cubist works, but it's still an excellent collection.

Continue south along the Carrer de Montcada to find one of the city's finest churches, **Santa María del Mar**. As the name suggests, at this point you are almost back on the waterfront.

Just to the east of here is the **Ciutadella**, named after a prison erected by the French in 1714 and torn down with much glee in 1869. It is now a lovely mature park, famous as the home of Barcelona Zoo, where you can visit Snowflake, the albino gorilla, plus performing dolphins and a killer whale.

Gaudí's Barcelona

From La Rambla the Bus Turistic continues north through the modern part of the city known as **L'Eixample** (the 'expansion', built mostly between 1860 and 1920). This district is famous for its Modernist architecture and the ones not to miss are all on Passeig de Gràcia: no. 35, **Casa Lleó Morera,** by Domènech i Montaner; no. 41, **Casa Amatller** by Puig i Cadafalch; no. 43, **Casa Batlló** by Gaudí; no. 92, **Casa Milà** (also known as La Pedrera) by Gaudí. The latter two are both extraordinary buildings with all of Gaudí's inventive, surrealistic hallmarks.

For more of the master of Modernism, rejoin the bus to the city's most famous landmark – the church of **Sagrada Familia** (Holy Family). No matter how many pictures you have seen of this unfinished masterpiece, you will not be let

Gaudí's Sagrada Familia, the world's most enigmatic church. A dream-like fusion of High Gothic and Art Nouveau, it may never be completed.

down by the reality. The basic shape is firmly rooted in the city's Gothic tradition, but no Gothic church has stonework that drips like melted candlewax, nor has sculptures of snails, vines and tortoises, nor has 100m (330ft) tall towers that resemble perforated cigars. An elevator and steps take you all the way up to see the detail on the amazing towers including Gaudí's famous 'broken-plate mosaics'.

The church is unfinished, and as Gaudí's plans were destroyed during the Civil War, no one knows what his exact intentions were. Work continues, but at a snail's pace, and it seems very unlikely that Sagrada Familia will be finished in the forseeable future.

There is more of Gaudí's work north of Sagrada Familia at the **Parc Güell**. His patron, Count Güell, intended to create a community of villas within the 2.4-ha (6-acre) park here, and in 1900 he gave Gaudí *carte blanche* to produce something original. The result is a compendium of the designer's most distinctive devices – dragons, drunken columns (86 of them support the roof of what was to have been the colony's covered market), a serpentine wall and tiled mosaic bench around a raised plaza, mask-eyes as windows, and so on. The villa plan never took off and the property became a popular family park in 1923. You can visit the house in which Gaudí lived for a while, and which now serves as a museum.

*P*arc Güell, another unfinished Gaudí masterpiece, has delighted locals and tourists for seven decades.

North of the City

If you get a bright clear day and you want a view of Barcelona that puts Montjuïc into the 'mere molehill' category, catch the bus to **Tibidabo** and change onto the city's last tram service. The famous 1900-vintage **Tramvía blau** (blue tram) will take you almost to the top of this 542m (1,778ft) peak overlooking Barcelona. Another five minutes on a funicular leads to the summit. There is a good amusement park here which combines the best of old and new technology rides.

If you still have an appetite for religious buildings, the **Monestir de Pedralbes** (on the north eastern edge of the city centre) boasts a superb Gothic church and a charming two-storey cloister.

A temple dedicated to an altogether different Spanish passion, though one that is hardly less devout, lies just south of here. The 120,000-seat Camp Nou stadium is famous all over the football world as the home of **Barcelona F.C.** (known to their enthusiastic followers simply as 'Barça'). Tours of the ground and the club's Museu del Futbol are fast becoming a major attraction.

All of the above mentioned sights can be seen on the Bus Turistic route. Catch the first and the last shuttles and you can see a good number of them in a single day, but it is a better idea to spend at least one night here. The city is famous for its choice of restaurants and *tapas* bars, plus its vibrant nightlife. If you want to know what's going on, pick up a copy of *Guià del Ocio*. The Barri Gòtic is the ideal place to stay, within walking distance of most of the action.

Barcelona is connected to all the Costa Dorada resorts by fast and frequent train services, so don't drive here unless you really have to.

Costa Dorada

The Costa Dorada takes its name from the fine golden (*daurada*) beaches that stretch almost without a break for over 241km (150 miles) along this calm Mediterranean shoreline.

Technically, the Costa Dorada begins at the Ebro Delta in the south and ends some 16km (10 miles) south of Sitges, where the Costa Garraf begins. This continues north as the Costa del Barcelona and flows into the Costa del Maresme. The name may change but the long golden sands remain the same.

Sitges

This is the most sophisticated resort on the Costa Dorada, yet it has managed to retain most of its old-world charm and a definite identity, avoiding the ravages of late 20th-century tourism architecture. The old town, built around a promontory, is a delight. Surmounting this appears to be a mediaeval palace, bearing the romantic name, **Palau Mar i cel**, meaning the 'palace of the sea and sky'. It bears the gargoyles and galleries of a Notre Dame, and is so tall that some of the narrow alleyways below

---

PABLO CASALS

The great cellist, Pablo (Pau) Casals (1876-1973), was born in El Vendrell (about halfway between Sitges and Tarragona). He was one of the great musicians of this century, tirelessly performing well into his eighties, a champion of human rights and a staunch advocate of Catalan independence. His old summer house is open to the public at the beach quarter of Sant Salvador. In addition to musical memorabilia, the house holds a fine collection of Catalan art. Concerts are held periodically at the auditorium opposite.

are permanently in shadow. Yet despite its Gothic appearance it was actually built in the second decade of this century. Inside, you can enjoy a fine collection of paintings and *objets d'art* from around the world, plus romantic sea views through picture windows.

Adjacent is the splendid art and wrought ironwork collection of Santiago Rusiñol, a leading exponent of Modernisme, who named his studio-home **Cau Ferrat** (the 'iron lair') after his work. Here, other leading sculptors and painters of the day would meet and the beginnings of Sitges as a fashionable artists' and intellectuals' colony was forged. Paintings by such luminaries as El Greco and Picasso, beautiful ceramics, crystal and much more is now imaginatively displayed in one of Spain's most exquisite small museums.

Dominating the point is the **parish church**, built between the 16th and 18th centuries. It may not be an architectural gem, in fact it is quite plain by day, but its dramatic setting more than compensates. By night it is beautifully illuminated.

The old town slopes inland from the church, its narrow streets home to whitewashed houses, antiques and art galleries, colourful local shops, excellent restaurants, cafés and lively bars.

There is another good museum in Sitges. The **Museu Romàntic** is an aristocratic mansion lavishly decorated in 19th-century style and full of interesting contemporary objects – clocks, working music boxes and a renowned collection of dolls.

The far end of the town is quiet. Here, wealthy families from Barcelona enjoy tranquillity behind high-trimmed hedges, but it is the young, trendy Barcelonans who make Sitges such a fashionable and lively spot. The fiestas here are particularly colourful and **Carnaval** is especially outrageous. At the other end of the spectrum, however, Sitges is also renowned for its **Corpus Christi** celebrations.

Vilafranca del Penedès

The town of **Vilafranca del Penedès** is situated on a fertile plain, midway between Barcelona and Tarragona, and over the last two centuries has literally grown its own success story. Nowadays, the Penedès is one of Spain's best-known wine regions.

There are no bodegas to visit in the centre of town, but you will find one of Spain's very best wine museums. You don't have to be a connoisseur to appreciate the lively exhibits at the **Museu del Vino**. Dioramas illustrate wine through the ages and you can see huge wooden winepresses which were crushing the grapes when the Romans were in the province. Another hall displays glass bottles and jugs which have slaked centuries of thirst, and there is even an art gallery devoted to the noble vine.

The wine museum shares its quarters with the **Museu Municipal**, which is

---

CASTELLERS IN SPAIN

The most spectacular of Catalonia's many folklore troupes are the castellers. These are men and boys who climb barefoot on to one another's shoulders to form human towers rising up to seven storeys high. The most pampered participant is the young boy who scampers to the very top of the tower and takes the crowd's cheers. The unsung, invisible heroes, however, are the behemoths at the very bottom of the pile who hold up the pyramid.

Castellers' appearances are not that common, so catch them while you can. The team from Valls are acclaimed as being the kings of the castellers.

These ancient casks, in Vilafranca's Museu del Vino, have been maturing and dispensing Penedès wine for many centuries.

devoted to geology, archaeology, natural history and Catalan religious art. The building is an attraction in its own right. It was formerly a mediaeval palace of the counts of Barcelona and the kings of Aragon.

Look out from the third-floor windows and you will see a monument to another of the town's passions – a five-storey human pyramid team of castellers. But Vilafranca is not just for oenophiles or balancing acts. Its leafy *rambla* and old town centre are full of character, particularly on a Saturday when it hosts one of the region's most colourful general **markets**.

Visit the splendid **Basilica of Santa Maria**, the adjacent Palais Baltà, and the **church of Sant Francesc**, famous for its Catalan Gothic treasures. Pick up a map from the helpful tourist office in the town hall and ask them about visits to nearby vineyards.

Tarragona

The Romans landed in **Tarragona** (they called it *Tarraco*) in the 3rd century BC and rapidly established it as an important military and political headquarters. It grew to a population of 30,000, coined its own money and by 27 BC was the capital of Hispania Citerior (later to become *Tarraconensis*), the largest Roman province in Spain. During its period of occupation a number of emperors lived here including such luminaries as Augustus and Hadrian. The legacy is some of the finest monuments to have survived from this period;

BLOOD OF CHRIST

If you have ever wondered where the wine that is used to celebrate Holy Communion comes from, the answer may well be Tarragona. De Muller, the city's largest and most prestigious wine concern have been specialist suppliers of altar wine (the symbolic blood of Christ) for generations. They export their organically produced sweet white wine all over the world and have been suppliers to the Vatican and many popes. In keeping with the changing taste of the market as a whole, altar wines have become drier in recent years.

the city walls, a great aqueduct, an amphitheatre, plus some fine museums and mosaics.

Tarragona's most impressive Roman monument is the **Pont del Diable** (Devil's Bridge) which lies some 4km (2.5 miles) north of the centre of town off the N240 Lleida (Lérida). The 'Devil's Bridge' is actually a perfectly preserved double-decker aqueduct spanning 217m (712ft) with a total of 11 lower-storey and 25 upper-storey arches, the highest of which rise up to 27m (88ft) from the ground. It was built in the 1st century as part of a complex network of canals that supplied Tarragona with water.

The Rambla Vella (old Rambla) neatly divides Tarragona in half. To the north is the old walled city, while parallel and to the south is the Rambla Nova (new Rambla) and the newer part of town.

Take a walk along the **Passeig Arqueològic** (archaeological promenade) which follows the top of the old city walls and passes three very solid Roman towers.

Within the walls is a labyrinthine mediaeval city, very Mediterranean, with flowerpots balancing on iron balconies, laundry drying in tall, dark narrow streets, and

*T*he impressive Pont del Diable, a few kilometres outside Tarragona, was built in the 1st century to bring water to the town.

canaries in cages on the walls. Patriotic red-and-yellow-striped Catalan flags fly from the balconies.

The **Museu Arqueològic** here is a modern, well-designed exhibition of delicate mosaics (don't miss the *Head of Medusa*), and Roman and Spanish artefacts.

The ancient, rough-hewn, tall, golden building adjacent to the museum is known as the **Pretori Romà** (Roman Praetorium), and is thought to have been part of the complex of Provincial administration buildings. It is certainly Roman in origin, though much restored in the Middle Ages, and it now houses the stylish and atmospheric **Museu d'Història** (history museum).

At the bottom level, you can walk a short way along a tunnel which linked the castle with the Roman **Circus** (part of which was on the site where the Plaça de la Font now stands) and acted as supporting vaults for the Circus tiers. Next door to the Pretori Romà are more remains of the Circus.

Walking from here towards the sea brings you to the ruins of the Roman **amphitheatre**, built into the hillside. Gladiators fought here, and on this site in AD 259 the first martyrdom of Christians on the peninsula took place (by fire). The most important ancient site beyond the city walls, the **Necròpoli i Museu Paleocristià** (Necropolis and Paleo-Christian Museum), is on the site of a cemetery for Tarragona's early Christians. It comprises a series of covered excavations. Over 2,000 graves have been uncovered here and a museum displays the best of the finds.

Mediaeval Tarragona's pride and joy is its **Catedral**. From the front aspect it looks rather disappointing, even small, but the great Gothic doorway, and above it, one of Europe's largest rose windows, give an indication that it is actually the largest cathedral in Catalonia. The cloister, constructed in the 12th and 13th centuries, is an attraction in its own right. Similar to those of the great local Cistercian monasteries it is big, airy and contains a pretty, sunny garden. Notice too the sculptural detail of the capitals all around the cloister. The cathedral's

Museu Diocesà boasts a fine collection of ecclesiastical art and ancient objects, including many impressive Flemish tapestries. The cathedral itself was built between 1171 and 1331, so its architectural style spans both Romanesque and Gothic. The overall effect, looking up to the great vaulted ceiling, is one of austere majesty. It is regarded as one of the finest cathedrals of this period in all Spain. The **main altarpiece**, and certain of the chapels are particularly noteworthy.

The narrow cobbled streets surrounding the cathedral have not changed much since the Middle Ages either: tiny houses in picturesque decay, shops selling tins and packets usually seen in museums of yesteryear, cross-legged artisans making brooms and wickerwork artefacts using time-honoured methods. Here you will find the **Casa Museu Castellarnau**, an 18th/19th-century mansion, recently renovated with sumptuous period fittings plus a small museum.

Back in the modern part of town, look out from the **Balco del Mediterrani** (Balcony of the Mediterranean) and you can see the port of Tarragona. This is one of the larger commercial ports in Spain and one of the busiest in the whole Mediterranean.

While the commercial port is not a tourist attraction, the adjacent fishing port is certainly worth a visit. Its waterfront district is unaccountably known as **El Serrall**, meaning the harem, but the only conspicuous wives are those sitting on wicker chairs mending the voluminous red fishing nets sprawled out along the quay. The area is famous for its fish restaurants.

Salou

Salou is by far the biggest resort on this coast and has few pretensions. It is a well-ordered, no-frills playground for north European package holiday-makers. The town's chief assets are its huge beaches, clean, well kept and offering every facility.

In the early evening, crowds gather to watch the town's **illuminated fountain** performing. It was designed by Buigas, (famous for his dancing fountains in Barcelona) and has become a symbol of Salou.

Cambrils

Salou's classy neighbour is an attractive fishing port turned resort. It has a long seafront and much of its charm centres on the large fleet of *bous* – small fishing boats carrying over-sized lamps for night duty – at anchor here. Their catches have helped turn Cambrils into a Catalan gourmet town. Its waterfront counts more good **restaurants** (and Michelin rosettes) than many a metropolis and attracts connoisseurs of good food from all over the region.

Set back from the waterfront is a small bustling centre full of character, with a fine indoor market and old, unspoiled streets to explore.

The Ebro Delta

The Ebro Delta is the largest wetlands in Catalonia and, after France's famous Carmague, the most important aquatic environment in the western Mediterranean. The delta was created from the mud travelling down the river Ebro all the way from Zaragoza. The river continues to throw up new land and the delta expands some 10m (33ft) into the sea each year. It now covers an area of over 320km^2 (123 square miles), of which 7,700 ha (19,000 acres) have been set aside as a protected Natural Park.

The Ebro Delta is a rich agricultural district famous for its rice, although many other vegetable crops and fruit also flourish in the rich alluvial soil inland.

Follow the road to **Deltebre** (formerly named La Cava) where there is a tourist office. In addition to supplying general information and maps, they will also be able to advise you on the best places to see birds at the time of your visit. Enquire about boat excursions which leave from Deltebre (you can also hire boats to tour the delta from Amposta).

Unless you are a bird-watcher, the principal beauty of the Ebro is its wide-open peace and calm, and vignettes of a slower way of life that has almost disappeared: tiny, thatched whitewashed houses; ramshackle smallholders' huts; rice workers sowing and reaping by hand; villagers cycling languorously between the paddies. Look for horses drawing

---

BIRD-WATCHING IN THE EBRO DELTA

The Ebro Delta is a major breeding ground for water-fowl, waders and seabirds, and is an important resting site for winter migrants. The population totals 50–100,000, and includes representatives of 60 per cent of all species found in Europe. The most common types are from the duck and coot families, although you will also see little egrets and, if you are lucky, flamingoes.

The best places for watching are the remotest parts of the reserve: Punta de la Banya (on the Peninsula dels Alfacs, a breeding point for flamingoes); Punta del Fangar; Ile de Buda (take a boat trip); La Tancada and Salines salt lagoons (which attract flamingoes). Dawn and dusk are the best times of day, and the best time of year is October and November following the rice harvest, but there is interest all year round. Call at the tourist office for the latest information.

plough-like contraptions which are winnowing the chaff from the grain.

When visiting the delta in spring, summer or early autumn, remember to carry mosquito-repellent.

Sant Carles de la Ràpita is the main town of the delta (population 10,000) though it is totally unlike any of the tiny, very southern agricultural settlements. Its large natural harbour serves a prosperous fishing fleet and a modest ship-building industry. What makes the town really stand out is its gigantic main square. It is so enormous for such a small town that there aren't even enough public buildings, shops and offices to fill its perimeter; many of the buildings are just private houses. The square was a brainstorm of Charles III who envisaged Sant Carles as being a port of great significance. The project died with him in 1788, but the great melancholy square remains.

Tortosa

Tortosa held a key strategic role for many centuries as the last major town before the sea, guarding the Ebro river which runs far into the Spanish interior. The elaborate fortress at the top of the town was built by the Moors who held out at length during the Reconquest of 1148. Under the rule of the Aragonese kings, this became a royal residence known as the Castle of San Juan. Today it is better known by its Arabic name **La Zuda** (or Suda) and houses a *parador*. It is well worth the steep ascent, as this is the only vantage point from which you can take in the whole city, and particularly the cathedral.

From ground level the **cathedral** is tightly hemmed in and is almost possible to miss. From above it is a splendid sight, haunched on its buttresses as if it is flexing itself to push up above the old town (the remains of the old city walls are visible from here). It was built between the 14th and the 16th centuries, and is a classic example of Catalan Gothic. Inside is a beautiful 14th-century triptych and two 15th-century carved stone pulpits.

A rice farmer shares the Ebro Delta with the migratory birds who attract serious hunters in season. Attempts to turn the River Ebro into Aragon's outlet to the sea have been dormant for years. As for the rice, it will go into paella, one of the masterpieces of east coast cuisine.

20TH-CENTURY MASTERS

Spain's greatest 20th-century artists were multi-media geniuses who created everything from paintings and engravings to ceramics and movies. They found their muse in the hungry Paris days and lived long, remarkably productive lives. Picasso died at 91, Miró at 90 and Dalí was 84.

The century's artistic titan, Pablo Ruiz y **Picasso** (1881–1973), went through phases from blue to pink to black and invented many a school of art. Born in Málaga, he spent his early years in La Coruña and Barcelona. From the age of 20 he signed his works with his mother's maiden name. Thanks to his inexhaustible output and controversial fame, Picasso's underlined signature became almost as familiar worldwide as the calligraphy of Coca-Cola. His tempestuous private life (shared by a series of seven women) was often reflected in his work, joyous or haunted. Perhaps his most revolutionary phase was Cubism, in which he fragmented the subject and reassembled its parts.

Picasso soon turned to other styles, but Juan **Gris**, another Spaniard in Paris, made Cubism his life. In 1906 Gris moved into the ramshackle house Picasso and other Bohemians occupied in Montmartre. When the frail, shy Gris died at the age of 40, Picasso was a pallbearer.

During the Spanish Civil War Picasso created his most unforgettable painting, the vast canvas dedicated to the bombing of the Basque town of Guernica. Picasso always refused to comment on its meaning, but the picture tells its own story of the horror and

Unfinished business: the studio of Joan Miró, Palma de Mallorca.

agony of war. At the opposite edge of the emotional spectrum, Picasso is also remembered for a happy image: a few inimitable brush strokes evoking the dove of peace.

Joan **Miró** (1893–1983) met his Frenchified countryman Picasso in Paris and spent many years in France, but he never lost his Catalan roots. Born in Barcelona, he had to struggle to become an artist. His parents forced him into the business world, but after he suffered a nervous breakdown they allowed him to go to art school. In Paris he dallied with the Dadaists, painted something like naïve art, then found his own patch of surrealism. In the 1920s he knew all the intellectual celebrities in Paris, from Ezra Pound to Henry Miller, from Max Ernst to Ernest Hemingway (Miró's unlikely sparring partner at a boxing club). The world warmed to his increasingly luminous colours and deceptively haphazard, childishly rendered forms. His dreamy, sometimes nightmarish abstractions were instantly identifiable as Miró, and in 1941 he was a star of New York's recently built Museum of Modern Art. Like Picasso, his versatility extended to ballet design, ceramics and sculpture.

Salvador **Dalí** (1904–1989) lived so outrageously that his art was often obscured by flashes of what looked like charlatanism. Even before his first trip to Paris in 1927 his surrealistic style was recognizably Dalí. While collaborating with Luis Buñuel on the shocking film, *Un Chien Andalou*, Dalí met Gala, who was to become his wife and all-purpose model. Although Dalí lived most of his life in Catalonia, the moustachioed monarchist disdained Catalan nationalism. His will bequeathed everything to Spain.

Dalí's classical draughtsmanship appeased audiences otherwise repelled by what he had done to the objects in his paintings. His melted watches, eviscerated bodies and unearthly landscapes captivated Europe, then America (where he took refuge in World War II). His astonishing pictures and provocative public relations stunts made Dalí a household name. History will have the last word on his stridently self-proclaimed genius.

A huge 3-D optical illusion by a whimsical Dalí; Picasso feeling blue in Barcelona at age 22.

Orange Blossoms and Golden Beaches

You can thank the Romans and particularly the Moors, who ruled eastern Iberia for centuries, for the fertile countryside here: flowering almond, olive and citrus orchards, and exotic intrusions such as date palms and rice paddies. There are wonderful beaches too. The only drawbacks are the crowds and the heavy tourist development on this coast.

For touristic purposes, the shore divides into *costas* as poetic as the 'orange-blossom' (*azahar*) coast, and as prosaic as the 'white' (*blanca*) and 'warm' (*cálida*) coasts. This 'branding' approach is the clearest signal that the holiday trade makes hay along this part of the Mediterranean. Not all the development is as intense as that of the Costa Blanca's famous boom town, Benidorm.

As always, there are plenty of alternatives away from the beaches and burger bars: unspoiled villages, mountain castles, and historic cities with important cathedrals and museums. In fact, a sightseeing

These Castellón fishwives are so busy mending the nets that they turn their back on a splendid sight, the Peñíscola peninsula topped by its 14th-century castle.

itinerary as full as you could want, and all within easy reach of the sands.

Costa del Azahar

The Orange Blossom Coast begins just south of the Tarragona border and stretches for 112km (70 miles) down a coast exceptionally well endowed with beaches. *Costa del Azahar* doesn't exactly trip off the tourist tongue, but the orchards do come down practically to the beach and there are oranges as far as the horizon. They grow enough citrus fruit here to wipe out scurvy around the world. The reality is less beautiful than the image, however. You may find that once you have seen one orange grove you've seen them all, and kilometre upon kilometre of them can be pretty monotonous. If you arrive when the blossom is on the trees, however, (which occurs three times a year), they are a beautiful sight.

EAST

N

Morella
Vinarós
Benicarló
Peñíscola
Teruel
Cuenca
Castellón
de la Plana
Segorbe
Sagunto
Requena
Valencia
Júcar
Gandia
Albacete
N430
Ontinyent
Denia
Almansa
Alcoy
Jávea
Cabo
de la
Nao
Guadalest
Calpe
Altea
Benidorm
Villajoyosa
Hellín
Yecla
Elda
Segura
Alicante
Elche
Caravaca
de la Cruz
Mula
Orihuela
Murcia
Mar Menor
La Manga
Lorca
N342
Cartagena

| 0 | 80km |
| 0 | 50 miles |

Land above 1,500m (4,900ft)

Morella

Tucked away in the north eastern corner of Valencia province, this small fortified mountain town figures on few tourists' itineraries. However, it is a good day out if you are staying in Peñíscola, with a memorable drive inland.

There is plenty of interest to be found in the narrow mediaeval streets as they wind their way upwards; the 14th-century Gothic Basilica of Santa María La Mayor, the former convent of Santo Domingo, the Monastery of San Francisco, and eventually the ruined castle.

The views from here are wonderful, and the town's workaday rustic atmosphere is a real refresher after the commercialized coast.

Peñíscola

The name is possibly a corruption of the Latin for 'peninsula' which describes the town's setting perfectly, if prosaically. **Peñíscola** is built on a huge rock, rising above the sea, crowned by a mediaeval castle and sloping down to gardens and a hamlet of whitewashed houses within its walls. As in many towns along the coast, tourist facilities have been established to exploit the almost limitless beach potential, and trinket shops and the like tend to overwhelm the native core. But it's a pretty place nonetheless, and even better by night when floodlit.

The **castle** was built by the Knights Templar on the ruins of a Moorish fortress. It has two claims to fame. The first is that Pope Benedict XIII found asylum in the castle after being dismissed from his position, and stayed here until his death in 1423. The second is that parts of the movie *El Cid*, starring Charlton Heston, were filmed here. The castle's layout is complicated and fun to explore. There are restored ramparts, tunnels, a church, a Gothic hall, and sensational sea views.

There are two popular fishing port-cum-beach resorts north of Peñíscola; Vinaroz, at the northernmost tip of this costa and, **Benicarló**, which practically abuts Peñíscola. This little town has an old castle and a pretty 18th-century church, with an octagonal bell tower and magnificent front door. When the sizeable local fleet of trawlers returns to the port, a siren announces the big event of the day, the fish auction.

Castellón de la Plana

The provincial capital grew at its present location after the area's reconquest from the Moors in 1233. Historic buildings here include a heavily restored cathedral (terribly damaged in the Civil War), an octagonal 16th-century clock tower and the 18th-century town hall. See also the Provincial Museum of Fine Arts. The city's outlet to the sea, El Grau (El Grao), is a busy port; while nearby beaches have caught the eye of holiday developers.

Sagunto

Sagunto was the tinder-box that ignited the Second Punic War, and its ramparts which crown the town bear witness to tragic events. In 219 BC the Carthaginian commander, Hannibal, attacked the Roman town of *Saguntum*, apparently in disregard of a treaty. The populace were besieged for nine months, and when all hope of rescue by Rome was gone, the women, children and elderly committed suicide in a huge fire, while the men fought to the death. The Romans declared all-out war, recaptured *Saguntum*, and redeveloped the town on a grand scale.

You can see the importance of Saguntum at the heavily restored **Roman theatre**, built into the hillside. School children enjoy testing the theatre's acoustics with screams; it's all very evocative of ancient Rome. Alongside the theatre a modest archaeological museum delves back into Iberian sculpture, Roman ceramics, mosaics, inscriptions and statues, and mediaeval relics.

Sagunto's **acropolis**, which sprawls for hundreds of yards on top of the hill above the town, shows signs of half a dozen civilizations, starting with the Iberians. Most of the fortifications, however, are Moorish. The panorama from this vantage point, called the Castell de Sagunt, sweeps from the citrus orchards to the sea.

Valencia

An infinity of orange trees surrounds Spain's third-biggest city, erstwhile capital of a kingdom. Despite this, it is an unprepossessing place with drab, sprawling suburbs and, like most of Spain's big cities, it is a driver's nightmare. Valencia caters less for visitors than either Madrid or Barcelona, and lacks their panache and vitality. Nonetheless, the city's crowded historic centre, framed by parks and gardens, is still a good place to spend a couple of days.

Valencia is over 2,000 years old, founded in 138 BC by the Romans. The Visigoths displaced the Roman Empire here in AD 413, followed three centuries later by the Moors. The city flourished as the capital of a far-flung Moorish kingdom until the Spanish hero El Cid captured it at the end of the 11th century and became Duke of Valencia. The Moors subsequently retook control after less than a decade and stayed in place until the city's final reconquest in 1238 by James I of Aragon. Valencia remained a kingdom under Aragon until the merger with Castile in 1497.

No sooner had Christianity been restored than plans were laid for **La Seo** (the cathedral). Construction continued, on and off, for centuries, and the result is quite a patchwork of styles. The main portal is baroque, while around the corner, the **apostles' portal** is a French Gothic beauty, and the third doorway is Romanesque. A trademark of the cathedral, and the city, is the tall octagonal **tower** called the *Miguelete* or *Micalet*, a Gothic

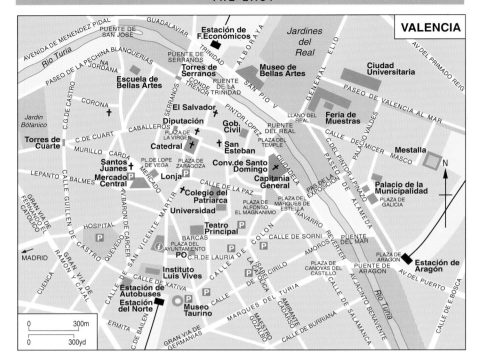

VALENCIA

treasure designed in 1381. Inside is a Flamboyant Gothic lantern, a periscope of windows thrust skyward to brighten everything in sight. The unusual point about this is that the windows are not glass, but alabaster, which gives an altogether different, diffused lighting. You can climb the tower for excellent views over Valencia's rooftops. Above the altar in the old chapter house, a chalice from the

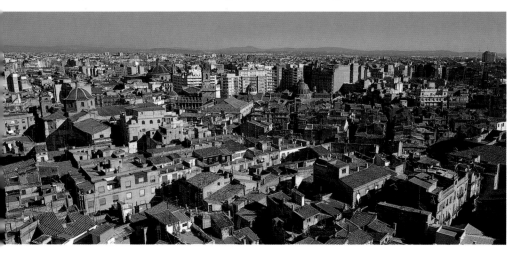

STILL WATERS

In the extraordinarily fertile region of the *Huerta de Valencia*, which surrounds the city, millions of orange trees grow, and grow, and grow. There are three juicy harvests per year. The secret of citrus success is the balmy climate, but the orchards require a plentiful water supply, too. Channelling the river Turia, the Romans organized the first irrigation system here, which was expanded and perfected by the Moors. Although after the Reconquest, most of the Moors were expelled, the victorious Christians were forced to retain the services of Moorish gardeners as only they knew the secrets of successful irrigation.

For a thousand years, disputes over the exploitation of the available water have been settled by the Water Tribunal, which still convenes every Thursday at noon on the steps of the Apostles' Portal of Valencia's Cathedral. There are no lawyers, no briefs, just oral decisions (in the Valencian dialect) which are honoured by all.

*O*ranges, oranges
*everywhere in this part of Spain,
but you'll find orange juice a
surprisingly expensive drink!*

Roman era is claimed to be the cup that Jesus drank from at the Last Supper, the legendary Holy Grail.

The **Lonja de la Seda** (Silk Exchange), a 15th-century masterpiece of civil Gothic design, is the city's cathedral to Mammon. This is where Valencia's mediaeval silk merchants haggled in a setting that would make any stock market in the world envious. The main hall, with thin spiralled pillars supporting ogival arches, is superb.

*A*ncient red-tiled roofs
*and modern office blocks jostle
for a place on the Valencia
skyline. Beyond lie the fertile
plains of the Huerta.*

Here too you can ascend steps for a bird's-eye view of the city. Across the street, the Modernist-looking central market (built in 1928) is another great tribute to trading. Domes and stained-glass windows are not usually reserved for food markets but this, after all, is the destination of the cream of the crop from Valencia's own *huerta* (literally 'the garden', but in this case the great cultivated plains of the Valencian hinterland). It's a cornucopia of comestibles – fruit, vegetables, fish and meat destined for the city's kitchens.

Valencia boasts several museums. The **Museo Nacional de Cerámica**, housed in an astonishing old palace, has assembled more than you might think it was possible to know about the history of ceramic art. Among the highlights are hundreds of inspired glazed tiles (*azulejos*) and tile ensembles. Children love the three 18th-century coaches parked on the ground floor, including the sumptuous carriage which was the personal transport of the palace's owner, the Marquess of Dos Aguas. The exterior of the palace is an overwhelming 18th-century rococo extravaganza. They say that the architect went mad – stare at it for long enough and you may understand why.

By contrast, the city's major art collection, the **Museo Provincial de Bellas Artes** is housed in an unprepossessing palace (on the edge of the park called Jardines del Real). In addition to an extraordinary work by Bosch, and paintings by Velázquez, Goya, El Greco and many other Spanish masters, it has the definitive

Everywhere along the coast, the views are marvellous. On the promontory of the old town of Benidorm, tourists sit where a castle once stood.

collection of 15th-century Valencian art. Influenced by Flemish and Italian techniques, Valencia's mediaeval artists produced impressive religious paintings in abundance. It is one of the country's finest provincial galleries. Fans of modern art should visit the Instituto Valenciano de Arte Moderno (IVAM). Two other specialist collections of note are the Museo Taurino (on the subject of bullfighting) and the **Fallas Museu**, where grotesque,

> ### PUTTING VALENCIA TO THE TORCH
>
> What started as simple festive bonfires a few centuries ago has evolved into Valencia's unique carnival, the *Fallas*, (from the word for 'torches') a week of revelry climaxing every 19 March, St Joseph's Day.
>
> What makes Valencia's celebration so special is the amount of artistic talent, effort and money that goes into creating the hundreds of satirical papier-mâché effigies (*niños*) which ride on floats destined for the flames. The fireworks cost millions of pesetas and there are even daytime previews, louder than a battle, and just as smoky. The very best *niños* are saved from the bonfire each year and are put on display in the Fallas Museu just south east of the old city centre.

award-winning, papier-mâché festival figures reside.

Gandía

Gandía was the birthplace of the devout 16th-century duke of Borja (the Italian branch of the family were the notorious Borgias) and several times a day, guided tours visit his **Palacio de los Duques**, now a Jesuit college. The duke (1510-72) turned priest and led an expansion of Jesuit operations through Europe and the western hemisphere. He was canonized in 1671. The palace houses splendid tapestries, paintings and period pieces, but the craftsmanship of the palace itself is equally as impressive as the exhibits.

There are beaches just beyond the town, popular with locals and tourists alike.

Costa Blanca

Perhaps surprisingly, it was not a PR whizz-kid who first dubbed the coast of

Alicante province the Costa Blanca. Some 2,500 years ago, Greek traders founded a colony here and named it *Akra Leuka*, 'White Headland'. The brilliant light, the hot, dry climate and the miles of fine sandy beaches make the White Coast one of Spain's liveliest tourist zones.

The beaches sprawl to the north and south of the town of **Denia**, named after a Roman temple to the goddess Diana (the remains are on view in the town hall).

The family resort of **Jávea** was described as 'environmentally nearly perfect' by the World Health Organization, and has a fine beach and a pleasant old quarter (do call in at the Casa de Cultura). The coast from here extends rockily to eastward-thrusting **Cabo de la Nao**, with fine sea views.

Calpe

This former fishing village set on a steep hill enjoys a spectacular situation at the base of the **Peñón de Ifach**, a volcanic peak resembling a mini-Gibraltar. If you are fit, it's a long but attainable trek, or you can cheat by driving up through the tunnel. Many tourists simply content themselves staring up at the rock from Calpe's fine sandy beaches. Overdevelopment has robbed the town of most of its character, though old parts do still remain at the top of the hill.

Altea

Altea sits high above the main road, its old houses climbing steeply to a carefully preserved old quarter which sits around a large attractive square. It is home to a thriving artistic community and is virtually unchanged in the face of the tourist tide. From here you can see the alternative: Benidorm's soaring skyline of mass tourism.

Benidorm

Benidorm – the very name has come to symbolize the worst excesses of packaged tourism. It has a skyline akin to Manhattan, all the sophistication of Daytona Beach or Blackpool, and in high season is so crowded that you have to queue to get onto the beach! Benidorm is also one of the great success stories of international tourist development. Take an obscure fishing village with a desirable climate and 7km (4 miles) of golden sands, add a few skyscrapers, and hey presto! The action here is as cosmopolitan as *smorgasbord*, German lager and 'tea like mother makes'. Benidorm knows what the package-tour invaders want and provides it cheerfully and efficiently, round the clock, without pretension.

Surprisingly, the original fishermen's quarter still exists and is a major saving grace. British and German bars have infiltrated, but here at least is a little bit of old Spain. It rises to a promontory and from the attractive **Balcón de Mer** you can look back at the magnificent crescent **beaches** to the north and south and the wind-sculptured mountains behind. When pressed to name the 'best' beach in Spain many a travel article has (often grudgingly) awarded this accolade to Benidorm. No matter that the sand has been shipped over from Africa. Try it out of season and you may agree. Just offshore, boats visit the Isla de Benidorm, a bird sanctuary.

Guadalest

A favourite excursion from Benidorm, **Guadalest** is the famous eagles' nest village-fortress of the Moors, built some twelve centuries ago. It stands 547m (1,800ft) above sea-level on top of rocky pinnacles, and there is only one way into this stronghold: via a tunnel carved through the solid rock. Not surprisingly, Guadalest was never conquered by force. The well-preserved village (including a plethora of day-tripper shops and some bizarre micro-museums) is pleasant enough, but the real attraction is the magnificent **view** over the valley below.

Villajoyosa

Houses painted pretty pastel shades of blue, pink, red, yellow or green line the palm-lined esplanade near the old fishing port. This is not trendy, Miami Beach-style Art Deco; the colours simply served as landmarks for the returning fishermen.

There are good beaches lying to the west of town.

In the last week of July the resort drops everything for the best Moors and Christians fiesta on this coast. Parades, cannonades and a recreated naval battle commemorate a 16th-century victory over Algerian pirates.

A licante's Castillo de Santa Bárbara looks down from its impressive position onto a busy Mediterranean port.

229

Alicante

With a population of more than a quarter of a million, **Alicante** is a typical bustling Mediterranean port with a splendid palm-lined promenade and lots of outdoor cafés. The spacious popular beach of Playa Postiguet, which lies below the castle, is a bonus.

Alicante's history looks right down at you from the **Castillo de Santa Bárbara**, on top of cliffs that squeeze the city towards the sea. The castle not only appears invulnerable; you wonder how it got there at all. Somehow the Carthaginians built the first fort on this hilltop in the 3rd century BC, and it was greatly expanded by subsequent regimes. You can drive up the steep, winding road to the summit, or take the lift built into the hillside across the busy coast road from the beach. There is a small museum of *niñots* here (Carnival figures), most of which are grotesque enough to put you off your *tapas*. The kids will probably love them.

Other impressive architecture includes the multibalconied, baroque **Ayuntamiento** (town hall) and a block away, the splendid **Iglesia Colegial de San Nicolás de Bari** with a baroque façade.

In the modernized halls of a 17th-century palace, the **Museo de Arte de Siglo XX** (Museum of 20th-century Art) is an excellent collection specializing in Spanish works, including Miró, Picasso and Dalí. Next door is the 14th-century **Iglesia de Santa María** (which is also baroque-faced).

Alicante is full of character, and perfect for just wandering around, particularly the old **Barrio de Santa Cruz**. Surprisingly, as the gateway to the Costa Blanca, the town is hardly bothered at all by foreign tourists. Perhaps it is a little too Spanish for their tastes. A few phrases of the native tongue are essential rather than optional here.

Elche

On many road signs, the town's name is a terse *Elx*, which is what the Moors called it. **Elche** is famous for the largest **date palm plantation** in Europe. It is claimed that centuries before the Muslim occupation, these trees were introduced by the Carthaginians, or perhaps even by the Phoenicians. However, it was the Moors who tended them with their famous irrigation systems, and gave Elche its present character. Today many tens of thousands of elegant palms surround the city.

The restful **Parque Municipal** has superb palm trees as well as a citrus alley and a noisy frog pond. The tourist office is on the edge of the park.

Next to this is a splendid grouping of several historic buildings. The huge 17th-century baroque **Basilica of Iglesia de Santa María** is unmissable. The **Palacio de Altamira**, a former royal holiday residence, is now a national monument, and is home to an archaeological museum.

In Elche's prettiest precinct, the **Hort del Cura** (Priest's Garden), grow celebrated palm trees, pomegranate and orange trees and a small cactus forest you would hate to get lost in. The star attraction is the 150-year-old, seven-branch, male Imperial Palm, girdled together to hold it upright.

Europe's biggest bunch of dates is to be found in Elche. Dates were first introduced here in about 300 BC, then were tended by the Arabs. Today, thousands of elegant palms surround the city.

Wherever you may be in Spain on Palm Sunday, the fronds you see come from Elche. As for the dates themselves, you can taste them anywhere, but it's a memorable treat to sample them beneath the graceful towering trees which provide them.

Orihuela

Orihuela lies about half-way between Elche and Murcia, but out of sight and sound of the busy N-340 highway. The number of elegant mansions and historic buildings in this small attractive city suggests that it has seen better days.

The old university, on the northern outskirts, was constructed in the 16th and 17th centuries. It is now a school, the **Colegio de Santo Domingo**. You can visit its cloisters and beautifully tiled refectory.

The Gothic **cathedral**, begun in the early 14th century, with spiral rib vaulting and ornamental grillework, is considered the region's second finest cathedral, after the one at Murcia. Ask to see the Velázquez masterpiece, the *Temptation of St Thomas Aquinas*, displayed right in the heart of the cathedral behind a series of locked doors.

Other buildings worth a look include the Iglesias Santas Justa y Rufina, the 18th-century Bishop's Palace and the Biblioteca Pública, which holds the town museum. Like Elche, Orihuela is also known for its fertile land. The Río Segura irrigates its citrus orchards and there is a palm grove here as well.

Costa Cálida

Even the water is warmer on the Warm Coast, and the most famous stretch is that of the **Mar Menor**, the 'Little Sea'. This vast lagoon is almost entirely sheltered from the open Mediterranean by a 22km (14-mile) long narrow spit. The shallow isolation of the Mar Menor (no more than 7m/23ft deep at any point) means a high salt and iodine content and even in winter water temperatures average a very tolerable 18°C (65° F).

High-rise resort facilities have multiplied on the sandy breakwater walling off the Mar Menor. It's known as **La Manga** (the sleeve) and is internationally famous for Club La Manga, a splendidly equipped holiday sporting complex. The lagoon is also renowned for its water-sport facilities, but sporting life aside, the Mar Menor is a pretty soulless place.

Cartagena

This is the principal port on this coast, and is also an important naval base. Its name refers to the Carthaginians, who captured the town two millennia ago. **Cartagena**'s harbour is so well protected that it is almost landlocked, and it was once renowned as one of the safest ports in the Mediterranean. The Castillo de la

Concepción, built at the end of the 14th century on the hill overlooking the port, offered further security, but today only ruins are left. Still, it's worth the drive up for the views. En route you will pass more ruins, the remains of the 13th-century church of Santa María.

Take a stroll around the alleys of the old town and see which ships are in the port. On the front is a submarine straight from the pages of a Jules Verne novel, which local inventor Isaac Peral built in 1888. There is a good clean beach quite close to the town.

Murcia

The capital of the Costa Cálida, **Murcia** lies well inland, though on a river, and is a city of modern prosperous pleasant boulevards combined with a fine old town of narrow alleyways.

At the heart of historic Murcia is the landmark 14th-century **Catedral de Santa María**, one of Spain's finest. Its concave baroque façade is a masterpiece and the 18th-century bell tower tapers grandly to a cupola and turret. Inside the Cathedral is the outstanding **Capilla de los Vélez** (Chapel of the Vélez family), with all manner of florid decoration.

Elsewhere in the cathedral is a good museum where you can admire the colourful wood sculptures of Francisco Salzillo (1797-1883), Murcia's greatest artist. You can see more of his works at the **Salzillo Museum** on Calle de San Andrés, and if you are here during Holy Week you will see his much revered *pasos* (sculptural ensembles) carried through the streets. Don't leave the cathedral without climbing its tower for splendid **views** over the town.

Calle de la Trapéria, the old town's principal shopping street, now pedestrianized, is a lovely ramble, running down to the cathedral and riverfront. The street's highlight is the **Casino de Murcia**, which is a private club, though not for gambling. It is housed in an altogether astonishing 19th-century building and the steward will normally let you in without any fuss. The entrance hall to this splendid, quite florid folly is a copy of the Hall of the Ambassadors in Seville's Alcázar. Ladies should take the opportunity to visit the toilets, where cherubs smile down from the ceiling.

Murcia has three other small museums to visit, the best of these being the **Museo Provincial de Bellas Artes** (Provincial Museum of Fine Arts) on Calle Obispo Frutos.

The Soul of Spain

Andalusia is everybody's idea of the 'real' Spain: white villages among the olive groves, cities of historic splendour and romance, booming beach resorts. Southern Spain is the home of flamenco, gazpacho, the bullfight, and those sultry beauties with flashing dark eyes. It is also an adopted home of British ex-pats, tawdry high-rise hotels, and the playground of the super-rich. There's not much you can't do or see here. If you have the energy, you can even swim on the coast in the morning and ski in the mountains in the afternoon.

Andalusia (*Andalucía* in Spanish) is an autonomous region composed of the country's eight southernmost provinces, adding up to one-sixth of Spain's total area and population. It's hot and dry most of the time, which accounts for its great coastal popularity, though inland this can make it unbearable.

The civilizing Romans built roads and aqueducts; they brought their language, their laws, and, eventually, Christianity. The most profound foreign influence on

*T*he head decoration and earrings may be for special occasions, but the smile is everyday wear for this beauty from Andalusia.

Andalusia, however, came from the Moors, whose occupation of this area lasted longer than in any other part of the country. Muslim-controlled Andalusia enjoyed prosperity, technological advance, intellectual attainments and tolerance. After the Reconquest, the south played a leading role in Spain's Golden Age of discovery and empire.

Costa de Almería

This is Spain's dustbowl. A searing, parched place where water-supply problems and inaccessibility have kept tourist development at bay until very recently. The towns in the vanguard of the tourist trade are **Mojácar** and **Roquetas da Mar**, but away from these settlements things are

SOUTH

N

Badajoz
Mérida

Penarroya
Pueblonuevo
Pozoblanco
La Carolina
Bailén
NIV
Úbeda
Villacarrillo
N322
N630
N420
Cazalla de
la Sierra
Córdoba
Andújar
Baeza
Cazorla
N432
N324
N433
Aracena
C431
Guadalquivir
Jaén
N323
Lorca
Palos de
la Frontera
Itálica
Santiponce
Carmona
NIV
Écija
Montilla
Alcala la Real
Baza
N342
N435
N431
Ayamonte
A49
N333
N337
N432
N340
Huelva
Moguer
Sevilla
El Rocío
N333
N334
Loja
Granada
Guadix
Sierra Nevada
Garrucha
La Rábida
Acebuches
Sorbas
DOÑANA
NAT. PARK
A4
Zahara de
la Sierra
N342
Antequera
Alhama
Solynieve
3,478m
Capileira
Trevélez
N324
Tabernas
N340
Mójacar
Sanlúcar de
Barrameda
Jerez de
la Frontera
Vélez-
Málaga
Cave of
Nerja
Bubión
N340
Rota
El Puerto de S. María
Arcos de la
Frontera
Medina-
Sidonia
C341
Ronda
Monda
Mijas
Málaga
N340
Nerja
Almuñécar
Salobreña
N323
Almería
Cádiz
Gaucín
C339
Torremolinos
Marbella
Motril
Roquetas
de Mar
Vejér de
la Frontera
N340
Jimena de
la Frontera
Castellar
Casares
Estepona
Puerto Banús
Fuengirola
Capo Trafalgar
Algeciras
Tarifa
Gibraltar

ATLANTIC
OCEAN

Ceuta
MEDITERRANEAN
SEA
Tanger

0   80km
0   50 miles

▲ Mountain
☐ National Park
☐ Land above 2,000m (6,550ft)

much as they always have been. The former is a charming white village on a hill. The Moorish influence is visible in the cubic houses, some with domes. So far the development is low and relatively restrained. The latter is little more than a stretch of beach with high-rise hotels. Another fledgling resort is **Garrucha**, which has little more than a long beach and a yacht harbour.

The main road from Murcia to the provincial capital of Almería steers clear of the coast, offering instead extraordinary inland scenery. **Sorbas** is a town in the middle of nowhere, the more so since it is surrounded by the sinuous bed of the Río Aguas. High above the cliff face, the white houses seem to hang in the sky. By now the countryside has become red and slightly menacing and near the little town of **Tabernas**, with its Moorish houses and castle ruins, the scenery is so engrossing that the area is called **Mini-Hollywood.** American and Spanish film companies have shot a number of cowboy films in this American Western-like desert setting, including *A Fistful of Dollars*. The sets remain and have been converted into a tourist attraction where shoot-outs and hold-ups are now daily fare.

Almería

As you would expect from the name (the giveaway is the 'al') **Almería** spent its formative centuries under Moorish rule. *Al-Mariyah* is Arabic for 'mirror', perhaps

Clint Eastwood was here. The man with no name starred in A Fistful of Dollars, *his first 'Spaghetti Western', in this town with no name.*

a reference to the mirror-clear waters of the Gulf of Almería.

It is a modern city, although its **Alcazaba**, an 8th-century Moorish fortress, overhangs the town and the port. In its day it was fabled to have been the equal of Granada, but little remains of that glorious period. The stronghold is even bigger than it looks from below: 35ha (87 acres) of ruined fortifications and a garden where everything from geraniums to cacti grows. The buildings in the inner redoubt were all but levelled by a 16th-century earthquake. However, the crenellated ochre outer walls and a section of the turreted ramparts stand firm.

Just inland from the harbour front stands the forbiddingly fortified Gothic **cathedral**. Completed in the mid-16th century, this bastion of the faith bolstered Almería's seaward defences in an age when Barbary pirates were the scourge of this coast. Heading to the port, the **Paseo de Almería** is a good place for strolling and shopping, with outdoor cafés to vary the pace.

Costa del Sol

The Costa del Sol claims to enjoy 326 days of sunshine per year, which is pretty close to most tourists' idea of heaven. So, even though the beaches tend to be narrow and grey, this sprawl of resort hotels, holiday villages, *urbanizaciones* and time-share developments continues its cosmopolitan growth. Everybody wants a piece of the action, a place in the sun – from cheap and cheerful European package tourists to the seriously rich from all corners of the world. What's more, today's tourist is tomorrow's resident – there are some 300,000 ex-pat foreigners in this

*S*urrounded by the fertile hill country of inland Andalusia, a white village stands out as if the target of a celestial searchlight. The Moors ruled here for centuries, setting the pattern for narrow streets of whitewashed houses concealing cool, flowered patios.

area (mostly British). For better or worse, the bonanza rolls on. Our coverage of the coast continues from east to west through the provinces of Málaga and Granada.

Almuñécar

The double life of **Almuñécar** bounces between the overdeveloped beach and the attractive old town above, inviolate on its small hill, topped by a Moorish castle. Almuñécar has always been famous for its

238

red pottery; you can still see the artisans at work. The town was founded by the Phoenicians, who called it *Sexi* – with a name like that, you may find it surprising that there has not been more tourist development.

Nerja

East of Málaga, where the beaches are less expansive than to the west, this is the only sizeable resort of any note. Hotels and hostels cluster around Nerja's **Balcón de Europa**, an attractive palm-fringed promenade built on top of a cliff that juts out into the sea, with pretty beaches to port and starboard.

It is a favourite among holiday-makers who want to feel they are in part of old Spain, but with the reassurances of English tea-shops. The narrow old streets are attractive, and Nerja is a good compromise of tradition and tourism.

The mysterious caves of Nerja. Concerts and ballet are performed here in summer.

The area's principal attraction is the **Cueva de Nerja**, a truly cavernous hole in the ground 4km (2-3 miles) east of town. It was discovered in 1959 by a group of boys out hunting bats. Evidence including wall paintings and tools shows that the stalactite-encrusted cave has been inhabited, on and off, since Cro-Magnon days. Inside, one cathedral-like vault boasts the world's longest stalactite, measuring 59m (195ft) from roof to floor.

Málaga

More than 3,000 years ago Phoenician traders founded *Malaka*, the future **Málaga**, at the strategic spot where the Río Guadalmedina joins the Mediterranean. Later, the settlement expanded under Carthaginians and Romans. In the invasion year of 711 the Moors seized Málaga and built it into one of Andalusia's great cities. Almost at the end of the Reconquest, in 1487, it was finally returned to the Christian fold after a dreadful siege of three and a half months.

Earlier this century it was a favourite of the British, who at that time had no alternative pre-packaged Costa del Sol destinations. These days, tourists from beach resorts all along the coast still head for Málaga for a taste of the real Spain: twisting, narrow streets, waterfront promenades, an old Moorish fortress, and bullfights. Certainly, if you can't get to either Seville, Granada or Córdoba, then Málaga should be on your itinerary. The only cloud on the horizon is the bad reputation that the city has acquired for petty crime against tourists, but if you take all the usual precautions, you should not have any problems.

The ancient fort atop pine-clad **Gibralfaro** (Lighthouse Hill) looks down on the bullring; whether there is a *corrida* or a pop concert in session, the sound zooms right up. The spectacular view from Gibralfaro reaches from the Mediterranean horizon to the stony mountains north of the metropolis. Much ravaged by wars and the passage of centuries, it is now just a shell filled by a wild garden.

A footpath leads uphill from the Paseo

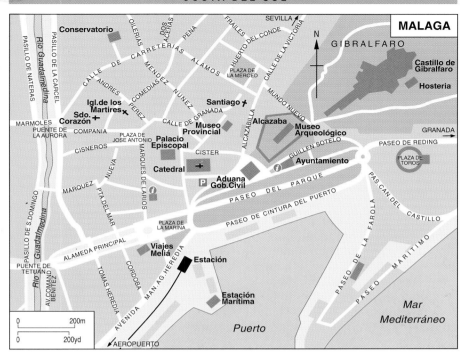

del Parque to the summit, but pickpockets and worse have been known to lurk along the way; to be on the safe side, go by taxi, bus or car.

The **Paseo del Parque**, which is built on land reclaimed from the sea, parallels the waterfront. Tall palm and plane trees, beautiful bougainvillaea, and aloe and geranium luxuriate in this tropical garden alongside the modern port. Midway along the avenue, Plaza de la Aduana gives on to the **Alcazaba**, a Moorish fortress. Across from the entrance lie the partially excavated ruins of a Roman theatre. The climb up the hillside to the Puerta del Cristo (Gateway of Christ) can be slightly tiring, but you will be on historic soil. This is where the first mass was celebrated after the Reconquest. Higher still, the former royal palace of the Moors contains a modest museum of archaeology.

Málaga's **cathedral** is known as the 'little lady with one arm' because it has one tall tower and the forlorn stump of another; work on the second 'arm' stopped in 1783. Under construction for three centuries, the Renaissance building incorporates baroque and neoclassical elements.

The **Museo de Bellas Artes** nearby in Calle de San Agustín shows, among other things, Málaga through the eyes of local artists. The most celebrated of them, Pablo Picasso, has a room of his own here. The museum also preserves some of the furniture from the house in Plaza de la Merced where Picasso was born in 1881.

Torremolinos

With its beaches, bars, restaurants, nightclubs, discos and throngs of tourists, **Torremolinos** is the fun capital of the

241

Costa del Sol. It has a reputation akin to that of Benidorm, a no-nonsense party sort of place taking good care of package-tourist business. From the beach of La Carihuela, the few remaining fishermen still set out at dawn in their gaily painted wooden *barques*. The catch, traditionally fried in crispy batter, ends up on the tables of the lively seafront restaurants.

*H*oliday playground of the rich and famous, Marbella may be more associated with luxury yachts than humble fishing craft these days, but behind the glamour, life for the local fishermen goes on much as it has done for centuries.

The adjacent resort of Fuengirola is a similarly popular place, although this is more geared for families, and lacks the pace and some of the eccentric local characters of Torremolinos.

Mijas

The picturesque village of **Mijas**, with its steep streets of whitewashed houses, is one of the most popular destinations for *costa* coach parties. Here the appearance of a typical corner of rural Andalusia has been preserved, albeit surrounded by modern villas and developments. The authenticity of the village may have been debased to cater for its numerous visitors but it is undoubtedly still a very attractive place. Except for *burro* (donkey) 'taxis', traffic is barred from the core of the village. The souvenir shops overflow with woven goods, tooled leather and ceramic articles of all kinds.

Mijas claims to have Spain's only square bullring, dating back to Moorish times.

Marbella

This is the aristocrat among the resorts of the Costa del Sol. Royalty and celebrities have been gravitating here for decades, and lesser mortals visit to see how the other half lives. Not surprisingly, prices are higher than anywhere else along the coast, but the standards are superior in accommodation, service and cuisine.

Marbella encompasses 28km (17 miles) of beachfront, built up with exclusive hotel complexes, and a **marina** with mooring space for hundreds of pleasure craft. North of the main road, in the old town, small shops are scattered through the warren of twisting streets. There are historic churches and a storybook Moorish fortress.

Monuments of the new Marbella cling to the hills on the western outskirts. A slightly enlarged copy of the Washington White House, is the holiday residence of the king of Saudi Arabia. Within hailing distance can be found many princely palaces, although most of them are well concealed. On a neighbouring rise is Marbella's modernistic mosque. Five hundred years after the Reconquest, direction signs in Arabic can again be seen in Andalusia.

They say it was Isabella of Castile who coined the name Marbella, from the Spanish for 'beautiful sea'. It is certainly an improvement on the old Phoenician name of *Salduba* (Salt City).

Puerto Banús

This is Spain's Saint-Tropez. A thousand yachts crowd the marina, some so big that

---

LITTLE BRITAIN

Beery pubs supplant earthy *tapas* bars and tea in the afternoon is more common than *café solo* on the tiny British enclave that is Gibraltar.

The Rock *(el Peñon)*, as it is known, is a narrow peninsula measuring just 6km² (21 square miles), but it has known more than its fair share of political and historical turmoil. The ancients considered it one of the Pillars of Hercules, marking the limits of the known world. To pass beyond it was to sail to certain death over the great waterfall at the edge of the world (another pillar was across the strait in Morocco).

In 711 the Moorish invasion of Iberia started here, led by Tariq ibn Ziyad, who named the peninsula after himself: Gibel-Tariq, Tariq's Rock, whence the modern 'Gibraltar'.

Spain reconquered Gibraltar in 1462, only to lose it to Britain in the 18th-century War of the Spanish Succession. As a crucial base for the Royal Navy, 'Gib' won honours in several wars. Spain, now a partner of Britain in the European Community and NATO, would like to regain sovereignty, but the Gibraltarians overwhelmingly profess allegiance to the United Kingdom.

For more than 15 years Spain blockaded the land border, but in 1985 it was opened, and it is now easy to visit Gibraltar for sightseeing, duty-free shopping and casino gambling. Most tours take in the ruins of the Moorish castle, the view from the Europa Point lighthouse, and the historic Trafalgar cemetery (Nelson's body was brought to Gibraltar after the fateful battle, and pickled in rum for its onward journey to England). The highlight is the cable-car ride to the top of the rock with its marvellous views – stopping half-way for a look at the famous Barbary apes. According to local superstition, if these apes ever leave the Rock, British dominance will end.

Don't forget to take your passport, however brief your intended visit.

Although there's a certain formality at the posh resort of Puerto Banús, shoes are not obligatory for wading.

they bear flags of convenience. It is the kind of resort where the first item on the menu is Russian caviar. Beyond the over-priced restaurants is a line-up of chic nightclubs and shops, where the beautiful people hang out.

Estepona

The last of the big resorts on the western flank of the coast, **Estepona** provides all the essentials for a sporty modern holiday – beaches, golf courses, marina – in an en-gaging small-town atmosphere. Of Roman origin, Estepona preserves the remains of Moorish fortifications and watchtowers.

Algeciras

The Moors landed here in 711 and you can still see their influence in old **Algeciras**. Otherwise it's all business in this high-rise town, an international gateway prospering from coast-road traffic and the ferry and hy-drofoil links with Tangiers, Morocco, and the Spanish North African enclave of Ceuta. Probably the best thing about Algeciras is the view across the bay to Gibraltar's memorable silhouette. The highway westwards climbs sharply, offer-ing some thrilling seascapes.

Costa de la Luz

The Atlantic-facing coast of southern Spain, called the Coast of Light, runs from the Strait of Gibraltar up to the Portuguese border. Seafaring folk who know the whims and perils of the open ocean share this shore with a relative trickle of tourists. This is a remote side of Andalusia, a long way from the bustle of the Costa del Sol, and with comparatively few tourist facil-ities. It does, however, have much to of-fer in the way of historic towns (including easy access to Seville), Spain's best na-tional park and long uncrowded beaches.

Those in search of a suntan, however, take note – it's very windy here.

Tarifa

North Africa is just a short hop of 13km (8 miles) away from **Tarifa**, Spain's southern extremity. Morocco's Rif mountains hang on the horizon, and Tangier is often clearly visible. Parts of the old Moorish walls still stand, along with the 10th-century fortress, now known as the **Castillo de Guzmán el Bueno**, after Alonso Pérez de Guzmán, a 13th-century Christian commander. Legend has it that he was called to the castle ramparts and told if he did not surrender Tarifa to the besieging Moors his son, held hostage, would be murdered. With a fine sense of melodrama he chose 'honour without a son, to a son with dishonour' and threw down his own knife to be used for the fatal deed.

From the castle ramparts you can look over to the Rock of Gibraltar and you may well see accomplished windsurfers, revelling in the gusty conditions – this is no place for beginners. The strong wind on the Costa de la Luz may be the scourge of sunbathers, but it has turned Tarifa into one of Europe's prime windsurfing locations.

Vejér de la Frontera

This is a beautiful unspoiled *pueblo blanco* sitting high on a bluff above the main road. There isn't a great deal you can actually visit here, but the whitewashed alleys of houses with black-grilled windows and bright red geraniums are travel-poster Andalusia at its best. It is definitely a town for exploring on foot.

The suffix *de la frontera* is common to many towns and villages in this part of Spain, and recalls the fact that the town was on the mediaeval border between the forces of Christians and Moors. Immediately due east of here, the Spanish and French fleets sailed in 1805 to fight the British at Cape Trafalgar. Britain won a famous victory that day, but in the process lost their favourite naval son.

Cádiz

Rolling Atlantic waves crash against the rocky defences of this narrow peninsula city, basking in the sunshine. The Atlantic Ocean has shaped the history of **Cádiz**. It was founded about 3,000 years ago by Phoenician traders from Tyre, on account of its excellent harbour, and is therefore one of the world's oldest cities. Christopher Columbus, too, valued the location, and it was from here that he departed on his second and fourth voyages to America. Later, when treasure-laden Spanish fleets took refuge, Cádiz was attacked by

---

COLUMBUS COUNTRY

The Río Tinto area around the industrial port city of Huelva is where Christopher Columbus started some of his travels. You can follow his trail in the area.

Near refineries on the road from Huelva to La Rábida, a giant waterside **monument** represents Columbus at the helm.

The Franciscan monastery at **La Rábida** is where he stayed, waiting for Ferdinand and Isabella to approve his project. He found an ally in the monastery's prior, who also believed that the world was round, and made representations on his behalf. Monks take visitors around the Mudéjar-style monastery daily (except Mondays), so you can visit the chapel where Columbus prayed.

A broad new boulevard leads into the pleasant little town of **Palos de la Frontera**. This is where Columbus is said to have stocked up with water and headed for America. The river has long since silted up, and Palos is surrounded by farmland. A monument marks the water source, and a canal several hundred metres from there is being dug to the river. Finally, Columbus recruited crewmen in the nearby town of **Moguer**.

Barbary pirates and the British; both Sir Francis Drake and the Earl of Essex left scars on the city.

In 1812, while Napoleon's troops were besieging Cádiz, the very first Spanish constitution was proclaimed. The delegates met in the **Oratorio de San Felipe Neri**, a domed church in the maze of the old town. You can hardly see the building itself for the memorial plaques vying for prominence on the façade.

The historic centre of the ancient seafaring town has definitely seen better days and the term 'seedy' has often been used to describe Cádiz. Here, opinions differ. Is it 'seedy' in a characterful way that only adds to its allure, or is it 'seedy' in an unappealing way? Its old streets certainly invite exploration by visitors. Do this by day, at least initially, and make up your own mind.

The baroque **cathedral**, overlooking the ocean, has a landmark dome glazed yellow. Its lavish treasury features a monster-sized monstrance made of a ton of silver. In the crypt is the tomb of the composer Manuel de Falla, who was born in Cádiz in 1876.

The Mueso de Bellas Artes is well worth a visit, particularly if you're a fan of the works of Zurbarán.

Sanlúcar de Barrameda
Here, where the Guadalquivir meets the Atlantic, Columbus's third trip to the Indies started; Magellan launched his round-the-world expedition and Pizarro sailed off to conquer Peru, but you would never guess it from today's quiet streets and fishing port.

Modern Sanlúcar is famous on account of the vineyards on the hills near by. They go to produce *Manzanilla*, a rich wine similar to sherry. The sea breezes are supposed to supply Manzanilla's distinctive salty tang.

Doñana National Park
The **Parque Nacional de Doñana** is the largest and most famous of the protected Spanish national parks. This wild conservation zone is made up of three environments: sand dunes (where parts of *Lawrence of Arabia* were filmed), pine areas and marshes. Until recent times, royal hunting parties used to fan out over the region, shooting exotic birds, deer and wild boar. Now the wildlife – including more than 250 bird species, transient or permanent – is protected. Among the

*T*he spectacular bee-eater is a colourful visitor to the Doñana National Park between May and August.

EL ROCIO
One of Spain's biggest, most enthusiastic religious festivals – the Romería del Rocío – takes place in the obscure community of El Rocío ('the Dew'), on the edge of Doñana National Park. The Whitsun (Pentecost) pilgrimage attracts more than a million colourful participants from all over Spain; they come by car, tractor, horse-carriage, ox-cart, on horseback or on foot. What brings them all to this otherwise inconspicuous village is a religious statue to which many miracles are attributed. The relic, the *Virgin of the Dew*, is said to have survived the Muslim occupation hidden in the marsh and has subsequently resisted all attempts to move it elsewhere.

rarities to be seen here: imperial eagle, purple gallinule and crested coot. Lynx are also found here.

The only way to see the park is by a guided tour. This is aimed at non-specialists, and what you see depends very much on the season, and what's afoot. Tours start from the reception centre at El Acebuche. For further details and reservations, phone (955) 43 04 32 as far in advance as possible.

Ayamonte

The Costa de la Luz and Spain end at the Guadiana River. The frontier town of **Ayamonte** is bigger than you might think at first. The *Ayuntamiento* (town hall) has a classic open-air patio with palm trees, a fountain, arches and tiled walls. From the *parador* on a bluff above Ayamonte you get an eye-filling view of the white town, the meandering river, and, across the way, Portugal looking curiously flat.

In the rolling hill country of Andalusia, the late 20th century has brought sweeping changes to agriculture, thanks in large part to bold irrigation projects. But the colour of farmhouses is still white.

carry your passport with you, even for a day trip, and do ensure that your car insurance is still valid across the border in Portugal.

Inland Andalusia

Beyond the beaches, Andalusia climbs to continental Spain's tallest peak, the Mulhacén at 3,482m (11,424ft). The population, however, concentrates in the lowlands, especially in the fertile triangle of the Guadalquivir valley. Our survey of the towns and cities of inland Andalusia takes a leisurely circular route, clockwise, starting in the hills west of Marbella.

Ronda

Clinging to a clifftop sundered by a deep gorge, **Ronda** is a strong competitor for the title of Spain's most dramatically sited town. The dizzying emplacement has always appealed to strategists. The ancient Iberians settled here, and then the Romans dug in. Under the Moors, Ronda proved impregnable for well over seven centuries.

The **gorge** that cleaves the city, called the Tajo, plunges over 150m (nearly 500ft) down to the surly Río Guadalevín. In a macabre episode during the Civil War, hundreds of Nationalist sympathizers were hurled to their deaths in the

The Portuguese town of Vila Real de Santo António is only 15 minutes away by ferry, or slightly longer if you choose to drive over the border via the impressive new suspension bridge just to the north. This would be your best bet if you were continuing west to the Algarve (it is a worthwhile day trip to Tavira, 30km, or Faro, 50km) or north towards Lisbon (which is a full day's drive). Whichever way you choose to travel, don't forget to

The vertiginous gorge at Ronda plunges down to the remains of old Arab Mills.

abyss, as recalled by Hemingway in *For Whom the Bell Tolls*.

For the best prospect of the Tajo and the patchwork of fields beyond, check out the view from the **Puente Nuevo** (New Bridge). It has spanned the ravine for more than two centuries, leading to the *Ciudad*, the old Moorish enclave. Ronda's Moorish kings – and Christian conquerors – used to live in the **Palacio de Mondragón**. Beyond the Renaissance portal, spacious courtyards with horseshoe arches and Arabic inscriptions reveal the real origins of this stately structure.

Ronda's chief mosque survives a street or two away as the church of **Santa María la Mayor**. The minaret was con-

verted into a bell tower, and a Gothic nave was tacked on to the original structure. Walk back across the chasm to the post-Reconquest part of town and you'll find Ronda's neoclassical **Plaza de Toros** (bullring). It's one of the oldest in Spain. A Ronda man, Francisco Romero, spelled out the rules of bullfighting in the 18th century; his father is said to have 'invented' the red rag that provokes the bull. This bullring is venerated as the cradle of the *corrida*, and whatever your views on the ritual, it is worth a visit. There's a small museum here, which is also entertaining for the non-aficionado.

Arcos de la Frontera

Another hill town in an extraordinary spot, **Arcos de la Frontera** also attracted ancient Iberian settlers.

At the top of the hill are the town hall, two churches and a *parador*. The fourth side of the square, a railing at the edge of a cliff, offers a stupendous view over rural Spain at its best – rolling hills of orchards, olive groves and vineyards and, directly below, the life-giving Río Guadalete. Roam the steep, narrow streets of the old town, with its Moorish and Gothic buildings. Like Vejer de la Frontera it's picture postcard Spain.

Jerez de la Frontera

Old wines and young horses bring fame to Jerez, which is the biggest town in the province of Cádiz.

The English, never very good at foreign languages, corrupted 'Jerez' to sherry, and

An unusual water fountain in the picturesque village of Grazalema.

the locally produced wine has borne the name ever since. Several of the many **bodegas** (wineries) in Jerez invite tourists to see how sherry is blended and aged in dark, aromatic halls. At Pedro Domecq they are proud to show you their most historic casks, and you will be in good company – visitors have ranged from the Duke of Wellington to Plácido Domingo. Meanwhile Gonzalez-Byass treats tourists to the tricks of its wine-tippling mice. Don't worry if you can't get into one of the 'big' names. As long as you turn up at the helpful tourist information office on a weekday morning, you will be directed to the nearest tour (there are no tours at the weekends or at any time during August). The hospitality of the *bodegas* is as generous as the bouquet of their wines: every tour ends with a comprehensive tasting session, and probably a small sample to take away.

As for the horses, the **Royal Andalusian School of Equestrian Art** (*Real Escuela Andaluza de Arte Ecuestre*) has the smartest, prettiest, lightest-footed

---

SHERRY: THE ENGLISH DRINK

Just over 400 years ago, Sir Francis Drake forcibly brought sherry to the attention of the English public. In a raid on Cádiz, the swashbuckling Drake seized nearly 3,000 barrels of the admirable aperitif. Then known as 'sack' or 'sherry-sack', it soon graced all the fashionable tables of London.

Shakespeare also thought enough of sack to praise it at length in *Henry IV, Part Two*. High-living Sir John Falstaff ends a long monologue extolling the amber nectar with this endorsement: 'If I had a thousand sons, the first human principle I would teach them should be to forswear thin potations, and to addict themselves to sack.'

mounts you may ever have seen. Every Thursday at noon the Jerez riding school puts on a beautifully orchestrated dressage show by horses that strut, goose-step, leap (sometimes encouraged by a thwack on the legs) and dance. If you like horses, it will be seventh heaven. If not, you may find it is as interesting as watching sherry mature. Turn up during the rest of the working week, and you can watch midday training sessions. Best of all, try to make it to Jerez for the annual **Spring Horse Fair**. This is when the aristocratic sherry barons get up on their horses and strut their stuff. There is a very strong Anglo influence to Jerez, as many bodegas were founded by British immigrants, and this is quite clear at the Horse Fair.

By way of historical monuments, the 11th-century walls of the Moorish **Alcázar** are now surrounded by gardens. Below the

hilltop fortress, the 18th-century **Colegiata** contains, appropriately, a precious image of Cristo de la Viña (Christ of the Vineyards). Other sights to see in Jerez include a **Museum of Flamenco** and a highly-rated **Clock museum**.

Seville

Romantic, spiritual, sensual **Seville** is as grand as an opera, and it has certainly inspired more operas than any other city – *The Barber of Seville*, *The Marriage of Figaro*, *Don Juan*, *Fidelio* and *Carmen* to name the most famous.

Seville has many faces: Moorish and Christian, stately boulevards and narrow alleys, tranquil gardens as fragrant as orange blossoms and cafés as noisy as anywhere on the peninsula (and that is saying

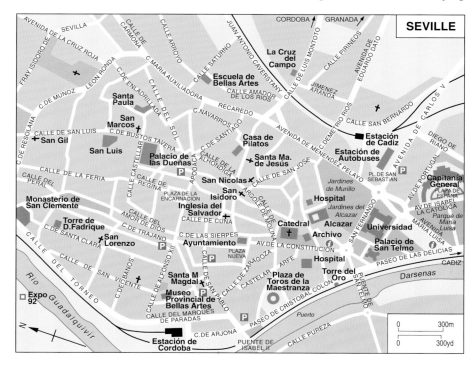

SPRINGTIME IN SEVILLE

Since the 16th century, the most solemn week in Spain's Christian calendar has been the occasion for tremendous festivities in Seville. The **Semana Santa** (Holy Week) **processions**, with masked penitents in sinister black pointed hoods (recalling the Inquisition), ornate candle-lit religious scenes carried on the shoulders of the faithful, and plaintive music, fill the streets for eight days. Finally, jubilant church bells signal the relief and joy of Easter.

Soon after the pageantry and fervour of Holy Week, Seville drops everything for the **Feria de Abril** (April Fair). Andalusia's most colourful celebration is a kaleidoscope of flamenco, bullfights, horses, flowers and wine.

Be sure to book months ahead if you want to stay in Seville during this period.

something). But they are all parts of the heart and soul of Spain. Capital of flamenco, a bastion of bullfighting, birthplace of Velázquez and Murillo, Seville is the fourth-biggest but most Spanish of Spain's cities.

The history of Seville leaps from success to success, under the Romans, the Visigoths and the Moors. After the Reconquest, Seville won a monopoly on trade with newly discovered America and great riches literally flowed straight into the city on the River Guadalquivir (Seville is still Spain's only major river port). During this Golden Age, a slogan developed: *Madrid is the capital of Spain but Seville is the capital of the world.* Seville is also a very forward-looking city. In 1992 it made the very most from hosting a very successful EXPO '92, not only by marketing itself to every major country in the world, but by building a whole new transport infrastructure to equip itself for future challenges.

In 1401, the Great Mosque of Seville was razed to make way for a colossal **cathedral** which became the largest Gothic church in the world. (Fortunately the minaret was saved.) There are five naves and more than 30 chapels, including the plateresque **Capilla Real** (Royal Chapel), the last resting place of the 13th-century King Ferdinand III, who delivered Seville from the Moors and was later canonized. Closed off by an 18th-century grille, the chapel is so beautiful that it is worth squeezing up against the screen for a good look. The most famous tomb in here is to the man who still brings the city fabulous wealth nearly five centuries after his death. No wonder the **Columbus tomb** is so ornate. Alongside the cathedral, the celebrated **Giralda** tower, formerly the minaret to the demolished mosque, is the city's lofty symbol. It's a hike up 34 flights of ramps (designed for horses) and one flight of steps to the top of the 98m (322ft) tower. Stop along the way for a breather and some unusual views of the cathedral's pinnacles and cityscapes beyond.

The **Alcázar** of Pedro the Cruel is a sumptuous monument from the 14th

COLUMBUS'S TRAVELS

It seems that even in death Christopher Columbus was exceedingly well travelled. He died in Valladolid (incredibly, alone and virtually forgotten) in 1506, and was interred for the next 27 years in the monastery of La Cartuja in Seville. The rest of his posthumous journey is fogged by historical confusion, but the bones were shipped off to Santo Domingo and maybe Cuba. After the defeat in the Spanish-American War, his presumed remains sailed back to Seville, where he finally received the heroic tomb that he might have expected.

century. The ceilings and walls of its halls provide a magnificent, if sometimes overpowering, concentration of Mudéjar abandon. Whereas the Alhambra in Granada was built by Moors for Moorish kings, this rambling palace was built by Moors for Christian kings. Beyond the richly embellished salons and apartments, the terraced **gardens**, scattered with pools and pavilions, are a visitor attraction in their own right.

Bordering on the Alcázar, the **Barrio de Santa Cruz** contains the essence of picturesque old Seville. The whitewashed walls in this labyrinth of narrow streets exude the fragrance of flowers, history and charm. Just wander at will, peering into the many lovely patios as you pass. On the edge of this district more Mudéjar sensations await in a typical 15th-century Andalusian palace, the privately owned **Casa de Pilatos** (Pilate's House). In case you are wondering as to the name and why the elegant patio has niches for the busts of Roman emperors, the design for the house was supposedly

*A*rabesques in old Seville: the spacious Patio of the Doncellas (ladies-in-waiting) in the Alcázar is a Renaissance impression of the Moorish style. In the 14th century, Pedro the Cruel recruited Mudéjar architects and artisans to redo an old Moorish palace. Expansions, repairs and revisions went on intermittently for several centuries. It may be a marriage of Christian and Moorish styles with some rather mixed results but on the whole it is one made in heaven.

modelled on Pontius Pilate's house in the Holy Land.

If the Giralda is Seville's most photographed monument, then the most picturesque is the **Plaza de España**, in María Luisa Park. Not a plaza in the conventional sense, it is semi-circular shaped and features a fanciful reconstruction of the palace of Pedro the Cruel. Gorgeous *azulejos* encrust the walls below this arcaded neo-Mudéjar fantasy, and tile-covered bridges criss-cross a canal in front of it. You can hire boats to be a part of the scene. The whole thing was built for the World Fair of 1929 (sadly curtailed because of the Great Depression). The Fair's pavilions still remain however and house two important city museums. The **Museo Arqueológico** is particularly good on the city's ancient history and houses many impressive remains from the Roman site of **Itálica** (10km/6 miles to the north west – a good excursion for fans of Roman digs, with a very impressive amphitheatre). The **Museo de Artes y Costumbres Populares** (Museum of Folk Arts and Costumes) concentrates on the colourful daily life of old Andalusia.

Just south of the Giralda is the **Hospital de la Santa Caridad** (Holy Charity Hospital). This hospital for the poor was founded in the 17th century and the highlight is its splendid church. Murillo pictures adorn the inside walls, Murillo *azulejos* dazzle on the exterior.

There is more magnificent art at the **Museo de Bellas Artes** (Fine Arts Museum) recently renovated and housed in an old convent. It's the best gallery this side of Madrid, and houses works by many big Spanish names plus foreign artist such as Rubens, Bosch, Titian and Veronese.

La Cartuja, an island in the Guadalquivir, has gained a landmark 21st-century suspension bridge in exchange for hosting EXPO '92, which celebrated the 500th anniversary of the first outing to America. The site had historical as well as logistical relevance as Columbus is said to have planned his voyage during a stay at the island's Carthusian monastery.

As for that infamous *femme fatale*, Carmen, the royal tobacco factory where she is supposed to have rolled cigars on her thigh is an enormous, square, 18th-century structure behind a moat, now the campus of the **University**.

A final word of caution. Although Seville is often the favourite tourist city in all Spain, there are certain drawbacks of which you should be aware. The city is notorious for petty crime. Always watch your personal belongings very carefully and never park your car on the street unless you have to. Better still, don't drive here. Always book ahead as the city gets incredibly busy at peak periods. Don't come here at the height of summer as it is unbearably hot and humid. And finally, it's a very expensive place.

*F*lowers brighten *everyday life in the narrow alleys of Seville, the world capital of flamenco. The local form of the dance, called the Sevillana, is also popular in Madrid.*

Córdoba

Córdoba is above all a Moorish city: its star attraction is the biggest and best mosque ever to be built by the Moors. Yet centuries before the Moors came, it had also enjoyed another golden age as the

The fabulous interior of the world's greatest mosque at Córdoba. The beautiful invention of the double-arch construction is the mother of necessity. When the Moors were building the mosque they used existing Roman columns – but these were not tall enough to give the required height, so they simply added another tier.

capital of Rome's *Hispania Ulterior*. It was once the biggest Roman city on the Iberian peninsula, although today there are few Roman remains. By the 10th century, the capital of the caliphate was as big and brilliant as any city in Europe. In the Middle Ages, indigenous Christians and Jews helped Córdoba blossom under Muslim rule as a centre of culture, science and art.

After the Reconquest, the Spaniards customarily levelled mosques and built churches on top of the rubble. In Córdoba, happily, they spared one of the world's biggest and most beautiful mosques, but they did build a cathedral inside it! The result is called the **Mezquita-Catedral**. The original Great Mosque, begun in the year 785 by Emir Abd-er-Rahman I, grew to its present humbling proportions under the 10th-century leader al-Mansur.

The exterior is quite unprepossessing and gives no hint of what is to come. A high wall surrounds the sacred enclosure and you reach the mosque through the ceremonial forecourt with its fountains and orange and palm trees. Inside, in the half-light, an enchanted forest of hundreds of **columns** seems to extend to infinity. The columns of marble, onyx and jasper are topped by arches upon arches, in red and white stripes. At the end of the main aisle, tendrils of stone twine around the 10th-century **mihrab** (prayer niche) where the caliph attended to his prayers. It is hard to gauge size in such a forest of stone, but the Mezquita is big by any standards, and is

not much smaller than St Peter's Cathedral in Rome. Almost hidden away in the very centre of these acres of beauty is the **cathedral**, a spectacular sequel in Gothic and baroque styles, pointedly rising far above its surroundings. Charles V was responsible for its building but perhaps later realized his folly. Legend has it that he admonished the builders, 'You have destroyed something unique to build something commonplace'. Which is a bit harsh on the cathedral as it is something of a florid masterpiece (the mahogany **choir stalls** in particular are splendidly carved). It remains, however, a shame that it was built here, of all places.

South west of the mosque, on the river, the **Alcázar** was actually built by a Christian king, Alfonso XI. There are pleasant patios, Roman relics, terraced gardens and, best of all, wonderful views from the ramparts.

Cross the river by the Roman bridge and visit the 14th-century **Torre de la Calahorra**. It is now a historical museum, and will fill you in on the town's Moorish history. You could even visit here first to prepare yourself for the Mezquita.

To absorb the full flavour of Córdoba there is no substitute for wandering the narrow streets and alleys of the **Barrio de la Judería** (Jewish Quarter), in which a small 14th-century synagogue can still be found. You will need all your peripheral vision not to miss glimpses of cool, flowered patios, so perfect they seem show-windows for traditional Spanish life.

Just to the north east is the town's best historical museum, the **Museo Arquéo-logico**. Other places of interest include the **Palacio del Marqués de Viana**, possibly Córdoba's finest private house, and two museums. In the **Museo Taurino** (Bull-fighting Museum) you can learn about the tragic demise of the city's favourite native *torero*, Manolete, while the Museo de Bellas Artes (Fine Arts Museum) is devoted to gentler pursuits.

Around Córdoba

Jaén

The province of Jaén, east of Córdoba, provides some of Spain's finest scenic contrasts. Harsh mountains stare down at undulating hills, covered with thousands of luxuriant olive groves, refreshed by giant irrigation projects.

The provincial capital, Jaén, spreads beneath a picturesque, ancient, Moorish castle, now converted to a *parador*. However, there is little to see in town. The **cathedral** has a vast Renaissance façade, which contrasts with the narrow streets and little squares and the provincial museum specializes in archaeology, notably Iberian and Roman relics. For a closer look at 11th-century life, see Jaén's **Arab baths**, the largest in Spain (though not as interesting as those of the Alhambra).

Baeza

There are not many towns of 15,000 inhabitants can list over 50 worthwhile historic buildings, but charming **Baeza** is very special. It played an important role in the Moorish period, then prospered after the Reconquest.

Life is somewhat quieter today: the main square, much too big for a town this size, is surrounded by buildings ranging from very agreeable to very distinguished. Just off the square, the **Fountain of the Lions**, composed of recycled Ibero-Roman statuary, marks the Plaza del Populo. The tourist office, housed in a 16th-century mansion, has maps of suggested walks through Baeza's prized collection of golden stone churches, monasteries and palaces.

Úbeda

Nearly twice the size of Baeza, **Úbeda** is just as engaging, and grander still. This was an important headquarters during the Reconquest and many Spanish nobles involved in the struggle liked Úbeda well enough to build their palaces here.

As you enter the town, it may appear disconcertingly modern; follow the signs to the *Zona Monumental*.

The showcase square is the **Plaza Vázquez de Molina**, which houses all the following architectural treasures.

The 16th-century **Sacra Capilla del Salvador** (Sacred Chapel of the Saviour) is the town's finest church. It is a private chapel but is open for visits. Another 16th-century gem is the former **Palace of the Dean of Málaga**, which became one of the first *paradores* in 1930; the old town is so undefiled by commercial infringements that you might miss the understated *parador* sign. Beyond is the Renaissance **Palacio de las Cadenas** (Palace of Chains), the name referring to its decorations. Opposite, in the 13th-century church of **Santa María de los Reales Alcázares**, the patio of the old mosque has given way to a Gothic cloister.

There are several more historic plazas in Úbeda. Just pick up a map from the tourist office. If you appreciate good architecture in quiet unaffected surroundings, the town is a joy.

Granada

Two factors have combined to make **Granada** inspiringly different from Andalusia's other Moorish cities: its site at the foot of the slopes of the snow-capped Sierra Nevada, and its stubborn historical resistance.

For more than two centuries, while the rest of Spain was busy building Gothic cathedrals and heating up the Inquisition, Granada remained a self-sufficient island of Islam, encircled by the unfinished Reconquest. Moors seeking safety from

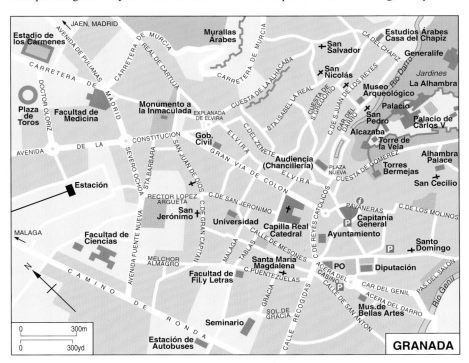

vanquished Córdoba and Seville swelled the population. Some of these refugees were great craftsmen, pitching in their talents to make mediaeval Granada a showcase city. When Ferdinand and Isabella accepted the keys to conquered Granada in January 1492, they discovered such splendour that they adopted the **Alhambra** for their own uses.

The Alhambra is actually a series of palaces, built in the 14th century. It was guarded by a sturdy **Alcazaba** (fort) while

They say that the Moorish king who gave up the Alhambra wept as he looked backwards to his vanquished palace. The very best views are from the hill of the Albaicín district opposite. The snowy Sierra Nevada provides the perfect backdrop.

by contrast its magnificent gardens provided a refuge for a civilization under siege. After the Reconquest, the citadel of the **Alhambra** suffered centuries of vicissitudes and years of neglect, but recently it has been restored, and now shines

again as the most magnificent mediaeval palace the Arabs ever built – anywhere. 'Nothing in life is sadder than to be blind in the Alhambra', reads the old inscription.

It is a long, steep, wooded climb up to the top; ignore the persistent would-be 'car-park attendants' who try to usher you off the road well before the Alhambra's official car parks. The ticket office is not well marked (it is to the left as you enter up into the compound) but once you have found it, it is a relief to know that your ticket is good for two days so that you don't have to cram everything in. It is worth noting that the Alhambra is also open at certain times in the evening, so if you would like a romantic floodlit viewing enquire at the ticket office about opening times.

You enter through the former council chamber (*Mexuar*) and a patio into the Arabian-Nights **Patio de los Arrayanes** (Court of the Myrtle Trees). The reflecting pool, a focus for photographers, is populated by a pack of plump goldfish. In the **Salón de Embajadores**, the royal audience chamber, the walls, five storeys high, are decorated with the most delicate examples of Arabic filigree and calligraphy. At the centre of the elegantly arcaded **Patio de los Leones** (Court of Lions)

The fabulous decoration of the Patio of the Mexuar – one of the Alhambra's finest rooms, leading into the 'official business' area of the mediaeval palace (previous page).

stands a fountain supported by a dozen cascading stone lions. Splendid rooms radiate out on every side, inviting leisurely exploration. The joy of the Alhambra is the detail of its beautiful ornamentation, mostly in frail stucco and wood, but do not expect to see much in the way of furnishings or regal trappings. It is largely an empty house.

Other highlights include the **Royal Baths**, where beams of sunlight peep through star-shaped holes and the lovely patio of the **Daraxa Garden** where Washington Irving once had rooms (unfortunately closed to the public). Romantics should pick up a copy of *Tales from the Alhambra* (1829) by Irving (the man who created Rip Van Winkle). His yarns brought attention to the Alhambra and helped save it from its decline to ruin.

As at Córdoba, a section of the palace was arrogantly razed to make way for Christian designs. Once again the culprit was Charles V. The **Palacio de Carlos V** was built by Pedro Machuca, a student of Michelangelo, to give the king a Renaissance roof over his head. A distinguished piece of work it may be, but after the delicacy and beauty of the Moorish palace, it seems a leaden lump. However, it does house two museums, of which the **Museo Nacional de Arte Hispano-musulmán**, (National Museum of Hispano-Muslim Art) is the best. This features some exquisite examples of the local Moorish arts and crafts, from an inlaid throne to ceramic masterpieces.

The **Alcazaba**, the military fortress, is the oldest part of the Alhambra and only the outer walls and towers survive. There is little to see and no historical interpretation. Still, it is a mighty place and the view from the top of the Torre de la Vela (watch tower) is the kind of prospect that wars were waged for. It reaches from the snowy mountains to the lovely forested hills, down to the tile-roofed warrens of old Granada, and the plain beyond. Better still, enjoy the view in reverse, from the hill of the Albaicín district opposite. When the sun sets and intensifies the colours of the ochre-coloured walls you will understand the name *al-hamra* ('the red one').

The Alhambra's famous gardens, the **Generalife** (pronounced *khay-nay-rah-lee-feh*) take their name from the Arabic for 'architect's garden' or 'sublime orchard', the latter being more appropriate. Here the king would seek refuge from the pomp and protocol of the Alhambra, musing among the fountains, trees, flowers, and the romance of an inimitable view over his realm. In the grounds of the summer palace, oleander, rhododendron and roses thrive, fountains play and cascades tumble.

After seeing the Alhambra, take a taxi to the top of the hill opposite, which holds the **Albaicín** district. This is Granada's most picturesque and oldest quarter, itself dating back to the Moors. Walk back down the hill, seeking out the best views of the Alhambra (probably from the square of the church of San Nicolás), and taking in the whitewashed houses, alfresco restaurants and cafés. At the bottom of the hill are some little-visited **Arab**

Baths. In anywhere else apart from Granada they would be a major attraction.

In the centre of town, Granada's white and gold cathedral, designed by Diego de Siloé, is as imposing as ordered, but the freestanding **Capilla Real** to one side steals its thunder. The great masterpiece of Enrique de Egas, the Renaissance chapel serves as the **mausoleum** of the Catholic Monarchs. The façade, with its twisted columns and blind arcade, displays remarkable qualities of dignity and refinement, and this applies just as truly to the interior. Behind a glorious wrought-iron screen, the white marble effigies of Ferdinand and Isabella lie on the right-hand side of the chancel, with those of their daughter, Joan the Mad, and her husband, Philip the Fair. Look into the crypt below to see the simplicity of their actual lead caskets. Under glass in the **sacristy** are Ferdinand's blunt-tipped sword, with a small gold handle a child could barely get a grip on, and Isabella's jewelless crown. They seem such paltry, almost ironic, artefacts to celebrate the memory of two monarchs who shaped the history not only of Spain, but much of the New World. On the walls of the sacristy hang superb 15th-century works of art from Isabella's personal collection, including Rogier van der Weyden's moving *Pietà* and his *Nativity*, an intimate homely scene; an emblematic *Head of Christ* by Dierick Bouts; and Botticelli's *Christ in the Garden*. These were all pious objects of the queen's devotions.

Sierra Nevada and The Alpujarras

If you have seen Granada, or perhaps a picture of the Alhambra, then you have probably seen the Sierra Nevada. The picturesque snow-capped mountains in the distance are just over an hour's drive south east. The road rises to over 3,352m (11,000ft) making it the highest navigable road in Europe, and it is only open in summer. It's quite a test of driving, and the views are tremendous, but the goal of most visitors who come this way is the ski-resort of **Sol y Nieve**. There is a ski jump here, but overall the amenities are more suitable for beginners or intermediate skiers.

The Alpujarras are the south-facing slopes of the Sierra Nevada. They are probably the wildest part of all southern Spain, and it was here that the Moors made their final retreat after the fall of Granada. The villages consequently look as Moorish as the *pueblo blancos* in the lower valleys, though features such as open patios are understandably eschewed in these chillier climes. Do pay a visit to **Bubión** and especially **Capileira**, which has already been 'discovered' to a small degree, and is touted by some to become the next Mijas. Isolation is, of course, the big stumbling block to coach parties.

If you are the active sort, this is marvellous hiking country, from mere rambling to serious climbing. Horse riding is another speciality of the area.

Cradle of the Conquistadores

Stranded half-way between the sea and Madrid, Estremadura has always languished as an economic backwater, and is relatively unknown to most Spaniards, let alone tourists. It is a harsh and unyielding land, and it has bred men of similar qualities. Some of these Estremadurans were also extremely ambitious, courageous, and ruthlessly dedicated to conquest. From these ranges they crossed the sea to subdue and destroy ancient civilizations, create new cities in their own image and to carry back to the homeland gold and riches beyond their wildest dreams.

Estremadura

The wide open land of the Spanish west (Extremadura in Spanish) was the birthplace of the *conquistadores,* the adventurers who colonized a new continent. Among their most celebrated native sons *(extremeños)*, were Cortés who colonized Mexico, Pizarro who conquered Peru, and de Soto who discovered the Mississippi.

In Estremadura there are said to be over 3,000 storks' nests. The old walled town of Cáceres has more than its fair share but that may be because it has more towers, spires and tall elegant buildings than most.

Nowadays, young men leave Estremadura for the same economic reasons, but they usually choose to make their fortunes less dangerously, in Madrid's offices or northern European factories.

Estremadura's heyday came in the time of ancient Rome. Along with all of present-day Portugal, the region belonged to Roman *Lusitania*. The capital of this province was the small city of Mérida, then grandly known as *Augusta Emerita* in honour of the emperor and his legionaries, who settled here. Two important rivers – the Guadiana and the Tagus – flow through the region on their way to Portugal and the Atlantic ocean. Great efforts have been made to tap these waterways for irrigation, but beyond a few green spots, Estremadura remains parched. It is still underpopulated unless you count the migratory flocks of

269

sheep among the holm and cork oaks; lamb is always on the menu. The farmers also keep pigs and make ham and sausage with a national reputation.

The definition of Estremadura ('land beyond the Río Duero') was flexible in the Middle Ages, when it encompassed a much larger area than the modern boundaries. Below, we stretch the borders to include a couple of charming, historic towns in Salamanca province, and this chapter is arranged in south-to-north order, starting in a part of the region indistinguishable from Andalusia.

Zafra

The most attractive of southern Estremadura's towns, the white houses of **Zafra** recall its Moorish origins. So too does the design of the town's mediaeval castle, previously an *alcázar*, now a sumptuous *parador* which still holds a fine gilded chapel. It is named 'Hernán Cortés' in honour of the well-known conqueror of Mexico, who stayed in the castle before his excursion to the New World. Next to the *parador* is the small old town centre which converges on two attractive arcaded plazas.

Badajoz

This close to the Portuguese border, you are as likely to find baked codfish on the menu as local lamb. Ever since the ancient Romans founded it at a sensitive strategic location, **Badajoz** (now the biggest city in Estremadura) has often been a town at war, most recently and tragically in the Civil War, when its bullring became a mass execution site.

The ancient **Puerta de Palmas** gateway, a small fortress in itself, leads to the walled city, with its narrow mediaeval streets. Another arch used to bar the way to the gardened **citadel** on Orinace hill, overlooking the Guadiana river. This is where the rulers of the Moorish kingdom of Badajoz held sway.

The **cathedral**, with its heavy walls and pinnacled tower, was built in the 13th century. The Gothic architecture was later modified with Renaissance effects. Inside are impressive choir stalls, paintings, tapestries and tombstones. On the same square is the town's **Museo Provincial de Bellas Artes** which boasts some good Flemish tapestries. There is another museum near by, the Museo Arquéologico, housed in a 16th-century mosque.

Mérida

Today **Mérida** is a sleepy modern town of no great distinction but it was once an imperial capital dubbed the Rome of Spain and still boasts the greatest number of Roman remains in any Spanish town.

The town was founded in 25 BC and grew rich and influential as the capital of the province of *Lusitania*. After the fall of the Romans, the Visigoths further enhanced the city until in AD 713 it fell to the Moors. The caliph, disappointed by his new subjects' revolutionary tendencies, let the town decline.

The *pièce de résistance* of the town is its partially restored **Teatro Romano**, seating over 5,500 spectators. For acoustics and visibility the design has never been bettered. Mérida's theatre was built in the 1st century BC, under the sponsorship of Agrippa, the son-in-law of the Emperor Augustus. The show went on (tragedy, comedy or mime) until late into the 4th century AD. Under new management, classical Roman and Greek plays are again being produced here; an inspiring way to spend a summer evening under the stars.

The elliptical **Anfiteatro**, next door (also known as the Circus Maximus), was designed to hold 15,000 fans of gladiatorial combat and chariot races. Perhaps not surprisingly, blood and thunder shows always drew bigger crowds than the more intellectual offerings. The theatre was even flooded at times to recreate great naval victories (in miniature, of course).

Just across the street from the park leading to the theatre and arena is an

The Roman wall and floor mosaics at Mérida are probably the finest that you will come across in Spain.

excellent award-winning new museum. No mere local project, this is the **Museo Nacional de Arte Romano**. On show are statues, vases, locally minted coins (always a sign of an important town) and even paintings discovered on the podium of the arena.

Around town are many other Roman monuments: what's left of a patrician villa next to the arena; a temple to Diana; Trajan's Arch; an aqueduct; and a bridge 0.8km (½ mile) long, with 64 granite arches, spanning the Guadiana. The **hornito**, 'little oven', is a small temple where a 13-year-old martyr, Santa Eulalia, is said to have been burnt alive by the Romans.

Guadalupe

From afar, the turrets, spires and crenellations of the rambling monastery announce an impressive shrine. Physically,

It's a pleasant place to visit but you probably wouldn't want to make your living here. Land for farming was once given to veterans of the Roman legions as a retirement pension. In modern times enterprising irrigation schemes have greened the Estremaduran hills, but little else has changed for traditional farmers and life is still tough on the land.

THE LEGEND OF GUADALUPE

Experts say that the venerated effigy of the Virgin of Guadalupe was carved at the end of the 12th century. According to legend, however, it is well over twice that age.

In the mediaeval version, the statue had been carved by St Luke himself. Then, late in the 6th century, the icon stood in the private chapel of Pope Gregory the Great in Rome. The pope sent the statue to Seville, but just before the Moors overran the city in AD 711 the relic was evacuated northwards. It was buried for safekeeping alongside the Guadalupe river, but in the chaos of those days it was lost.

Then, in the 13th century, a shepherd named Gil Cordero had a miraculous vision: the Virgin herself directed him to the spot where the statue was buried. Soon a shrine was built, then a chapel, a church, and eventually the vast citadel-monastery. The elaborately dressed and crowned statue has attracted millions of ordinary pilgrims, primarily from Spain and Spanish America, as well as celebrities from Ferdinand and Isabella to Pope John Paul II.

as well as economically, the institution totally dominates the very small town spread at its feet; the main square of **Guadalupe** descends from the monastery's steps. The narrow streets of the village, whose prosperity has always depended on the pilgrim traffic, retains its traditional face; bird cages and flowerpots brighten the balconies of the old houses.

Everything here revolves around the wooden statue of the Virgin of Guadalupe.

*G*uadalupe monastery –
*Spain's second most important
Marian shrine after Montserrat.
The feast day of the Virgin,
October 12, draws huge crowds.*

It's a familiar enough story, involving visions, a chance discovery and miraculous intercessions on behalf of Spanish forces in times of strife. The Virgin became the shrine and inspiration of the *conquistadores* and their riches in turn built a powerful institution and a missionary training school for the conversion of the New World. When Columbus brought back a couple of token American Indians, they were baptized here to symbolize the Christianization of the New World. Columbus also named the Caribbean island Guadeloupe after this town. Even today, here in the back of beyond, it remains Spain's fourth most important pilgrimage site.

The **monastery** complex covers an area of about 2 ha (5 acres). There are so many irregularities and extensions that the floor plan looks like a child's doodle. The Flamboyant façade, flanked by stern, square, defensive towers, offers some airy Mudéjar stonework. The church was begun in the 14th century and enlarged four centuries later.

To see the rest of the complex, including the revered statue and the riches around it, you have to join a tour. The guides tend to speak only Spanish, but some exhibits are labelled in English as well. You'll see the 15th-century Mudéjar cloister, an embroidery museum, the Gothic cloister, and the chapter house and sacristy, with a remarkable collection of paintings by Zurbarán, among others.

Trujillo

The hilltop skyline of **Trujillo**, seen from afar, is one of those magical sights that revives the spirits of the tired traveller. Even up close, the town does not disappoint. There are no modern intrusions here to mar the great sense of history.

Although Spain has historic towns with far more imposing architecture, Trujillo's main square must win a prize for relaxed charm. The eccentrically shaped **Plaza Mayor** is a happy meeting place of distinguished and ordinary buildings.

The most elegant of these, on the southwest corner of the square, is the **Palacio del Marqués de la Conquista**, built by Pizarro's half-brother (and son-in-law), Hernando. Along with seals of honour on the walls, look for the bas-relief portraits of Francisco and Hernando and their South American Indian brides. With their historic escutcheons, portals, windows and patios, half a dozen palaces around the town reward close study.

SONS OF TRUJILLO

Of all the *conquistador* towns, none are prouder of their sons' exploits than Trujillo. The most famous were the Pizarros who conquered Peru, but other, lesser-known natives were Diego García de Paredes and Francisco de las Casas, who both founded towns called Trujillo, in Venezuela and Honduras respectively, and Francis Orellana, the first navigator of the Amazon.

Diego García in particular had a fearsome reputation. He was known as the Estremadura Samson and among his legendary feats of strength he is said to have picked up the font in Santa María Mayor to carry holy water to his mother. This is the same font that Francisco de Pizarro was baptised in and the tombs of the Pizarros and that of García are also in this church.

Diagonally across the square, you cannot miss the bronze equestrian **statue** of Francisco Pizarro (cast in 1927, by two American sculptors), the scourge of the Incas. Both rider and horse wear armoured helmets. Behind them, the town clock looks out from the corner tower of the Gothic church of **San Martín**; storks nest above it, evidently immune to the jolt of the gongs. When you are exploring the long, dark nave of this church, which is paved with historic tombstones, mind the step: half-way to the altar, the floor level suddenly rises.

The Romanesque and Gothic church of **Santa María la Mayor,** up the hill, boasts a fine Hispano-Flemish style retable by Fernando Gallego. On the balcony, note two VIP-sized stone seats, built for the Catholic Monarchs, Ferdinand and Isabella, who attended a royal funeral here. There are several *conquistador* tombs in the church. On the hilltop, the heavily fortified **castillo** began as a Roman fort and later became a Moorish *alcazaba.* Above the keyhole-shaped main gate, in a glassed-in niche, stands the Virgin of Victory, the local patron. The view over Trujillo from here is the best in town.

Cáceres

The old walled city of **Cáceres**, capital of the province of the same name, is one big national monument, a magnificent assembly of mellow stone churches, palaces and towers.

T his sculpture on the corner of Hernando Pizarro's mansion in Trujillo illustrates the subjugation of the New World. Above, the glory; below, the despair.

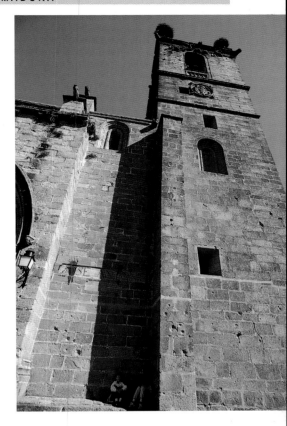

T his sturdy tower in Cáceres sums up the conquistador *qualities of strength, ambition and longevity.*

Before it became a feast of mediaeval architecture, Cáceres was a Roman town, and the Roman wall looks now much as it did then. You are bound to gravitate to the **Plaza Mayor**, along the town wall, as this is the centre of local life, especially at the hour of the *paseo.* Cáceres has all the historical attributes of Trujillo, but being a provincial capital and a college town, is much livelier. The crowd bulges into the side-streets; conversations reverberate; husks of chewed sunflower seeds shower onto the pavements. As night falls, the historic buildings are illuminated, providing a dignified backdrop to the relaxed ritual.

The skyline used to be more vertical. Many an aristocratic or nouveau-riche family crowned its mansion with an ego-expanding fortified tower. Petty feuds ensued, and in an effort to ease tension, Queen Isabella ordered that they should be truncated. Later the rules were eased, and there are heights enough to interest a great number of storks, for which the town is famous. One of the most visible towers is part of the Toledo-Moctezuma mansion, formerly the home of a follower of Cortés, who married the daughter of the Aztec emperor.

Go through the Arco de la Estrella (Star Arch) into the **old town** and wander among the mediaeval mansions, towers and churches. Look out for the details on these rough-stone mansions: heraldic shields, Renaissance windows and filigreed roof decorations. Inside you may well catch a glimpse of a pretty patio. The Casa de las Veletas (Weathervane House) has been turned into an excellent provincial **museum** of archaeology and ethnology including some historical local costumes and customs. In the basement is the original 11th-century Moorish cistern of the *alcázar*.

Alcántara

In its day, the **six-arched bridge** over the Tagus near here was world renowned for its elegant engineering. It boasts extraordinarily high arches, is 194m (636ft) long and altogether so impressive that the town was named after it: *al-Qantara* is Arabic for 'the bridge'. The Romans built it in AD 106 during the reign of the Spanish-born Emperor Trajan.

The name of the town in turn was given to the Order of Knights who defended their fortress here against the Moors in the 13th century. With a membership up to 100,000, the Order figured prominently in two centuries of struggle for the Reconquest of Spain. The convent of San Benito is a legacy of those times.

East of Alcántara the Tagus has been dammed, giving the landscape a dramatic facelift. Beside its aesthetic contribution to the area, the lake also provides good recreational possibilities.

Plasencia

When King Alfonso VIII of Castile liberated this hilltop town from the Moors in the 12th century, he renamed it **Plasencia**, and fortified it with a city wall that included 68 towers. Plasencia's importance has slipped since then, but the bristling silhouette still stands. The old mansions and churches retain their historic allure.

The **cathedral** works its architectural way from Romanesque to Gothic. It rates among Estremadura's most significant churches for its rich ornamentation, starting with plateresque embellishment on the exterior. The choir stalls, carved to illustrate Bible stories and scenes from mediaeval life, are particularly notable. In the old town are aristocratic houses and full-blown palaces, as well as narrow streets lined with simple white houses. Plasencia is an important agricultural centre although it only comes alive on a Tuesday, which is market day.

La Alberca

Just north of the Estremadura border in León region, this charming, unpretentious rural settlement is another

'Estremaduran town' (it's actually in Salamanca province) which has been declared a national monument. Donkeys are at work in the main streets, whitewashed houses overhang the narrow alleys, with flowers brightening the flimsy-looking wooden balconies. You may see the bean harvest spread out to dry in the middle of La Alberca's unassuming Plaza Pública, a far cry from the grandeur of main squares elsewhere. Black-clad housewives wait patiently behind trays of pollen and homemade nougat and honey. Try to be here on 15 August, when the whole town turns out in traditional costume. It is celebrated throughout Spain as the Feast of the Assumption but they say no one does it better than the people of La Alberca.

Only 14km (9 miles) west from La Alberca, the **Peña de Francia** is a peak with a Dominican monastery (closed in winter) at the summit. A paved road winds to the top (altitude 1,723m/5,653ft), spreading at your feet an incomparable **view** of the whole of neighbouring Castile and more.

Why the French name ('Rock of France')? It is suggested that French pilgrims joined in the Reconquest here, then settled down in the area. The shrine of the *Virgen Morena* (Dark Virgin), a statue discovered in the 15th century, is a popular modern-day pilgrimage.

Ciudad Rodrigo

You can literally walk all the way around the pleasant, ancient hill town of **Ciudad Rodrigo** (also in Salamanca) in a few minutes. Just take the path on top of the mediaeval defensive wall encircling the old city. It measures just over 2km (1 mile) and is only interrupted by a *parador* housed in the town's old castle.

Ciudad Rodrigo's Plaza Mayor is distinguished by the **Casa Consistorial** (the town hall), a 16th-century arcaded palace with a belfry. A smaller palace on the square has rather come down in the world; its ground floor now serves as a general store. There are perhaps a dozen worthy old mansions in the town, most with interesting features to examine – such as escutcheons, grillework, stone-masonry, and perhaps an inviting patio.

The exterior of the **cathedral**, begun in the 12th century, is full of fine sculptural details, especially around the west portal. Inside, the choir stalls are richly carved by the same craftsman, Rodrigo Alemán, who distinguished himself at Plasencia, Ávila, Toledo and Zamora. However, the Rodrigo in the name of Ciudad Rodrigo is another fellow completely. This Rodrigo is Count Rodrigo González Girón, who gave the town a big boost in the 12th century.

British visitors to Ciudad Rodrigo may like to note there is a long-standing historical link with the city. Ever since the Duke of Wellington defeated Napoleon's forces here in 1812 during the War of Independence (Peninsula War) every Duke of Wellington has also carried the honorary title: Duke of Ciudad Rodrigo.

The best-known landmark of Ciudad Rodrigo is an archaeological monument beyond the walls. **Las Tres Columnas** (the Three Columns), in a triangular configuration, seem to have made up the corner of a Roman temple.

Here in the border country, so close to Portugal, the countryside is very sparsely settled. The most activity that you are likely to see is modern-day cowboys tending rambling cattle herds among low, generous oak trees.

THE CONQUISTADORES

They came from the harsh soil of Estremadura and went forth ruthlessly to explore and exploit the New World. Many of the Conquistadores, who launched Spain's Golden Age in the 16th century, grew up virtually as neighbours. They came from small towns no farther apart than New York and Philadelphia or London and Birmingham. They braved the unknown—and unimaginable hardship and danger. A few returned rich and bemedalled. Most of the other notables died in Spanish America, victims of hostile receptions or the intrigues of their own countrymen.

Francisco **Pizarro**, born in the 1470s in *Trujillo,* is said to have worked as a swineherd before signing on for early expeditions to the Caribbean and South America. He thrived as a colonist in Panama, then set forth down the uncharted Pacific coast to Peru. In a battle with the primitively armed Incas, Pizarro captured their ruler, Atahualpa. Having accepted a huge ransom

Hometown statue of Francisco Pizarro.

in gold and silver paid for Atahualpa's release, the Spaniards executed him. The Inca empire fell apart and Pizarro, known as the Great Marquis, became the not necessarily beloved ruler of Peru. Rivalries among the colonial masters seethed. In 1541, in his palace in Lima, the city he had founded, Pizarro was assassinated.

Fame and fortune in the New World was a family affair for the Pizarros. Francisco's half-brother, **Gonzalo,** after helping subdue the Incas, explored Ecuador. He made history as the leader of the first revolt by colonists against Spanish rule. But the viceroy captured him and he was decapitated. Two other brothers, **Hernando** and **Juan,** joined the Pizarro family business. Juan perished in an Indian siege. Hernando, the governor of Cuzco, was the only one of the four to retire. He died peacefully, of old age, back home in Estremadura.

The first European to set eyes on the Pacific, Vasco Núñez de **Balboa,** was born around 1475 far from any sea in *Jerez de los Caballeros,* Estremadura. Balboa became an explorer almost by default. A career as a pioneer farmer in the Caribbean failed and, to flee his creditors, he stowed away on a ship to Panama. From there he contrived to be put in charge of a daring expedition westwards through jungle and swamp. In September, 1513, from a mountain top, he sighted the "South Sea", which he claimed for the King of Castile. The rest of his career was anything but pacific. Intrigues among the colonists put him in the dock on trumped-up charges of rebellion and high treason. By order of his own father-in-law, Balboa was beheaded in 1519.

The small Estremadura town of *Medellín,* in Badajoz province, was the birthplace, in 1485, of the conqueror of Mexico, Hernán **Cortés**. Well educated, the son of a distinguished family, he sowed some notorious wild oats before sailing for the Caribbean at the age of 19. From Cuba, which he helped conquer, Cortés led an 11-ship expedition to the east coast of Mexico. The local Indians, soon subdued, presented the Spaniards with a gift of 20 maidens. One of them, renamed Doña Marina, became the interpreter, political adviser and, eventually, mistress of Cortés.

Scuttling his fleet to discourage defec-

Vasco Núñez de Balboa gets his first glimpse of the Pacific Ocean.

tions, the Conquistador marched his troops to the Aztec capital, the rich, beautiful city of Tenochtitlán. It was a three month ordeal, through jungles and over mountains. The Aztecs, who had never seen horses, much less guns, were awed into submission. Cortés took the ultimate hostage: Montezuma, the gentle ruler of a barbaric society. The final conquest of Mexico, more complex and costly than anticipated, took another year. King Charles V, who received a generous slice of all the Mexican gold, promoted Cortés to the rank of a marquis and Captain-General of New Spain. But the later years were anticlimax, and the great Conquistador died in obscurity in 1547.

Francisco **Orellana** helped a fellow *Trujillo* man, Pizarro, conquer Peru. Next he founded the city of Guayaquil, Ecuador. In 1541, searching through thick and thin for El Dorado, he became the first European to explore the Amazon River, which he named. On the way back for a second visit, Orellana's ship capsized and he was drowned. By an ironic twist of politics, the lands he mapped for Spain now belong to Portugal.

Born in *Villanueva de la Serena*, Estremadura, around 1500, Pedro de **Valdivia** explored Chile. He founded the cities of Santiago, La Concepción and (at last surmounting the modesty problem) Valdivia. A couple of years later his forces lost a battle with a revolting tribe of Indians. Captured, Valdivia was very slowly tortured to death.

Balboa's brother-in-law, Hernando **de Soto,** seems to have been born around the year 1500 in *Jerez de los Caballeros*. Rich and well educated, he took part in the conquest of Central America. As an officer in Pizarro's Peruvian operation he became the friend of the Inca chief Atahualpa. When Pizarro betrayed the king, de Soto, disillusioned, went home to Estremadura. But adventure called, and he mounted a thousand-man expedition to the southern part of North America. In the course of explorations all the way from Florida to Oklahoma, de Soto's band were the first Europeans to explore the Mississippi river. De Soto survived many a battle and hardship but he fell victim to a fever. They buried him in the river he had put on the map.

Spain's Sunny Islands

The empire, once covering three-quarters of the known world, has slimmed to realistic, democratic dimensions, but Spain still flies the flag in the Mediterranean and the Atlantic. Its two alluring archipelagos, now autonomous regions, have found their vocation in tourism. Both have received a bad press in recent years due to overdevelopment but you have only to scratch the surface to find wonderful natural scenery, local colour, and peace and tranquillity.

In the western Mediterranean, the Balearics comprise a sunny cross-section of landscapes from mountainous Majorca to low-slung, sleepy Formentera. In the Atlantic, just off the coast of North Africa, the volcanic Canaries thrive as a semi-tropical escape for those in search of winter sun. Here too the islands vary greatly, from lush and damp to wind-blown desert. Within each of the archipelagos every island has its own character.

Carnival time in Tenerife is as much fun for the locals who take part as it is for the tourists.

The Balearics

Foreigners have been making themselves at home on the Balearic Islands since the Carthaginians settled here some 25 centuries ago. Romans, Vandals, Byzantines, Saracens and Moors have all enjoyed their moment in the sun. Since the Reconquest in the 13th century, however, things have been generally quiet, barring the incursions of the Barbary pirates and, more recently, swarms of pale-faced package tourists.

Majorca

For decades, **Majorca** (*Mallorca* in Spanish) has been Europe's playground. Nearly 5 million visitors crowd on to the island each year; it is the largest tourism concentration in the world, and almost inevitably, not all is rosy in this holiday-

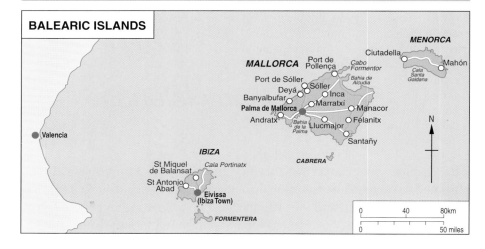

BALEARIC ISLANDS

*P*alma's magnificent cathedral La Seu dominates the bay. Inside you can admire one of the world's largest rose windows and work by Gaudí.

trade Garden of Eden. Fortunately for those who want to avoid the excesses of modern-day tourism however, the Benny Hill Bars and the Bavarian Bierkellers are mostly confined to the southern Bay of Palma and, to a lesser extent, the northern

Bay of Alcudia, so there's still plenty of unspoiled Majorca to enjoy. The island may look like a small dot on a map, but it's 72km (45 miles) from north to south and 96km (60 miles) from east to west. Driving along all those hairpin bends will make it feel even bigger. More good news is that Majorcans have recently woken up to the environmental damage that over-development has wreaked on the island and 'green' measures are being adopted. With regard to beaches, however, the island already has an enviable record – boasting 23 Blue Flags.

Well over half of the total population of Majorca lives in the animated and cosmopolitan capital city, **Palma de Mallorca**. It is the only Balearic city of any size, and for atmosphere and authentic Spanish flavour, it is a match for many a mainland metropolis. Before the serious sightseeing, start on Palma's tree-shaded central promenade, called **Es Born** (the islanders speak in a Mallorquí dialect of Catalan). This elongated plaza, once the scene of jousting tournaments, is the hub of the city's social life. At the top of Es Born is Avinguda Rei Jaume III, a street of sleek, expensive shops.

The **Palacio Almudaina** was once the residence of the Moorish kings. After the Reconquest it was rebuilt for the mediaeval kings of Majorca (briefly an autonomous kingdom). Catch up on your Balearic history in the museum housed in one wing of the palace. Overshadowing the delicately arched and covered balconies of the palace is **La Seu**, a magnificent Gothic cathedral which also compares very favourably to anything the mainland can offer. Construction started in 1229, but the job went on for hundreds of years after this. Unlike most Spanish cathedrals, this one has an open plan with a continuous view from end

*S*pinning and cloth work goes back centuries on Majorca. Embroidered linen is still one of he island's best buys.

to end; the choir stalls have been moved out of the way.

High above the eminently avoidable beachside suburb of El Terreno stands a sturdy symbol of Majorca, the cylindrical keep of the **Castillo de Bellver**. In its own pine-wooded park, the fortress has commanded the sea and land approaches to the city since the 14th century. It is a wonderful piece of military architecture, and now houses a small museum, but it's also well worth coming up here for the views.

Majorca's coast couldn't be more varied, 965km (600 miles) of long white beaches (mostly without high-rise hotels), tiny coves, and cliffs to take your breath away. The best scenery and the favourite haunt of independent travellers is the north-west coast, known as the Tramuntana. Here there are few beaches and the mountains often drop sheer into the sea. The view from the hairpin

TO THE CENTRE OF THE EARTH

The most popular tourist excursion on Majorca is a trip to the caves. The coastline is in fact riddled with caves, a good way to escape the hot sun. A two-hour guided tour of the popular **Cuevas del Drach** (Dragon's Caves), stretching for more than 1½km (1 mile), takes in all the expertly lit, fanciful shapes, with names like Ruined Castle and Diana's Bath. There's a surprise treat in store on the large underground lake when the lights go out! The **Cuevas de Hams** (Caves of the Hooks) show nature in a more whimsical mood. The seemingly impossible shapes of stalactites and stalagmites have been formed by centuries of dripping water fanned by vagrant air currents.

It is said that the experience of a third Majorcan set of caves, the **Cuevas de Artá**, so impressed one visitor, Jules Verne, that he went away and wrote *Journey to the Centre of the Earth*.

corniche, which is acknowledged as one of the world's finest, is sometimes hair-raising. This type of terrain is, of course, the best possible barrier to any large-scale tourism development.

On the southern coast, close to the western tip of the island, is Port d'Andratx (pronounced Andratch); a broad, wonderfully sheltered bay more at home to yachts than fishing boats these days. At Banyalbufar the hillsides have been tamed since Moorish times into some of the finest **terraces** on the island. Near here you will find **La Granja**, which is a cross between a stately home, a traditional farmhouse, a craft-centre and a museum of rural life.

Valldemosa is a town transformed by the visit of Frédéric Chopin and his lover, George Sand, in 1838-9. They stayed in the monastery of **Sa Cartuja**, but it was hardly a happy residence. Chopin was ill, the weather was cold, wet and bad for his chest and George Sand described the local people as 'barbarians, thieves and monkeys' (from *A Winter in Majorca*). After three months they left. The locals probably didn't think too highly of George either – a scandalous woman who had deserted her husband. Yet, quite inexplicably, a veritable tourist industry has grown up around the couple. They come by the coachload to the monastery to see

the cell the couple rented (it is actually an attractive suite with garden), and memorabilia relating to them. It is worth a trip, however, if only to see the monastery.

Just north of here is the beautiful estate of **Son Marroig**, a house that belonged to an Austrian Archduke who, unlike Chopin, fell in love with the island and stayed.

Deía, a pretty hilltop town of honey-coloured stone, is most probably the

A round the town of Banyalbufar, in western Majorca, the hillsides have been tamed since Moorish times into some of the finest terraces on the island.

Minorca is not famed for its night-life, but with sunsets like these who needs loud music and flashing lights?

island's most attractive town and is a good base for visiting the Tranmuntana region. Robert Graves lived the latter years of his life in this artists' colony and died here in 1985.

At **Sóller** and its seaside twin, Port de Sóller, the mountains relent. The biggest bay on this coast makes a fine harbour. Sóller and Palma are linked by a delightful narrow-gauge **railway** straight from the pages of an Agatha Christie novel, all polished wood and gleaming brass. The hour-long journey passes through orchards and spectacular mountain scenery.

accommodation that doesn't overpower the landscape and a reasonable, but far from rowdy nightlife.

For stupendous scenery visit the cliffs of **Cabo Formentor**, the northernmost projection of the island. Everyone pauses on the road for the views, and there is a beautiful pine-shaded sandy cove below.

Minorca

Minorca (*Menorca* in Spanish) is one-fifth the area of its more illustrious neighbour, has one-tenth of its population and receives the same small fraction of visitors. Comparisons with Majorca may be irrelevant but many holiday-makers, seduced by the the unspoilt parts of Majorca, do choose to try Minorca. This is a tranquil, low-key island; the natural scenery is by no means as dramatic as on Majorca and sightseeing (aside from ancient mini-Stonehenge sites) is virtually nil, but if you want a relaxed bolt-hole from 20th-century civilization, this may be it.

Most tourist development is to the west of the island. The north is more scenic but many beaches, both north and south, can only be reached on foot or by four-wheel drive vehicles. The best beach and resort on the island is **Cala Santa Galdana**, a beautiful horseshoe cove, developed in a restrained fashion in keeping with the island. **Fornells**, on the north coast, is

Another novel form of transport leads down to Port de Sóller – an old San Francisco-style open-sided tram.

The coast road twists and turns violently, and at one point of the journey, appropriately close to Sa Calobra ('the snake'), the road even passes under itself in a knot.

Port de Pollença is the sort of seaside resort that has given Majorca a good name; a beautiful beach, a wide choice of

---

SAUCE OF INSPIRATION

They say Minorca is Spain's best-kept secret, and modesty does seem to be a speciality of the island. Who, aside from past visitors, would know that the island gave the rest of the world one of the tastiest and most versatile of all sauces? The name is a derivation of 'sauce of Mahón', *salsa mahonesa*, which we know better as mayonnaise.

PREHISTORIC REMAINS

Around the island of Minorca are hundreds of prehistoric sites, including massive T-shapes, made of two great blocks of subtly carved stone, known as *taulas*. These Bronze Age structures are presumed to have held some religious significance, possibly the centre-pieces of temples. There are also hundreds of rock mounds or towers called *talaiots*, and burial chambers, or *navetas*, in the shape of up-turned boats. You'll find the best of these at Torelló (next to the airport); Torre d'en Gaumés, Talatí de d'Alt, Rafal Rubi Nou and Torralba d'En Salort (all west of Mahón); and near Ciutadella, Naveta d'es Tudons.

As at many such sites around the world, how they were lifted into position is a weighty mystery in itself.

another low-key resort still very much alive as a fishing village.

The strategically important deep-water harbour of **Mahón** (*Maó* in Menorquí) caught the eye of the British in 1708 and they occupied it for much of the 18th century. Walk through the older parts of the city and you could almost be in Georgian England. Elegant façades with sash windows and original rippled glass, plus a gin distillery, calls to mind old-time Plymouth. The little city clusters on the cliffs above the port and stretches along the quayside. Broad ceremonial steps lead from one level to another. Driving here is a one-way nightmare, so explore on foot. Don't leave Mahón without taking a boat trip of the harbour.

Ciudadela (*Ciutadella*), on the west coast, also has its own fine harbour but unlike Mahón, the whitewashed streets of Minorca's ecclesiastical capital radiate a charm that is more akin to Andalusia than old England. **Ses Arcades**, the street leading to the 14th-century Gothic cathedral, is all archways and completely Moorish. Visit the **city museum** in the *Ayuntamiento* (town hall) which provides a curious rag-bag of the island's history. Here, too, driving is not recommended.

Ibiza

The famous White Island, a long-time favourite of Europe's hippies, now also caters to the seriously hip of all persuasions. Fashion victims from Spain and the Continent, the 'beautiful people', a sizeable gay community and the usual retinue of film stars, rock musicians and artists party here from midnight until 10 o'clock the following morning. And of course, Ibiza also packs in the package tourists. Beyond the beaches and the all-nighters, however, the island also merits attention for its old capital. **Ibiza Town** (*Eivissa*), the island's capital city, is the loveliest in the Balearics. Its ancient walled town, **Dalt Vila**, is a cobbled maze on a hillside, with all its houses whitewashed by local byelaw. Among the tiny bars, shops, hippy markets and restaurants you'll glimpse many a charming view over the sea. Ibiza's **fortifications**, 16th-century bulwarks on top of the remains of Moorish walls, are almost completely intact.

Colonized by Carthage in the 7th century BC, the island held on to the old

*T*he port of Ciutadella, Minorca, now shared by pleasure craft and fishing boats. Part of the catch goes to restaurants just a few yards away – some housed in caverns in the base of the harbour bastion. The port area is a focus of Ciutadella nightlife.

traditions long after the Romans vanquished Hannibal. The capital has two **archaeological museums**, one opposite the cathedral and the other beyond the walls in the lower town. They add up to a truly great treasury of Carthaginian art, especially the terracotta statuettes. The latter, the Puig des Molins, is built adjacent to a necropolis and tours of the burial chambers are given. If you would prefer something a little more up to date, look in at the Museo d'Arte Contemporáneo.

The beaches start immediately south of town but the best, and certainly the trendiest on the island are generally agreed to be those at **Ses Salinas**, close to the airport. Other pleasant spots include **Portinatx** (pronounced Port-EE-natch) and San Miguel in

*T*he most beautiful city in the Balearics, Eivissa or Ibiza Town, is famous as a playground for Europe's young trendies, but it also retains its traditional elements.

*T*he town of Ibiza and harbour seen from the bay.

the north. You can see regular displays of folk dancing and visit caves at the latter.

Just north of Ibiza town is **Santa Eulalia del Riu**, a relaxed though quite developed resort, with something of the character of the capital, although on a lower key.

Last and very definitely least is the tourist capital of San Antonio (Sant Antoni) Abad, a skyline of high-rise hotels and holiday apartments around a large attractive bay. This town is specifically geared towards pleasing the package tourist, and, site apart, is probably best left to those who revel in its mixture of fun and sun.

Formentera

The 11km (7 mile) sea voyage from Ibiza takes seventy-five minutes by boat, or around half that by hydrofoil. Either way, it's often a bumpy ride. There is no airport here, and very little water, which has seriously hindered any large-scale development. Building on Formentera is, in any case, restricted to a maximum height of four storeys.

Once the sole retreat of the backpacker and the beach bum, the island is now catering for package tourists too. They come for much the same reasons – unimpaired horizons and endless uncommercialized nudist beaches. Windsurfing aside, there is little to do here.

The Canary Islands

The Canaries are seven specks of rock, scattered over 480km (300 miles) in the middle of the vast Atlantic Ocean. To the east lies the Sahara, from where the beaches of Fuerteventura have blown; to the north east lies the North of Africa, from where the Guanches – the original Canarians – once came. To the north lies Spain, from where latter-day lawmakers have laid the foundations for modern Canaries life.

Nowadays English, German and Scandinavian tourists descend on the islands all year round. The warm subtropical Canarian climate is the perfect cure for those north-European winter blues.

The diversity of landscapes on the different islands is quite amazing. While Fuerteventura is truly a desert island –

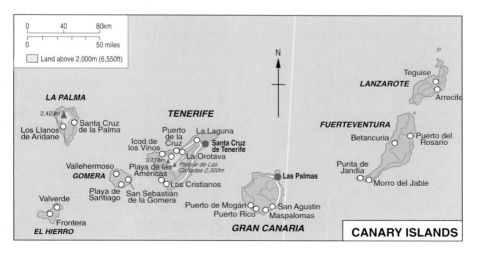

293

windswept, sandy and bare, La Palma is verdant, lush and fertile. If the strikingly beautiful interiors of Tenerife, Gran Canaria and Gomera are Gardens of Eden, then the stark *malpais* (badlands) of Lanzarote are surely the Valleys of Hell. The Canaries are volcanic islands and volcanic islands are never dull. La Palma erupted as recently as 1971. On Lanzarote you can not only gaze on the awesome scenery created by earth-shattering events which occurred centuries ago; you can watch your lunch cooking over the heat of the volcano beneath your feet.

The delights of Tenerife, Gran Canaria and Lanzarote are well documented in most travel agents' brochures and all can accommodate most general holiday requirements. The lesser-known islands of Gomera, El Hierro and La Palma are for the more inquisitive and the hardier travellers. There are relatively few comfortable hotels, no international restaurants and – best of all, as far as many are concerned – very few tourists. If you enjoying walking through beautiful mountain scenery for days on end, if you don't mind conversing with the aid of a phrase-book in the local village bar and your idea of nightlife is gazing at the north star, then one of these islands may be your Shangri-La.

Tenerife

Tenerife is not only the largest of the Canaries geographically, it also offers the tourist more sightseeing, more attractions, more towns and cities to explore and more contrasts than any of the other islands. Where else in the Atlantic can you explore a banana plantation then drive for just 45 minutes half-way up a mountain for a snowball fight?

The mountain in question is Mount Teide (it rhymes with lady), at 3,717m (12,200ft) the tallest in all Spain. The symbol of the island, it can be seen from many vantage points all over Tenerife but for the very best views you need to be high above its ring of clouds.

Tenerife has been welcoming visitors from cold northern climes since the 19th century. The focus, however, has changed from the cloudy green north coast where Puerto de la Cruz was once the favourite resort (it still is enormously popular) to the hot, dry arid south. By day the beaches are thronged with glistening bodies, by night the streets throb to a new sort of holiday-maker's beat, far removed from the travellers who used to visit the island on doctor's orders.

Santa Cruz de Tenerife is the capital of Tenerife and the administrative centre for the westerly Canaries. It is not a city in which too many tourists spend a great deal of time. Which is a pity, because although there are few tourist attractions and the city is not especially beautiful, it has an undeniable authentic Spanish charm, proud of its colonial heritage.

The city's best museum is the **Museo Municipal de Bellas Artes** which lies on Calle Béthencourt Alfonso and includes some fine Spanish and Flemish works. The adjacent church of San Francisco is also worth a visit.

Close to the seafront is the **Iglesia Matriz de la Concepción** (Church of the Immaculate Conception). Dating from the early 16th century, this is the town's most important historical building and contains several interesting historical relics, including Nelson's faded battle flag (he lost part of his arm in a sea battle just off Santa Cruz).

One of the most charming aspects of the city is its picturesque squares and gardens. Situated conveniently at the very end

of Calle Castillo, the main shopping street is the flower-decked square of **Plaza Weyler**, a perfect spot for a drink and a snack. If ceramics are to your taste, walk a short way along Avenida 25 de Julio to the Plaza of the same name to admire the delightful, museum-piece, tiled benches here. Many are adorned with colourful ceramic advertising messages from the 1920s. The city's finest park, **Parque García Sanabria** is a few metres along the same street. Cool and shaded on a hot day, it is famous for its fountains and its floral clock.

Follow the coast road for 9km (6 miles) and, incongruously located just past the oil terminal, is the best beach on the island. **Las Teresitas** is a beautiful golden crescent of Saharan sand stretching almost 1½ kilometres (1 mile) and measuring some 100m (330ft) wide.

The Caldera (volcanic crater) de Las Cañadas en route to the summit of Mount Teide. A section has been cut through the old volcano for the road.

Puerto de la Cruz, or Puerto, as it is often abbreviated to, has neither good beaches nor the abundant sunshine of the south, yet for many travellers it is the most complete resort on the island. Like Santa Cruz, it has been attracting convalescing north Europeans for over a century, and, also like the capital, it maintains much of its colonial grandeur. The seafront promenade from the surfing beach of Playa Martiánez along to the **Puerto Pesquero** (the old fishing port) has been quite heavily commercialized but not spoiled, and the atmosphere is lively without being boisterous.

The problem of Puerto's beachlessness has been brilliantly addressed by the César Manrique-designed **Lago de Martiánez**. This 3ha (8-acre) complex of tropical swimming lagoons, cascading fountains and sunbathing terraces is cleverly landscaped with lush palms and black and white volcanic rockery to fit perfectly into the seafront, where the surf crashes spectacularly against the rocks.

The charming pedestrianized street of **Calle de San Telmo** descends into town passing the delightful tiny white 18th-century Ermita de San Telmo. A little further on is the majestic 17th-century **Iglesia de la Peña de Francia** (Church of the Rock of France).

The main square, **Plaza Charco**, is the hub of both tourist and local life and its numerous cafés, restaurants and shops are busy at all hours. Just off the square, the old town around the Puerto Pesquero is remarkably oblivious to modern change. The major tourist attractions lie just outside town. The biggest is **Loro Parque**, which houses the world's largest collection (over 230 species) of parrot, in beautiful subtropical gardens. Other amusements include performing dolphins, a 180° film screen, flamingoes and performing parrots. The oldest attraction is undoubtedly the **Jardín Botánico** (the Botanical Garden), founded by royal decree in 1788 and located on the road to La Orotava. This dense and dark jungle covers some 2½ha (6 acres). There are palms of every variety, and the centrepiece is a huge South American fig tree whose enormous branches and roots have become intertwined into one great outlandish tree-house. There is no great display of colour here, but everywhere on the island

---

HERE BE DRAGONS!

The Dragon Tree is a strange primitive plant, peculiar to the Canary Islands and Madeira. King of them all is the *Drago Milenario* (the thousand-year-old Dragon Tree) at Icod de los Vinos on the north coast of Tenerife. This is the largest specimen standing – nearly 17m (56ft) tall and with a girth of 6m (20ft). Its age, however, cannot be verified, as unlike other trees the *Drago* does not have age rings. Local estimates vary between 2,000 and 3,000 years old, although some sceptics believe it may only be 500 years old. Its bizarre spiky foliage and its blood-red sap imbued it with all sorts of magical properties in the eyes of the local natives, and even today alternative healers perform strange rites involving the tree.

---

the roadsides are fragrant with honeysuckle and mimosa; they blush with bougainvillaea, poinsettia and jacaranda.

On the same road is **Banañera El Guanche**, a fascinating insight into how a Canarian banana plantation operates. It also boasts a superb collection of exotic trees, shrubs, flowers and cacti from all over the world.

Set high on a steep hill above Puerto de la Cruz is the remarkably well-preserved old town of **La Orotava**. Stately mansions, ancient churches and cobbled streets are its trademark with not a tourist blandishment in sight. The twin towers, baroque façade and Byzantine dome of the **Iglesia Nuestra Señor de la Concepción** dominates a fascinating roofscape which, aside from the occasional TV aerial, has been unchanged for centuries. Don't miss the **Casa de Los Balcones** (House of the Balconies). The balconies in question are actually on the inside of the house's courtyard, and are some of the finest examples of their kind. This splendid 17th-century mansion and the

Casa de Turista (1590) opposite are now dedicated to Canary handicrafts.

The former was also the living quarters of a wealthy family, and their apartments have recently been opened to the public.

The highlight of the island, in every sense, is the ascent of **Mount Teide**. The entrance to the mountainous National Park is **El Portillo de las Cañadas**. There is a Visitor Centre and a small exhibition area. If you wish to walk in the park, pick up a leaflet or ask about the daily guided walks that are conducted. Note that during winter the environment can become quite hostile and that you should never undertake winter walks without consulting the Visitor Centre first. It is quite likely that you will be in the clouds, temperatures are very low and in winter there may well be snow on the ground. The landscape becomes very lunar-like and it was around here that some of the filming for *Planet of the Apes* took place.

As you continue ever upwards you will eventually drive through the clouds and bright warm sunshine will greet you again. The ascent to the top of Mount Teide can be made by **cable-car** (*teleférico*) or by climbing. Most choose cable-car. Note, however, that in summer the queues are very long and even after leaving the cable-car there is still another 160m (500ft) to climb to the very summit (3717m/ 12,200ft). Once at the top you should be able to count off all the other Canary Islands and on a good day see North Africa. Sulphurous fumes will remind you that a volcano is beneath your feet. Don't worry – it has been dormant since the end of the 17th century.

The most popular tourist destinations in Tenerife are the adjacent resorts of **Los Cristianos** and **Playa de Las Américas**. Los Cristianos used to be a quiet fishing port with a quiet little beach. It now plays host to hundreds of thousands of mainly British and German holiday-makers each year, and its small beach is woefully inadequate. All sorts of pleasure craft can be hired here; deep-sea fishing for shark and swordfish, piratical expeditions aboard a fully rigged tallship or a **boat safari** in search of pilot whales and dolphins.

Playa de las Américas was born in the 1970s and has literally grown from a desolate shoreline to the high-rise, high-energy, highly-packaged resort it is today. Here the bars are not Spanish, nor even international; they are either German or British, often adorned with football colours. If your idea of a holiday is to mix solely with people of your own nationality and to avoid 'foreign food' ('No Spanish cooking here' some signs proudly proclaim) then this is the place for you. You will also have to be pretty tolerant of leech-like time-share touts who are a constant nuisance at both resorts.

Gran Canaria

In spite of its name, **Gran Canaria** is only the third-biggest of the Canaries, but it's second to none for its perfect beaches and sophisticated night-life, for its history and hubbub, marvellous natural scenery, sightseeing and shopping.

Almost circular in shape, Gran Canaria is in profile the classic volcanic cone. It is small enough to get to know quite well within a week or two, yet its mountainous character causes the climate to change radically with latitude and altitude. You can leave a wet and chilly Las Palmas at 9am and by 10am be greeting a hot sunny day in Maspalomas.

Gran Canaria has been called a continent in miniature. The coastline ranges from awe-inspiring cliffs to golden dunes. Inland you can choose between stark mountains and tranquil valleys. Travelling from the din of Las Palmas to the quietude of a languorous provincial village could easily bring on culture shock. Bustling **Las Palmas** is more than just a provincial capital. As the largest city in the Canaries, it is a major commercial and historical centre, a cosmopolitan resort and a vital seaport all rolled into one.

Up to a thousand ships a month can arrive at the port to take on fuel, unload cargo (these days mostly oil and petroleum) or just give the crew a break. Gone, however, are the romantic days of the 1960s and '70s when grand liners such as the *Queen Elizabeth* and *Queen Mary* were regular visitors here. Due to the changing nature of cargo and port handling, the colourful presence of sailors of many nations is also less apparent now than it used to be.

The real hub of Las Palmas is **Santa Catalina Park**. One gigantic outdoor café, it buzzes day and night with almost every language in the world. Exotically gowned visitors from West Africa sip tea or ply their wares, while tourists with peeling noses down excesses of bargain-priced gin and brandy and the Spaniards themselves avidly digest the local and national newspapers.

A short walk through the dust and the exhaust fume-filled streets leads to **Playa de las Canteras**. This superb golden strip stretches for 3-5km (2-3 miles), and a natural reef 180m (600ft) offshore means that the water couldn't be calmer. But the beach, like the city, has seen better tourist days and is losing

T here is a striking contrast on Gran Canaria between the rugged, natural beauty of the islands, and the developed coastal plain with its marvellous beaches.

COLUMBUS IN GRAN CANARIA

There are still parts of the old Vegueta district of Las Palmas where Columbus would be quite at home if he came back tomorrow. He prayed at the Ermita de San Antonio Abad before he set off on his first Voyage of Discovery to the New World, and close by on Calle Colón (Columbus's name in Spanish), is the beautiful 15th-century house of Casa Colón. This elegant house with a charming courtyard was formerly the residence of the island's first governor, and Columbus is said to have stayed here on three occasions. Now an atmospheric museum, it recreates the Age of Discovery with exhibits of navigational instruments, charts, weapons and a selection of everyday items of the period.

holiday trade to the smarter modern resorts of the warmer south.

The southern resorts of San Agustin, Playa del Inglés and Maspalomas are often all lumped together under the collective name of Maspalomas. It is rather disconcerting to learn that this three-in-one resort is the biggest holiday complex in all of Spain, let alone just the Canaries, but each resort does have its own characteristics.

San Agustin is a restrained area of pleasant low-rise apartments, catering for the more mature and discerning holiday-maker. Above, the streets are neat and tidy, below there is a quiet black-sand beach backed by low cliffs.

Playa del Inglés is altogether more robust, as the very name (Beach of the English) might suggest. In winter, however, there are just as many German visitors here. This is an unashamedly fun- and sun-resort of high-rise hotels, *Centro Commerciales* (shopping malls) and fast-food restaurants. It has, however, been established for several years, and the raw concrete edges are now being smoothed away. The night-life can be hectic, and at the last count there were some 50 discos here. The golden beach stretches for some 16km (10 miles), so there is room enough for everyone and all water sports.

Maspalomas itself is famous for its dunes, which are sufficiently large and unspoiled to constitute a local mini-Sahara of great beauty. **Palmito Park**, situated in a picturesque gorge some 13km (8 miles) north of Maspalomas, is an excellent day out for all the family. Performing parrots amuse with conjuring and circus tricks and caged birds of every possible hue and colour are kept in beautiful gardens. The real stars, however, are the exotic free-flying residents, including brilliantly coloured parrots and toucans.

Puerto Rico is the most attractive beach resort on this coast. It, too, has been grossly overdeveloped in terms of numbers of accommodations on the surrounding hillsides, so its lovely sheltered golden beach can become unbearably crowded. Out of season, however, it is recommended. Puerto Rico is famous for its water sports, and there is also an attractive marina here.

Puerto de Mogán is an object lesson to all Canarian resort developers in how to provide accommodation that is functional, attractive and totally in sympathy with its surroundings. The holiday accommodation here is an interpretation of local town houses, ablaze with bougainvillaea, and arranged in pedestrian-only squares with narrow alleyways and arches leading to a very attractive marina. This is lined with stylish cafés and restaurants, jazz and piano bars, and small boutiques. The northern coastal zone of Gran Canaria is banana-land. Row upon row of green terraced plantations slope gently down from the mountains to the edge of the sea.

The mountainous centre of the island makes for very tiring driving; you will rarely get out of the lower gears, but the wonderful panoramas are ample reward. Pine forests, almond groves, gnarled mountains, sheer cliffs and cloudy mountain tops beckon.

Arguably the best, and certainly the most popular vantage point is the **Cruz de Tejeda**, at 1,463m (4,800ft). This is one of the few points inland where you are almost guaranteed to meet fellow tourists. A small cluster of cafés, fruit and souvenir stalls and a man with his donkeys sit waiting at the summit for the coach parties. It is hardly high-pressure tourism, however, and the elegant *parador* (restaurant only) is a welcome refreshment stop.

The magnificent panorama includes two rock formations once worshipped by the Guanches. The most distinctive is the statuesque **Roque Nublo** (1,817m/ 5,961ft), the other is the Roque Betaiga. As it is the hub of the island there are any number of routes to and from the Cruz de Tejeda – almost all have something to offer the visitor.

Lanzarote

Lanzarote is a startling island and represents man's triumph over a hostile environment. Its pock-marked lunar-like surface is dotted with over 300 volcanoes, yet onions, potatoes, tomatoes, melons and grapes all spring in abundance from the black volcanic ash. The daily scene of *Lanzaroteños* (or *Conejeros* as they are sometimes called) toiling successfully in such an apparently desolate landscape warms the heart.

It is not only in the fields that the island is succeeding. Later on to the tourist scene than either Gran Canaria or Tenerife, Lanzarote seems to have learned from the excesses of its sister islands. Here, small is beautiful and harmony with the environment is the philosophy.

The island's major resort is **Puerto del Carmen**. Its long golden beach stretches for several kilometres and comfortably accommodates its visitors. The sea is calm and ideal for families. Restaurants, bars and shops line the Avenida de las Playas in Lanzarote's one outbreak of mass commercialism. Yet Spanish bars and restaurants can still be found on 'the strip'.

The highlight of your trip to Lanzarote and the magical ingredient that makes this island so special is to be found in the **Montañas de Fuego** (Mountains of Fire). The Parque Nacional Timanfaya, which

encompasses the mountains starts just north of Yaiza, and its boundary is marked by an impish devil motif. This national park of desolation was formed largely over the course of sixteen cataclysmic months during 1730 and 1731. Eleven villages were buried for ever and many of the people left the island for Gran Canaria.

Just inside the *malpais* (volcanic badlands) of the park **camels** take tourists on a short ride up and down a volcanic hill. Whether or not you think the ride is

worthwhile, the hubbub in the car park (which doubles as a 'camel park') is not to be missed. Chaotic and quite exotic, it could almost be mistaken for a North African bazaar. Until not so long ago camels were still used as beasts of burden in the fields of Lanzarote.

Your introduction to the inner sanctum of the Montañas de Fuego leaves you in no doubt that at least one of these volcanoes is not dead, just sleeping. In fact, the very one that you are standing on! A guide demonstrates this by pouring water

View from the splendid Mirador del Río on the northern tip of Lanzarote, looking to the island of Graciosa. Boat trips go to the deserted beaches here from Orzola.

down a tube into the earth, then beating a hasty retreat. A few seconds later a geyser erupts with an almighty whoosh, startling the diners in the adjacent restaurant. You can watch the cooking being done over an enormous barbecue which uses the volcano as its fuel.

Cars are not allowed any further into the park, and from here coach tours depart to explore the incredible landscape. The adjectives *lunar* and *alien* are worked to exhaustion and still scarcely do justice to the dramatic scenery. Suffice to say that by the time the theme-music to *2001 A Space Odyssey* is played at the end of your tour, you will be convinced that you have just visited another world.

The **Costa Teguise**, just north of Arrecife (the island's undistinguished capital) is a totally modern conglomeration comprising several *urbanizaciones* with time-share apartments, hotels and apartments designed for a wealthy clientèle. There are a handful of good sandy beaches, particularly Playa Cucheras, where water sports thrive and windsurfing

---

THE MAGIC OF MANRIQUE

César Manrique is probably Lanzarote's greatest artist, designer, landscaper, conservationist and all-round cultural mandarin. Born on the island in 1920 and trained primarily in Madrid, there is hardly a visitor attraction of any worth on the island that somehow does not bear his signature. In his own words his works are 'dreams that capture the sublime natural beauty of Lanzarote' and right up until his death in 1992, he was constantly striving to ensure that tourism developments kept in harmony with the island's own character. Simplicity is the Manrique hallmark – whitewashed walls, natural building materials, classical or local music, local food and wine. Lanzarote will miss him.

---

is particularly prominent. The coast road east passes the town of Guatiza where prickly pears abound. Here the island's tourism guru, César Manrique, has cultivated the spiny flora into a beautiful **Jardín de Cactus** complete with a working windmill.

There is more Manrique magic to admire at the caves of **Jameos del Agua**. Here his landscaping skills have embellished and transformed a grotto and an underground lagoon into a short fantasy journey. Ethereal mood music accompanies your descent into the cave, lushly planted with luxuriant foliage. Peer into the black lagoon and you can pick out the extremely rare tiny albino spider crabs which live here. Finally you emerge from the cave into a South Seas paradise!

The adjacent **Cueva de los Verdes** (Green Cave) is part of the same system, blasted through the earth by exploding lava. A guided tour includes some memorable sound and light effects that evoke the menacing volcano most effectively.

Fuerteventura

Beaches on **Fuerteventura** still outnumber hotels. At the last count there were 152 pristine golden stretches surrounding this arid rock. Situated less than 100km (60 miles) off the coast of North Africa, most of the sand on Fuerteventura is blown here from the Sahara, so this is quite literally a 'desert island'.

Fuerteventura is barren and windswept to the point of desolation, or grandeur, depending on your point of view. Its landscape may not have the variety and contrasts of neighbouring Lanzarote but most travellers still find some inspiration in its primeval appearance. The beaches here are probably the best in the Canaries, and resorts for most tastes are springing up.

Water sports aside though, there isn't much to do or see. Which may be fine as long as you know that in advance.

Betancuria, the most attractive and most-visited town on the island is an oasis in a harsh land. Although the river bed here is almost perpetually dry, the town is fortunate in having a high water table. Because of its theoretical invulnerability at the heart of the island, it was made Fuerteventura's first capital in the early 15th century. However, in 1539 the ravaging Berber pirates somehow overcame the mountains (which provide a difficult drive even today) and destroyed the original cathedral. The present 17th-century church, **Iglesia de Santa María**, is a splendid building and hosts many interesting treasures. At the southern tip of the island are the seemingly infinite beaches of **Jandía**. The most beautiful are those of the **Costa**

The long soft sandy beaches of Playa de Jandía, Fuerteventura, are often deserted. The dunes behind can rise as high as a house.

Calma, not blighted as yet by overdevelopment. The Playa de Sotavento is world famous as a windsurfing destination with activity focused on the F2 school at the Los Goriones Hotel. Here the beach is very wide, very flat, usually very empty and, as the tides go out, also very wet. The dunes behind and a little further to the south, however, are much photographed and form an idyllic beach backdrop.

Urbanizaciones spread relentlessly all the way down the coast to **Morro del**

Jable. This pleasant small town dips down to the sea along a dry river-bed and a small promenade offers a choice of bars and restaurants.

There are more fine beaches towards the southern tip of the island but you will need a jeep to traverse the rocky paths that lead there.

La Gomera

The short journey across the water from the throbbing resorts of south Tenerife to the island of **Gomera** can take as little as 40 minutes, but in terms of tourism, it is a step back in time of many decades.

Gomera is the only Canary Island without a commercial airport – but that is about to change. Construction is now well advanced and within the next few years the island atmosphere may well change forever. Tourism has increased dramatically in recent years, though from a very small base and Gomera remains unspoiled and authentic, a Shangri-La of steep green terraced hills and tranquil valleys. In this world of irreversible 'progress' you may be quite relieved to find roads completely free of advertising signs, *urbanizaciones* and souvenir stalls.

The boat and the hydrofoil dock at **San Sebastián**, the small town capital of the island, notable for its Columbus associations. The Columbiana starts in the main square. A simple pavement mosaic shows the route of Columbus's voyage and next to the large tree is the Casa de Aduana (the old Customs House). By tradition Columbus drew water from the well here (Pozo de Colón), took it to the New World and used it to baptise America.

Leading off the square, the Calle del Medio is the only street of any consequence in town, and features more connections with the great navigator. The **Iglesia de la Asunción**, built between 1490 and 1510, looks and feels so old that you can almost see Columbus praying in a dark recess, which is what a plaque here tells us he did back in 1492. A little way up the street is the modest Casa Columbina/Casa de Colón which is supposedly where he stayed in Gomera. Exhibitions are held here. High above the town sits a *parador*.

The highest peak on the island is the Alto de Garajonay at 1,487m (4,878ft) and touring the island seems to be entering a maze of eerie crags. One hilltop may be within waving distance of the next, but driving between them is a dizzying ordeal of twists and turns.

There is a handful of pleasant friendly settlements to explore and the **Garajonay**

WHISTLE DOWN THE WIND

La Gomera has a mountainous landscape, riven by deep gullies, and so posed a frustrating problem of how to communicate to someone who was so close (as the crow flies) and yet so far (as the paths go). The ingenious Gomerans solved this a long time before the telephone came to the island.

For ages, gossip and messages have been transmitted across the ravines by the language of *El Silbo* (the whistle). This is a real language of regulated tones and rhythms, representing words, whistled with or without the aid of fingers in the mouth, at great volume. Only a small minority of Gomerans keep the language alive. Many younger people may understand it, but they cannot converse in *silbo*.

If you are not on a coach tour of the island, but want to see *silbo* in action go along to Las Rosas restaurant at the village of the same name, where regular demonstrations are given to coach parties.

National Park (a World Heritage site) is a delight for walkers.

The south of the island boasts the one and only beach resort of **Playa de Santiago**, a deliberately low-key tranquil place and also the beautiful multi-tiered valley of **Valle Gran Rey**.

La Palma

La Palma, the most north westerly of the Canaries has two nicknames – La Isla Bonita and La Isla Verde. Beautiful it certainly is, and very green too. Not only in the physical sense but also ecologically. Tourism development is strictly controlled and even unnecessary light is kept from the night sky in order that the world-renowned La Palma observatory may function unhindered by artificial light sources.

The island not only has a beautiful face; its statistics are also very impressive. The highest peak, Roque de los Muchachos, rises to 2,423m (7,950ft) above sea level. That makes it the steepest island in the world in relation to its total area.

At the heart of La Palma is the **Caldera de Taburiente**. This giant crater has a circumference of some 27km (17 miles), a diameter of over 83km (52 miles) and a depth of 700m (2,300ft). It was created some 400,000 years ago, and has since been colonized by nature into a green, fertile valley. It is perfect walking country with some marvellous views.

The island capital, **Santa Cruz de la Palma**, is an appealing small town – clean and bright with traditional and modern architecture side by side. New buildings blend harmoniously with old colonial houses and their wooden balconies, painted green, brown or faded red.

There are basically only two routes from here, a northern or a southern loop of the island. The southern is the best, passing the 17th-century **Santuario de Nuestra Señhora de las Nieves** (Sanctuary of Our Lady of the Snows) and onto the magnificent Caldera de Taburiente.

The northern loop also enjoys dramatic scenery, and culminates in the **observatory** (closed to the public) on top of the Roque de los Muchachos.

El Hierro

Until the voyages of Columbus, geographers considered **El Hierro** the end of the world. In Canarian tourism terms, it still is. A daily 35-minute flight connects the island with Tenerife, but tourist traffic is very limited. There are hardly any tourist facilities, no natural spectacles, no good beaches and swimming conditions are poor. On the plus side, El Hierro is pretty (though no more beautiful than the other islands), very quiet and totally unspoiled. For many travellers the latter is reason enough to visit this tiny rock.

Valverde, the island capital won't deter you for too long: it's a tiny, very provincial place. Make your first stop the splendid **Mirador de la Peña**, 8km (5 miles) due west of the airport. It's the one and only attraction on the island. Those familiar with the work of César Manrique (*see* page 302) will need no introduction to its peaceful simple style. The views from here are magnificent and there is also a good restaurant. Below is the stretch of north coast known as **El Golfo**, actually part of an immense volcanic crater, half of which is beneath the sea. Frustratingly, although it's only a few hundred metres as the crow flies, you have to go all the way back on yourself in a giant loop to get there. Consider spending the night at the remote *parador* south of Valverde, instead of trying to rush the island in a day.

Joining in the Fun

Spain isn't just for seeing, it's also for doing. Whatever you get up to – bargaining in the *rastro*, betting on *jai-alai* in the Basque Country or dancing the *sardana* in Catalonia, you'll be absorbing the vitality and passion of the people, their pastimes and their culture.

Sport

With its seas and mountains, Spain offers every kind of sporting and leisure opportunity, as strenuous or as relaxing as you want, summer or winter. In Andalusia you can even ski in the mountains and swim in the sea on the same day.

On the Beach
Spain boasts hundreds of miles of sandy beaches (ranging from fine, golden grains to the coarse black volcanic variety), and pebbly and rocky shores too, excellent for snorkelling. These include some of the most attractive beaches in Europe, and over 100 of them have been given the EC Blue Flag seal of approval.

The best-quality beaches are often the most developed, Benidorm being the most extreme example, but even slightly out of season even the famous *costas'* beaches are usually very pleasant. In season, with a little enterprise you can still discover nearly deserted coves, or head off to the less developed coasts such as Costa de Almería or Costa de la Luz.

The main tourist beaches offer the full range of facilities: water sports, restaurants, bars, changing rooms, showers, deck-chairs and parasols. A few beaches are reserved for nudists. On busy

*O*ne of Spain's more relaxing pastimes – a game of boules in a shady square – but note the unusual local variation of the game

beaches, flags are hoisted to advise swimmers of sea conditions: a green flag means it's safe for swimming, while red means danger.

Windsurfing is the boom sport along the coasts. At almost any resort of size you will be able to hire a rig, possibly a wetsuit and maybe some tuition. Large resorts generally have more than one windsurfing school competing for trade. Advanced windsurfers should head for Tarifa (the southern-most tip of Spain), Mundaka and Sopelana beaches (on the north coast between Santander and San Sebastián), or the beaches of Jandía on the south of Fuerteventura (Canary Islands).

Water-skiing is less popular these days, partly on account of rising fuel prices, but is still always available in large resorts. The Balearics, La Manga (Murcia), the Costa Dorada and the Costa Brava are good places to go. Here too you can indulge yourself in jetskiing, parascending and riding the 'water sausage'. No skills are required for the latter two, just a sense of adventure.

Scuba diving prospers particularly off the Costa Brava, the Costa Almería and the Balearic islands, with their rocky coasts and clear water. There are also four underwater nature parks: the Formigues Islands and the Medes Islands (Gerona), the Tabarca Marine Reserve (Alicante) and the Proyecto Bentos (the Canary Islands). Diving centres operate in several resorts. They can arrange for the necessary diving permits, provide boats, equipment and, in many cases, tuition – though this is expensive.

Boating enthusiasts will find that most tourist beaches have a variety of craft for hire – light catamarans are very popular. Sailing is particularly popular on the Costa Brava, in the Balearics and the Canaries,

the Bay of Cádiz and the area around Santander and Laredo in the Bay of Biscay. You will also find marinas all along the coasts; Catalonia alone has two dozen yacht clubs and sporting ports. Here too you may well be able to organize water sports and big-game fishing trips (shark and swordfish are caught off the Costa del Sol).

Fishing from rocks along the coastline is popular, but results are better if you hire

a boat and head for open water. If you are accompanied by a local fisherman, or at least take some local advice, you should find what you're looking for more quickly. Cheap fishing tackle is available in most resorts.

You can fish inland too. The *Mapa de Pesca Fluvial*, issued by the tourist board, shows where to hook different varieties of freshwater fish (mainly salmon, trout and pike, though chub, barbel carp and black

*O*n the beach at
*Paguera, Majorca, everything you
need is right at hand, from
umbrellas and deck chairs to
pedal boats and water skis. Closer
to the capital, Palma, the beaches
become more crowded.*

A grown-up way to play in the sand in Spain. The rules of the game are the same as at home, but the scenery may be anything from palms to pines to snow-capped mountains. In the Canaries an 18-hole course skirts the crater of an extinct volcano.

bass also swim in Spanish freshwaters), and also gives details of season dates and licences. Castile, Catalonia, Aragón and Green Spain are the best areas.

Sports Ashore

Spain is world famous for **golf**, with more than 90 courses on the mainland and islands at the last count, although this figure will soon be 100-plus. Not every pro is a Seve Ballesteros, but the quality of in-

For better value, consider the east coast, where the Valencian courses of El Saler (once voted the best course in Europe) and nearby, the Gary Player-devised El Escorpian are both highly rated. Further north on the Cost Brava, Pals is a beautiful course, also highly regarded by the pros. Elsewhere on the mainland there are a dozen courses surrounding Madrid, but nearly all resort towns have a golf course within driving distance.

The most complete sporting resort in Spain is the La Manga Club on the Costa Calída, south of Murcia, with three championship courses for players of all abilities. (Horse riding, water sports and tennis are also superbly catered for here.)

Of the islands, Majorca is the best served with 9 courses (plus another 5 on the way) of which Santa Ponsa and Poniente are the pick of the bunch. The

struction is generally high. The greatest concentration of courses is on the Costa del Sol with 24 courses – half of these are concentrated in the short distance between Málaga and Estepona alone. The best is Valderrama at Sotogrande (Tony Jacklin was the resident director here for many years), while Las Brisas is a great favourite with British showbiz personalities. Not surprisingly, these are two of the most expensive courses.

THE WORLD'S FASTEST BALL GAME

For a rousingly different experience, go to a *frontón* to watch the ancient Basque ball game, *jai-alai* (pronounced high-a-lie), also known as *pelota*. Players use woven straw scoops to combine the functions of glove and catapult, snagging the whizzing ball and blasting it back against the far wall at speeds up to 303kph (188mph). The basic rules of the game are akin to tennis or squash. The ball may only bounce once on the floor, and a point is won when the opponent fails to return. A game comprises 7-9 points. The system of betting, which engrosses most of the audience, is likely to remain a mystery unless you are fluent in both Spanish and betting parlance. Bookies negotiate the odds by hand signals and slang, tossing receipts to their clients inside tennis balls. Even the referee, on the dangerous side of the protective screen, has been known to place a discreet bet during the match.

Club de Golf Las Palmas, on Gran Canaria, merits a special mention for its stunning setting. It is also Spain's oldest golf club.

The national tourist office will be happy to send you a map of Spain locating and detailing all major courses.

Tennis is another favourite sport in Spain, but unless you know you will be able to play under floodlights it may be best to avoid the hottest months of the year. Many hotels, apartments and villa complexes have their own tennis courts, and some centres have resident professionals. The Costa del Sol is probably the biggest centre for tennis tuition with past heroes such as Lew Hoad and Manolo Santana turning their vast experience to tuition. La Manga Club excels here too, with one of the best-equipped tennis centres in Europe, boasting 17 courts, most of them floodlit.

Even before the days of El Cid, **horse-riding** was a Spanish speciality. Andalusia springs readily to mind, but there are ranches all over the country where you can hire horses and lessons. Many of these cater to tourists, providing a quiet seaside jog or, for more advanced riders, skilled instruction and stimulating cross-country excursions. For the experienced and saddle-fit, there are often overnight mountain treks, just a short distance from the busy *costas*.

You may not immediately think of Spain for a **skiing** holiday, but it is attracting an increasing number of devotees to its 27 resorts. Over half of these are in the Pyrenees (including Andorra). There are 4 resorts just north of Madrid, another 4 in the Cantabrian mountains, close to the north coast, while Europe's southernmost, and possibly sunniest skiing takes place in the Sierra Nevada, only just over an hour

---

PYRENEAN ACTIVITIES

Real outdoor types should head for the Pyrenees, where the range of sporting activities is probably greater than anywhere in Spain. The area is most famous for its ski resorts, but not far from the mountains there are the usual warm weather activities of windsurfing (various suitable locations) plus a round of golf at San Sebastián.

After you have exhausted these, consider some of the following: diving, at Banyuls; surfing, cross the border to Biarritz; paragliding – the *only* way to descend a mountain according to its devotees; white-water rafting; canyoning and caving.

---

from Granada. The Pyrenean resorts are particularly good, and feature sophisticated ski-lifts and testing runs that can match the best in the Alps. The very best are Baqueira Beret (Lérida), Candanchú (Aragón) and La Molina (Gerona). However the sun-drenched ski-resorts here cannot always guarantee snow, and climatic factors make the French side of the range more dependable than the Spanish side. Not surprisingly the central areas are also better than those on the coast. For a skier's map of Spain, contact the Spanish National Tourist office. The same office also provides a list of *Holidays of Special Interest*, which lists tour operators specializing in skiing, golf, riding, tennis, fishing, and most water sports.

For mountain climbing and serious walking, you can't beat the Pyrenees, though there are many more mountainous regions and areas of great natural beauty for hikers all over the interior.

You don't have to be in the country too long to realize that Spain's No. 1 spectator sport is **football** (soccer). Most cafés are adorned with football colours and on the night of a match they will be crowded

312

with passionate fans cheering or booing every kick and tackle. Street celebrations are commonplace after important (and sometimes not so important) victories. Matches are usually held in the evenings; the animated post-mortem goes on, over cigars and *coñac*, far into the night. Tickets are sold at the stadium but when internationally known teams like Real Madrid or Barcelona ('Barça') are playing, you have to apply well in advance.

Horse racing fans should note that the main courses are La Zarzuela in Madrid, Lasarte in San Sebastián and Pineda down south in Seville.

Shopping

Modern Spain has long since climbed out of the bargain basement; the more European the country becomes, the higher the prices seem to soar. Aim to come home with something different, rather than concentrating on finding a bargain by home standards and you'll have a much more rewarding time. There are always those cheap and cheerful, kitsch Spanish souvenirs (such as straw donkeys, bullfight posters etc.), which will serve to remind you of a good holiday.

For a quick survey of what Spaniards are buying, browse through the big department stores: **El Corte Inglés** and **Galerías Preciados.** They have branches in almost every sizeable town, with easy-to-find souvenir and gift departments.

Unlike most Spanish businesses, these chains stay open non-stop across the lunch-and-siesta break until about 8pm in the evening. More than a dozen cities have branches of *Artespaña*, the official network of showplaces for Spanish artisans. They stock classy handicrafts – from artis-tic ceramics and furniture to a full suit of armour.

The shopping choices are predictably wider in the big cities, which also offer more reasonable prices than the resort areas. For regional specialities, the best buys are usually on the spot: the biggest choice of Toledo steel, clearly, can be found in Toledo; your bottle of sherry will certainly be more meaningful if you buy it at the *bodega* in Jerez (though it may be slightly cheaper in the supermarket next door).

For exclusive fashions and jewellery, the top shopping streets are Madrid's Serrano and Castellana and Barcelona's Passeig de Gràcia, though the trendy over-spill goes far beyond. Upmarket resorts like Marbella and San Sebastián also offer lavish opportunities for luxury shopping.

Antiques abound in Madrid's *Rastro* (which also serves as a transit camp for some unbelievable junk). Barcelona's near equivalent to the Rastro is the Els Encants flea market and Las Palmas on Gran Canaria holds a good *rastro* with a very African flavour every Sunday morning. Good-natured haggling over the price is all but obligatory in these open-air bric-a-brac markets. As ever in these types of places, beware of pick-pockets.

Any local or village market is Spain is likely to be a colourful affair, and is worth attending to browse over the colourful fruit and vegetables, maybe the fish, and above all to experience the hustle and bustle of ordinary people going about their everyday lives. If you are self-catering, this is where you should shop too (food prices are not negotiable). One of the most colourful fruit and veg market in all Spain is that of La Boqueria on Las Ramblas in Barcelona – though by its very location, this is hardly typical. Ask the local tourist office for a list of market days in your locality.

Best Buys in Brief

Alcohol. For liquid souvenirs, look for bargains in brandy, *cava* (Spanish champagne), sherry, table wines, dessert wines and local liqueurs such as the herbal concoctions in Galicia or *anisette* from Chinchón. Many liqueurs are sold in decorative bottles.

Antiques. Beware among the tempting, theoretically authentic *antigüedades:* paintings, polychrome sculptures, illuminated mediaeval psalters, handmade rugs, furniture, porcelain and crystal. You can always take home a rusty old door key suitable for a haunted house, or a kitchen iron of undeniably pre-electric vintage.

Artificial pearls from Majorca are so cleverly made that not even experts can tell the difference until they feel the smoothness. Rub them along your teeth – the real ones are rougher.

Ceramics. Each region produces its own distinctive shapes, colours and designs, traditional or cheerfully modern. Among the standouts: the blue-and-white classics from Manises, near Valencia; the blue-and-yellow products of Talavera de la Reina; and *avant-garde* ideas from

Sargadelos, Galicia. Or take home a hand-painted, illustrated *azulejo* (wall tile of Moorish origins).

Damascene. Study the intricacies of inlaid gold designs in steel knives, scissors, thimbles, jewellery. This art, begun in Damascus, lives on in Toledo.

Embroidery. In many a village the women spend their days at the kind of needlework their grandmothers taught them: handkerchiefs, tablecloths, pillowcases. Look for lace *mantillas*, those lightweight shawls for covering shoulders and sometimes heads – as Spanish as their name.

Fans. The collapsible kind, as fluttered by *señoritas* over the centuries. The best are illustrated with hand-painted scenes and include real lace.

Fashions. Madrid and Barcelona are currently two of the most fashionable places in Europe, while the Ibiza look has long been trendy. If you prefer old-fashioned fashion, you can even buy a real flamenco dress; they come in a rainbow of colours. For men: custom-made shirts and suits. Off-the-peg children's clothes are charming but expensive.

Foodstuffs. You can take home an after-taste of Spain, mostly sweet – almonds (roasted or sugar-glazed), dates, figs, *turrón* (nougat), *chochos* (cinnamon jaw-breakers from Salamanca), *membrillo* (quince paste or jelly), or locally celebrated pastries. Olives, and virgin olive oil may be bargains.

Glassware. On the island of Majorca, glassmaking is a tourist attraction. If you miss the demonstration, you can see the results of all the huffing and puffing – blue, green or amber bowls, glasses, pots and pitchers – in stores all around the mainland.

Hats. Just for fun: a broad-brimmed Andalusian hat, a Basque beret, a sombrero or a bullfighter's hat.

Ironwork. Heavy on the baggage scales, but wrought-iron lanterns, candlesticks and lamps may be a bright idea.

Jewellery. From cheap but decorative bracelets by itinerant artisans to expensive silver or titanium necklaces in sophisticated modern designs, Spain can satisfy most tastes.

Knives. For a pointed present, penknives, daggers and swords from Toledo, where the Crusaders bought theirs.

Leather. Top-flight raw material, processing and workmanship account for the renown of Spanish leather products at their best. Whether you are looking for a sturdy wallet or the handbag of a lifetime, you will find exactly what you want. Also fine gloves, belts, coats and shoes: but they are no longer cheap.

Paintings. Gone are the days when Spain's best artists lived in exile. In the current air of freedom and creativity, the muse is back. Madrid has developed into one of Europe's leading contemporary art markets, and Barcelona has dozens of important galleries. Many more provincial centres, and even fashionable seaside resorts, follow the trend.

Rugs. From the south come inventively designed, meticulously woven, colourful floor-coverings: tiny throw-rugs or big, thick carpets. Some are so original they are worth putting up as wall hangings.

Valencian porcelain. Collectors of Lladró (it's a little like Capo di Monte, but cheaper) can stock up in its hometown; less detailed models (but they are not

There's an endless choice of wine skins for every tourist's taste.

A 16th-century figurine peers, not quite angelically, at prospective buyers in a Toledo antique shop.

seconds) from the same workshop go under the name *Nao*.

Woodwork. Spanish carvers have been whittling sublime statues, altars and choir stalls for centuries. Look for reproductions of classic saintly figures. Downmarket, there is no shortage of Don Quixote statuettes. Olive wood makes salad bowls, pepper mills, chess boards and beads. If portability is irrelevant, consider buying some Spanish furniture –

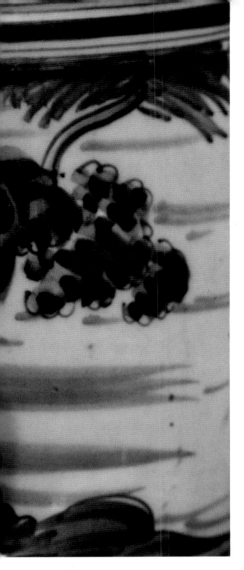

reproductions of classic styles or enterprising modern designs.

Entertainment

The challenge here is keeping the pace, or changing your own routine to get on an even footing. Since Spaniards don't usually start thinking about a leisurely dinner until 9 or 10pm (earlier in the resorts, later elsewhere) the night-life tends to keep going far later than in other countries. The sleepless, prowling 'cats' of Madrid are Europe's champion night-owls, but smaller Spanish cities aren't far behind. From opera to girlie show, from flamenco to disco, every kind of entertainment is on tap. All you need is enough time and plenty of energy.

There are basically two types of Spanish night-life on offer to the foreign visitor. The first type is almost exclusively aimed at the package market. On the *costas* this usually takes the form of large-scale venues which stage Las Vegas/ Parisian-style cabaret spectaculars (such as the Benidorm Palace, or the Scala on Gran Canaria). Not too dissimilar from these are many of the 18 casinos in Spain (on your way in they will ask to see your passport). Obviously gambling is the big thing here and this attracts many local high-rollers in addition to holiday-makers of all nationalities, but there is also often a large glitzy cabaret content to Spanish casinos.

A variation on the cabaret theme may be to add folklore to the usual international entertainment and give it a local setting and atmosphere, such as a Majorcan country manor, or a Tenerife cave. Barbecues and 'country feasts' held in rustic settlements with folklore entertainers are other perennial packaged favourites (the latter is usually a complete misnomer, where mediocre food is washed down with as much rough wine as you can drink).

Quite obviously the locals, or indeed many Spanish tourists, wouldn't be seen dead patronizing these north European-sponsored evenings, so where do they go? There are the usual trendy bars, night-clubs and discos, which are universal currency. In Barcelona many a humble

GAMBLING THE NIGHT AWAY

Spanish casinos come in various shapes and sizes. Some are very grand with rows of cypresses, fountains and ornamental gates leading to authentic mansions. Others are thoroughly modern with few pretensions to the type of aristocratic old-world glamour seen in James Bond films. The casino games are usually roulette (European and American), *la boule* (a roulette-style game), *baccarat/chemin de fer*, *punto-banco* and blackjack. Even if you are not gambling, it is fascinating to watch the monied clientèle trying to become even more monied, and the lightning reflexes of the unsmiling croupiers as they scoop away the poor punters' gaming chips. If you intend visiting you will need either your passport, identity card or driver's licence. A tie is not always necessary, but you should dress smartly. The safest rule for amateurs is to set your limit in advance and to stick rigidly to that limit.

Casinos also put on regular international cabaret and some stage occasional classical music, dance and opera performances.

drinking bar has been taken to an art form. In fact if Gaudí were alive today, he would not be commissioned for churches or private mansions, but for Barcelona's *bars modernos* ('designer bars'). Add to the bars an abundant supply of state-of-the-art discos and currently Barcelona is one of the most fashionable nightspots in Europe. Elsewhere on the fashion bar/disco scene, Madrid is the city that never sleeps (and would hotly dispute any claim that Barcelona is this year's in-place) while Ibiza is the pride of the Mediterranean. In case you were wondering what is the difference, 'Discos' usually last longer into the next morning than do 'music bars' and are correspondingly more expensive. Drinks prices can be extortionate, so be careful.

There is a half-way house between the *costa* glitz-palaces and the truly Spanish designer bars, and they are the establishments where the majority of locals and more enterprising tourists meet – the humble bar or café. From sunrise to the middle of the night – from the first coffee to the last brandy (and often vice-versa) – the café-bar is a very special institution. In practice there is little difference between what is a bar and what is a café aside from the bias of the 'bar' towards alcoholic drink.

Most bars are noisy places, in keeping with the general decibel level in Spain as a whole. The ubiquitous TV is almost always switched on, a radio or tape may well be playing simultaneously and the infuriating gaming machine in the corner pumps out in electronic stacatto tones the first few bars to Colonel Bogey as the locals try to hit the jackpot. It is no wonder that Spaniards often seem to be shouting at each other for no reason! The bars and cafés are the meeting places for locals and tourists, either to swop the day's news in pidgin-English, Spanish or German or to shout animatedly at the TV screen whenever the football is on. The price of a beer or a coffee buys you a ring-side seat for as long as you care to stay; no-one will rush you to leave or to buy another drink.

Flamenco

Throbbing guitars, snapping fingers, stamping heels, and songs that gush from the soul put the passion in **flamenco**, Spain's best-known entertainment. Many songs resemble the wailing of Arab music – which may be a clue to flamenco's centuries-old origins. Flamenco nightclubs attract local enthusiasts as well as tourists who don't usually go to nightclubs or stay up late. The anguished chants and compelling rhythms generate an electricity that crosses all frontiers of nationality or language.

There are two main groups of songs: one, bouncier and more cheerful, is known as the *cante chico*. The second group of songs, called *cante jondo*, deals with love, death, all the human drama, done in the slow, piercing style of the great flamenco singers. Purists say the talent in a *tablao flamenco* (floorshow) in Madrid is rarely up to top standard. The show-biz version available in coastal resorts is even less authentic. For the real thing, you have to go to flamenco's birthplace, Andalusia, and

THE FIESTA BRAVA

Even among Spaniards, bullfighting excites controversy. Is it an art, a spectacle, a metaphysical experience – or ritually choreographed slaughter? However you judge the *fiesta brava*, the bullfight has long been a symbol of Spain – flamboyance and fate, and violence with grace.

The Spanish writer and philosopher José Ortega y Gasset, much concerned with the soul of Spain, wrote of 'the tragic friendship, going back three millennia, between the Spanish man and the brave bull'. In truth, nobody can say when the first Spaniard fought the first bull. Something anticipating the bullfight was known among the ancient Celtiberian people. The first operating bullrings were the amphitheatres that had crumbled after the fall of the Roman empire; elsewhere in Spain, bullfights were held in the town square.

The rules of bullfighting were codified in the 18th century at Ronda. It was never meant to be a sport, for no one regards bullfighting as a contest between equals; it is one man's wits against the brawn and instinct of a specially bred beast. The odds are weighted heavily against the bull, for whom the conclusion is foregone. Yet, every time the *torero* enters the ring, he knows his own life is in danger. Some of the most admired bullfighters have been killed by brave bulls. The municipal museum of Córdoba is largely devoted to the life and death of a local hero, Manolete, fatally gored at the age of 30; elsewhere in town he rates a triumphal statue.

Starting, traditionally, at exactly 5 o'clock in the afternoon, the scenario of the *corrida* is straightforward. To the accompaniment of a fanfare of trumpets and clarinets, the *matadors* and their teams arrive in fanciful, even effeminate uniforms. (Don't call the *torero* a *toreador*; it's a word invented to suit the lyrics of Bizet's *Carmen*.) After the opening procession, the first bull of the afternoon enters the ring. The fighter sizes up the bull's intelligence and agility and begins to tire him using the big red and yellow *capote*. After these preliminaries the *picador*, a mounted spearman in Sancho Panza costume, lances the bull's shoulder muscles.

In the second *tercio* (the second of the drama's three ritual acts) the deft *bandarilleros* risk a goring as they stab long beribboned darts into the animal's shoulders.

In the final, fatal *tercio* the matador taunts the bull with the small, dark-red *muleta* cape, eventually dominating him. Finally, as the panting bull awaits the inevitable, the matador unveils his sword and lunges for the kill.

Depending upon the skill and courage shown by the matador, he may be awarded an ear, two ears or, rarely, the top prize, two ears plus the tail of the bull he has just dispatched. If he has disappointed the audience, he is likely to be sent off in silence or with catcalls.

Bullfight fans consider a *corrida* an extemporaneous poem about the mystery of life and death. Critics condemn the spectacle as the most barbarous form of cruelty to animals. To assuage the opponents, it has been suggested that Spain adopt the rules of neighbouring Portugal, where the bull leaves the ring on his own four feet. But many a devout supporter of the *fiesta brava* would reply: 'Over my dead body'.

search out the specialist bars and small clubs frequented by Spanish connoisseurs.

Some flamenco troupes go from bar to bar throughout the night so if you enjoy the show simply follow them!

Cultural Activities

Spaniards take **opera** very seriously; consider José Carreras, Plácido Domingo, Victoria de los Angeles, Teresa Berganza and Montserrat Caballé. There are three great venues. Barcelona's opera house, the Gran Teatre del Liceu, described as the finest theatre in the world when it opened in 1857, is the grand old lady in this respect. Madrid's Teatro Real reopened as an opera house after extensive renovations in 1992, and Seville also dedicated a new Teatro de la Maestranza in the celebratory year.

Madrid is the home of *zarzuela*, the uniquely Spanish form of operetta, first presented in the 17th century at the palace of La Zarzuela, the royal family's residence. These musical plays come in two varieties, light-hearted and serious. Even if you don't understand the language, an evening of *zarzuela* can still be entertaining. For **concerts**, Madrid's new Auditorio Nacional de Música is the home of the Spanish National Orchestra. In Barcelona major concerts take place at the wildly *art nouveau* Palau de la Música Catalana. Concerts and recitals in cities often take place in historic surroundings, such as churches and palaces.

Spain's tradition of **drama** is long and prolific; Lope de Vega wrote or co-wrote something like 1,800 plays, and Tirso de Molina, who created the character Don Juan, also turned out hundreds of scripts. Spanish and foreign plays, classical and contemporary, can be seen in theatres all over the country. Madrid alone has dozens of theatres, often offering two performances per night.

Television and other distractions have drastically cut the size of the Spanish **cinema** audience. Almost all the foreign films shown commercially in Spain have been dubbed into Spanish. In the big cities, however a certain number of cinemas show foreign films (usually controversial or 'art' films) in the original version, labelled 'v.o.' with Spanish subtitles. If your Spanish is adequate, you can catch up on the works of contemporary filmmakers like Victor Erice, Carlos Saura and Pedro Almodóvar.

For Children

Long sunny days and soft sandy beaches means that much of coastal Spain is a favourite family destination. Many hotels have special features for very young guests, ranging from organized pool-side games and outings to baby-sitting. When the appeal of seawater and sandcastles starts to wear thin, try some of the following:

Make a splash. Water parks are usually the favourite activity off the beach all over tourist Spain (at the last count there were over 30, so there is bound to be one close to you). While energetic kids hurl themselves down the 'kamikaze' or ride the

Look closely at these bar-room bullfighting pictures and 'Death in the Afternoon' takes on a new meaning. The corrida may appear to be a one-sided contest but the torero is forever dicing with danger.

'super toboggan', those feeling particularly lazy can top up on their sun-tanning in landscaped gardens. Additional park attractions often include mini-golf and ten-pin bowling.

Go-karting. Go-kart tracks are also common along the *costas*, providing fun on four wheels for the over fours. There's no problem in selecting the wrong gear (they don't have any) and being so low to the ground they cannot tip over. As they are slung so low, they do give a great sensation of speed. Dad needn't feel left out: there are often high-speed karts for adults too.

A night out. The Spanish take their children out at night, so why not do likewise? There are many suitable tourist excursions, one of the favourite old clichés being the 'mediaeval tournament'. Knights joust for the fair damsel's hand while you tuck into a rustic 'mediaeval' dinner. Swop knights for buccaneers and you get Pirate Adventure, Benidorm's favourite night out. Older children will probably also enjoy the colour, noise and movement of the flamenco show. There are few, if any, restrictions on children coming out with you into bars and restaurants, and joining the adult world can be fun in itself. Large hotels may also organize children's evening activities.

¡Fiesta! Older children will love the fireworks, the devils and dragons, the giant papier-mâché figures and whatever else is on parade during the fiesta. Carnival is a particularly colourful event, where the local children usually end up with the best costumes. There is nothing to stop you dressing up and joining in. Many tourists do; parties are always better when you take part rather than just watch.

The Fun of the Fair. There are *Parque de Atraciones* in most big towns or resorts where the rides range from the old-fashioned carousel and big-wheel to high-tech thrills.

Barcelona's two funfairs (one at Montjuïc, the other at Tibidabo) deserve a special mention. Both have first-class rides, both enjoy hilltop locations with marvellous views, and it's an adventure getting up to each of them. It's a thrilling cable-car ride up to Montjuïc, while Tibidabo is a slower haul, starting on an old-fashioned tramcar then changing to funicular railway.

Animal life. The Barcelona Zoo, with its famous albino gorilla and a killer whale and dolphin show is acclaimed as one of Europe's finest zoos. Elsewhere on the *costas*, marine parks are becoming popular, often featuring performing dolphins, sea-lions and parrots. The Canary Islands are particularly good, with beautifully landscaped near-natural marine and bird-life parks on Tenerife, Gran Canaria and Lanzarote.

*H*otels with stunning views, such as this one at Coll de Lilla in Catalonia, abound in Spain. The following pages list a good selection of the better hotels at a variety of prices that we recommend

The Right Place at the Right Price

While hotels and restaurants throughout the world tend more and more to uniformity, Spanish accommodation and cuisine can still provide a welcome change. Our selection of some of the best hotels and restaurants in Spain and her islands is listed alphabetically by town. Book in advance for both hotels and restaurants in high season or during a fiesta period (when accommodation prices soar).

There is a central reservation point for *paradores* in Madrid. Contact:

Paradores de España
Central de Reservas
Velázquez, 18
28001 Madrid
Tel. (01) 435 97 00;
fax (01) 435 99 44

Paradores also have representatives in other countries. In the UK contact:

Keytel International
Tel. 0171 402 8182

In the USA or Canada contact:

Marketing Ahead, New York
Tel. 212 686 9213

Enquire at the Spanish National Tourist Office in other countries.

Hotels

The star rating in brackets after each entry refers to the official government grading system (*see* ACCOMMODATION).

As a basic guide to room prices, we have used the following symbols (for a double room with bath/shower in high season), but do be aware that you can negotiate prices for more than one night and out of high season room rates can fall sharply:

▯	below 6,000 ptas
▯ ▯	6,000-8,500 ptas
▯ ▯ ▯	8,500-12,000 ptas
▯ ▯ ▯ ▯	12,000-17,000 ptas
▯ ▯ ▯ ▯ ▯	above 17,000 ptas

Mainland Hotels

Aiguablava
Parador Costa Brava   ▯ ▯ ▯ ▯
(4 stars)
17255 Aigua Blava
Tel. (972) 62 21 62;
fax (972) 62 21 66
87 rooms. A thoroughly modern parador in a terrific setting high on a small promontory, above peaceful coves and beaches. Outdoor swimming pool.

Alarcon
Parador Marqués   ▯ ▯ ▯ ▯
de Villena (4 stars)
Avdo. Amigos del Castillo, s/n,
16213 Alarcon
Tel. (966) 33 13 50;
fax (966) 33 11 07
11 rooms. Old castle, originally an 8th century Arab fortress, by the Madrid to Valencia road.

Alcañiz
Parador   ▯ ▯ ▯ ▯
La Concordia (4 stars)
Castillo de Calatravas,
44600 Alcañiz
Tel. (974) 83 04 00;
fax (974) 83 03 66
12 rooms. Charming hotel in a castle of the Calatrava Knights, on a hill overlooking the town.

Algeciras
Reina Cristina (4 stars)   ▯ ▯ ▯ ▯
Paseo de la Conferencia
11207 Algeciras
Tel. (956) 60 26 22;
fax (956) 60 33 23
162 rooms. This locally famous hotel enjoys a picturesque park location. Outdoor and indoor swimming pools, terrace, sauna, tennis.

Alicante
Meliá Alicante (4 stars)   ▯ ▯ ▯ ▯
Playa Postiguet, 03001 Alicante
Tel. (96) 520 60 60
fax (96) 520 47 56
545 rooms. Centrally located, between a rocky outcrop and the sea.

Hotel Palas (3 stars)
Calle Cervantes, 5, Plaza de Mar
03002 Alicante
Tel. (96) 520 93 10;
fax (96) 514 01 20
49 rooms. 19th-century hotel full of character. Stylish; large bedrooms.

Almagro
Parador de Almagro
(4 stars)
Ronda de San Francisco
13270 Almagro
(Ciudad Real 22km/13 miles)
Tel. (926) 86 01 00;
fax (926) 86 01 50
55 rooms. Beautifully converted 16th-century convent with beamed public rooms and large but cosy bedrooms. Ask for a room overlooking the courtyard. Swimming pool.

Arcos de la Frontera
Parador Casa
del Corregidor (3 stars)
Plaza de España
11630 Arcos de la Frontera
Tel. (956) 70 05 00;
fax (956) 70 11 16
24 rooms. Modernized mansion with spacious rooms, enjoying a splendid cliff-top location and panoramic views. Good restaurant.

Cortijo Fain
(2 stars)
Carretera de Algar,
Tel/fax (987) 70 11 67
6 rooms. Small farmhouse set in an olive grove, converted into a charming hotel. 3km from Arcos.

Astorga
Gaudí (3 stars)
Eduardo de Castro, 24700 Astorga
Tel. (987) 61 56 54;
fax (987) 61 50 40
35 rooms. Stylish hotel, many rooms overlooking the cathedral and the Gaudí palace. Good restaurant.

Ávila
Palacio Valderrábanos
(4 stars)
Plaza de la Catedral, 9
05001 Ávila
Tel. (918) 21 10 23;
fax (918) 25 16 91
73 rooms. Historic building furnished in grand style. Ask for a room with a cathedral view, or room 229 in the old watch tower.

Barcelona
Gran Hotel Calderón
(4 stars)
Rambla de Catalunya, 26
08007 Barcelona
Tel. (93) 301 00 00;
fax (93) 317 31 57
244 rooms. Modern high-rise tower offering stunning views over the whole city. Indoor, outdoor pools plus sauna and exercise rooms.

Hotel Claris (5 stars)
Pau Claris, 08009 Barcelona
Tel. (93) 487 62 62;
fax (93) 215 79 70
124 rooms, Modernist palace in central location, near the Museum of Egyptology, with roof top pool.

Hotel Colón (4 stars)
Avenida Catedral, 7
08002 Barcelona
Tel. (93) 310 14 04;
fax (93) 317 29 15
151 rooms. This charming town house boasts an unbeatable location opposite the cathedral. Ask for one of the two front rooms overlooking the cathedral plaza, where the sardana is danced every Sunday.

Hotel Gran Derby (5 stars)
Loreto 28
Tel. (93) 322 32 152;
fax (93) 419 68 20
43 rooms. An ultra-modern hotel in a quiet location outside the centre.

Duques de Bergara
(4 stars)
Bergara, 11, 08002 Barcelona
Tel. (93) 301 51 51;
fax (93) 317 34 32
56 rooms. A late 19th-century Modernist mansion, only recently converted into a hotel. Tasteful combination of old- and new-style décor.

Hotel España (2 stars)
Sant Pau, 9-11
Tel. (93) 318 17 58;
fax (93) 317 11 34
84 rooms. An architectural gem, the España is a must if you are looking for atmosphere. Come for a meal in the splendid Modernist restaurant.

Gaudí (3 stars)
Carrer Nou de la Rambla, 12
08001 Barcelona
Tel. (93) 317 90 32;
fax (93) 412 26 36
73 rooms. Opposite Gaudí's Palau Güell just off La Rambla, this is a comfortable modern hotel.

Hotel Gótico (3 stars)
Jaume I, 14
08002 Barcelona
Tel. (93) 315 22 11;
fax (93) 315 38 19
70 rooms. An attractive hotel well placed in the heart of the Barri Gòtic. The rooms are simple, but tastefully decorated in rustic style.

Hotel Gran Vía (3 stars)
Gran Vía de les
Cortes Catalanes, 642
08007 Barcelona
Tel. (93) 318 19 00;
fax (93) 318 99 97
48 rooms. Delightful 19th-century town house brim-full of old-world charm. The public rooms are richly furnished and decorated throughout with Art Nouveau fittings.

Hotel Gravina (3 stars)
Gravina, 12
08001 Barcelona
Tel. (93) 301 68 68;
fax (93)317 28 38
80 rooms. Conveniently situated near Plaça Catalunya, the Gravina's classical façade conceals a very modern interior. The rooms are on the small side but spotlessly clean.

Gran Hotel
Havana (4 stars)
Gran Via, 647
09010 Barcelona
Tel. (93) 412 11 15;
fax (93) 412 26 11
141 rooms. A magnificent hotel with all modern facilities, in a convenient location.

Majestic (4 stars)
Passeig de Gràcia, 70
08005 Barcelona
Tel. (93) 488 17 17;
fax (93) 418 18 80
336 rooms. A picturesque townhouse hotel with a modern extension, rooftop terrace and swimming pool. Good location.

Hotel Oriente (3 stars)
La Rambla, 45-47
Tel. (93)302 25 58;
fax (93) 412 38 19
142 rooms. Barcelona's most venerable hotel still preserves its old-world glamour and style. The ballroom incorporates part of an old Franciscan monastery; wonderful Modernist restaurant. The rooms are fairly ordinary, but large and comfortable.

Royal (4 stars)
La Rambla, 117
08002 Barcelona
Tel. (93) 301 94 00;
fax (93) 317 31 79
Good position at the top of La Rambla, rooms tastefully appointed, if somewhat small. All the usual amenities at a reasonable price for the location. 108 rooms.

Hotel San Agustín (2 stars)
Plaça Sant Agustí, 3
Tel. (93) 318 16 58;
fax (93)317 29 28
70 rooms. Charming hotel converted from a convent about a century ago; tastefully refurbished.

Hotel Suizo (3 stars)
Plaça de l' Angel, 12
08002 Barcelona
Tel. (93) 315 41 11;
fax (93) 315 38 19
48 rooms. Just off Vía Laietana on the edge of the Barri Gòtic, the Suizo enjoys a prime location. Its recently renovated rooms, each with own balcony, are spacious, bright and cheerful.

Bayona
Parador Conde de Gondomar (4 stars)
Ctra. de Bayona, km 1,6
36300 Bayona
Tel. (986) 35 50 00;
fax (986) 35 50 76
124 rooms. Typical, elegant Galician country mansion rebuilt within an old castle with fine estuary views. Swimming pool, garden, tennis court.

Benidorm
Hotel Alameda (3 stars)
Alameda, 13
03500 Benidorm
Tel. (96) 585 56 50;
fax (96) 585 56 54
68 rooms. Good central location in the old part of town. Large rooms, friendly staff.

Bilbao
Hotel Villa de Bilbao (5 stars)
Gran Via 87, Bilbao
Tel. (94) 441 60 00;
fax (94) 441 65 29
142 rooms. Centrally located with all facilities and a fine Basque restaurant.

Burgos
Landa Palace (5 stars)
Ctra. N-1 Madrid-Irún, km 236
09000 Burgos
Tel. (947) 20 63 43;
fax (947) 26 46 76
42 rooms. Luxury hotel mostly built in the 1960s to resemble a mediaeval-Gothic fantasy. Large rooms superbly decorated, antiques and plants abound. Outdoor and indoor pools. Excellent cuisine.

Mesón del Cid (3 stars)
Plaza Santa Maria, 8
09003 Burgos
Tel. (947) 20 87 15;
fax (947) 26 94 60
29 rooms. Modern but picturesque hotel in a central location, stylishly decorated to reflect the El Cid theme. Ask for a room with a cathedral view.

Norte y Londres (2 stars)
Plaza Alonso Martinez, 10
09003 Burgos
Tel. (947) 26 41 25; fax 27 73 75
50 rooms. Good value recently renovated rooms in a pleasant turn-of-the century establishment. Quiet but central location in old town.

Cáceres
Meliá Cáceres (4 stars)
Plaza San Juan, 13
10001 Caceres
Tel. (927) 21 58 00;
fax (927) 21 40 70
86 rooms. Part of the Meliá hotel chain, sensitively converted from an old palace. Ask for a first-floor room for original features.

Cádiz
Francia y Paris (3 stars)
Plaza de San Fransisco, 2
11004 Cádiz
Tel. (956) 22 23 48;
fax (956) 22 24 31
69 rooms. Charming freshly renovated belle-époque hotel located on a popular traffic-free plaza.

Parador Atlántico (4 stars)
Duque de Nájera, 9
11002 Cádiz
Tel. (956) 22 69 05;
fax (956) 21 45 82
153 rooms. Bland, modern six-storey block but attractive, comfortable rooms and handy central location. Swimming pool, garden.

Cambrils
Cambrils Princess (3 stars)
Carretera de Salou a Cambrils
43850 Cambrils
Tel. (977) 36 42 83;
fax (977) 36 53 51
400 rooms. Smart Princess chain hotel in a relatively quiet location, albeit on the main road, 2km from Cambrils, only a few metres from the beach. Swimming pool, sun terraces, tennis court, crazy golf. Popular with tour operators.

Hotel Mónica (3 stars)
Galcerán Marquet, 3
43850 Cambrils
tel. (977) 36 01 16;
fax (977) 79 36 78
56 rooms. A smart, comfortable, small hotel in the quiet back streets only a stone's throw from the centre. Cheerful rooms and lawned garden with palm trees and outdoor swimming pool. Squash court. (Half-board minimum tariff in high season).

Hotel Tropicana (2 stars)
Avenida Diputación
43850 Cambrils
Tel. (977) 36 01 12;
fax (977) 26 01 12
28 rooms. Modest, comfortable small hotel set on the main road just before the centre of Cambrils and opposite the beach. Attractive lawned garden with swimming pool.

Cardona
Parador Duques de Cardona (4 stars)
08261 Cardona
Tel. (93) 869 12 75;
fax (93) 869 16 36
60 rooms. Possibly Spain's favourite parador, set in a romantic hill-top castle with parts dating from the 9th century. Views of the mountains. Splendid mediaeval atmosphere. Outstanding restaurant.

Carmona
Parador Alcázar del Rey Don Pedro (4 stars)
41410 Carmona
Tel. (95) 414 17 12;
fax (95) 414 17 12
65 rooms. Splendid reconstruction of the old Alcázar of Pedro the Cruel with extensive views over the plain and to Seville (38km). Stately public areas, comfortable rooms in period style. Swimming pool.

**Hotel Palacio Casa
de Carmona (5 stars)**
Plaza de Lasso, 1, 41410 Carmona
Tel. (95) 414 33 00;
fax (95) 414 37 52
*30 rooms. One of the most beautiful
hotels in Spain. 16th-century palace
with antiques in every room, and
modern facilities discreetly incorporated in the original building.*

Chinchón
**Parador de Chinchón
(4 stars)**
Avenida Generalísimo, 1
28370 Chinchón
Tel. (91) 894 08 36;
fax (91) 894 09 08
*38 rooms. Peaceful location in a
17th-century Augustinian convent,
of which the chapel remains. Swimming pool, cloisters and garden.*

Ciudad Rodrigo
Parador Enrique II (3 stars)
Plaza del Castillo, 1
37500 Ciudad Rodrigo
Tel. (923) 46 01 50;
fax (923) 46 04 04
*27 rooms. Spartan rooms in atmo-
spheric 12th-century castle. Ask for
a room with a river view, or room 10
– circular with a domed roof.*

Córdoba
**Parador de la Arruzafa
(4 stars)**
Avenida de la Arruzafa, s/n
14012 Córdoba
Tel. (957) 27 59 00;
fax (957) 28 04 09
*94 rooms. Modern building in a pic-
turesque location with views over
the town. Attractive garden and terrace with pool and tennis court.*

Gonzalez (2 stars)
Manriquez, 3
14008 Córdoba
Tel. (957) 47 98 19;
fax (957) 48 61 87
*16 rooms. Charming family hotel in
part of 16th-century palace. Public
areas full of antiques. Most rooms
look on to a lovely Arabesque patio.*

Meliá Córdoba
Jardines de la Victoria
14004 Córdoba
Tel. (957) 29 81 47; tlx. 76591
*147 rooms. Picturesque, central lo-
cation. Pleasant flowered terrace,
swimming pool, garden.*

La Coruña
Hotel Finisterre (4 stars)
Paseo del Parrote, 22
15001 La Coruña
Tel. (981) 20 54 00;
fax (981) 20 84 62
*127 rooms. The town's best hotel,
recently renovated with pleasantly
refurbished bedrooms. Splendid position with view of the bay. Heated
swimming pool.*

Cuenca
**Hotel La Cuva del Fraile
(3 stars)**
Hoz del Huécar, 16001 Cuenca
Tel. (966) 21 15 71;
fax (966) 25 60 47
*63 rooms. Modernized historic
building with pool, tennis court, cy-
cles for hire, children's play area.*

Posada de San José (2 stars)
Julián Romero, 4, 16001 Cuenca
Tel/fax (966) 21 13 00
*25 rooms. Charming hotel full of
character, in a 17th-century convent. Picturesque, with antiques and
sloping floors. Marvellous view.*

Elche
Huerto del Cura (4 stars)
Porta de la Morera, 14
03203 Elche
Tel. (96) 545 80 40;
fax (96) 542 19 10
*70 rooms. This modern parador-
style hotel enjoys a picturesque
location inside the town's date plantation. Lush garden, swimming pool,
tennis, sauna, good restaurant.*

Estepona
El Pilar (Pension)
Plaza de las Flores, 22
29680 Estepona
Tel. (95) 280 00 18; no fax
*16 simple but comfortable rooms,
recently renovated. Picturesque location on a quiet square in the old
town and close to the beach.*

Figueras
Ampurdán (3 stars)
Ctra. Gral Madrid Francia, km 763
17600 Figueras
Tel. (972) 50 05 62;
fax (972) 50 93 58
*42 rooms. This centrally located ho-
tel was a great favourite of the famous Catalan, Josep Pla.Garden,
terrace. Execellent cuisine.*

Fuengirola
Florida (3 stars)
Paseo Marítimo
29640 Fuengirola
Tel. (95) 247 61 00;
fax (95) 258 15 29
*116 rooms. Comfortable modern ho-
tel in central location. Pool and
garden.*

Girona
**Hotel Sol Girona
(4 stars)**
Barcelona 112
17003 Girona
Tel. (972) 40 05 00;
fax (972) 24 32 33
*114 rooms. A modern hotel with all
the usual facilities, in a good central
location.*

Gijón
**Parador Molino Viejo
(4 stars)**
Parque de Isabel la Catolica
33204 Gijón
Tel. (98) 537 05 11;
fax (98) 537 02 33
*40 rooms. The parador is housed in
a converted water mill in a park.
Peaceful spot with elegant rooms.
Garden, terrace.*

Granada
**Alhambra Palace
(4 stars)**
Peña Partida, 2
18009 Granada
Tel. (958) 22 14 68;
fax (958) 22 64 04
*132 rooms. Extravagant neo-
Moorish creation enjoying views
over Granada and the Sierra
Nevada. Garden, terrace.*

América (1 star)
Real de la Alhambra, 53
18009 Granada
Tel. (958) 22 74 71;
fax (958) 22 74 70
*13 rooms. Family-run hotel within
the Alhambra compound; vine-cov-
ered patio dining area. Excellent
value for its position. Small rooms.*

Guadalupe (3 stars)
Avenida de los Alijares
18009 Granada
Tel. (958) 22 34 23;
fax (958) 22 37 98
*58 rooms. Good location next to Al-
hambra. Modern hotel with large
characterful rooms.*

Hotel Meliá Granada
(4 stars)
Angel Ganvet, 7, 18009 Granada
Tel. (958) 22 74 00;
fax (958) 22 74 03
197 rooms. In the city centre, near the cathedral, with fitness centre and fine restaurant.

Parador San Francisco
(4 stars)
Alhambra, 18009 Granada
Tel. (958) 22 14 40;
fax (958) 22 22 64
39 rooms. A parador now occupies the convent within the Alhambra grounds, enjoying views over the Generalife gardens. Garden, terrace. Book months ahead.

Guadalupe
Hospedaría del Real
Monasterio (2 stars)
Plaza Juan Carlos I
10140 Guadalupe
Tel. (927) 36 70 00;
fax (927) 36 71 77
40 rooms. Stay in the monastery's own hotel. Many of the bedrooms are converted from 16th-century monks' cells, set around a delightful courtyard.

Parador Zurbarán
(4 stars)
Marqués de la Romana, 10
10140 Guadalupe
Tel. (927) 36 70 75;
fax (927) 36 70 76
40 rooms. Originally a 14th-century Pilgrim's hospice this simple white-washed structure has been converted into a parador.

Guillena
Cortijo Torre de la Reina
(4 stars)
Torre de la Reina, Guillena, Sevilla
Tel. (95) 578 91 62;
fax (95) 578 92 42
12 rooms. Small, charming hotel with a marvellous restaurant, in a 13th-century building.

Huesca
Pedro I de Aragón
(3 stars)
Del Parque, 34, 22003 Huesca
Tel. (974) 22 03 00;
fax (974) 22 00 94
52 rooms. The only hotel in town to rate more than two stars. Central location. Garden.

Jaca
Conde Aznar (2 stars)
Paseo General Franco, 3
22700 Jaca
Tel. (974) 36 10 50;
fax (974) 36 07 97
23 rooms. Comfortable, friendly, old-world, family-run hotel.

Jerez de la Frontera
Hotel Capele (3 stars)
Corredera, 58
11402 Jerez de la Frontera
Tel. (956) 34 64 00;
tlx. (956) 75032
30 rooms. Behind the drab town-house façade lies a very smart, comfortable and welcoming hotel with many traditional features.

Jerez (4 stars)
Avenida Alvaro Domecq, 35
11405 Jerez de la Frontera
Tel. (956) 30 06 00;
fax (956) 30 50 01
121 rooms. Luxury hotel in attractive gardens with swimming pool and tennis courts.

León
Conde Luna (4 stars)
Independencia, 7, 24003 León
Tel. (987) 20 65 12;
fax (987) 21 27 52
154 rooms. A modern, rather undistinguished hotel, but in a central location and well equipped with garage, heated swimming pool, sauna.

Parador San Marcos
(5 stars)
Plaza San Marcos, 7, 24001 León
Tel. (987) 23 73 00; fax 23 34 58
253 rooms. The old 16th-century monastery is now a national monument and holds one of Spain's finest and most luxurious paradores. Ask for a room in the old part (very atmospheric with tapestry-covered stone walls).

Lloret de Mar
Santa Marta (4 stars)
Playa de Santa Cristina
17310 Lloret de Mar
Tel. (972) 36 49 04;
fax (972) 36 92 80
78 rooms. Splendid location in its own park, next to Santa Cristina Beach, away from the bustle of the town. Swimming pool and tennis court.

Logroño
Hostal Marqués de
Vallejo (2 stars)
Marqués de Vallejo, 8
26001 Logroño
Tel. (941) 24 83 33;
fax (941) 24 02 88
30 rooms. Simple lodgings in an old town house; friendly, family-run and recently renovated. Pine furniture in bedrooms. No restaurant.

Lugo
Gran Hotel Lugo (4 stars)
Avenida Ramón Ferreiro, 21
27002 Lugo
Tel. (982) 22 41 52;
fax (982) 24 16 60
168 rooms. Comfortable hotel in the town's residential area. Swimming pool, terrace.

Madrid
Arosa (4 stars)
De la Salud, 21
28013 Madrid
Tel. (91) 532 16 00;
fax (91) 531 31 27
126 rooms. Variety of rooms ranging from the grand old style of the original building to sleek and modern refurbished quarters. Good central location on Gran Vía. Swimming pool. No restaurant.

Barajas (5 stars)
Avenida Logroño, 305
28000 Madrid
Tel. (91) 747 77 00;
fax (91) 747 87 17
230 rooms. A modern luxury hotel near the airport with good facilities. Swimming pool, gym, golf-course, garden, sauna. Night-club.

Carlos V (3 stars)
Maestro Vitoria, 5
28013 Madrid
Tel. (91) 531 41 00;
fax (91) 531 37 61
67 rooms. Central location next to the Puerta del Sol. Elegant historic building with splendid public rooms, ordinary modern bedrooms. No restaurant.

Palace (5 stars)
Plaza las Cortes, 7
28014 Madrid
Tel. (91) 429 75 51;
fax (91) 429 82 66
500 rooms. Sumptuous belle-époque building with every modern luxury and a relaxed approach.

HOTELS

Paris (2 stars)
Alcalá, 2, 28014 Madrid
Tel. (91) 521 64 96;
fax (91) 429 82 66
114 rooms. Old favourite in an historic building in a convenient central location.

Serrano (4 stars)
Marqués de Villamejor, 8
28006 Madrid
Tel. (91) 435 52 00;
fax (91) 435 48 49
34 rooms. Small, traditional hotel in a central location.

Tryp Monte Real (5 stars)
Arroyo Fresno, 17, Madrid
Tel. (91) 316 21 40;
fax (91) 316 39 34
77 rooms. This elegant, modern hotel is slightly out of town, in tranquil surroundings. Impressive interiors hung with tapestries and art works.

Málaga
Parador de Gibralfaro (3 stars)
29016 Málaga
Tel. (95) 222 19 02;
fax (95) 222 19 04
12 rooms. Wonderful location above town with views to Gibraltar. Simple rooms and facilities.

Marbella
Pensión Enriqueta (2 stars)
Los Caballeros, 18
29600 Marbella
Tel. (95) 282 75 52; no fax
123 rooms. Friendly establishment in a quiet pedestrianized street.

El Fuerte (4 stars)
Avenida El Fuerte
29600 Marbella
Tel. (95) 286 15 00;
fax (95) 282 44 11
262 rooms. Long-established hotel in an historic building. Large comfortable bedrooms. Swimming pool, terrace, mini-golf, tennis.

Marbella Club (4 stars)
Ctra. Cádiz-Málaga, km. 178, 200
29600 Marbella
Tel. (95) 277 13 00; fax 282 98 84
95 rooms. Luxury and exclusivity are the hallmarks of this hang-out of the famous. Beautiful, sub-tropical gardens, swimming pool, heated swimming pool, tennis courts, fitness centre, sauna. Night-club.

Mérida
Emperatriz (3 stars)
Plaza de España, 19
06800 Mérida
Tel. (924) 31 31 11;
fax (924) 30 03 76
41 rooms. A characterful 16th-century palace with a tiled foyer and central patio garden. Rooms furnished in similar historic style

Parador Vía de la Plata (4 stars)
Plaza de la Constitución, 3
06800 Mérida
Tel. (924) 31 38 00; fax 31 92 08
82 rooms. Former baroque convent on the site of the old Roman Praetorian Guard Palace. Pleasant bar and garden. Friendly management. Good regional food.

Murcia
Hotel Meliá Siete Coronas (4 stars)
Paseo de Garay, 30003 Murcia
Tel. (988) 21 77 71;
fax (988) 22 12 94
156 rooms. Everything you would expect of a Meliá hotel; close to beaches and places of interest.

Nerja
Balcón de Europa (3 stars)
Paseo Balcón de Europa, 1
29780 Nerja
Tel. (952) 52 08 00;
fax (952) 52 44 90
105 rooms. Picturesque location, built into the cliff face. This simple hotel is quiet and traditional. Garden, terrace, sauna, mini-golf.

Olite
Parador Principe de Viana (de Olite) (3 stars)
Plaza de los Teobaldos, 2
31390 Olite
Tel. (948) 74 00 00;
fax (948) 74 02 01
43 rooms. Atmospheric palatial suites and public rooms in a restored castle, once home to the kings of Navarre. Double rooms are housed in a new extension.

Oviedo
Hotel de la Reconquista (5 stars)
Gil de Jaz, 16, 33004 Oviedo
Tel. (985) 524 11 00;
fax (985) 524 11 66
142 rooms.Luxury hotel in magnificent 18th-century building. Stylish with antique furnishings.

Pamplona
Ciudad de Pamplona (3 stars)
Iturrama, 21, 31007 Pamplona
Tel. (948) 26 60 11;
fax (948) 17 36 26
117 rooms. Functional chain hotel in a quiet residential part of town.

Iruña Palace Hotel Tres Reyes (4 stars)
Jardines de la Taconera
Tel. (948) 22 66 00;
fax (948) 22 29 30
313 rooms. Modern hotel in the centre of town; all rooms have balcony, all modern facilities.

Peñiscola
Hosteria del Mar (3 stars)
Ctra. Benicarló-Peñiscola, km 6
12598 Peñiscola
Tel. (964) 48 06 00;
fax (964) 48 13 63
85 rooms. An old Castile theme has been given to this modern parador-like hostal. Good facilities including swimming pool, garden, tennis.

Pontevedra
Parador Casa del Barón (3 stars)
Maceda, 36002 Pontevedra
Tel. (986) 85 58 00;
fax (986) 85 21 95
47 rooms. This old 18th-century baronial house still drips with chandeliers, tapestries and gilt and provides a very elegant hotel setting.

Ronda
Parador de Ronda (4 stars)
Plaza de España, 29400 Ronda
Tel. (95) 287 75 00;
fax (95) 287 80 80
79 rooms. A new hotel in an impressive location on the edge of the 'Tajo' gorge. Good range of facilities including swimming pool.

Polo (3 stars)
Mariano Soubirón, 8
29400 Ronda
Tel. (95) 287 24 47;
fax (95) 287 43 78
33 rooms. Plain but cheerful and well run, good bedrooms and bathrooms; central location.

329

Reina Victoria (4 stars)
Jerez, 25, 29400 Ronda
Tel. (95) 287 12 40;
fax (95) 281 10 75
88 rooms. The town's 'grand old lady' enjoys a superb view over the valley. Public rooms are grand but faded, bedrooms are a reasonable size. Swimming pool, garden, terrace.

Rosas

Coral Playa (3 stars)
Avinguda de Rhode, 28
17480 Rosas
Tel. (972) 25 62 50;
fax (972) 25 66 12
123 rooms. Simple four-storey hotel used by up-market tour operators, right on the beach.

Salamanca

Monterrey (4 stars)
Azafranal, 21
37001 Salamanca
Tel./fax (923) 21 44 00
89 rooms. Old world elegance, if a little faded, in the heart of the city.

**Parador de Salamanca
(4 stars)**
Teso de la Feria, 2
37000 Salamanca
Tel. (923) 26 87 00;
fax (923) 21 54 38
108 rooms. An ugly, modern block but enjoying a splendid panoramic view of the city. Good large rooms, garden, terrace, swimming pool and tennis court.

Salou

Hotel Planas (2 stars)
Plaza Bonet, 3, 43840 Salou
Tel. (977) 38 01 08
100 rooms. Modern, quite comfortable rooms (though with modest public areas) and despite being in the centre of town, retains a quiet atmosphere. Meals are served on the attractive tree-shaded terrace.

Salou Princess (3 stars)
Avenida de Andorra
43840 Salou
Tel. (977) 38 22 02;
(977) fax 38 34 10
288 rooms. Elegant modern hotel located on the town's quieter stretch of beach, but still close to the centre. Well-equipped rooms, attractive sun terraces and swimming pools.

San Sebastián

Costa Vasca (4 stars)
Avenida Pio Baroja, 15
20008 San Sebastián
Tel. (943) 21 10 11;
fax (943) 21 24 28
203 rooms. Reasonably priced good lodgings just out of the centre in a quiet location near Playa Ondaretta. Swimming pool, garden, tennis.

María Cristina (5 stars)
Paseo de la República Argentina, 4
20004 San Sebastián
Tel. (943) 42 49 00;
fax (943) 42 39 14
139 rooms. This belle-époque beauty is the city's finest hotel with all luxuries including air conditioning, and traditional high standards (though few sporting facilities).

Monte Igueldo (4 stars)
Monte Igueldo
20008 San Sebastián
Tel. (943) 21 02 11;
fax (943) 21 50 28
125 rooms. Modern hotel in a picturesque and peaceful location, enjoying a superb view of the city, bay and sea. Swimming pool, garden, terrace.

Niza (3 stars)
Zubieta, 56
20017 San Sebastián
Tel. (943) 42 66 63;
fax (943) 42 66 63
41 rooms. Arty types will enjoy this hotel as it owned by a renowned Basque sculptor, and is a showcase of modern art and fine antiques.

Santander

Roma (3 stars)
Avenida de los Hoteles, 5
39005 Santander
Tel. (942) 27 27 00;
fax (942) 27 27 51
47 rooms. Elegant hotel which has maintained high standards and tasteful décor. Quiet location.

Santiago de Compostela

Compostela (4 stars)
General Franco, 1
15702 Santiago de Compostela
Tel. (981) 58 57 00;
fax (981) 56 32 69
99 rooms. Very comfortable hotel in an historic building. No restaurant.

Peregrino (4 stars)
Avenida Rosalía de Castro
15706 Santiago de Compostela
Tel. (981) 52 18 50;
fax (981) 52 17 77
148 rooms. Comfortable hotel 1km (half a mile) from city centre. Pool, views, garden, terrace.

**Los Reyes Católicos
(5 stars)**
Plaza del Obradoiro, 1
15705 Santiago de Compostela
16-23000
Tel. (981) 58 22 00;
fax (981) 56 30 94
136 rooms. This magnificent building was founded in 1499 to give shelter to pilgrims and is therefore claimed to be the world's oldest hotel. Bedrooms surround patios, public rooms resemble museums.

Hostal Suso (2 stars)
Rua del Villar, 65
15700 Santiago de Compostela
Tel. (981) 58 66 11; no fax
9 rooms. This charming family-run hostal enjoys a fine location on one of the city's oldest (pedestrianized) streets. Simple rooms.

Santillana del Mar

Hotel Altamira (3 stars)
Calle Cantón, 1
39330 Santillana del Mar
Tel. (942) 81 80 25;
fax (942) 84 01 36
32 rooms. This 17th-century stone mansion has been beautifully restored and decorated with antiques. Better value than the parador.

Parador Gil Blas (3 star)
Plaza Ramón Pelayo, 11
39330 Santillana del Mar
Tel. (942) 81 80 00;
fax (942) 81 83 91
56 rooms. Charming country mansion built in the 15th and 16th centuries. Totally in character with the picturesque, mediaeval village of Santillana. Beautiful rooms, particularly those overlooking the garden.

Los Infantes (3 stars)
Avenida Le Dorat, 1
39330 Santillana del Mar
Tel. (942) 81 81 00;
fax (942) 84 01 03
30 rooms. Fine 18th-century stone building with grand public rooms but modern bedrooms (suites are an exception). Pleasant terrace.

Segovia

Los Linajes (3 stars)
Dr Velasco, 9
40003 Segovia
Tel. (921) 46 04 75;
fax (921) 46 04 79
55 rooms. Modern hotel built into the hillside, with a mock-mediaeval façade. The higher you go, the better the view. Garden, pleasant terrace with swimming pool. Nightclub (weekends).

Parador de Segovia (4 stars)
Apartado de Correos 106
40003 Segovia
Tel. (921) 44 37 37;
fax (921) 43 73 62
80 rooms. A very modern parador, with contemporary artwork and furnishings plus a superb view of Segovia from all rooms. Indoor and outdoor pool, garden, terrace.

Las Sirenas (2 stars)
Juan Bravo, 30, 40001 Segovia
Tel. (921) 43 40 11;
fax (921) 43 06 33
39 rooms. A charming, if faded 1950s hotel. Quiet, central location.

Seville

Alfonso XIII (5 star)
San Fernando, 2,
41004 Seville
Tel. (95) 422 28 50;
fax (95) 421 60 33
149 rooms. The haunt of royals and film stars, this opulent palace was built in 1909-29 and is the last word in overblown pseudo-Moorish splendour. Every facility including swimming pool, garden, terrace.

Becquer (3 stars)
Reyes Cátolicos, 4,
41001 Seville
Tel. (95) 422 89 00;
fax (95) 421 44 00
120 rooms. Well-equipped modern hotel in a good central location.

Doña Maria (4 stars)
Don Remondo, 19
41004 Seville
Tel. (95) 422 49 90;
fax (95) 421 95 46
61 rooms. Delightful hotel in a 19th-century town house superbly positioned with a view of the cathedral, and elegantly decorated, right down to the painted bed headboards (some bedrooms are

disappointing – ask to view). Unusual rooftop swimming pool and terrace. No restaurant.

Hotel Meliá Sevilla (4 stars)
Doctor Pedro de Castro, 1
41004 Seville
Tel. (95) 442 15 11;
fax (95) 442 16 08
678 rooms. Pretty, central location next to the Plaza de España. All modern facilities.

Murillo (2 stars)
Lope de Rueda, 7
41004 Seville
Tel. (95) 421 60 95;
fax (95) 421 96 16
57 rooms. An old curiosity shop of antiques and unusual objects lurking behind an ordinary townhouse façade in the middle of the Barrio de Santa Cruz. Bedrooms are quite plain.

Simon (1 star)
García Vinuesa, 19
41001 Seville
Tel. (95) 422 66 60;
fax (95) 456 22 41
68 rooms. Three 18th-19th-century town houses make up this hotel which is high on charm, with a typical Andalusian courtyard, if low on luxury (ask to see the bedrooms, most are pretty and plain). Central, often noisy location.

Sitges

Antemare (4 stars)
Verge de Montserrat, 48-50
08870 Sitges
Tel. (93) 894 70 00;
fax (93) 894 63 01
112 rooms. Six apartment-like buildings make up the elegant Antemare, established for over 60 years in the heart of the town's quiet residential district. Swimming pools and many fitness facilities.

Romántic (2 star pension)
Sant Isidre, 33
08870 Sitges
Tel. (93) 894 83 75;
fax (93) 894 81 67
55 rooms. Three 19th-century villas have been combined to form a gem of a hotel in the quiet back streets. Tiles, sculptures, wicker and greenery blend Modernisme with old Cuba in the public areas and a delightful garden and bar. Traditionally furnished rooms. Very popular with the gay community.

La Santa María (3 stars)
Paseo de la Ribera, 52
08870 Sitges
Tel. (93) 894 09 99;
fax (93) 894 78 71
35 rooms. On the seafront in the busiest part of town. Recently renovated, attractive bedrooms, traditionally furnished public areas and an excellent restaurant. Helpful, friendly owners.

Sitges Park (3 stars)
Calle Jesús, 16, 08870 Sitges
Tel. (93) 894 02 50;
fax (93) 894 08 39
87 rooms. Behind the street entrance of this very central hotel is a fairy-tale Modernist 'Gothic' tower, plus a beautiful palm-shaded terrace and swimming pool. Rooms are fairly basic.

El Xalet (2 stars)
Isla de Cuba, 35, 08870 Sitges
Tel. (93) 11 00 70
11 rooms. A gorgeous late 19th-century Modernist building. Lovely swimming pool and garden and a charming period dining-room. Bedrooms have antique furniture, air conditioning and all mod cons.

Soria

Parador Antonio Machado (4 stars)
Parque del Castillo, 42005 Soria
Tel. (975) 21 34 45;
fax (975) 21 28 49
34 rooms. An unusual, chic, light, modern parador offering splendid views of Soria. Garden.

Parador Fernando de Aragón (3 stars)
50680 Sos del Rey Católico
Tel. (976) 88 80 11;
fax (976) 88 81 00
65 rooms. Modern parador which blends in well with this small interesting town. Excellent views from the fourth-floor restaurant terrace. Fine Aragonese food.

Tarragona

Hotel Astari (3 stars)
Vía Augusta, 95
43000 Tarragona
Tel. (977) 23 69 00;
fax (977) 23 69 00
83 rooms. A comfortable efficiently managed hotel. Pleasant swimming pool and terrace bar with sea views and outdoor dining.

Hotel Imperial Tarraco
(4 stars)
Rambla Vella, 2, 43000 Tarragona
Tel. (977) 23 30 40;
fax (977) 21 65 66
170 rooms. Accustomed to business-men rather than tourists, but its good facilities and central cliff-top situation make for a pleasant short stay. Swimming pool, tennis court.

Hotel Marina (1 star)
Vía Augusta, 151
4300 Tarragona
Tel. (977) 23 30 27;
fax (977) 23 33 09
26 rooms. Small, modern establish-ment with a leafy front garden, re-sembles a private house. Modest, clean rooms plus terrace and tennis court. Conveniently placed for the Platja de l'Arabassada.

Toledo
La Almazara (2 stars)
Ctera de Cuerva km 3.5
45080 Toledo
Tel. (925) 22 38 66; no fax
21 rooms. Delightful hill-top coun-try retreat. Many personal touches give a cosy, warm atmosphere to this 16th-century country house. Splendid views. No restaurant.

Hostal de Cardenal (3 stars)
Paseo de Recaredo, 24
45004 Toledo
Tel. (925) 22 49 00;
fax (925) 22 29 91
27 rooms. A beautifully converted 18th-century bishop's palace, now home to Toledo's most distinctive hotel. Very stylish bedrooms and public areas, very popular.

Los Cigarrales (2 stars)
Ctra. Circunvalación, 32
45000 Toledo
Tel. (925) 22 16 72;
fax (925) 21 55 46
36 rooms. An old farmhouse a short drive (or walk) from town, con-verted into a simple but smart hotel and restaurant.

Hotel Maria Cristina
(3 stars)
Marqués de Mendigonia, 1
48003 Toledo
Tel. (925) 21 32 02;
fax (925) 21 26 50
65 rooms. A renovated 15th-century hospital near two historic gates, this hotel reflects all the charm of the city.

Parador Conde de Orgaz
(4 stars)
Cerro del Emperador
45000 Toledo
Tel. (925) 22 18 50;
fax (925) 22 51 66
77 rooms. A fine re-creation of a typical mediaeval Toledo country house with attractive bedrooms, 20 of which enjoy wonderful views over the city (so too does the restaurant). Swimming pool and terrace.

Torremolinos
Miami (2 stars)
Aladino, 14
29620 Torremolinos
Tel. (95) 238 52 55; no fax
26 rooms. This friendly Andalusian villa is an oasis of peace and local style, almost literally so around its courtyard swimming pool, shaded by palm and banana trees. Public areas full of antiques and curios, rooms plain and simple. No restau-rant.

Tortosa
Castillo de La Zuda
Parador (4 stars)
Tortosa
Tel. (977) 44 44 50;
fax (977) 44 44 58
82 rooms. A beautifully restored mediaeval castle in a majestic posi-tion overlooking the town, cathedral and Ebro valley. Public areas are rather gloomy; bedrooms are deco-rated in comfortable local rustic style. Swimming pool.

Tossa de Mar
Diana (2 stars)
Plaza d'España, 6
17320 Tossa de Mar
Tel. (972) 34 18 86;
fax (972) 34 11 03
21 rooms. The main attraction of this charming town house is the stamp of the Modernist architec-tural genius, Antoni Gaudí who de-signed many of its features. Very stylish and recently refurbished.

Pensión Horta Rosel (2 stars)
Pola, 29
17320 Tossa de Mar
Tel. (972) 34 04 32; no fax
29 rooms. An old whitewashed cot-tage provides simple comfortable bedrooms, looked after by the charming hostess. Open late May to October. No restaurant.

Úbeda
Parador Condestable
Dávalos (4 stars)
Plaza de Vázquez de Molina, 1
23400 Úbeda
Tel. (953) 75 03 45;
fax (953) 75 12 59
31 rooms. The centrepiece of this magnificent palace built in the 16th and 17th centuries is its glassed-in patio. Attention to detail is evident in public rooms and bedrooms and a friendly, lively atmosphere per-vades.

Valencia
Excelsior (3 stars)
Barcelonina, 5, 46002 Valencia
Tel. (96) 351 46 12;
fax (96) 352 34 78
65 rooms. Charming old hotel with a sense of character. Gleaming brass and old wood fittings, pleas-ant bedrooms. Central location.

Parador Luis Vives
(de El Saler) (4 stars)
Crtera Saler, km 16,
Avda de los Pinares, 151
46012 Valencia
Tel. (96) 161 11 86;
fax (96) 162 70 16
58 rooms. Modern parador in a peaceful spot amid pines and sand dunes a few miles outside town. Good for sporty types; excellent golf-course (adjacent) plus swim-ming pool and tennis court.

Reina Victoria (4 stars)
Barcas, 4, 46002 Valencia
Tel/fax (96) 352 04 87
97 rooms. Grand neoclassical pub-lic rooms are a feature of this his-toric building in a good central lo-cation.

Valladolid
Imperial (2 stars)
Peso, 4, 47001 Valladolid
Tel. (983) 33 03 00;
fax (983) 33 08 13
81 rooms. Comfortable hotel in a former 16th-century palace. Central location.

Olid Meliá (4 stars)
Plaza de San Miguel, 10
47003 Valladolid
Tel. (983) 35 72 00;
fax (983) 33 68 28
211 rooms. The best choice in the city centre, albeit quite a functional chain hotel. Central location.

Vich

Parador de Vich (4 stars)
08500 Vich
Tel. (93) 888 72 11;
fax (93) 888 73 11
36 rooms. This re-creation of an old Catalan farmhouse enjoys a spectacula, peaceful location high in the mountains. Grand public rooms, and bedrooms in local style. Swimming pool, garden, tennis court.

Vitoria

Hotel Dato (2 stars)
Eduardo Dato, 28
01005 Vitoria
Tel. (945) 14 72 30;
fax (945) 24 23 22
14 rooms. Comfortable town house built in 1903, decorated in Art-Nouveau style by the very personable owner. Some rooms feature the vernacular mirador style of glazed-in balcony. No restaurant.

Zamora

**Parador de Zamora
(Condes de Alba y Aliste)
(4 stars)**
Plaza de Viriato, 5
49014 Zamora
Tel. (988) 51 44 97;
fax (988) 53 00 63
27 rooms. 15th-century Renaissance palace with magnificent glazed-in patio. Antiques and pot-plants abound and much of the original structure and fittings remain. Characterful bedrooms all in old part. Swimming pool, terrace.

**Hostería Real de Zamora
(3 stars)**
Cuesta de Pizarro, 7
49001 Zamora
Tel. (988) 53 45 45;
fax (988) 53 45 22
16 rooms. This 15th-century building, the reputed home of Pizarro, has just opened as a hotel. Good bedrooms, some with river views.

Zaragoza

**Meliá Zaragoza Corona
(4 stars)**
Avda. César Augusto, 19
50004 Zaragoza
Tel. (976) 43 01 11;
fax (976) 44 07 34
In the heart of the ancient city, with extensive facilities including penthouse pool, nightclub and sauna gymnasium.

Paris (3 stars)
Pedro María Ric, 14,
50008 Zaragoza
Tel. (976) 23 65 37;
fax (976) 22 53 97
62 rooms. Good modern hotel with all facilities, recently renovated and decorated, in a central location.

Hotel Sauce (2 stars)
Espoz y Mina, 33
50003 Zaragoza
Tel. (976) 39 01 00;
fax (976) 39 85 97
20 rooms. Charming whitewashed house tastefully decorated with stylish and cosy bedrooms. Café, no restaurant.

Balearic Islands

Ibiza

Hostal El Corsario (3 stars)
Poniente, 5
07800 Ibiza town
Tel. (971) 30 12 48; no fax
14 rooms. A characterful, rather Bohemian sort of place decorated in old Ibizan style. Some rooms have antique fittings and fixtures, pleasant terrace.

Hacienda (5 stars)
Urb. Na Xamena
07815 San Miguel
Tel. (971) 33 45 00;
fax (971) 33 45 14
54 rooms. The island's most luxurious hotel, set in a peaceful hillside retreat with wonderful views. Traditional décor and grand bedrooms.

Ses Estaques (3 stars)
Ses Estaques
07840 Santa Eulalia del Río
Tel. (971) 33 00 69; no fax
159 rooms. Smart modern four-storey hotel used by package tour operators, directed with a personal touch by a husband and wife team.

Majorca

L'Hermitage (4 stars)
Carretera de Sollerich
07349 Orient
Tel./fax (971) 61 33 00
20 rooms. Country-house style hotel built onto a former 17th-century convent, in a delightful secluded setting. Swimming pool, tennis courts. Excellent French cooking.

Mar i Vent (3 stars)
Calle Mayor
07191 Banyalbufar
Tel. (971) 61 00 25; no fax
30 rooms. Charming, friendly family-run hotel with wonderful views of the coast and hillside terraces. Homely décor with antiques and hand-carved beds.

Punta Negre (4 stars)
Carretera de Andraiz, km 12
Costa d'en Blanes
Tel. (971) 68 07 62;
fax (971) 68 39 19
69 rooms. Modern hotel with splendid views over bay of Palma and lush gardens leading to tiny coves.

La Residencia (4 stars)
Son Moragues, 07179 Deia
Tel. (971) 63 90 11; fax 63 39 70
27 rooms. A famous country house set in gorgeous gardens. Service and rooms are impeccable. Pool, terraces, outstanding restaurant.

Ses Rotges (2 stars)
Calle Rafael Blanes, 21
07590 Cala Ratjada
Tel. (971) 56 31 08; fax; 56 43 45
24 rooms. Attractive mansion-like hotel, managed by French brothers. Beautiful courtyard with abundant flora; splendid restaurant.

Son Vida (5 stars)
Son Vida
07015 Palma
Tel. (971) 79 00 00; fax 79 00 17
165 rooms. The core of this deluxe hotel is a 13th-century castle. Antiques abound, magnificent views and setting. Three pools, four tennis courts, golf-course adjacent.

Menorca

Hostal Biniali (3 stars)
Carretera S'Vestra
07710 San Luis
Tel. (971) 15 17 24; fax 15 03 52
9 rooms. Old country house with a homely feel and friendly Irish manageress. Antiques adorn the rooms, which have excellent views. Garden, swimming pool. Superb restaurant.

Port Mahón (4 stars)
Avenida Fort de l'eau
07701 Mahón
Tel (971) 36 26 00; fax 35 10 50
74 rooms. Modern, comfortable, friendly hotel overlooking the port. Traditionally furnished, pretty bedrooms. Swimming pool.

S'Algar (3 stars)
Urbanización S'Algar
07710 San Luis
Tel. (971) 15 17 00;
fax (971) 35 04 65
*106 rooms. Modern hotel in a
peaceful setting; good sports facilities. Pleasant rooms and terraces.*

Canary Islands

Fuerteventura
**Parador de Fuerteventura
(3 stars)**
Playa Blanca, 48
Tel. (928) 85 11 50;
fax (928) 85 11 58
*50 rooms. A modern hotel located
right on the ocean front.*

Gomera
**Conde de la Gomera
Parador (4 stars)**
Balcón de la Villa y Puerto
38800 San Sebastián
Tel. (922) 87 11 00;
fax (922) 87 11 16
*42 rooms. This comfortable country
manor is beautifully furnished and
enjoys a breathtaking cliff-top site
with panoramic views.*

Hotel Tecina (4 stars)
Lomada de Tecina
35811 Playa de Santiago
Tel. (922) 89 51 88
*434 rooms. This stylish, low-rise
complex effectively forms the only
resort on the island.*

Gran Canaria
Club de Mar (2 keys)
Playa de Mogán
35140 Puerto Mogán
Tel. (928) 56 50 66; fax 74 02 23
*160 rooms. Situated in the mini-
village of hotels and apartments
around the beautiful marina of
Puerto Mogán and designed to
blend in with the local style.*

**Meliá Tamarindos
(5 stars)**
Calle Retama, 3
San Agustin
Tel. (928) 76 26 00;
fax (928) 76 22 64
*318 rooms. The lovely gardens of
this splendid hotel face on to the
beach of this affluent resort. Famous for its casino and night-club.*

Reina Isabel (5 stars)
Calle Alfredo L Jones, 40
35008 Las Palmas
Tel. (928) 26 01 00;
fax (928) 27 45 58
*233 rooms. The capital's most luxu-
rious hotel with excellent restaurant, roof-top pool and night-club.*

Santa Catalina (5 stars)
Parque Doramas,
León y Castillo, 227
35005 Las Palmas
Tel. (928) 24 30 40;
fax (928) 24 27 64
*208 rooms. Beautiful historic build-
ing patronised by Spanish and
British royalty, enjoys a splendid
leafy position.*

El Hierro
**Parador El Hierro
(3 stars)**
Las Playas, 38900 El Hierro
Tel. (922) 55 80 36;
fax (922) 55 80 86
*47 rooms. Secluded 20-year-old
building at the end of a long dead-
end road, with swimming pool, perfect for getting away from it all.*

Lanzarote
**Hotel Los Fariones
(4 stars)**
Acatife, 2,
Urbanización Playa Blanca
35510 Puerto del Carmen
Tel. (928) 51 01 75;
fax (928) 51 02 02
*237 rooms. Long-established hotel
sited on the best part of this fine
beach with virtually its own secluded cove and a luxurious palm
garden in its grounds. Quiet atmosphere despite central location.*

**Meliá Salinas
(5 stars)**
Costa Tequise
Tel. (928) 59 00 40;
fax (928) 59 03 90
*310 rooms. All rooms have sea
view, swimming pools and daily
poolside luncheon buffet.*

**Apartments Tahiche
(3 keys)**
Plaza Montaña Clara
35509 Costa Teguise
Tel. (928) 59 01 17
*238 apts. Attractive three-storey
complex in green and white local
architectural style, 300m (1,000ft)
from both beach and resort centre.*

**Playa Flamingo Apartments
(2 keys)**
Urbanización Montaña Roja,
Playa Blanca
35570 Yaiza.
Tel. (928) 51 73 69
*305 apts. These attractive low-level
apartments enjoy a fine beach-side
setting. Moorish -style exteriors.*

La Palma
**Parador Santa Cruz de la
Palma (3 stars)**
Avenida Marítíma, 34
38726 Santa Cruz de la Palma
Tel. (922) 41 23 40;
fax (922) 41 18 56
*32 rooms. A modest but attractive
parador that blends into the
weather-beaten balconied
buildings lining the sea-front.*

Tenerife
**Parador de Cañadas del
Teide (2 stars)**
Cañadas del Teide
Tel. (922) 38 64 15;
fax (922) 23 25 03
*17 rooms. This chalet-style parador
enjoys an incomparable setting in
the foothills of Mount Teide next to
Los Roques. Rustic, wooden furnishings make for comfort rather
than luxury.*

Jardín Tropical (4 stars)
Urbanización San Eugenio,
38660 Playa de las Américas
Tel. (922) 79 41 11;
fax (922) 79 44 51
*376 rooms. This Moorish fantasy is
probably the most beautiful building
on the south coast. Beautiful gardens, lovely décor, good position.*

Mencey (5 stars)
Avenida Dr José Naveiras, 38
38001 Santa Cruz
Tel. (922) 27 67 00; fax 28 00 17
*298 rooms. Probably the finest hotel
in the islands and on a par with the
world's great hotels. Patios and
balconies, antiques and art.*

Monopol (3 stars)
Calle Quintana, 15
38400 Puerto de la Cruz
Tel. (922) 38 46 11; fax 37 03 10
*100 rooms. A charming, character-
ful, old family-run establishment in
the centre of town; with Canarian
balcony façade and tropical-style
patio. Simple modern facilities plus
roof-top pool.*

Restaurants

It is advisable to book in advance for dinner (and perhaps lunch) at all establishments during the high season.

Prices given are for an average à la carte selection per person, without any wine or other drinks. Luxury items such as lobster will obviously cost more. Many restaurants have cheaper fixed price menus so don't be put off an establishment if the prices seem just out of your range.

under 2,500 ptas
2,500-3,500 ptas
3,500-4,500 ptas
over 4,500 ptas

Mainland Restaurants

Alicante
Dársena
Paseo del Puerto
03001 Alicante
Tel. (96) 520 75 89
Enjoy rice and fish specialities overlooking the marina. Try the bouillabaise. Attractive, outdoor terrrace. Closed Monday and Sunday evenings.

El Delfín
Esplanada de España,12
03002 Alicante
Tel. (96) 521 49 11
Alicante's finest food. Valencian fish specialities served in modern, surroundings. Book the upstairs window seats for esplanade views.

Altafulla
Hotel Faristol
Calle San Martin, 5
Altafulla
Tel. (977) 65 00 77
A beautifully restored Catalan mansion where meals are served in an atmospheric dining room or in a lovely walled garden. House specialities include rabbit in almond sauce, seafood mousse with cava. Open weekends only, October to July.

Aranjuez
Casa Pablo
Almíbar, 20
28300 Aranjuez
Tel. (91) 891 14 51
Typical Castilian tavern-style décor. Hearty roasts. Closed August.

Arcos de la Frontera
El Convento
Calle Maldonado, 2
11630 Arcos de la Frontera
Tel. (956) 70 23 33
Award-winning regional cooking in a rustic 16th-century mansion.

Ávila
Méson del Rastro
El Rastro, 1
05001 Ávila
Tel. (918) 21 12 18
Simple Castilian home cooking in a large country-style dining room. Lively, friendly atmosphere, particularly at lunchtime.

Piquio
Calle de Estrada, 4
05000 Ávila
Tel. (918) 21 14 18
Popular local restaurant with Castilian specialities and good tapas.

Barcelona
Agut
Gignas, 16
Barcelona
Tel. (93) 315 17 09
Top quality Catalan cuisine in an intimate 1930s setting. Excellent menu del día. Very popular, but not the most relaxed environment.

Amaya
Rambla Santa Mónica, 20-24
08002 Barcelona
Tel (93) 302 61 38
Some of the best Basque cooking in the city can be found at this friendly establishment. Particularly good on Sundays. Look for cococha a las vasca (Basque barbels) and chipirones del norte (baby squid).

Botafumeiro
Major de Grácia, 81
08012 Barcelona
Tel. (93) 218 42 30
Perfectly prepared and presented fish and shellfish dishes from Galicia: reputedly the best restaurant in Barcelona for this cuisine. Closed Sunday evening and Monday.

Los Caracoles
Escudellers, 14
08002 Barcelona
Tel. (93) 302 31 85
This restaurant típico is a minor legend, and serves classic Catalan cuisine at a reasonable price. It is patronized by opera and theatre personalities, whose signed photos decorate the walls.

La Cuineta
Carrer Paradis, 4
08002 Barcelona
Tel. (93) 315 01 11
This atmospheric restaurant is set in the 17th-century vaults of a wine cellar in the heart of the Barri Gòtic. Excellent traditional Catalan cuisine; the bacalla (salt cod) is very popular. Closed Mondays.

Egipte
Jerusalem, 3
Barcelona
Tel. (93) 317 74 80
Just behind La Rambla's Boqueria market, the ever-popular Egipte serves well-prepared Catalan dishes, including huge desserts. Arrive early for a table on the balcony. Closed Sundays. (If you cannot get in here, try its young trendy sister restaurant, also called Egipte, near the Liceo at Rambla de les Flors, 79.)

Eldorado Petit
Dolors Monserdà, 51
08017 Barcelona
Tel. (93) 204 51 53
One of Barcelona's finest restaurants, serving inspired and lavish Catalan food, traditional and innovative dishes, in opulent surroundings One Michelin rosette. Outdoor dining. Closed 2 weeks August and Sunday.

El Gran Café
Avinyó, 9
08002 Barcelona
Tel. (93) 318 79 86
A delightful 1920s-style restaurant on two floors, close to Las Ramblas, serving French and Catalan food. Live pianist in the evenings. Closed Saturday lunch, Sundays and all August.

Jaume de Provença
Provença, 88
08029 Barcelona
Tel. (93) 230 00 29
Good value excellent Catalan cuisine; modern décor. Closed August, Sunday evening and Monday.

Petit Paris
Paris, 196
08036 Barcelona
Tel. (93) 218 26 78
Just ten tables make up this small restaurant, which serves excellent Catalan cuisine.

Reno
Tuset, 27
08006 Barcelona
Tel. (93) 200 91 29
Catalan and French cuisine; served to politicians and business types at lunchtime, to the general public in the evenings, in sombre traditional surroundings. Good dessert menu and excellent selection of wines. Late opening for a smart restaurant.

Les Set Portes
Passeig de Isabel II, 14
08003 Barcelona
Tel. (93) 319 30 33
A venerable institution, now designated as an architectural monument and little changed since it opened in 1836. A reasonably priced, extensive menu of Catalan food caters for up to 1,000 diners in any of the restaurant's seven rooms, from 1pm to 1am.

Viá Veneto
Ganduxer, 10 y 12
08021 Barcelona
Tel. (93) 200 72 44
Award-winning and inspired French and Catalan cuisine (one Michelin rosette) is served in elegant belle-époque surroundings. Renowned dessert menu. Closed Saturday lunch and Sunday except July and August.

Benalmádena
La Rueda
San Miguel 1
Benalmádena
Tel. (95) 244 82 21
Popular with local residents. Menus include both international dishes and tasty local specialities. Terrace dining. Closed Tuesday.

Benidorm
Don Luis
Avenida Dr. Orts Llorca,
Edificio Zeus
03500 Benidorm
Tel. (96) 585 46 73
Elegant, modern restaurant with good Italian cuisine. Outdoor dining.

Tiffany's
Avenida Mediterraneo, 51,
Edificio Coblanca, 3
03500 Benidorm
Tel. (96) 585 44 68
Classic Spanish cuisine plus some interesting international dishes are served at this popular elegant restaurant (dinner only). Piano music. Closed January.

Bilbao
Goizeko-Kabi
Particular de Estraunza, 4
48011 Bilbao
Tel. (94) 441 50 04
One Michelin rosette. Try the ensalada de bogavante, *the house-style* bacalao, *or roast woodcock with armagnac. Closed Sunday.*

Burgos
Casa Ojeda
Vitoria, 5
09004 Burgos
Tel. (947) 20 90 52
Famous local institution; snack on tapas sitting outside or try Castilian and international food in its elegant restaurant. Closed Sunday evening.

Cáceres
Figón de Eustaquio
Plaza de San Juan, 12
10003 Cáceres
Tel. (927) 24 81 94
Traditional rich and unusual Estremaduran and Spanish dishes are served in this locally famous family-owned restaurant. Rustic décor.

Cádiz
El Faro
San Félix, 15
11002 Cádiz
Tel. (956) 21 10 68
Splendid fish dishes and Andalusian food is the speciality of the locally famous proprietor of this popular establishment.

Cambrils
Berganti
Consolat del Mar, 6
43850 Cambrils
Tel. (977) 79 13 37
Small and friendly with an outdoor terrace, a good and reasonably priced fish restaurant. Several types of zarzuela, *good value lobster specials.*

Eugenia
Consolat de Mar, 80
43850 Cambrils
Tel. (977) 36 01 68
Enjoy excellent fish and seafood on a shady terrace or eat inside the elegant, old-world dining room. Eugenia's owner is the town mayor, a friendly mine of information on all aspects of Cambrils.

Joan Gatell-Casa Gatell
Paseo Miramar, 26
43850 Cambrils
Tel. (977) 36 00 57
Superb seafront restaurant which has been awarded a Michelin rosette, owned and managed by the town's pioneering culinary Gatell family; try the entremeses Gatell, the bouillabaise *or the* arroz marinera. *Ask for a table by the window on the first floor. Closed Sunday night, Mondays.*

Mas Gallau
Carretera Valencia-Barcelona, km 4
43850 Cambrils
Tel. (977) 36 05 88
Superb setting in an atmospheric recreation of a beamed and stuccoed traditional Catalan masia *(farmhouse). Extensive Spanish regional menu, try* escudella *followed by rabbit or pig's feet with* escargots à la Catalane.

Córdoba
Almudaina
Jardines de los Santos Mártires, 1
14004 Córdoba
Tel. (957) 47 43 42
Situated in a typical 15th-century Andalusian building with patio, this excellent restaurant specializes in local produce with unusually interesting vegetable dishes. Outdoor dining. Closed Sunday evening.

El Caballo Rojo
Cardenal Herrero, 28
14003 Córdoba
Tel. (957) 47 53 75
Good traditional Andalusian cuisine, including some interesting old Moorish influences, can be enjoyed in this well-known and tastefully decorated restaurant.

El Churrasco
Romero, 16
14003 Córdoba
Tel. (957) 29 08 19
Córdoba's most famous restaurant, decorated with local handicrafts

and antiques. Try the eponymous churrasco *(a grilled pork dish with hot pepper sauce)*, dorada *baked in salt, or simply snack on tapas. Outdoor dining on an elegant patio.*

La Coruña
Coral
Estrella, 2
15003 La Coruña
Tel. (981) 22 10 82
A comfortable traditional restaurant specializing in fish fresh off the dock. Closed Sunday (except in summer).

Yéboles
Calle Troncoso, 14,
Zone Plaza María Ptia
15000 La Coruña
Tel. (981) 20 62 20
Popular informal meeting point, tapas *and snack bar plus restaurant. Closed Wednesday.*

Cuenca
El Figón de Pedro
Cervantes, 13
16004 Cuenca
Tel. (966) 22 68 21
Excellent cuisine in traditional Castilian surroundings. Closed Sunday evening.

Méson Casas Colgadas
Canónigos
16001 Cuenca
Tel. (966) 22 35 09
Fine regional and international food but the view is everything, hanging precariously above the town's famous ravine. Closed Monday evening.

Elche
El Escondrijo
Ctra. de Elche, km 8
03200 Elche
Tel. (96) 568 08 25
Regional and French cuisine. Closed first 2 weeks September and Sunday evening.

Estella
Navarra
Gustavo de Maeztu, 16
31200 Estella
Tel. (948) 55 10 69
Good Navarrese food served in mediaeval surroundings. Outdoor dining. Closed Sunday evening and Monday.

Figueras
Mas Pau
Avinyonet de Puigventós
17742 Figueras
Tel. (972) 54 61 54
Attractive and characterful rustic restaurant in old farmhouse (also recommended for accommodation). French-Catalan cuisine; famous for its prawns.

Hotel Ampurdan
Carretera de Francia (N2)
17600 Figueras
Tel. (972) 50 05 62
Hotel restaurant of wide renown specialising in local cuisine, including wonderfully rich game dishes. Excellent wine selection with a range of local wines.

Fuengirola
Romy
Moncayo, Edificio Perlilla,
Fuengirola
Tel. (95) 246 41 31
Lively restaurant with terrace on pedestrianized street, serving excellent value zarzuela, *garlic prawns and grilled meats.*

Fuenterrabía
Ramón Roteta
Irún, s/n
20280 Fuenterrabía
Tel. (943) 64 16 93
Chef-owner Ramón Roteta welcomes you personally to the cosy restaurant which was formerly his house. Outstanding Basque cuisine with a fish and seafood emphasis has earned him one Michelin rosette. Outdoor dining. Closed Sunday evening and Thursday (except evenings in summer).

Gerona
La Penyora
Nou del Teatre, 3
17004 Gerona
Tel. (972) 21 89 48
This small restaurant-cum-art gallery serves delicious 'market cuisine', depending on the availability of the best ingredients. Try the garbanzos *(chick-pea stew).*

Cal Ros
Cort Real 9
Cosy country-style restaurant by the city wall, serving warming local dishes.

Granada
Alacena de las Monjas
Plaza del Padre Suárez, 5
18008 Granada
Tel. (958) 22 40 28
Atmospheric restaurant in a 16th-century vaulted building, specializing in regional dishes. Closed Sundays and in August.

Carmen de San Miguel
Plaza de Torres Bermejas, 3
18009 Granada
Tel. (958) 22 67 23
Beautifully situated on the Alhambra hill. Panoramic views and outdoor dining from a Spanish-international menu. Closed Sunday in winter.

El Amir
General Narváez, Granada
North African restaurant serving felafel, couscous, baba ganoush *and other specialities.*

Mirador de Morayma
Calejón de las Vacas, Albaicín,
Granada
Tel. (958) 22 82 90
Romantic Andalucian restaurant with fine views over the city. Closed Sunday evening and Monday.

Ruta del Veleta
Ctra. Sierra Nevada, km. 5,400
Cenes de la Vega
18190 Granada
Tel. (958) 48 12 01
One of the most highly rated restaurants in the Granada area, serving cuisine from all over Spain. Closed Sunday evening.

Sevilla
Oficios, 12
18001 Granada
Tel. (958) 22 12 23
This traditional and characterful Andalusian restaurant is perhaps the most famous in Granada. García Llorca came here to meet like-minded poets and intellectuals. Closed Sunday evening.

Jaca
La Cocina Aragonesa
Cervantes, 5
22700 Jaca
Tel. (974) 36 10 50
The town's best restaurant has a good reputation for fresh seasonal produce. Try its game or wild mushroom dishes. Regional décor. Closed Tuesday.

Jerez de la Frontera

Tendido 6
Circo, 10
11405 Jerez de la Frontera
Tel. (956) 34 48 35
*Generous helpings of traditional
local food are served on a covered
Andalusian patio with decor and
memorabilia celebrating local festive events. Closed Sunday in summer, Sunday evening rest of year.*

Venta Antonio
Ctra. de Jerez-Sanlúcar, km 5
11405 Jerez de la Frontera
Tel. (956) 33 05 35
*Good cuisine. Seafood specialities.
Closed Monday (except in spring
and summer).*

León

**Meson Leones del
Racimo de Oro**
Caffo Badillo, 2, 24006 León
Tel. (987) 25 75 75
*Good, earthy country cooking is the
fare in this charming rustic restau-
rant, set in a 17th-century building.
Lovely summer terrace. Closed Sun-
day evening and Tuesday.*

Lérida

Molí de la Nora
Ctra. Puigcerdà-Andorra, km 7
25000 Lérida
Tel. (973) 19 00 17
*A rustic place with an attractive ter-
race. Try the dorada baked in salt,
served with a piquant sauce. Closed
Sunday evening and Monday from
October to March.*

Logroño

La Merced
Marqués de San Nicolás, 109
26001 Logroño
Tel. (941) 22 11 66
*An oustandingly beautiful restau-
rant in a former palace with antique
furniture. Nine dining rooms serve
wonderful regional country food
and a selection from every bodega
in Rioja. Closed 3 weeks August and
Sunday.*

Lugo

Mesón de Alberto
Cruz, 4
27001 Lugo
Tel. (982) 22 83 10
*Good Galician cuisine. Closed Sun-
day out of season.*

Madrid

Botín
Cuchilleros, 17
28000 Madrid
Tel. (91) 266 42 17
*The world's oldest restaurant,
established 1725; lovely old
interior. Traditional roasts are
the house speciality.*

Casa d'a Troya
Emiliano Barral
28043 Madrid
Tel. (91) 416 44 55
*Superb Galician cuisine has earned
this establishment one Michelin
rosette. Try the pulpo or merluza a
la gallega. Closed last 2 weeks July,
August and Sunday.*

Casa Lucio
Cava Baja, 35, 28005 Madrid
Tel. (91) 365 32 52
*Very upmarket tapas bar where the
King and many other luminaries are
known to eat. Try the churrasco de
la casa, a 1lb sizzling steak. Closed
August and Saturday lunchtime.*

El Cenador del Prado
Prado, 4
28014 Madrid
Tel. (91) 429 15 61
*Excellent nueva cocina in one of the
city's most outstanding, and most
romantic of restaurants. One Michelin rosette. Closed 2 weeks August,
Sunday and Saturday lunchtime.*

Jockey
Amador de los Ríos, 6
28010 Madrid
Tel. (91) 319 24 35
*Superb continental cuisine has been
served here in elegant surroundings
for some 50 years. One Michelin
rosette. Closed August and Sunday.*

El Mentidero de la Villa
Santo Tomé, 6
28004 Madrid
Tel. (91) 308 12 85
*Romantic restaurant with clever
trompe l'oeil murals. Inventive and
interesting French-inspired menu.
Closed last fortnight August, Saturday lunchtime and Sunday.*

El Pescador
José Ortega y Gasset, 75
28006 Madrid
Tel. (91) 402 12 90
*One of the best places in Madrid for
choice and quality of seafood. One
Michelin rosette. Simple rustic dé-
cor. Closed August and Sunday.*

Príncipe de Viana
Manuel de Falla, 5
28036 Madrid
Tel. (91) 457 15 49
*Excellent Basque/Navarrese cuisine
in comfortable luxurious surroundings, popular with the bejewelled
set. One Michelin rosette. Outdoor
dining. Closed August, Sunday and
Saturday lunchtime.*

El Schotis
Cava Baja, 11
28005 Madrid
Tel. (91) 265 32 30
*Good, long Spanish menu but the
house speciality is steak brought to
you on a sizzling platter for you to
cook as you like it. Closed August
and Monday.*

Zalacaín
Alvarez de Baena, 4
28006 Madrid
Tel. (91) 561 48 40
*The best restaurant in Spain accord-
ing to many. Three Michelin stars
have been awarded for its magnificent Spanish (Basque-Navarrese)
international haute cuisine, impec-
cably served in beautiful, though not
overpowering, surroundings. Closed
August, Sunday and Saturday
lunchtime.*

Málaga

Antigua Casa Guardia
Alameda Principal 18
29016 Málaga
*One of the oldest tapas bars in
Málaga, serving a good range
of traditional tapas and wines from
the barrel.*

Antonio Martín
Paseo Marítimo
29016 Málaga
Tel. (95) 222 21 13
*A family establishment for over a
century, the Martíns serve the best
local seafood and fish and rice
dishes on an attractive waterside
terrace. (Hemingway was a regular
here.) Closed Sunday evening in
winter.*

Café de Paris
Vélez Málaga, 8
29016 Málaga
Tel. (95) 222 50 43
*This elegant restaurant, facing the
beach, is the most comfortable in
town. Creative cuisine and a wide
choice. Closed three weeks July and
Sunday.*

338

Meson El Chinitas
Moreno Monroy 4,
29016 Málaga
Tel. (95) 221 09 72
Attractive restaurant in the heart of the Old Town, serving Andalucian and Málagueño specialities.

La Taberna del Pintor
Maestranza, 6
29016 Málaga
Tel. (95) 221 53 15
Cosy restaurant with rustic décor, specializing in roast and grilled meats.

Marbella
La Fonda
Plaza del Santo Cristo, 10
29600 Marbella
Tel. (95) 277 25 12
One of this coast's finest restaurants. One Michelin rosette. Try the marinated sardines, house-style dorada or veal in Málaga wine. Charming Andalusian patio. Dinner only. Closed Sunday.

La Hacienda
Ctra. Cádiz-Málaga, km 193
29600 Marbella
Tel. (95) 283 12 67
This Belgian-run establishment serves excellent cuisine, either in a delightfully rustic dining room, or on its splendid patio. Closed Monday lunchtime in August; Monday and Tuesday rest of year.

La Meridiana
Camino de la Cruz s/n, Marbella
Tel. (95) 277 61 90
One of the best restaurants on the Costa del Sol. Top international cuisine and impeccable service.

Mérida
Nicolás
Félix Valverde Lillo, 13,
06800 Mérida
Tel. (924) 31 96 101
Quality regional cuisine including some excellent soups and stews. Closed Sunday.

Mijas
El Mirlo Blanco
Plaza de la Constitución, Mijas
Tel. (95) 248 57 00
Traditional basque specialities. Attractive restaurant with terrace dining, overlooking the village square.

Murcia
El Rincón de Pepe
Apóstoles, 34
30001 Murcia
Tel. (968) 21 22 39
The best restaurant in town, if not the province. A varied mix of seafood, regional specialities, Mediterranean and nouvelle styles have earned one Michelin rosette. Closed most Sundays June-August.

Orense
Sanmiguel
San Miguel, 12-14
32005 Orense
Tel. (988) 22 12 45
Fine Galician fish and seafood is served here in the town's best restaurant. Pleasant terrace. Closed Tuesday.

Oviedo
Casa Fermin
San Francisco, 8
33003 Oviedo
Tel. (985) 521 64 52;
fax (985) 522 92 12
Superb seafood has earned Casa Fermin one Michelin rosette. Closed Sunday.

Pamplona
Josetxo
Plaza del Príncipe de Viana, 1
31002 Pamplona
Tel. (948) 22 20 97
Classic Navarrese cuisine, excellent service and luxurious décor has earned the town's best restaurant one Michelin star. Closed August and Sunday.

Shanti
Castillo de Maya, 39
31003 Pamplona
Tel. (948) 23 10 04
Good Navarrese home cooking at a reasonable price, enjoyed by tourists and locals. Closed July, Sunday and Monday evenings.

Peñiscola
Casa Severino
Urb. Las Atalayas
12598 Peñiscola
Tel. (964) 48 07 03
An attractive villa set in the hills just outside Peñiscola, serving good fish and seafood dishes. Closed November and Wednesday (except July, August).

Pontevedra
Casa Solla
Carretera de la Toja
36000 Pontevedra
Tel. (986) 85 26 78
Excellent local cuisine (one Michelin rosette) featuring such dishes as stuffed squid, hake with fines herbes, veal in leek sauce. Outdoor dining. Closed Sunday and Thursday evenings.

Ronda
Don Miguel
Plaza de España, 3
29400 Ronda
Tel. (95) 287 10 90
Good Andalusian cuisine (try the venison or other game dishes). Although the food is excellent the restaurant is most popular just for the view from the terrace overlooking the famous gorge. Closed Sunday June-August.

Pedro Romero
Virgen de la Paz, 18
29400 Ronda
Tel. (95) 287 11 10
Perhaps the next best place to eat in Ronda (after Don Miguel) although the location is not as outstanding; local dishes served in typical restaurant.

Rosas
Hacienda El Bulli
Cala Montjoi, Apt. 30
17480 Rosas
Tel. (972) 25 76 51
Ranch-style restaurant with a terrace overlooking the bay, serving some of the best food on this coast. The views are wonderful but the restaurant (11 miles from Rosas) can only be reached by a long bumpy ride through the hills. (two Michelin rosettes).

Salamanca
Chez Victor
Espoz y Mina, 26
37002 Salamanca
Tel. (923) 21 31 23
Salamanca's best restaurant is owned and run by a Parisian master-chef, and has won a rare Michelin star. Serves classic and nouvelle French dishes, but also Salamancan inspired cuisine. His dessert los tres chocolates is a legend! Closed August, Sunday evening and Monday.

Río de la Plata
Plaza del Peso, 1
37001 Salamanca
Tel. (923) 21 90 05
Small, charming restaurant serving traditional Castilian dishes as well as seafood. Closed Monday and July.

Salou
Casa Font
Calle Colon, 17
Tel. (977) 38 04 35
Long-established gourmet restaurant, one of the best in Salou, serving quality Mediterranean and international cuisine. Dining room overlooks the beach. Closed Monday.

La Goleta
Platja des Capellans
Tel. (977) 38 35 66
Elegant and romantic restaurant with terrace, facing the beach. Specializes in Spanish-international cuisine, with interesting dishes such as partridge in pickle sauce or prawns in Madeira.

San Sebastián
Arzak
Alto de Miracruz, 21
20015 San Sebastián
Tel. (943) 27 84 65
Outstanding traditional Basque cuisine has won this renowned restaurant three Michelin stars and parity with Madrid's Zalacaín as Spain's most fêted gourmet shrine. Superb game and seafood dishes. Closed Monday, Sunday evening, 2 weeks in June, all November.

Bretxa
General Echgüe, 5
20003 San Sebastián
Tel. (943) 42 05 49
A popular and reasonably priced grill restaurant in the old part of town, specializing in fish and seafood. Closed Sunday.

Casa Nicolasa
Aldamar, 4
20003 San Sebastián
Tel. (943) 42 17 62
One of this gourmet town's finest eating houses (one Michelin star) serving traditional Basque seafood plus some nueva cocina dishes. Closed Sunday, Monday evening (except August, September) and all February.

Jatetxea Rekondo
Paseo de Igueldo 57
20008 San Sebastián
Tel. (943) 21 29 07
Traditional, simple but quality dishes including game, grilled meats and fish. The outstanding wine cellar is one of the best in Spain. Closed Wednesdays and November.

Panier Fleuri
Paseo de Salamanca, 1
20013 San Sebastián
Tel. (943) 42 42 05
The haute cuisine here recently achieved a national award to add to the restaurant's Michelin rosette. Some excellent wines to match the food. Closed Wednesday, three weeks in June, and Sunday evening.

Santander
El Molino
Carretera N-611
Puente Arce
39470 Santander
Tel. (942) 57 50 55
Excellent cuisine, specializing in Cantabrian and seafood dishes, served in a beautifully renovated old mill, 13km (8 miles) from Santander. One Michelin rosette. Closed Sunday evening and Monday.

Puerto
Hernán Cortés
39003 Santander
Tel. (942) 21 93 93
Good restaurant specializing in Cantabrian seafood dishes. Food is prepared in the open over a charcoal grill.

Santiago de Compostela
Anexo Vilas
Avenida de Villagarcia, 21
15706 Santiago de Compostela
Tel. (981) 59 86 37
This family-run restaurant has been serving fine Galician food for 80 years. Closed Monday.

Don Gaiferos
Rua Nova, 23
15705 Santiago de Compostela
Tel. (981) 58 38 94
Local fish and seafood, plus international dishes are served in charming small bare-stone rooms in this elegant, relaxed restaurant. Closed Sunday.

Los Reyes Católicos
Plaza del Obradoiro, 1
15705 Santiago de Compostela
Tel. (981) 58 22 00
Galician and international dishes are served in the atmospheric arched undercroft of this wonderful historic building.

Santillana del Mar
Hotel Altamira
Calle Cantón, 1
39330 Santillana del Mar
Tel. (942) 81 80 25
This atmospheric restaurant, set in an atmospheric 17th-century stone mansion, is particularly noted for its fish dishes and Cantabrian regional cuisine.

Segovia
José María
Cronista Lecea, 11
40001 Segovia
Tel. (911) 43 44 84
Traditional Castilian fare (which matches the Mesón de Candidó) is served in a lively and trendy yet rustic atmosphere. Excellent suckling pig and noisy tapas bar with good selection of dishes.

Mesón de Cándido
Plaza del Azoguejo, 5
40001 Segovia
Tel. (911) 42 59 11
A locally renowned eating house (King Juan Carlos eats here occasionally) in a splendid mediaeval building underneath the famous Aqueduct. Typical Castilian roasts are the speciality, plus seasonal fish and game dishes.

Seville
La Albahaca
Plaza de Santa Cruz, 12
41000 Seville
Tel. (95) 422 07 14
Charming Andalusian mansion with restrained decor serving international and regional food. Try the pumpkin soup or the wild red partridge. Outdoor dining. Closed Sunday

La Dorada
Virgen de Aguas Santas, 6
41001 Seville
Tel. (95) 445 51 00
You don't have to choose fish in this lively maritime-themed restaurant (there's a short but good meat

*menu) but it would be a shame to miss dorada baked in rock salt (*a la sal*). Closed August and Sunday evening.*

Engaña Oriza
San Fernando, 41
41000 Seville
Tel. (954) 22 72 54
Now one of two restaurants in Seville to boast a Michelin rosette, serving excellent Basque and Andalusian cuisine. Closed Saturday lunchtime and all day Sunday.

Figón del Cabildo
Plaza de Cabildo
41001 Seville
Tel. (954) 22 01 17
Both modern and traditional local dishes are served here, including a good choice of fish and seafood. Try the eel and endive salad. Outdoor dining. Closed Sunday.

Ox's
Betis, 61
41010 Seville
Tel. (954) 27 95 85
Serious Basque cuisine is the attraction here. Try the fashionable kokotxas de merluza con salsa (hake cheeks with parsley sauce). Closed August and Sunday evening.

Pello Roteta
Farmacéutico Murillo Herrera, 10
41010 Seville
Tel. (95) 427 84 17
The excellent Basque cuisine has recently won the restaurant a Michelin rosette. Good fish dishes at very reasonable prices. Closed Sunday and mid-August to mid-September.

Río Grande
Betis, 70
41010 Seville
Tel. (95) 427 39 56
Superb location next to the river and opposite the Torre del Oro, particularly if you can get a conservatory table. Food is international with local touches, with fish the speciality.

Sitges
Casa Hidalgo
Carrer Sant Pau, 12
08870 Sitges
Tel. (93) 894 38 95
Traditional restaurant serving good selection of meat and fish dishes, including goat à la Castellana.

Mare Nostrum
Paseo de la Ribera, 60
08870 Sitges
Tel. (93) 894 33 93
Long-established, elegant sea-front restaurant, with a pleasant terrace and an attractive nautical-themed dining room. Regional dishes include shrimp romesco, hake with cava, chicken and crayfish. Closed Wednesday.

La Masia
Passeig Vilanova, 164-166
08870 Sitges
Tel. (93) 894 10 76
Splendid traditional farmhouse setting with garden terrace. Luminaries from near and far come for the huge portions of excellent local food.

La Santa Maria
Passeig de la Ribera, 52
08870 Sitges
Tel. 894 09 99
The most popular place in town – the front terrace of this seafront restaurant is always packed. Long menu, efficient service, huge portions, good at all times of the day. Try the paella or the zarzuela.

Soria
Mesón Castellano
Plaza Mayor, 2
42001 Soria
Tel. (975) 21 30 45
Hearty country fare is served at this formal grill-restaurant. Outdoor dining. Closed Sunday October-April.

Tarragona
Lers Fonts de Can Sala
Carretera de Valls (N240), 62
43000 Tarragona
Tel. (977) 22 85 75
Attractive restaurant decorated in rustic Catalan fashion, with a tree-shaded terrace. Specializes in Catalan cooking using fresh inland produce. Closed Tuesday.

Nàutico
Explanada del Port, El Serrallo
43000 Tarragona
Tel. (977) 24 00 62
The smartest restaurant in the port and the dining room of Catalonia's oldest sailing club. Relax with a drink on the balcony overlooking the port before enjoying a fish feast. Dining room haspanoramic views.

La Puda
Moll de Pescadors, 25, El Serrallo
43000 Tarragona
Tel. (977) 21 10 70
A no-frills fishermen's café with a cheerful area of gingham table-cloths set aside for more formal dining. Try the entremeses de la casa for a bit of everything, and look out for interesting daily specials.

Sol Ric
Vía Augusta, 227
43007 Tarragona
Tel. (977) 23 30 32
This excellent outdoor garden restaurant has been serving what many critics regard as the best food in Tarragona since 1959. Fish and shellfish dominate the menu, with romesco specials. Closed Sunday night and Mondays.

Les Voltes
Trinquet Vell, 12
43000 Tarragona
Tel. (977) 21 88 30
Atmospheric location within the actual vaults of the old Roman circus; high-tech fittings meeting ancient stone. Spanish and international cuisine. Try the arròs negre (black rice). Closed Sunday evening.

Toledo
Asador Adolfo
Calle de la Granada, 6
45001 Toledo
Tel. (925) 22 73 21
Splendid national award-winning Spanish haute cuisine in the beautiful setting of a 14th-15th century house near the cathedral. Closed Sunday evening.

Hostal de Cardenal
Paseo de Recaredo, 24
45004 Toledo
Tel. (925) 22 49 00
Traditional Spanish home-cooking with meaty game specials is served in the beautiful surroundings of an 18th-century bishop's palace (by the owners of the famous Botín, in Madrid).

Casa Aurelio
Sinagoga, 6
45001 Toledo
Tel. (925) 22 20 97
Friendly restaurant and tapas bar in a three-storey local house around a patio. Game dishes a speciality. (Note – there are at least two other Aurelio restaurants in Toledo!)

Torremolinos

Casa Guaquín
Carmen, 37
29620 Torremolinos
Tel. (952) 38 45 30
Enjoy the sea views and the fruit of the sea – try the fish a sal (baked in salt). Outdoor dining. Closed December and Thursday.

Taurino
Paseo Marítimo La Carihuela, Torremolinos
Tel. (95) 238 81 79
One of the best seafood restaurants on the promenade, where your dinner is cooked as you watch.

Tossa de Mar

Es Moli
Tarull, 5
17320 Tossa de Mar
Tel. (972) 34 14 14
Good imaginative cuisine (Catalan and house specials) is served on a delightful garden patio. Open mid-March to mid-October, closed Tuesday during April, May, October.

Tudela

El Choko
Plaza de los Fueros, 5
31500 Tudela
Tel. (948) 82 10 19
Typical Tudelan restaurant serving fine regional dishes; try the menestra de la Mejana (a mixed dish of local vegetables). Closed Monday.

Úbeda

Parador Condestable Dávalos
Plaza de Vázquez de Molina, 1
23400 Úbeda
Tel. (953) 75 03 45
Have a drink in the splendid courtyard before your meal in this former mediaeval palace. Regional specialities include andrajos (soup with noodles and salt-cod) and pumpkin fried with chilli and garlic).

Valencia

Les Graelles
Arquitecto Mora, 2
46002 Valencia
Tel. (96) 360 47 00
Excellent rice dishes (in huge portions) are the house speciality, but plenty of other interesting choices too. First-class service. Closed August and Sunday evening.

La Hacienda
Navarro Reverter, 12
46004 Valencia
Tel. (96) 373 18 59
Elegant nueva cocina is served in a small romantic dining room. The goose in blackcurrant sauce or hake in squid sauce are particularly good. Closed Easter week, Saturday lunchtime and Sunday.

Oscar Torrijo
Dr Sumsi, 4
46005 Valencia
Tel. (96) 373 29 49
Fine cuisine has won this establishment a Michelin rosette. Try the arroz de langosta and the mousse de chocolate. Closed Sunday and mid-August to mid-September.

Río Sil
Mosén Fermades, 10
46002 Valencia
Tel. (96) 352 97 64
A good atmospheric restaurant in the traditional tavern style . Try the famous local paella at a reasonable price.

Valladolid

Mesón Cervantes
Paseo de Zorrilla, 10
47006 Valladolid
Tel. (983) 33 71 02
Excellent Castilian cuisine in an elegant relaxing setting. Friendly, efficient service. Closed Sunday evening and August.

Vich

La Taula
Miquel Clariana, 4
08500 Vich
Tel. (93) 886 32 29
Good local food in an ancient building close to the cathedral. Closed: all February; first week in August; Sunday during June-October, Sunday evening rest of year; Monday all year.

Vigo

Sibaris
García Barbón, 168
36201 Vigo
Tel. (986) 22 15 26
Excellent Galician cuisine has led to the award of a Michelin rosette. Try the marinated sea-bass or the hake with tomato and rosemary. Closed Sunday and last week June, first week July.

Vitoria

Dos Hermanas
Madre Vedruna, 10
01008 Vitoria
Tel. (945) 13 29 34
Local and regional specialities are produced by this 100-year-old restaurant and supplemented by an interesting range of classic modern Basque and French dishes. Closed mid-August to mid-September and Sunday.

El Portalón
Correría, 151
01001 Vitoria
Tel. (945) 14 27 55
This attractive restaurant in a former 15th-century posada (lodgings) is owned and run by a prominent Basque sculptor who adorns the tables with superb Basque cuisine and the building with modern (and antique) art. Closed August and Sunday.

Zamora

París
Avenida de Portugal, 14
49002 Zamora
Tel. (988) 51 43 25
Popular restaurant where locals and tourists enjoy fine Castilian cuisine in a pleasant intimate atmosphere.

Zaragoza

Costa Vasca
Tte. Coronel Valenzuela, 13
50004 Zaragoza
Tel. (976) 21 73 39
Good Basque cuisine at a reasonable price. Closed Sunday and August.

Gurrea
San Ignacio de Loyola, 14
50008 Zaragoza
Tel. (976) 23 31 61
Imaginative local cuisine in luxurious surroundings. Menu changes daily. Closed Sunday and throughout August.

La Venta del Cachirulo
Crta N232, 4.5km
50011 Zaragoza
Tel. (976) 33 16 74
Typical Aragonese-style restaurant to the north of Zaragoza, serving regional dishes such as duck with cherries, using fresh local ingredients. Closed Sunday evening and 1-17 August.

Balearic Islands

Ibiza
La Masia d'en Sord
Carretera San Miguel
07800 Ibiza town
Tel. (971) 31 02 28
*Delightful 17th-century farmhouse
with romantic outdoor terrace and
suitably rustic indoor dining. The
huge house is divided into smaller
rooms for greater intimacy.
Mediterranean cuisine; specialities
include salmon cooked in cava.*

Sa Capella
Can Germana
07820 San Antonio Abad
Tel. (971) 34 00 57
*Sample traditional Ibizan home
cooking in the unusual and atmospheric setting of a former mediaeval chapel.*

Sa Cova
Calle Santa Lucia, 5
07800 Ibiza Town
No telephone
*Unusual restaurant which is actu-
ally built into a cave, with an outside terrace which has good views
of the cathedral. The menu changes
daily and meals can be cooked to
order. Very reasonably priced.*

S'Oficina
Avenida España, 6
07800 Ibiza Town
Tel. (971) 30 00 16
*One of Ibiza's best restaurants, spe-
cializing in Basque cuisine, with
huge tanks of live lobsters, fish and
shellfish. Terrace dining in summer.
Closed Sundays, also Saturdays in
winter.*

Majorca
Caballito de Mar
Paseo Sangrera, 5
07012 Palma
Tel. (971) 72 10 74
*This lively fish restaurant enjoys a
harbour terrace on the front near
the cathedral. Friendly service.*

Ca'n Quet
Crta Deiá, Deiá
Tel. (971) 63 91 96
*Renowned restaurant which draws
locals from Palma to enjoy such
delicacies as giant prawns wrapped
in puff pastry. Quality cuisine with
unique local touches. Closed
Monday.*

Koldo Royo
Paseo Marítimo, 3
07014 Palma
Tel. (971) 45 70 21
*The very best in Spanish nouvelle
cuisine has won the owner-chef a
Michelin rosette. The second floor
has fine views over the port.*

Hotel Ses Rotges
Calle Rafael Blanes, 21
07590 Cala Ratjada
Tel. (971) 56 31 08
*Superb French cooking has earned
the French brothers who run this
tasteful hotel one Michelin rosette.
Leave room for dessert.*

Son Tomas
Baronia, 17
07191 Banyalbufar
Tel. (971) 61 81 49
*Enjoy the wonderful views from the
terrace of this village restaurant,
while you tuck into the seafood.*

Minorca
Hostal Biniali
Carretera S'Vestra
07710 San Luis
Tel. (971) 15 17 34
*Varied and interesting Spanish-
international meals are served on a
delightful terrace in summer.*

Es Plá (lobster)
Pasaje Es Plá
07748 Fornells
Tel. (971) 37 66 55
*The island's most famous restaurant
due to the regular patronage of
King Juan Carlos who comes here
for the caldereta de langosta, a delicious lobster stew. If your wallet is
not up to the royal dish, there are
plenty of other good things to try.*

Gregal
Moll de Llevant, 306
07701 Mahón
Tel. (971) 36 66 06
*Fresh fish is the obvious dish here,
right on the port, but the Greek
dishes are good too (that's where
the owner comes from).*

Meson El Gallo
Carretera Cala Galdana 1.5km
Ferreríes
Tel. (971) 37 30 39
*Old farmhouse restaurant with a
faithful clientele, specializing in
Menorcan home cooking using fresh
local ingredients. Try the paella del
gallo. Closed Monday.*

Canary Islands

Fuerteventura
La Molina
Antigua
*Canarian specialities served in the
atmospheric restaurant next to the
windmill.*

Gran Canaria
El Cerdo Que Rie
Paseo de las Canteras, 31
35008 Las Palmas
*Excellent international and Spanish
food in informal colonial-style
surroundings; fondues and
flambés are the specialities of
The Laughing Pig.*

Jardín Canario
Carretera del Centro, Tafira Alta
35008 Las Palmas
Tel. (928) 35 16 45
*Canarian and international dishes
including many fish specialities with
splendid views over the tropical hillside garden.*

Dedo de Dios
The Harbour
Puerto de las Nieves
*Picture-window views of the small
fishing beach and the rock stack
Dedo de Dios (Finger of God).
Good fish, good salads.*

Parador de Cruz de Tejeda
Cruz de Tejeda
Tel. (928) 65 80 50
*Set amid the most beautiful moun-
tain scenery in the island, the
parador (no accommodation)
serves some of the very best in
Canarian cooking.*

La Parilla
Hotel Reina Isabel
Alfredo L Jones, 40
35008 Las Palmas
Tel. (928) 26 01 00
*Superb international food with a
view, on the eighth floor of this five-
star hotel. Try the Steak Reina
Isabel.*

San Agustin Beach Club
Playa de los Cocoteros
35100 San Agustin
Tel. (928) 76 04 00
*Fine international food plus the very
best shellfish is served in generous
portions either by the poolside or
inside the large elegant dining
room.*

El Hierro

Mirador de la Peña
Guarazoca
A splendid Mirador restaurant bene-fitting from the César Manrique de-signer treatment. Island and islands specialities are served in a tranquil, modern room with wonderful views over the coast of El Golfo.

Lanzarote

Barito Tapas Bar
Avenida de Las Playas
35510 Puerto del Carmen
No telephone reservations
Small, lively, bustling, authentic tapas bar where locals and holiday-makers literally rub shoulders.

Castillo de San José
between Puerto de los Marmolés and Puerto Naos, Arrecife,
Tel. (928) 81 23 21
Elegant, simple, César Manrique-designed restaurant with panoramic views to sea. Excellent Canarian food in a quiet, relaxed atmosphere.

La Era
Barranco, 3
35570 Yaiza
Tel. (928) 83 00 16
The last word in charming Canarian típicos. A whitewashed courtyard decked with flowers opens on to two tiny 17th-century rustic dining rooms, serving island specialities.

Jardín de Cactus
Guatiza
Tel. (928) 52 93 97
Good simple Canarian lunches are served on a lovely peaceful terrace shaded by a colourful awning over-looking the beautiful cactus gar-dens. Lunch only.

Montañas del Fuego
Parque Nacional de Timanfaya
Tel. (928) 84 00 57
All the cooking here is done from the heat of the volcano. Order grilled food and watch it cook. Im-pressive sweeping views over the lava fields.

La Sardina Flamenca
Centro Comercial Montaña
Tropical, Calle Toscon
35510 Puerto del Carmen
Tel. (928) 51 05 82
This attractive modern restaurant puts on a regular menu of the very best grilled fish, shellfish and meats accompanied by excellent flamenco dancing.

El Varadero
The Old Port
35510 Puerto del Carmen
Fine fish and a good selection of tapas are served in this atmospheric old boat-house style building. A live pianist and walls covered in art posters adds an almost Gallic charm.

Tenerife

El Botánico
Hotel Botánico,
Calle Richard J. Yeoward, La Paz.
38400 Puerto de la Cruz
Tel. (922) 38 14 00
Recommended for Sunday lunch buffet, beautifully laid out in the garden of this five-star hotel (weather permitting).

Mario
Edificio Rincón del Puerto
Plaza del Charco
38400 Puerto de la Cruz
Small fish restaurant decorated with nautical memorabilia. Eat your meal from a fishing boat! Closed Mondays.

Mi Vaca Y Yo
Cruz Verde, 3.
38400 Puerto de la Cruz
Tel. (922) 38 52 47
Superb international food in an exotic sub-tropical setting, special-izing in fresh grilled fish and sea-food. A great favourite with tourists. Closed July and lunchtimes.

La Rueda
Carretera General del Norte
Sauzal
38400 Puerto de la Cruz
Tel. (922) 56 29 81
Charcoal-grilled meats are the spe-ciality at this rustic family-run es-tablishment. Closed Wednesday.

Index

Page references in **bold** refer to main entries; those in *italic* refer to illustrations. Asterisks refer to entries for which there are maps.

INDEX

INDEX

039/609 RP

FMC

FUNDACIÓN MUNICIPAL DE CULTURA
-JOSÉ LUIS CANO-
c/ Teniente Miranda 118
11201 Algeciras
Tel. 956.63.00.36 / 956.63.03.02

Universidad
de Cádiz

Diseño: Dpto. Imagen Fundación
Imprime: INCOGRAFIC, S.A.L.

Algeciras
en
Primavera
1998